KNOW YOUR CHILD

KNOW
YOUR CHILD

AN AUTHORITATIVE
GUIDE FOR
TODAY'S PARENTS

STELLA CHESS, M.D.

ALEXANDER THOMAS, M.D.

Basic Books, Inc., Publishers

NEW YORK

Library of Congress Cataloging-in-Publication Data

Chess, Stella.
  Know your child.

  Bibliography: p. 377.
  Includes index.
  1. Child psychology.   2. Child development.
3. Parenting.   I. Thomas, Alexander, 1914–
II. Title.
HQ772.C418   1987   649'.1   86–47742
ISBN   0–465–03732–1

Contents

Preface   vii

PART I

CHILDREN ARE DIFFERENT, PARENTS ARE DIFFERENT

Chapter 1
The Mysteries of Human Development: New Questions,
New Answers   3

Chapter 2
Babies Are Different from the Start: Temperament and Its
Significance   21

Chapter 3
The Many Ways of Parenthood   39

Chapter 4
Goodness of Fit: The Key to Healthy Development   54

Chapter 5
Goodness of Fit: Practical Applications   71

PART II

THE DEVELOPING CHILD: INFANT TO ADOLESCENT

Chapter 6
Babies Are Human from the Start: The Beginnings of
Social-Cognitive Development   95

Chapter 7
Children Are Learning All the Time   117

Chapter 8
Cognitive and Emotional Development   137

Chapter 9
The Child's Self-Esteem   154

Chapter 10
Sex Differences and Gender Identity   178

Chapter 11
The Child Goes Off to School   196

Chapter 12
Middle Childhood and Adolescence   217

PART III

SPECIAL FAMILY ISSUES

Chapter 13
Special Children with Special Needs   241

Chapter 14
The Tyranny of the IQ Score   259

Chapter 15
The Parent as Teacher and Friend   278

Chapter 16
Brothers and Sisters Can Be Friends   305

Chapter 17
Other Family Issues   319

Chapter 18
Working Mothers and Their Children   341

Chapter 19
Where We Are Now   365

References   377
Index   387

Preface

PARENTS TODAY are deluged by books and magazine articles that give them specific prescriptions on how to raise their children. Most of these "expert" directives are based on the author's personal opinions and depend on a particular theory of child development with only fragments of actual supporting evidence. Often contradictory advice is given, but all are sure they have the recipe for producing a perfect child. Earnest parents who clutch at these books for the ultimate truths in raising their children will find a veritable Tower of Babel.

Our book is not one more compendium of recipes to produce the perfect child. Rather, our aim is to give parents accurate information based on solid scientific research in the field of child development, information they can use fruitfully as they care for their own children.

An explosion of new findings and ideas in the past quarter-century has radically changed and expanded our knowledge of the child's nature and the relationship between parent and child. We believe we are in a special position to evaluate these research studies, to judge critically which are valid and useful, and to translate the important research findings into a form both useful and understandable to parents. We have conducted a thirty-year study that traces the development of a large group of children from early infancy to adult life. Known as the New York Longitudinal Study, it has stimulated a number of related studies in many centers in this country and abroad. For the past twenty years we have also edited an annual volume of *Progress in Child Psychiatry and Child Development,* in which we review some one hundred professional journals each year and select for republication the most important articles. In addition, for over forty years our teaching positions and consultative practices with children and their parents have given us the opportunity to apply research findings to the prevention and treatment of psychological problems in children.

This book presents several major themes, from our own research and that of others, and cites the evidence to support each idea:

1. Babies are human from the start. Infants are born with a biological endowment that immediately enables them to enter into a social relationship with their parents and to begin actively learning about the world around them.

2. Babies are different from the start. This has been a major focus of our own research, and has been confirmed by many studies. One important set of individual differences is temperament. The child's temperament influences his or her responses to the parents' caregiving, as well as influencing the parents' own attitudes and behavior. In this way the relationship between child and parent is a two-way street; each continuously influences the other.

3. There are many different ways to be a good parent. Just as children have their individual characteristics, so do parents. No single magical recipe is best for all children. What is crucial for a child's healthy development is what we have called "goodness of fit"—that is, a good match between the parents' attitudes and expectations and the individual child's temperament and other characteristics.

We spell out these three themes in detail in the first part of the book, so that parents can apply them on a day-to-day basis with their children. Then we take up a number of other issues that concern parents, always with the question in mind: What have we learned from the best research in the field? We cover such questions as: What do we know about sex differences between girls and boys? Do the child's life experiences determine his or her future life? Are parents' mistakes irreversible? What are the effects on a child of a mother working outside the home? Can brothers and sisters be friends? What are the special problems of the handicapped child? How should we evaluate the meaning of an IQ score? How should parents handle divorce or adoption? What roles can fathers fulfill? What is the evidence for such concepts as "infant bonding," "attachment," and "cognitive stimulation"?

Where the evidence from good research studies is still unclear, we have offered our own opinion based on our knowledge of children, including our own children and grandchildren. We have been careful to distinguish between our own personal views, no matter how strongly we hold them, and information based on solid scientific research.

As we look back over the many challenges we have posed to untested and unproven theories of child development in the past thirty years, and the many arguments we have had with respected colleagues over these years, we are struck by one recurrent theme: We have consistently played the part of the parent's advocate. Over the years, one theory after another has been fashionable, in which the parent, usually the mother, has been held responsible for the child's psychological development. When examined carefully, these theories have all too often been built on conjecture, half-truth, or misinterpretations of the available evidence. We take satisfaction in the many professional papers and books we have written, and now this book, in which we challenge the ideology that identifies the mother as a scapegoat for her child's ills.

There are bad parents, but most parents are devoted to their children's welfare. When they fail in some way, it is most often due to ignorance or confusion rather than malice. Parents who *know their children,* and are not bewildered by the contradictory advice they read and hear, will usually be able to figure out the best approach to caregiving. That is why we have entitled this book *Know Your Child.*

We owe much to Jo Ann Miller, senior editor at Basic Books. She has worked with us tirelessly and thoughtfully, challenging our formulations when they were not documented, demanding that our discussions be clear to parents, and pointing out a number of ideas and issues that we had not treated adequately. Her editorial expertise and knowledge has helped tremendously to strengthen this book.

We are also grateful to Nina Gunzenhauser for her superb copyediting and excellent suggestions.

Our own research work has received generous support from the National Institute of Mental Health and other federal agencies, as well as the New York City Research Council and several private foundations. We have also been fortunate in the consistent support of the administration of our own institution, the New York University Medical Center.

Most of all, we are indebted to the youngsters and their parents of the New York Longitudinal Study, who have cooperated magnificently with us all through the years of this study, and continue to do so. Without their cooperation, whatever contribution we have made to the field of child development would have been impossible.

STELLA CHESS
ALEXANDER THOMAS

PART I

CHILDREN ARE DIFFERENT, PARENTS ARE DIFFERENT

1

The Mysteries of Human Development: New Questions, New Answers

WE HOLD our three-week-old granddaughter, Sarah, in our arms. She lies quietly and fixes our faces with her eyes, but she does not smile or show any sign of recognition. Her behavior is no different when her mother or father or a stranger holds her gently.

Seen from the outside, her life seems to consist of eating, sleeping, and bladder and bowel elimination. She moves about in her crib, and every once in a while she cries, but she is soothed when she is fed or caressed. What goes on inside her brain? How is she responding to the constant stream of sensations from the outside? Is it true, as the pioneer American psychologist William James put it one hundred years ago, that "the baby, assailed by eyes, ears, nose, skin, and entrails at once . . . feels that all is one great blooming, buzzing confusion" (1890)? Or, as psychoanalytic theory would have it, is Sarah being driven by the irrational, primitive asocial instincts of the "id" (Freud 1933)? Is she really not yet a human being, or at best imprisoned in a pathological mental state, akin to that dread psychiatric disorder of childhood known as autism? A leading child analyst, designating this state *normal autism,* sees the infant as "in a state of primitive hallucinatory disorientation, in which need satisfaction belongs to his own omnipotent *autistic* orbit" (Mahler, Pine, & Bergman 1975, p. 42). Or is she already possessed by complex and elaborate ideas such as omnipotence and narcissism, as some theorists would have it (A. Freud 1965)?

But perhaps Sarah is already a normal human being, busy using the unique human capacities and potentials with which she was born to organize her sensations and experiences into increasingly coherent and complex psychological structures. Perhaps she is not being "assailed" by these sensations, not in some pathological state of autism, not endowed with some mystical capacity for omnipotence and narcissism. Perhaps she is already going about the business of developing into a competent and capable youngster. How do we decide which theory is correct? How do we gather the facts that can tell us what is really happening inside the newborn baby's brain?

Our eldest grandson, Ricky, fourteen years old, visits us in our country home. He is a good student, highly motivated to learn, and an excellent athlete. He makes friends easily. He is by no means a paragon of virtue: He can tease his sisters and maneuver to get out of doing his share of household chores. But there is no maliciousness in his irritating behavior, and he responds cheerfully when called to task. He takes correction and criticism positively, whether of his academic performance, his table manners, or his grammar, and he is willing and able to change. He is friendly with our neighbor's son, Michael, two years younger, and encourages him in their play rather than lording it over him. When Michael had a tantrum over a minor frustration, Ricky told him in a friendly but earnest way that he was being silly and childish and should be more grown-up. Already Ricky is feeling the pressure for adult achievement. He announces that he will have to get a good job when he grows up. Why? He explains that he has heard his father complain about the cost of fuel oil and how much it costs to heat their house. As of now, he is not sure whether he wants to be a baseball player or a doctor, but he knows he will have to work hard to achieve either.

On the other hand, there is Eddie, thirteen years old, a boy in treatment with one of us. Born the first child of an affluent suburban family, with parents who wanted him and eagerly embraced their new roles and responsibilities as parents, Eddie was physically healthy and endowed with superior intelligence. His parents truly loved and respected each other, and the household was indeed a peaceful one. Eddie had everything going for him, yet his development was stormy, marked by turmoil, arguments and fights, poor academic performance, and difficulty in making and keeping friends.

Psychotherapy was imperative, but positive change has not been easy for him.

What has made for this radical difference between Ricky's and Eddie's development? Was it primarily the parents' doing when the children were very young, as popular theory from the past would have it? Or are the answers more complex and varied? Will our granddaughter, Sarah, grow into a Ricky, or will she be an Eddie, or an entirely different personality altogether, and what forces will determine the outcome? Are Ricky's and Eddie's personality characteristics already fixed for the future? If not, what are the possibilities for change, and what forces can create change either for good or bad?

We certainly do not have all the answers to these questions. Understanding the processes of human psychological development is perhaps the most complex and difficult task for scientific research, even more challenging than the study of the universe or of the world of subatomic particles. But in the past quarter century there has been a tremendous explosion in our knowledge of child and adolescent psychological development, and a similar expansion in the field of adult development is beginning. Research in psychiatry, developmental psychology, sociology, and neurobiology has produced findings with profound theoretical and practical implications. Old accepted theories are having to be modified and even radically revised. On the practical side, our new knowledge is affecting not only the advice we give to parents for the care and management of their normal children but the approach of the teacher to individual students and the therapeutic strategies of the mental health professional and pediatrician in dealing with children with behavior disorders.

Our goal in this book is to shed light on the mysteries of human development, so that we may better understand what three-week-old Sarah is experiencing when she rests so peacefully in our arms and why it is that children like Ricky and Eddie develop in such different ways. To answer these questions we will take the reader on a voyage of discovery as we explore the exciting new research, describe the practical implications of our new knowledge and theory, and highlight some of the questions that we still have to answer.

Mal de Mère: Scapegoating the Mother

Our own voyage of discovery into the mysteries of human development began more than thirty years ago. We were struck by the number of mothers in our practice who blamed themselves for their children's unhappiness or misbehavior or failure to develop in ways the mothers considered "normal." Regardless of the circumstances, the responsibility for the child's problems always seemed to be placed—by self-styled experts and by the parents themselves—squarely on the mother's shoulders.

One mother, Mrs. M., remains vivid in our memory. A young woman clearly in a state of great anxiety, she was convinced that she needed psychiatric treatment, because she couldn't handle her infant son, Bobby. "Why am I such a bad mother? I am ruining my baby, and I don't know what to do," she exclaimed tearfully. The baby, it turned out, had been hard to manage from the start: He screamed and squirmed through his first baths, he slept irregularly, and to his mother's utter dismay he refused new foods, crying and turning his head away when she offered them to him.

Although her husband and the pediatrician had tried to reassure her, a psychiatrist friend had furthered her distress by telling her that a normal baby with a loving, caring mother didn't behave this way. Bobby must be reacting to something unhealthy in her, he announced with certainty; unconsciously she must be hostile or insecure or both. And he quoted a prominent research psychologist, who claimed that young infants absorbed their mother's unconscious feelings "by contagion" (Escalona 1952, p. 46). That there was no evidence for these assertions didn't seem to bother the psychiatrist, who went on to recommend long-term psychotherapy to uncover Mrs. M.'s "unconscious hostility."

As we listened to Mrs. M's story, it became clear that she didn't need costly and probably ineffective psychotherapy. What she did need was a better understanding of the nature of babies, especially of the fact that babies differ in how they behave and how they react to the world around them. We explained that Bobby was a perfectly normal baby but that he needed plenty of time to adapt to new situations and new demands. To help her deal effectively with her child, we taught her to introduce new foods and new experiences very gradually and not to expect Bobby to take to them easily or quickly, as some of her friends' children did. When she saw that this worked with feeding, bathing, and even going to new places (we suggested that she bring along some of Bobby's favorite toys to help him feel at home), Mrs. M. was enormously relieved and no longer felt she was a bad mother.

During this period we were also consulted by the parents of Roger, a nine-year-old boy who was having difficulty learning to read. This time the parents were tyrannized not by a psychiatrist but by a teacher, who offered an impressive array of "evidence" that Roger's reading problems were "psychological" and strongly urged that he and his mother undergo psychotherapy. His mother had pressured Roger too much, the teacher insisted; she had imposed unrealistic expectations on him and was generally overinvolved in his efforts to read. After all, she noted, Roger was a bright boy who did well in arithmetic and participated easily in class discussion, and so his inability to read must be psychological.

One aspect of Roger's mother's "overinvolvement"—the fact that he found it impossible to write compositions but could easily dictate ideas to her, which she then wrote down—gave us a clue to the real nature of his problem. It appeared that the mother's concerns were not the *cause* but rather the *effect* of Roger's reading difficulties. Almost twenty years earlier, in a now-classic study of language disabilities, Samuel Orton, a midwestern physician, had presented evidence that such learning problems could be caused by slowness in maturation of brain functions (1937). In mild cases, the problem could be short-lived; in severe cases, brain maturation in the language area could be permanently affected. Today there is a tendency to overascribe language difficulties to brain dysfunction, but in the 1950s Orton's ideas were virtually unknown, and most psychiatrists, psychologists, and educators clung to the idea that the cause of learning problems lay in some problem in the child's relationship with the mother.

It happened that one of us had reported on a group of children with just the sort of language disabilities that Orton described (Chess 1944), and as we looked closely at Roger's history and his present performance it occurred to us that he was probably suffering from a developmental lag in the maturation of the brain areas concerned with reading. We recommended special remedial instruction, not psychotherapy. With the help of a remedial teacher who was familiar with the idea that reading difficulties could have a biological rather than an emotional basis, Roger made excellent progress and within two years was up to grade level.

Why We Started Our Research Studies

Our experiences with Mrs. M., with Roger's parents, and with many others like them confirmed for us that the prevailing psychiatric dogma of blaming the mother neither added to our understanding of child development nor in any way helped parents to enjoy their children or raise them competently. Out of the many cases we had seen, there were a few psychiatrically ill or negligent parents who did undermine their children's emotional and physical well-being, but the vast majority of parents were well-meaning people who tried to be good parents and were hampered by the belief that everything that went wrong was their fault. Our experiences also brought up important questions to which we had no answers: Would Bobby continue in his pattern throughout his life? How could we systematically identify normal "problems" in a particular child's development so that the parents would not be held responsible for them? And, perhaps most important, how could we educate parents and professionals in general, as we had helped Bobby's and Roger's parents?

We had done our best with each individual family that came to us, but now we said to each other, "That is not enough. We have to find a way to tackle this issue on a broad and decisive level, and not just case by case. We can't avoid this responsibility any longer."

We knew that we were taking on a formidable task. The "blame the mother" ideology (and sometimes fathers were also included) dominated the mental health field in the 1950s and ran rampant in the ideas of most mental health professionals and other child care experts. We call it an ideology rather than a theory, because it was a fixed system of ideas whose premises were not to be questioned, whereas a scientific theory is always considered incomplete and open to challenge and change.

To say that this ideology ran rampant is, if anything, an understatement. Mothers were blamed for everything that went wrong with their children, whether it was a simple behavior disorder, school difficulties, adolescent delinquency, a more serious psychiatric disturbance, or one of a number of physical illnesses. New terms were even invented. There was the "schizophrenogenic mother," who unconsciously exerted such a malignant influence that her child grew up to develop schizophrenia. There was the "double bind," in which the mother gave contradictory messages to her child—such as saying "I love you" but acting as if she hated him—that so confused the child that he developed severe mental disturbance. There were the "refrigerator parents," who were so cold and unfeeling that their child developed autism, that most malignant mental illness that starts in early childhood. A leading center for the treatment of children suffering from severe asthma invented the "parentectomy," the necessary separation of the child from the parents who were the cause of the asthma. Other ideas blaming the parent multiplied even when no new word was manufactured. The adolescent delinquent was considered to be only acting out the "unconscious wishes" of his parent, an idea presented as gospel truth in one professional paper after another. What was the proof? None was required, since the explanations fit neatly into the prevailing ideology; that was proof enough.

The Influence of Freud and Pavlov

What produced this ideology? Primarily it was the influence of psychoanalysis, founded by Sigmund Freud, and secondarily that of behaviorism, based on the brilliant work of the Russian neurophysiologist Ivan Pavlov.

The beginnings of the study of human psychological development, both normal and abnormal, were fashioned almost a century ago by the creative and seminal work of Freud and Pavlov. Both demolished the established mechanical concepts of the time, in which the infant was considered to be a *homunculus,* an adult in miniature who possessed all the physical and psychological attributes that would characterize him as an adult. Both Freud and Pavlov, however, emphasized the process of the interaction of biology and the environment in shaping a person's behavioral characteristics. Both traced the effects of life experiences in transforming simple patterns to more complex ones. Both provided methods for the study of human psychological functioning that proved to be enormously productive in their hands and those of succeeding generations.

From perhaps the 1930s on, Freud and psychoanalysis became highly attractive to mental health professionals in this country. Freud pointed up the meaning and purpose to be found even in many behaviors that appeared accidental or trivial. He showed how behavior can be determined by motivations that lie outside of awareness and how anxiety, conflict, and defense mechanisms influence human goals, feelings, thoughts, and fantasies. He elaborated a system of treatment of a host of psychological disorders through such techniques as dream interpretation, the insistence on free association (the patient's verbalizing whatever thoughts came to mind), and the analysis of transference (the patient's emotional reactions and behavior toward the analyst).

It is hard to imagine now what excitement and interest Freud's ideas produced in this country a half-century ago when they became familiar to mental health professionals, as well as to writers, philosophers, and others concerned with the question of how a child matures psychologically. Here was a dynamic view of the growth of a human being, instead of the static and sterile view of the constitutional-heredity schools. As young psychiatrists, both of us underwent psychoanalytic training, because it was assumed to be essential to understanding and treating our patients. The only question was whether one chose training in a psychoanalytic institute that adhered strictly to all of Freud's theories and treatment techniques or whether one opted for training under teachers who were skeptical of some of Freud's ideas, such as his instinct theory or the need to treat a patient five days a week. We chose the latter kind of training, and as time has passed many analysts have come to admit the need for revisions of Freud's concepts in the light of our present knowledge.

Pavlov discovered the basic neurophysiological mechanism of the formation and modification of conditioned reflexes. This is the process in which inborn, unconditioned reflexes are modified or changed by their linkage with stimuli coming from the environment, and is one of a number of ways in which the child is influenced by and learns from the outside world. This work was influential in creating the discipline of behaviorism under the leadership of the American psychologist John Watson. Behaviorism attracted a number of psychologists and has been useful in the study of learning and in the treatment of certain specific psychological ailments, such as phobias (severe irrational fears). It ignored all the other basic subjective elements of the human mind however. Thoughts, feelings, conflicts, and fantasies—all were proclaimed by the behaviorists to be a "black box" that could not be investigated scientifically. Because of its limitations, behaviorism never had the influence that psychoanalysis developed, especially in this country.

Both psychoanalysts and behaviorists proclaimed that the first few years of life are decisive for the child's whole future life. Early mistakes made by the parents could do permanent, irreparable damage to the child. As the president of Barnard College put it in the early 1950s, "All the experts seem to be saying to young parents: 'Even the most innocent-appearing act or a carelessly spoken word may "harm" a child or "damage his future happiness." You hurt them by comparing them and praising them for being special. You hurt them by being too affectionate to them or by not being affectionate enough' " (quoted by Bruch 1954, p. 727). A mother had to be "mature" to avoid harming her baby. But from the psychoanalytic viewpoint that even apparently innocuous behavior often reflected unconscious conflicts, very few mothers could qualify as mature. A psychoanalytic study of twenty-two mothers randomly selected in the Boston area in the 1950s concluded that only one of the twenty-two could qualify as a "mature mother" (Pavanstedt 1961).

The Research Challenge

How were we to combat this "blame the mother" ideology? We did have an alternative approach. We were convinced that babies had innate differences and that these differences were perhaps as important as the family's influence in shaping the child's development. Perhaps that explained why any one set of child care principles worked out very well with some children, only moderately well with others, and not at all with still others, and why a different approach might work out well with the ones who had done badly with the first approach. Perhaps it explained why certain disturbed parents had healthy children, while other good parents had problem children. Perhaps it explained why a rigid, punitive parent produced a defiant, rebellious adolescent in one family and an inhibited, submissive one in another family. This was not to negate the influence of the parents, which in some cases was decisive. But how could we explain these different outcomes if the parents and the outside environment were the only factors shaping the child's development?

With few exceptions, our professional colleagues rejected these ideas. When we presented our case material, we usually met with the pat answer, "You haven't investigated the mother's unconscious enough. If you did, you would get a different answer." Or we were accused of going back to a discredited constitutionalist view of development.

Indeed, the prevalent ideology appeared impervious to challenge. All too often a mother with a problem child was confused, anxious, or guilty, or all three. To argue that this might at least sometimes be the mother's *response* to the child's behavior, rather than its *cause*, we needed powerful supporting evidence.

Such evidence had begun to appear, however. In 1949 Harold Orlansky, an anthropologist at Yale University, had published a comprehensive scholarly review of the research literature on the effects of different child care practices on the child's development, concluding that "personality development should be considered as a dynamic interaction of a unique organism undergoing maturation and a unique physical and social environment" (p. 39). This was the position that we and a small group of psychiatrists and psychologists were evolving separately and gradually. But Orlansky's critique was ignored, and he himself never followed up this work. Other specific studies were also shrugged off. For example, in a study of fifty infants, the psychiatrist and pediatrician Edith Jackson and her co-workers at Yale found no relationship between maternal practice in the areas of feeding and socialization and the child's behavior, either during the first year, when the mother's practices were monitored, or in the second year as a delayed effect (Klatskin, Jackson, & Wilkin 1956). Such reports were either ignored by most of the experts or explained away with the rationalization that the effects were buried in the infant's unconscious and would show up only in later life.

We were not the only psychiatrists disturbed by this "blame the mother" ideology and its harmful effects on highly committed and basically competent mothers. Hilde Bruch, a well-respected child psychiatrist then at Columbia University, wrote a powerful polemical article in which she incisively raised a cry of alarm:

Modern parent education is characterized by the experts pointing out in great detail all the mistakes parents have made and can possibly make, and substituting "scientific knowledge" for the tradition of the "good old days." An unrelieved picture of model parental behavior, a contrived image of artificial perfection of happiness, is held up before parents who try valiantly to reach the ever receding ideal of "good parenthood" like dogs after a mechanical rabbit. . . . The new teaching implies that parents are all-responsible and must assume the role of preventive Fate for their children. (1954, p. 723)

Yet Bruch too was ignored; her article caused not even a ripple of disturbance among the experts.

If Bruch, Orlansky, Jackson, and others were so easily dismissed, what chance did we have to campaign on behalf of the unjustly condemned mothers and bring a new viewpoint to the field of child development? We were young psychiatrists, with respected but still modest positions. We were not even research experts; we were primarily clinicians, concerned with the day-to-day treatment of patients, and medical school teachers.

We were familiar with the standards and demands of serious research from our reading and from the few clinical research papers we had each published. It was clear to us that only a study that met rigorous criteria could hope to succeed where the others had failed. We had to formulate our hypotheses clearly—that is, what we were trying to prove. We had to gather systematically the information that could either support or disprove our hypotheses. We had to transform this information into categories that could be defined clearly, scored, and rated quantitatively for purposes of statistical analysis. The categories we identified also had to be amenable to qualitative analysis—that is, to case-by-case comparisons that could identify similarities and contrasts in development that statistical analysis alone would not reveal. The methods of data-gathering and analysis, as well as the categories we identified and their definitions, had to be usable by other investigators, so that our findings could be either confirmed, modified, or disproved. And most important of all, we had to demonstrate that the categories we identified had functional meaning in the lives of the subjects we studied.

Our hypotheses were based on our observations of our own children and those of our relatives and friends, our impressions gained from treating our patients and reading the professional literature, and numerous discussions with each other:

1. From birth onward, babies vary in their behavior and their reactions to stimuli from the outside. These differences we called differences in the child's temperament. Differences in temperament are not caused, but may be influenced, by the way the mother or other caregiver handles the baby.
2. These differences are not haphazard or vague but can be grouped into specific categories that can be defined and rated. Some examples of categories: intensity or energy with which any sort of mood is expressed; rhythmicity, or the predictability or unpredictability of timing of biologic functions such as sleepiness, hunger, and defecation; activity level, or the frequency and speediness of movement throughout the day and night; and initial positive or negative response to a new situation or person, with quick or slow adaptability if the initial reaction is negative. (A complete list of the categories, their definitions, and their ratings are given in the next chapter.)
3. Babies and older children can be classified according to how they rate on these categories: mild or intense, high or low, quick or slow.
4. The rating of these categories is typical for each child, so that he tends to show them in different situations at different times. At the same time, unlike the now-discredited constitutionalist views, the expression of these categories is not fixed and immutable but can be modified by different life situations and experiences.
5. The child's expression of these categories influences the attitudes and behavior of his mother and other caregivers, as well as his own responses to their child care practices. In other words, child care is a two-way street, with child and caregiver influencing each other mutually and continuously, rather than a one-way street that runs only from caregiver to child.
6. It is this mutual interaction of the child with the caregiver, as well as with other influential people in his life, that determines the course of the child's development, and not just the child or the caregiver alone.

These hypotheses also recognized that other aspects of the child, such as special abilities, handicaps, or unusual life experiences, might also have important effects on the child's development.

We were by no means the first to put forward these ideas. Many students of child development had suggested that such inborn differences in infants existed, and some had identified specific differences in motor activity level, sleeping and eating patterns, and social responsiveness. (A summary of these reports can be found in Thomas, Chess, & Birch 1968.) These observations were usually restricted to one or another category, however. They did not attempt a systematic overview of the child's behavior, did not provide adequate guidelines by which others could duplicate their observations, and failed to examine the effect of the child's characteristics on the caregiver or their functional significance for the child's development. The state of knowledge in this field was so sparse and fragmentary that the Mid-Century White House Conference on Children and Youth reported in 1950:

All who have had the opportunity of watching children of like ages have been impressed with the high degree of individuality which each one shows. Even as newborn infants they differ not only in such physical characteristics as weight and height, but also in the manner in which they react to events. . . . At present, however, factually tested knowledge concerning individual differences among children is so scarce that there is doubt of the wisdom of including it in this report. (Witmer & Kotinsky 1952, p. 35)

Finding an adequate method to test our hypotheses was no easy task. The reports of other research studies did not help us. We could not find any that pointed to a way of obtaining a systematic, objective view of the essential characteristics of a baby's behavior. The other research reports we found were either speculations lacking in facts, with conclusions based on an unproven theory, or descriptions of fragments of infants' behaviors, insufficient for a broad systematic overview of the whole child, or judgments based on clinical hunches and impressions, with no information how another investigator could duplicate the impressions.

We talked to a neurophysiologist friend, asking him whether there were some physiological measure that we could use to show up differences in children's behavior. He smiled but shook his head no. "I'm glad it's your problem," he said, "and not mine." A pediatrician friend who was intrigued by our ideas made a series of observations in a newborn nursery for us. He came back with a discouraging report. The newborn babies varied so much in their behavior from hour to hour that he didn't think we could find what was "typical" for each one in the newborn state. We thought differences in conditioning might give us a clue—Pavlov had reported such differences in his animal experimentation—so we bought a half-dozen little bells and gave them to a group of mothers with new babies. For a week, each time the baby cried the mother was to tinkle the bell before feeding him. The results were disappointing. The tinkling of the bell didn't seem to affect the babies' crying or other behavior to any significant degree.

But the answer came as we checked with these mothers on the bell-tinkling experiment. They chattered on about their babies' behavior, not only in feeding but in sleep routines, in bathing, and in reactions to sudden noises and other events. At first we listened politely, but it quickly dawned on us that the mothers were giving us just the information we wanted: how the baby functioned in all the daily routines of living, as well as his behavior with anything new. Each baby was different, and as we listened, each one came alive as a unique individual.

The Research Methodology

The obvious often takes the longest to appreciate. After all, it is the parents as the infant's primary caregivers who know best the details of their child's behavior. Only an observer actually living in the house for days or weeks could duplicate this knowledge.

But this realization did not mean that we could simply take the parents' spontaneous reports and work with that information alone. Some parents wanted to talk about only some areas of their baby's behavior and had to be gently asked about other details. Some parents gave very brief descriptions and had to be encouraged to elaborate. Some were busy interpretating—"He loves this; he hates that"—and had to be pressed to give us the actual details of the baby's behavior.

We therefore developed a systematic, comprehensive interview that asked the parents for the factual details of the child's behavior in the routines of daily life—the first bath, feeding and sleep behavior and schedules, dressing and undressing, new foods, new people, new toys, new places and the subsequent adjustment, as well as illness and any other special events. These interviews became our primary method of obtaining information during the first three years of the child's life. In a number of the interviews both parents participated; in some only the mothers did. We insisted on detailed factual descriptions of each item and were not satisfied with the parents' interpretations. We always asked what the child did, not why the parent thought he did it. However, we did take note of the parents' interpretations, because they gave clues as

to the parents' attitudes and thinking, even if they did not describe the
child's behavior.

Parents varied greatly in the ease with which they gave us the information we requested. Some were clear, others rather vague; some reported
succinctly and to the point, others elaborated and digressed. But with
patient questioning we were able to obtain clear and detailed information
on the child's behavior in a variety of situations.

The question has been raised whether we could rely on the accuracy of
the parents' reports. After all, they might try to give us favorable impressions of their children. We avoided this potential pitfall by assuring each
parent that we considered the child to be normal and that different normal children behaved differently. We also made every effort to phrase
each question so that it was not judgmental. We did not ask, "Does he
get upset often?" but rather, "What kinds of situations upset him, and
how does he act when he is upset?" To check the parents' accuracy, two
observers separately went to the homes of eighteen of the children and
took detailed notes of the children's behavior over a two- or three-hour
period. These observations showed a significantly positive correlation
with the mothers' reports. Finally, because almost all the interviews were
done in the families' homes, we had many opportunities to watch a
child's behavior unobtrusively and found a close correlation with what
the mother was reporting. Our finding that parents can give accurate and
objective reports of their children's behavior has been confirmed by
other research workers (Costello 1975; Dunn & Kendrick 1980; Wilson &
Matheny 1983).

Our research objectives required that we undertake a longitudinal study,
observing and evaluating the behavior of our subjects over a substantial
period of time. Only this kind of investigation can reveal the full story of
an individual's behavior. Such a study is laborious and time-consuming,
and one must wait for years for definitive findings. A longitudinal study
also represents a gamble: For example, if it becomes clear when the subjects
are ten years old that certain information at age one or two years is crucial,
it is too late to go back and get this information.

There is no substitute for a longitudinal study, however. An investigator
may gain much useful information from a cross-sectional study—for example, a comparison between the behavior of one group of children at two
years and another group of children at five years. But such a study will not
reveal the life course of any individual child in this three-year period.
Child A might be high in a particular rating at two years and low at five,
and Child B the reverse, low at two years and high at five years. If only
the whole group trend is analyzed, these two children will cancel each

other out. Only a longitudinal study that follows each child over time will be able to detect such individual shifts, which may be crucial to the understanding of the differences in psychological development of different children.

Longitudinal studies are also important because parents cannot be relied upon to remember accurately events from past years. Memory plays tricks on all of us. One can have vivid memories of the past that one is sure are accurate and then be chagrined to discover that these events had occurred differently or not at all. We conducted an interesting experiment along these lines in our study. During the first-year interviews we asked and noted whether the child was a thumb-sucker or used a pacifier. When the children were three years of age, two researchers who had had no previous contact with the study asked each parent to remember whether the child had been a thumb-sucker or had used a pacifier in the first year of life. The parents' answers to this simple memory question were then compared with the actual facts, as given in the first-year interview. The results of this comparison were surprising. A number of parents had forgotten that their infants had been thumbsuckers. On the other hand, all the parents whose infants had not been a thumbsucker remembered this fact accurately. When it came to the use of a pacifier, the results were entirely reversed. No parent whose infant had used a pacifier had forgotten that, but some parents whose children had been thumbsuckers and had not used pacifiers now reported that their infants had used pacifiers. This finding puzzled us until one researcher hit upon the explanation: Benjamin Spock, whose child care manual was the Bible for these parents, was critical of thumb-sucking but approved of the use of a pacifier. The parents' distortions of memory clearly served the purpose of bringing their infants' behavior in line with Spock's recommendations (Robbins 1963). A number of other studies have also reported significant distortions of mothers' recall of their children's earlier years (Wenar 1963).

The clinician responsible for the immediate treatment of a patient must rely on the recollections of the patient or the parents, if no more accurate source of information is available. The research worker, however, has a different responsibility, the accumulation of pertinent and accurate data. In this task, memories of the past, if utilized at all, must be evaluated with great caution. Our interviews with parents, as well as other information we collected from other sources, therefore concentrated on reports of the child's behavior in the present and recent past.

The New York Longitudinal Study

We began our first and major study, the New York Longitudinal Study (NYLS), in 1956, although it took about five years to gather our total sample of 133 infants. In most cases, the first interview was done when the child was two or three months of age; a small number were started at slightly older ages. Subsequent interviews were conducted at three-month intervals during the first eighteen months of life, then at six-month intervals until five years of age, and then yearly until eight or nine years of age. Financial considerations then limited our subsequent follow-ups to those youngsters with behavior problems. At age sixteen or seventeen years 107 of our 133 subjects and their parents were interviewed separately. Those not interviewed at that time were primarily the youngest subjects; they were interviewed during the next follow-up period, when they were seventeen to nineteen years of age. In this last completed series of interviews, when the older subjects in the cohort were in early adult life, we were able to interview all 133 subjects and their living parents separately. We have now started a new follow-up of our subjects in their late twenties and early thirties.

We were not content to limit ourselves to the data obtained by our parent interviews, as valuable as these were. A yearly one- to two-hour period of observation of each child was conducted in nursery school, in kindergarten, and in the first grade. Whenever possible, it was scheduled to include a free-play period. The observations were made by a research staff member who had no previous knowledge of the child's history or behavior. The observer sat unobtrusively in a corner of the schoolroom and made a running account of the child's behavior in concrete descriptive terms. The child being observed had no knowledge that this was being done.

Up through the first grade a yearly teacher interview was also conducted by a different staff member, who again had no knowledge of the child's history. The teacher interview was modeled on the parent interview form and emphasized descriptive details of the child's day-to-day behavior in the various school routines and special events.

IQ testing was done at three and six years of age. We were interested in obtaining this measure of intellectual capacity, despite all its limitations. We were even more interested in obtaining information on each child's style of behavior in such a standard and formal test situation. We therefore placed an observer in the testing room, who made a detailed written account of the child's behavior and verbalization preceding, during, and immediately following the IQ test procedure. These additional data obtained from the school and test situations provided us with rich information on many aspects of the child's behavioral patterns and adaptive patterns, which could also be compared with his home behavior.

When the child was three years old, a special interview was held with each mother and father separately but simultaneously to determine their child care attitudes and practices, their goals for their children, and other related information. This information was an important systematic supplement to the impressions gained by the interviewers who did the sequential basic interviews. The basic interviews, which focused on the child's behavior, also revealed a great deal about the parents' personalities and their approaches to managing their children.

A primary objective of the NYLS was to determine whether and how individual behavioral characteristics of children influenced their psychological development, both in healthy and in unhealthy directions. With this in mind, we paid special attention to children in the project who developed behavior disorders. This concentration was important not only in helping the children with problems but in contributing to our understanding of normal development. It was in line with the medical tradition in which the study of many disorders, such as vitamin, hormone, and other biochemical disturbances, has given vital clues to the functional importance of these substances in the normal person.

The parents were told that one of us (S.C.) was always immediately available for clinical consultation when and if their child developed any kind of worrisome behavior. The parents who became concerned contacted me either through the staff interviewer or directly by telephone. In some cases it was clear that the child's behavior was essentially normal, and simple reassurance and advice were all that was required. Where there was any possibility that the behavior might represent an actual psychological problem, however, I did a full clinical evaluation, as I would with any case referred to me. This included a detailed history from the parents, a playroom session with the child, and special neurological or psychological studies where necessary. As in any other case, I made a clinical evaluation and diagnosis of the child's problem on the basis of this work-up. Only then did I review in detail all our information on the child, starting with the first interview in early infancy. With this review I was able to formulate a judgment about the origin of the problem and the factors that had contributed to it and to advise the parents, and the teachers where indicated, about the remedial treatment required. All children with behavior disorders were followed at regular intervals and reevaluated clinically whenever necessary.

Our Other Research Studies

Our major study, the NYLS, comprised a fairly homogenous middle- and upper-middle-class group of families; most of the parents had been born in this country. This similarity among the families had the advantage of minimizing differences in the children that could be caused by differences in sociocultural environments, but it raised the question of whether the findings from the NYLS could be generalized to other sociocultural groups. For this reason we also gathered data on a group of ninety-five children from stable working-class families with parents born in Puerto Rico but living in New York City. The interviewers and testing psychologists were also Puerto Rican. An identical research method was used with the Puerto Rican families as with the NYLS, except that we were able to follow the children only from infancy to six years of age. In addition, we also studied two samples of deviant children: one a group of fifty-two children with mild mental retardation living at home and the other a group of 243 children who had suffered various physical defects because of infection with the rubella virus (German measles) before birth. These two special groups allowed us to study the effects of individual behavioral differences combined with various mental and physical disturbances.

In the remainder of this book we will take up some of the specific issues raised by our research—from the ways children develop emotionally, socially, and cognitively to the ways families deal with special needs and special problems.* We will address specific questions that parents ask: Is it better for a baby if the mother stays home or if she goes to work outside the home? How well can we predict from a baby's first year what his further development will be? Thanks to recent research studies in child development, we can answer such questions with greater confidence than we could in the past. In the chapters that follow we will therefore bring in the findings not only of our own research but of others who have studied child development in a scientific and systematic way. On the basis of this solid evidence, we hope to question much of the conventional wisdom and to free both parents and professionals from the myths that have for too long enshrouded human development in mystery.

*Our discussion of our findings will be based, unless otherwise indicated, on the NYLS sample, the group we have studied the longest and most intensively, from the subjects' early infancy to early adulthood. We recommend that those interested in learning more about our findings read our *Temperament and Development* (Thomas & Chess, 1977) and *Origins and Evolution of Behavior Disorders* (Chess & Thomas, 1984).

2

Babies Are Different from the Start: Temperament and Its Significance

IN 1956 we began to gather detailed information on the behavior of individual infants, using the parent interview we had developed. Within a year we were convinced that we were on the right track. The parents could describe factually and specifically how their babies ate and slept, how they took to the bath, how they behaved when being dressed or undressed or just lying in their cribs, how they reacted to a soiled diaper or a loud noise, and how they took to new foods, toys, people, and places. The parents could also describe specifically what they themselves did when the infant was upset and how the baby responded to what the parent did. A typical dialogue in an interview might go as follows:

"What was your baby's first solid food?"
"Cereal, two weeks ago, when she was almost three months old."
"How did she take to the cereal?"
"She loved it. She lapped it up, opened her mouth, and took it all."
"Have you tried any other solids since?"
"Yes, I've given her several different fruits, and she took to each one the same as the cereal."

With another parent, there might be a different dialogue:

"What was your baby's first solid food?"

"It was cereal, when she was three months old, just after my first interview with you."

"How did she take to it?"

"She didn't. With the first taste she spit it out, cried loudly, and turned her head away. She would only take her bottle of milk."

"What did you do next?"

"I tried the cereal again the next day, and she had the same reaction."

"What then?"

"I waited a few days and then tried her on applesauce. She didn't like that either, but it wasn't as bad."

"What do you mean by 'not as bad'?"

"Well, she also spit it out, but she didn't cry or turn her head away. So I tried applesauce again the next day, and this time she didn't spit it out but just let it dribble out. But she wouldn't swallow it. I was a little encouraged, because she didn't make the big fuss she did with the cereal. So I offered her the applesauce every day and finally, after about a week, she began to swallow it. Now she loves it, just gobbles it up. I've tried other fruits, too, and she went through the same routine with each one as with the applesauce."

"Have you tried cereal again?"

"I did, after she was taking the applesauce well. But no go, she just spit it out and cried, just like the first time. The next day I mixed a little cereal in with the applesauce and she took that all right. Then I gradually put more and more cereal mixed in with the fruit, and she kept on taking it. After about two weeks, when the mixture was about half and half, I offered her cereal without the fruit. She took it, though not as eagerly as the fruit, and she's been taking it since almost every day."

It was also clear from the parents' descriptions that babies did differ in many ways, even in the first few months of life. Some infants cried softly while others tended to cry loudly. Some fussed or cried a great deal, others only a little. Some babies developed regular sleep and feeding schedules quickly and easily; others got hungry and sleepy at different times from day to day. Some moved their arms and legs and twisted their necks and bodies actively; others moved much less and lay quietly most of the time. Some took to new foods quickly and easily; others rejected most new foods and accepted them only after many trials. Some infants were startled easily by a loud noise and were uncomfortable with a wet diaper; others didn't seem to mind. Some were easily distracted when feeding if a person passed by or the telephone rang; others were not.

From these descriptions we were able to form pictures in our minds of the infants as organized, functioning human beings, each with an individual style of behavior and each very alert and responsive—though in different ways—to the environment in which they were beginning to grow up. They were certainly not miniature adults; rather, they were competent human beings at their own infant level of abilities and activities.

What Is Temperament?

Children differ behaviorally in a number of ways. They differ in the rates at which different abilities mature: when they can turn over, sit up, crawl, and walk; when they begin to talk, read, and write; when they begin to be able to understand abstract ideas. They also differ in the development of special interests and talents and in the kinds of aims and ambitions they formulate as they grow older. All these factors are important in a child's development, but they had been studied by many investigators and were not the focus of our own research. We were rather interested in individual differences in styles of responding to various stimuli and experiences, including what the children's caregivers did and expected, how other people behaved with them, and what new situations they encountered. We were also interested in the children's individual differences in carrying out the activities of their lives: sleeping and feeding, exploring objects, and so on with the more and more complex activities of older children. These differences in behavior had been given little attention by psychologists and psychiatrists, and yet they appeared to us to have great significance in shaping the child's psychological development.

Several research workers in the field of personality studies, especially the American psychologists Raymond Cattell (1950) and J. Paul Guilford (1959), had suggested what we thought was a usable way of categorizing different aspects of behavior: the *what*, the *why*, and the *how*. The *what* of behavior refers to the level of abilities and talents: how well a person performs an activity. The *why* of behavior refers to a person's motivations and goals. The *how* of behavior refers to behavioral style or temperament: the way in which a person does what she does.

It is the *how* of behavior, or temperament, that became the major though not the exclusive focus of our research study. Two children may dress and feed themselves equally well, ride a bicycle with the same skill, and have the same motives for engaging in these activities. Two adolescents may have similar academic interests, learn equally quickly, and have similar ambitions. Two adults may have the same technical expertise and motivation on their jobs. Yet these two children, adolescents, or adults may differ markedly in the quickness with which they move, the ease with which they approach a new physical environment, social situation, or task, the intensity and character of their mood expression, and the effort it takes to distract them when they are absorbed in an activity. In other words, their behavioral styles may be different.

Of course, the different aspects of behavior do not exist in separate watertight compartments. Abilities, motivations, and temperament all influence each other. A child whose temperament is to be persistent in the vast majority of her activities may be poorly motivated with regard to one specific task, such as learning to swim, perhaps because of a low level of ability for skilled muscular activity; as a result she may show low persistence in learning to swim. Conversely, another child who is typically much less persistent may be highly motivated to learn to swim and show great persistence in that particular task. Similarly, temperament may influence abilities or motivations. For a child with a high level of motor energy and muscular activity, being forced to sit quietly for hours at a time in her seat in school may lower her motivation for learning and prevent her academic abilities from reaching their full potential.

Because the expression of temperament may be influenced by motivation or abilities or by a specific situation, a person's temperament cannot be evaluated on the basis of behavior in only one setting or at only one time. Information must be gathered on the person's behavior in a number of situations and different times. With broad information such as we obtained in our parent and school interviews, it is possible to decide which behaviors are typical for an individual and which are not typical but shaped in some special way by an unusual situation or life experience.

The Origins of Temperament

What determines individual differences in temperament in the young infant? Research findings to date, using the standard method of twin studies, suggest some genetic influence (Buss & Plomin 1975; Torgersen & Kringlen 1978). In these studies, a group of identical twins, who have identical chromosomes and genetic characteristics, is compared with a group of nonidentical same-sexed twins, who share on the average only 50 percent of the same genetic characteristics. If the identical twins are more similar to each other with respect to some physical or behavioral characteristic, than the nonidentical twins are to each other, it is presumed that a genetic-hereditary factor is at least partially involved in determining that particular characteristic. This research technique was used by Torgersen and Kringlen as well as by Buss and Plomin. Torgersen and Kringlen studied a group of thirty-four Norwegian identical twins and sixteen nonidentical same-sex twins in infancy, using our categories and methods of rating. They found that in all of the temperamental variables measured, the identical twin pairs were more similar than the nonidentical same-sex twins (1978). Buss and Plomin, using a larger sample of twins in Colorado, and an approach to the collection of data and the categories of temperament that differed from ours, came to similar conclusions. Both sets of investigators also emphasized that the genetic factor only partly accounted for the child's temperament. Other biological factors, such as the influence of the intrauterine environment on the unborn child, or differences in handling by the parents might also have an effect.

It may very well be that identical twins, who have a close physical resemblance, may be treated more nearly alike by parents and others than are nonidentical twins, who resemble each other no more than do ordinary brothers or sisters. If so, the greater similarity in temperament of identical twins might be due to environmental as well as to genetic causes. There is, however, no firm evidence to support this speculation.

Brain damage before birth or during delivery does not appear to affect temperament in any striking fashion. A few studies suggest that chronic anxiety in the mother during the prenatal period may influence the newborn's temperament. Sociocultural factors appear to make a difference, although the evidence is still tentative. A few researchers have begun to explore possible correlations of temperament with various biochemical and physiological measures—a difficult but promising area of research.

It is our hypothesis that differences in temperament in the newborn and the very young infant are biologically determined, but then the infant's temperament is influenced by her interaction with her parents, which may either intensify or modify her original temperament. And as the child grows older, other environmental factors may accentuate, modify, or even change one or another temperamental attribute or pattern. This hypothesis is in line with the current view of development as a combination of the biological and environmental at all age periods, but it remains to be validated or modified. It is hoped that a number of studies now in progress at various research centers will provide the needed validation or modification.

Evaluating Temperament

As interested as we were in the relationship of temperament to other behavioral characteristics, our first task, after we began to accumulate the records of infant behavior from the parent interviews, was to use this information to identify, define, and rate the different categories of temperament. We had to decide which details of behavior were related so that they could be grouped under one general category or another. We had to define these categories in a way that would make sense to us and to others. And we had to develop a scheme of rating the details of the child's behavior, so that each child's temperament could be accurately and quantitatively scored. Judgments of temperament made impressionistically—that is, qualitatively—could also be valuable in assessing a child's behavior and tracing her development over time. But quantitative ratings were necessary in order to compare statistically the different children's temperaments at any one time or to correlate the evaluations of any one child's temperament at different ages. Quantitative ratings were also necessary for comparing the NYLS findings with those from other groups of children, whether our other samples (the Puerto Rican children, the mentally retarded group, or the children with congenital rubella) or groups of children that might be studied by other investigators using our ideas and methods.

Our clinical psychiatric training enabled us to scan the parent interviews and make impressionistic qualitative evaluations of the children's temperamental characteristics. We could describe a number of qualities quite clearly, but this was not sufficient. Definitions of the different categories of temperament had to be established in a way that would permit the records to be scored quantitatively. And a method of scoring had to be established that could utilize all the details of a child's behavior. This task we were not equipped by training or experience to undertake. We approached several competent research psychologists, but they felt the task was too complex to undertake. We were then fortunately able to consult Herbert Birch of the Albert Einstein Medical Center, who was already established as an outstanding research scientist in the fields of animal and human behavior. Birch was intrigued by our hypotheses and the method of data collection we had developed and agreed to undertake the task of developing a quantitative scheme for defining and scoring temperament. He succeeded quickly and brilliantly.

Birch took a group of our parent interviews for the infancy period, four for each of twenty children. Without any other knowledge of the children, he examined these reports in detail. He extracted a number of categories of behavior that could be identified in all the children but that showed a considerable range of variability among the different children. He established definitions for each category and identified the items of behavior that appeared to fit appropriately within each of these categories. For example, he identified a category that indicated the child's reaction to anything new and labeled this category *approach or withdrawal.* The items in this category included the first bath, the first contact with a new food, new toy, or new clothing, being held by a new person, and entering a new place.

Birch worked out this analysis without any prior knowledge of the categories and definitions we had developed. We then compared his categories and definitions with ours. We found a remarkable agreement, although there were some relatively minor differences in the labels of the categories and in the assignment of specific items of behavior to the categories. For our joint final decisions, we used three basic principles: (1) The category itself should have functional significance in the child's life, for which the two of us drew on our long clinical experience with children and their families; (2) Any item of behavior to be included should be amenable to quantitative scoring, a judgment in which Birch was the expert; and (3) An item of behavior should be included only if it varied substantially from one child to another. The amount of movement during sleep was an appropriate item, for example, because it could vary from very seldom to very frequent change in position during sleep.

Birch continued to work with our research studies as an active senior consultant and contributed a number of creative ideas and formulations to our longitudinal studies until his untimely death in 1973.

The Categories of Temperament

Out of this consensus nine categories of temperament were identified. Each can be rated on a scale from high to low. For the early childhood years a three-point scale was used: high, medium, and low. For the later childhood years and for adolescence and adulthood we expanded the scale to seven points, from very high to very low. It should be emphasized that all ratings, whether high, intermediate, or low, represented differences within the *normal* range of behavior. Thus temperamentally high activity is a normal trait, as distinguished from the pathological type of overactivity that we call hyperactivity. Superficially, the two may sometimes result in similar behavior, but hyperactivity is an abnormal psychiatric disorder that may arise from a number of causes and usually requires special treatment. It should also be remembered, in the examples given below, that most children's ratings were intermediate between the high and low ratings.

The nine categories with their definitions and typical examples of a high and low rating for each category for the infancy period (birth to two years), the preschool period (two to six years), and middle childhood (six to twelve years) are as follows:

1. *Activity level:* motor activity and the proportion of active and inactive periods
   Infancy
   High activity: "She kicks and splashes so much in the bath that the floor must be mopped afterward."
   Low activity: "She can turn over, but she doesn't do it much."
   Preschool
   High activity: "When a friend from nursery school comes to visit, she immediately starts a game of running around wildly."
   Low activity: "Given a choice of activities, she usually selects something quiet such as drawing or looking at a picture book."
   Middle childhood
   High activity: "When she comes home from school, she is immediately outside playing an active game."
   Low activity: "Typically she gets involved with a jigsaw puzzle and sits quietly working at it for hours."

2. *Rhythmicity (Regularity):* the predictability or unpredictability of the timing of biological functions, such as hunger, sleep-wake cycle, and bowel elimination
   Infancy
   Regularity: "Unless she is sick, her bowel movement comes predictably once a day immediately after breakfast."
   Irregularity: "I wouldn't know when to start toilet training, since bowel movements come at any time, and she has from one to three a day."
   Preschool
   Regularity: "Her big meal is always at lunch time."
   Irregularity: "Sometimes she falls asleep right after dinner, and on other days she keeps going till 9 or 10 P.M.—there is no predicting."
   Middle childhood
   Regularity: "She awakens like clockwork each morning; I never need to wake her for school."
   Irregularity: "Sometimes her big meal is lunch time, sometimes it's dinner, I never know."

3. *Approach or withdrawal:* the nature of the initial response to a new situation or stimulus—a new food, toy, person, or place. Approach responses are positive and may be displayed by mood expression (smiling, speech, facial expression) or motor activity (swallowing a new food, reaching for a new toy). Withdrawal reactions are negative and may be displayed by mood

expression (crying, fussing, speech, facial expression) or motor activity (moving away, spitting new food out, pushing new toy away).

Infancy

Approach: "She always smiles at a stranger."

Withdrawal: "When I introduce a new food, her first reaction is almost always to spit it out."

Preschool

Approach: "We went to her new play group yesterday, and she plunged right in."

Withdrawal: "She started nursery school two weeks ago. She wouldn't join the group and stood on the sidelines. It took her a week to begin to participate."

Middle childhood

Approach: "She came home from her new school the first day talking as if all the other pupils were already her friends."

Withdrawal: "The class just started fractions. As usual, she is sure she will never learn it. I reminded her that she always says that with a new subject, but then she masters it well."

4. *Adaptability:* long-term responses to new or altered situations. Here the concern is not the nature of the initial responses but the ease with which they are modified in desired directions.

Infancy

High adaptability: "When I first gave her cereal she spit it out, but it only took two or three times and she was eating it with gusto."

Low adaptability: "Every time I put her in her snowsuit, she screams and struggles until we are outside, and this has been going on all winter."

Preschool

High adaptability: "We moved to a new apartment last month, and she adjusted to her new room and new bed the first night."

Low adaptability: "She didn't like nursery school at first, and then it took her all fall to be content with it."

Middle childhood

High adaptability: "She went to a new summer play group this year. Although it was a totally new type of schedule, and she felt uncomfortable at first, it took her only a few days to get involved and feel comfortable."

Low adaptability: "We moved to a new neighborhood three months ago, and she is only just now beginning to make friends."

5. *Sensory Threshold:* the intensity level of stimulation necessary to evoke a discernible response, irrespective of the specific form the response may take.

Infancy

Low threshold: "If a door closes even softly, she starts and looks up."

High threshold: "She can bang her head and even raise a bump, but she doesn't change her behavior."

Preschool

Low threshold: "She complains about any pants if the waistband is the slightest bit tight."

High threshold: "Whether clothing texture is smooth or rough doesn't make any difference; she seems comfortable in every type."

Middle childhood

Low threshold: "She is the first one in any group to notice an odor or feel a change in the room temperature."

High threshold: "She came home from playing soccer with a blistered heel and hadn't noticed it, and didn't complain at all."

6. *Quality of Mood:* the amount of pleasant, joyful, and friendly behavior and mood expression, as contrasted with unpleasant crying and unfriendly behavior and mood expression

Infancy

Positive mood: "When she sees me take out her bottle of juice, she begins to smile and coo."

Negative mood: "Each night when put to sleep she cries at least five or ten minutes."

Preschool

Positive mood: "She got new shoes and she ran around bubbling with pleasure and showing them to everyone she met."

Negative mood: "She typically comes home from nursery school full of complaints about the other children."

Middle childhood

Positive mood: "She never objects to home chores and does whatever she is asked with a smile."

Negative mood: "School just started last week and she already has a list of grievances about each teacher."

7. *Intensity of Reactions:* the energy level of response, positive or negative

Infancy

Low intensity: "When she is upset she fusses but doesn't cry loudly."

High intensity: "If she hears music, she bubbles with loud laughter."

Preschool

Low intensity: "I know if she likes a new toy because she smiles quietly."

High intensity: "As soon as she has trouble with a puzzle, she screams and throws the pieces."

Middle childhood

Low intensity: "I know she was very upset at failing the test, but outwardly she appeared only a little subdued."

High intensity: "In the restaurant she couldn't get the food she wanted and screamed and made a big fuss."

8. *Distractibility:* the effectiveness of an outside stimulus in interfering with or changing the direction of the child's ongoing behavior

Infancy

Low distractibility: "When she is hungry and it takes a little while to get her food ready, it is not possible to get her involved in play. She just keeps crying until fed."

High distractibility: "If someone passes by while she is nursing, she not only looks but stops sucking until the person has gone."

Preschool

Low distractibility: "If she decides she wants to go out to play and it's raining, she will fuss and won't accept any substitute."

High distractibility: "She's not a nagger. If she wants special cookies at the

supermarket and they don't have them, she will ask once or twice but then will accept a substitute."
Middle childhood
Low distractibility: "Once she starts reading a book, we can't get her attention until she gets to the end of a chapter."
High distractibility: "Her homework takes a long time, as her attention repeatedly gets sidetracked."

9. *Persistence and attention span:* These two categories are usually related. Persistence refers to the continuation of an activity in the face of obstacles or difficulties. Attention span concerns the length of time a particular activity is pursued without interruption.
Infancy
Low persistence: "If the bead doesn't go on the string immediately, she gives up."
Short attention span: "Although she loves her teddy bear, she plays with it only a few minutes at a time."
High persistence: "She always tries to poke at electric outlets, and if I pull her away she immediately tries to go back."
Long attention span: "If I give her an old magazine, she will contentedly tear up paper for as long as a half hour."
Preschool
Low persistence: "She asked to be taught to draw a dog but lost interest after the first try."
Short attention span: "She likes to play with a new toy but concentrates on it only for a few minutes at a time."
High persistence: "If she is pushing her wagon around and it gets stuck, she struggles until it moves again. She doesn't give up."
Long attention span: "She can be absorbed playing in the sandbox for almost an hour."
Middle childhood
Low persistence: "She tried to learn to ice-skate, but after she fell a few times, she gave it up."
Short attention span: "She likes to read, but only a half hour at a time."
High persistence: "If she has a hard arithmetic problem for homework, she keeps after it and insists she has to figure it out herself."
Long attention span: "If she has a part in a school play, she can rehearse it for hours."

Three Patterns of Temperament

We have identified three combinations of temperamental attributes that occurred together in a number of the children in our longitudinal studies and appeared to influence a child's behavior as a pattern. We have called these combinations *the easy child, the difficult child,* and *the slow-to-warm-up child.*

The temperamentally easy child is characterized by regularity of biological functions, a positive approach to most new situations and people, easy adaptability to change, and a mild or moderately intense mood that is predominantly positive. These children quickly develop regular sleep and feeding schedules, take to most new foods easily, smile at strangers, adapt easily to a new school, accept minor frustrations with little fuss, and accept the rules of new games without trouble. Such a youngster is usually a joy to her parents, pediatricians, and teachers (although an occasional parent may worry that the child adjusts too easily and will be taken advantage of in the outside world). This group comprises about 40 percent of our NYLS sample.

At the opposite end of the temperamental spectrum is the difficult child, who is characterized by irregularity in biological functions, negative withdrawal reactions to many new situations and people, slow adaptability to change, and intense mood expressions that are frequently negative. These children typically have irregular sleep and feeding schedules. They are slow to accept many or most new foods, and new routines require prolonged adjustment periods. Periods of crying are relatively frequent and loud, and laughter is also characteristically loud. Frustration typically produces a violent tantrum. Parents, pediatricians, and nurses find such youngsters difficult indeed to handle. This group of children comprises about 10 percent of our sample. Mrs. M's infant son Bobby, whom we introduced in chapter 1, we would now call a typical temperamentally difficult child.

One point should be made regarding the temperamentally difficult child. We coined this term because we found in our study that parents with this type of child did have special difficulties in their management. Some parents, however, can adapt rather easily to such a child. Others will label a child "difficult" for other reasons, such as low sensory threshold, high distractibility, or extreme persistence. Also, what caregivers find irksome in our culture—a child who wakes up frequently and irregularly at night, for example—may not disturb a mother in a different culture with different priorities for her life. So the term "temperamentally difficult" should be distinguished from an individual mother's label of "a difficult child to manage." The two terms may or may not coincide.

It should also be emphasized that parents do not produce this temperamental pattern in a child, although the way parents respond to such a child may minimize or exaggerate the difficult features of the child's behavior. Given sufficient time and patient handling, these difficult children do adapt well, especially if the people and places in their world remain constant.

The third noteworthy temperamental pattern is that of the slow-to-warm-up child. These children respond negatively to new situations and people and adapt slowly. In contrast to temperamentally difficult children, however, these youngsters show mild rather than intense reactions and have a lesser tendency to irregular sleep and feeding schedules. When frustrated or upset, the child is likely to try to withdraw from the situation quietly or with mild fussing, rather than exploding with the violent tantrum of the difficult child. Slow-to-warm-up children can be called shy, so long as this term does not imply anxiety or timidity. They comprise about 15 percent of our sample.

As the above percentages (40, 10, and 15 percent) indicate, not all children fit into one of these three groups. Some children show other combinations of attributes, especially in the moderate range, that do not make for neat labels. Moreover, among those children who do fit one of these three patterns there is a wide range in the degree of its manifestation. Some children are easy in practically all situations; others are relatively easy but not always so. A few children are extremely difficult with all new situations and demands; others show only some of these characteristics and relatively mildly. Some children will warm up slowly in any new situation; others warm up slowly in certain types of new situations but quickly in others.

Certain temperamental qualities may combine in ways that have an impact in life situations. For example, a child with high distractibility and high persistence will generally complete tasks but perhaps not on time. In contrast, when high distractibility is combined with low persistence, promises to accomplish a task may be given in good faith but are not likely to be carried out. The combination of high activity and long attention span is a good formula for perfecting a motor skill such as bicycle riding, skiing, long-distance running, or building a house. But a child with high activity and high distractibility needs constant watching or she may be hurt or break things. As a final example, low sensory threshold with high persistence may lead to long fussing over slightly tight or rough clothing each morning, but under other circumstances this combination may lead to a sensitive awareness of the moods of others and a persistent positive concern to help out.

Our classification of temperament into the nine categories and our three patterns of easy, difficult, and slow-to-warm-up children have been confirmed by many other research studies in this country, in a number of European countries, and in Canada, Japan, India, Israel, Taiwan, and Kenya (Ciba Foundation 1982). These temperamental attributes have thus been identified in children with the widest range of cultural, national, and social class backgrounds. Some workers have suggested some modifications of our scheme of classification, and a few have proposed different categories, but the usefulness of these alternative approaches remains to be determined.

Temperament and Personality

When we began, in the 1950s, to explore the significance of the infant's own behavioral style for the course of psychological development, our psychiatric colleagues with few exceptions assumed we were returning to some outdated and discredited view of the infant as a *homunculus,* born with a predetermined personality. Polite, unconvinced nods met our insistence that constitution and environment—nature and nurture—were not mutually exclusive. On the contrary, we were told, the more we knew about the child's own temperament, the more clearly and thoroughly we would understand the influence of the parents and other environmental factors. Psychoanalytic colleagues were also critical of the importance we gave to psychological attributes that were not derived from motivational forces or instinctual drive states.

Our ideas received a different reception among pediatricians. From their own practical experience pediatricians knew that babies are different at birth. Many had also observed that these differences influence the manner in which the infant responds to specific child care practices and to illness or other special events. The pediatricians we knew welcomed and encouraged our plan to do a systematic study of behavior differences in children and their importance for psychological development. Several of these pediatricians were actively helpful to us in gathering a study sample and encouraging parents to participate in our project. Dr. William Carey became the first professional to use our early reports defining the different temperamental categories and patterns to develop a short temperament questionnaire form for parents. This form has proved highly useful for both research workers and clinicians and is now widely used. Dr. Carey has since developed questionnaires for older children, and we and others have also proposed various other questionnaire methods for assessing temperament at different age periods (Chess & Thomas 1986). By 1969, the Harvard pediatrician T. Berry Brazelton noted in the preface to his deservedly popular and influential book for parents, *Infants and Mothers,* that "Stella Chess and Alexander Thomas had made it 'de rigueur' to think of different styles of development in children" (1969, p. x). His book traces the differences in development over the first year of three babies with different activity levels—average, quiet, and active.

In recent years, our basic findings have been recognized and confirmed by an increasing number of mental health professionals as well as pediatricians. The concept of temperament has been applied to nursing practice, and its influence on teachers' attitudes and approaches has been studied systematically. Various mental health professionals and pediatricians have been exploring different methods of applying this knowledge in well-baby care as well as in the treatment of childhood behavior disorders. Research studies of temperament have become a major field of investigation in developmental psychology and psychiatry.

But this recognition of the importance of temperament should not lead to an attempt to equate temperament with personality. To do so would in truth be a return to the old notions of the *homunculus.* We consider personality to be a composite of the enduring psychological attributes that constitute the unique individuality of a person. Personality structure is formed from the many diverse elements that shape psychological development, all acting together: motivations, abilities and interests, temperament, goals and value systems, psychological defense mechanisms, and the impact of the family and the larger sociocultural environment.

Temperament is one of the important factors that helps to shape personality, and its influence varies from person to person. Because temperamental categories or patterns evidence themselves as responses to environmental events and attitudes, the final results of such interactions vary from one person to another. In some instances, one temperamental attribute or pattern may be important in personality development, in other cases a different temperamental attribute may be significant, in still others the important temperament pattern may be different again. Furthermore, the same temperament may lead to different personality outcomes, depending on all the other factors that are operating. The opposite is also true: Children with different temperaments may eventually have similar personalities, again depending on the other factors. We have seen instances of all these variations in personality outcome as we have followed the development of our subjects from infancy to adult life (Chess & Thomas 1984).

Another aspect of temperament of interest to us was its consistency over time. When we originally began to observe the temperament characteristics of our own children and other children we knew, we were impressed by the many dramatic instances in which one or another attribute remained the same as a child grew older. It was tempting to generalize from these observations to the idea that an older child's temperament, or even an adult's, could be predicted from a knowledge of her temperament in early childhood.

Like all other psychological attributes, however, such as intellectual competence, social patterns, adaptive mechanisms, and value systems, temperament in some people is consistent over time and in others changes at one time or another. So many factors help to shape the developmental course of any psychological attribute that the outcome can vary from one person to another. As we have followed our subjects, we have seen in some cases evidence of dramatic consistency in one or more attributes of temperament from one age period to another and in others indications of substantial change (Thomas & Chess 1977). The issue of consistency versus change over time is currently a topic of major interest in temperament research. The findings from these research studies, as they appear in the coming years, promise to increase our understanding of the meaning and significance of temperament for a child's psychological development.

Implications of Temperament for Parents

Our longitudinal studies, which have been confirmed by other research projects, have made it clear that the different categories and patterns of temperament are all within the normal range of behavior (Thomas & Chess 1977). This is a crucial point that we have had to emphasize to parents over and over again. Parents of a difficult or slow-to-warm-up child can easily conclude that their child is behaving abnormally. They blame either themselves or the child, or both. And whether they condemn themselves or the child, the parents are likely to put too much or too little pressure on the child, with unfavorable consequences for the child. All too often, mental health professionals who are not aware of how different normal children can be also make this mistake in judgment.

A child's temperament can actively influence the attitudes and behavior of her parents, other family members, playmates, and teachers and in turn help to shape their effect on her behavioral development.

The parents of a highly active child may regard her as undisciplined or disobedient because she doesn't sit still enough to suit them. A low-activity child may be considered sluggish and dull, because she moves so slowly. People may criticize a distractible child with low persistence for not having the "willpower" to stick to her homework or other activities to the very end without interruption. Parents may approve the way their highly persistent child plugs away at her tasks, no matter how difficult, but then be annoyed at her when she resists leaving her project to come to dinner or to get ready for a family outing.

The specific effect the child's temperament has on a child's behavior and on her parents will also vary from one age period to another. High distractibility may be an advantage in a young child, making it easier for the parents to divert her from potentially dangerous activities. At a later age, however, this same distractibility may make her forget prearranged appointments or activities, as she gets diverted on the way home or on the way downstairs to breakfast.

The importance of temperament will be spelled out with detailed examples in later chapters. Our findings have confirmed the basic hypothesis that motivated us to launch our longitudinal studies: A child plays an active role in her own development and is by no means a blank slate on which the parents and others inscribe her psychological development. To understand a child's behavior requires an understanding of her characteristics and the parents' characteristics, as well as of the influence of other family members and the outside world. All these factors interact at all age periods to produce the child's mental functioning. All are important, and no one factor can be said to be more important than any other.

Most parents can describe their child's temperament accurately. They can even apply appropriate designations, especially when a particular characteristic tends to be at one extreme or the other: "She doesn't move a lot, the way my friends' babies do"; "She's such an easy baby to take care of"; "Anything new upsets her, and I have to give her time to get used to it"; "She's very distractible, always turning her head when we're feeding her if she hears a noise or someone else is passing by. Half her food goes into her ear." Parents can make these informal generalizations even if they know nothing about our work on temperament. But many parents need help in dealing with their child's temperament. We have found it useful to provide parents with three guidelines:

1. Do not assume that if your child behaves differently from what you expected and hoped, you have been a "bad" parent. Your child's temperament may differ from the average even if you are a perfectly adequate parent. If you have this worry, ask yourself, "What is the *evidence* that I'm doing the wrong thing with my baby?" The fact that the baby is not responding as you hoped is not sufficient evidence for such a judgment. Also, be skeptical of an explanation that puts the blame on "your unconscious."

2. Don't assume that your child is deliberately behaving in a way that upsets you and could behave differently if she wanted to do so. Take note

of instances of behavior when this could not possibly be the case. For example, one mother of a highly distractible boy in our study was convinced that he just wanted to annoy her when he "forgot" to come home after school to go with her for a dental or medical appointment. But she herself told us of times when one of his friends had dropped by to remind him that he was supposed to be out at the ball field or the swimming pool with them and her son would exclaim, "Gosh, I got sidetracked and forgot. I'll be right there."

3. Don't make moralistic judgments about your child because of behavior that doesn't live up to a rigid standard you have set. One father of a temperamentally difficult girl in our study labeled her "a rotten kid" because she didn't adapt quickly to successive new rules and regulations of social living that were demanded of her. Another father condemned his highly distractible son, who also had a short attention span, as lacking willpower, because the boy couldn't sit still for several hours at a time going through his homework from beginning to end. The boy actually was intellectually bright and was doing very well in school. But the fact that the interruptions created by his temperament did not hinder his learning did not satisfy the father. "If I can sit and concentrate without interruption, he can, too."

Once the parents understand that their child's temperament requires some special handling, the question then comes up: "But how do we know what is the best approach?" We will take up this issue in detail in chapter 4. But first, having examined the differences among children, let us complete the picture by looking at how parenting styles differ.

3

The Many Ways of Parenthood

O UR PRIMARY INTEREST in launching the New York Longitudinal Study was to study individual differences in temperament in young infants and trace the significance of temperament for the child's psychological development. But our hypothesis was that the child's temperament was intimately related to the parents' caregiving practices and attitudes. The parents influenced the child and the child influenced the parents in a mutual give-and-take relationship. We were therefore also concerned with assessing the nature of the parents' activities, especially those related to their caregiving responsibilities.

Studying Parental Styles in the NYLS

We had a number of opportunities to gather information on the many different ways in which parents functioned. First, the parent interviews, although they focused on the child's behavior, also gave us a wealth of information on the parents themselves. The interviews always requested specific descriptive information of what the parent did in response to the child's behavior. For example, if the parent reported that the child awoke crying loudly at night, our next question would be "What did you do?" and then "How did the baby respond?" and "What did you do when the child responded in that way?" and so on until the sequence of interaction was complete. There would be questions of the same order if the parent described denying a child's request or the youngster's clinging to his mother the first day of nursery school or any other incident involving the parent's interaction with the child. In the course of these interviews many of the parents also made spontaneous judgments of their child's "personality." These subjective comments were not useful for rating the child's temperament, although at times the question "What makes you say that?" elicited objective descriptive information on the child's behavior. But these judgments did provide insights into the parents' attitudes toward the child.

In addition we had the separate interviews when the child was three years old, which focused on the parents' attitudes and caregiving practices. These interviews were rated quantitatively and subjected to a statistical analysis that identified a number of caregiving characteristics on which the parents as a group showed substantial variation: (1) parental approval, tolerance, and acceptance of the child versus disapproval, intolerance, and rejection; (2) parental conflict or lack of conflict with each other, especially over caregiving practices; (3) parental strictness versus permissiveness; (4) degree of parental concern and protectiveness; and (5) consistent versus inconsistent discipline.

Finally, in those children who showed evidence of a behavior disorder, the clinical interview with the parents probed for the details of the parents' attitudes and handling of the child.

A number of investigators have studied different styles of parenthood and their correlation with the child's development (Baumrind 1979; Chamberlin 1974). Various labels have been given to different types of parents: *authoritarian, authoritative, permissive, accommodative, overprotective, flexible, rigid,* and *rejecting,* to name only a few. A number of these adjectives could be applied to our NYLS parents, but our concern has been that researchers have used these labels without considering the influence of the child on the parent. The studies have usually assumed a one-way street, from parent to child. They have also often made global judgments about categories into which the parents are presumed to fit at all times. But a parent can be permissive in certain situations and authoritative in others, or flexible on certain issues and rigid on others. And the basic question is the same for parents as for children: Is there only one good way to be a good parent? Is there one style of parenthood that is "best," that will produce the "ideal child"? Or is this a false goal, a search for the pot of gold at the end of the rainbow?

Our own data, as well as a review of other studies, give an emphatic answer to these questions. There is no single style of parenthood that is best for all children. There are many ways of being a good parent. And there are many ways of being a difficult or even psychologically disturbed parent.

In our study, we correlated statistically the three-year ratings of parental attitudes and practices with our ratings of the level of overall adjustment and psychological functioning when the child reached early adulthood. Only parent conflict at age three showed a significant correlation. The higher the parental conflict score at age three, the lower the youngster's adult adjustment. This was a finding for the group as a whole and, like all statistical correlations, did not identify the individual subjects with different outcomes—those in whom low or high age three parental conflict made no difference in adult outcome, or when high conflict had existed in young adults with a high level of adjustment or vice versa. However, we did not find correlation with early adult outcome for the other parental ratings—degrees of approval, tolerance and acceptance of the child, permissiveness, parental protectiveness, or consistent discipline.

Other Research Into Parenting

Diana Baumrind, of the University of California at Berkeley, is one of the few major investigators in this area who has reported a definitive relationship between parental attitudes and the child's pattern of behavior (1968, 1979). In her studies, which were carefully done, she described three types of parents: (1) authoritarian parents, who try to shape, control, and evaluate the child's behavior in accordance with a preestablished absolute standard of behavior; (2) permissive parents, who respond to the child's behavior in a nonpunishing, accepting, and affirmative manner; and (3) authoritative parents, whom Baumrind considered to be the most nurturant. The authoritative parents were most responsive to their children's demands for attention, but they did not yield to unreasonable demands. They also expected mature, independent behavior from the child, appropriate to his developmental level. Such parents tended to have the most socially competent children. Baumrind reported that authoritarian parents tended to have children who were less happy, as well as moody, apprehensive, passively hostile, and vulnerable to stress; the permissive parents tended to have children who were impulsive-aggressive. Baumrind did not consider the effect of the child's temperament on the parents' attitudes, however. Moreover, her findings were of tendencies, with many mixtures that did not conform to her overall simple scheme.

Other studies besides our own have questioned this kind of close correlation between parental styles and outcome in the children. One of the most important longitudinal studies has been the Harvard Grant study (Vaillent 1977) in which ninety-five Harvard sophomores from the years 1939–44 have been followed into middle life. Detailed accounts of each subject's early life were obtained from the subjects themselves and their mothers. Because the early life data were obtained retrospectively, they were subject to the distortions of memory that this kind of recall can bring, but the information obtained was of factual, descriptive details, which minimize such distortions of recall. This study found that an overall rating of a happy versus an unhappy childhood did correlate with outcome in adult life. The conclusions emphasized, however, that "when the childhoods of the Best and Worst outcomes in the Grant study were compared, there were many surprises. When identified in advance, finger-nail biting, early toilet training, the 'tainted family tree,' even that old standby—the cold rejecting mother—failed to predict emotionally ill adults" (p. 285).

Robert Chamberlin of the University of Rochester studied seventy-two mothers of two-year-old children recruited from pediatric practices (1974). They were rated by interview as either authoritarian or accommodative in their child-rearing styles. In forty cases the ratings were confirmed by home observations by an independent observer. Ratings of the children were obtained through interviews with the mothers. These ratings were subjected to statistical analysis, and three childhood patterns were identified: friendly-outgoing, dependent-inhibited, and aggressive-resistant— patterns similar to those obtained in other studies. (In this case overall personality traits were being evaluated, and not temperament.) Chamberlin found a minimal relationship between maternal style and child behavior and felt that the different parental approaches appeared to be related to different life styles that should be respected by the physician. He concluded wisely that "attempts to change a child-rearing approach should be based on clear evidence that a particular pattern is having harmful effects on a particular type of child rather than on ideologic grounds" (p. 292).

Finally, we can mention a very recent report by two leading research workers in the field of child development, Judith Dunn, of Cambridge University, and Robert Plomin, of the University of Colorado (Dunn, Plomin, & Nettles 1985). (Dunn was in residence in Colorado at the time of this study.) In each of forty-six families, they studied the mother and two children, each child at age twelve months. For these families, the average age difference between the two children was fifty-five months. Each mother's behavior was observed intensively in the home with each child, and the observations were rated on three scales: (1) affection and acceptance of the child; (2) verbal expression of feelings; and (3) maternal control and behavior. Dunn and Plomin found that each mother showed very similar behavior toward her two children, even though the observations were made on the average of fifty-five months apart, and even though the range of differences among mothers was considerable. But we know, especially from our studies and from other temperament research, as well as from studies of other aspects of the behaviors of twelve-month-old children, that two children of this age in the same family *are* often different in their behavior. And it is in the child's first year of life, as many theorists have asserted, that we would expect the mother's influence to be especially strong. She is usually a powerful nurturing figure even if she works outside the home, and has an intense relationship with the infant before the child begins to have important peer relationships or begins to go to nursery school. This study therefore suggests that even in the first year of life, the individual child's development, which leads to significant behavior differences by twelve months of age, is not decisively determined by the mother. The mother and father may be important influences, but they are not decisive. This study also lends additional evidence to the judgment that individual differences in temperament in early childhood are not determined by parental attitudes or child-rearing practices.

Styles of Parenting

Parents and families are different. Some parents are permissive with regard to manners and social niceties; others have strict standards for their children. Some parents express affection openly; others are reserved. Some spend a great deal of time with their children in activities of joint interest; others are less involved. Some parents and children confide easily in each other on intimate personal issues; others do little of this kind of communication. Some parents go in for early weaning and training; others are casual about them or even feel that early weaning and toilet training are undesirable.

Some fathers play a very active part in their babies' daily care. They take turns with the mother in feeding, changing, and dressing the baby, putting him to bed, and getting up at night when he cries. Others concentrate on certain special activities with their young children, like taking night calls, roughhouse play, and excursions. (Fathers who keep their distance from their babies and don't get involved are another matter; both father and child are likely to suffer.)

Some children are brought up in a tight nuclear family—father, mother, and at most one brother or sister. Others live in an extended family, with several brothers and sisters and with grandparents and perhaps other relatives, like uncles, aunts, and cousins, living in the same house or very close by.

There are mothers who go back to work outside the home within a few weeks after the birth of the baby. There are other mothers who devote their time to their children and do not return to work until the youngsters are in school full-time, if at all. The high divorce rate also makes for many kinds of arrangements for children: custody with the mother, custody with the father, or joint custody.

Recent years have seen the emergence of a group of mature, self-supporting single women who have a child and bring him up without a father in the household. Also challenging the necessity of a nuclear family are experiments with communal family living. Small as these trends are, they do exist, and babies are being brought up either with a single mother or in a community of parents. (We are not referring here to the isolated and poverty-stricken teenage single mother, who all too often has neither the psychological nor the financial resources to bring up a child on her own. In addition, many such mothers do not receive adequate support, if any, from community agencies.)

In tracing the interplay of parents and children in different families, we have found it useful to use our own categories of styles of parenthood. These are not new; they have been described by others, sometimes with the same labels and sometimes with different labels but with the same meaning. In using these categories, we have tried to differentiate those elements that the parent has brought to his or her caregiving style from those that have been in reaction to the child's behavior. In most cases, both elements are present and work together in the parent's style of functioning.

The Secure Parent

Many parents feel and act secure in taking care of their children. They have learned the basic techniques of baby care from relatives and friends or from classes for expectant parents: how to diaper, how to burp the baby in the middle of a feeding, how to hold the young infant while bathing him, and so on. They have also probably observed from watching other babies that each one seems a little different in his behavior and reactions, so that finding the best approach to their own baby may take a period of trial and error. If they make mistakes, they can change, and no real harm has been done. They assume that they will cope successfully with their responsibilities as parents, just as they have with other duties and tasks in life. They expect that this new mission of parenthood will not be just a chore but a truly creative activity that will bring a special sense of self-fulfillment.

Such parents are ready to experiment with a new approach if the baby does not appear content with what they are doing. They are not afraid of making mistakes; they know that no disasters will occur. On the other hand, if the baby appears chronically discontented or is not thriving, they are ready to seek expert advice; they are not afraid that doing so will expose them as unfit to be parents.

This does not mean that all secure parents bring up their infants in the same manner. Quite the contrary. The parents' own life style, their preferences, and their schedules mesh with the baby's own individual behavioral style to create all kinds of variations in actual handling. Let us take two actual mothers with their first children, Mrs. A., with a baby daughter, Brenda, and Mrs. B., with a baby son, Brad. Brenda's mother gave up her job and decided to breast-feed, which she did successfully. Her friends approved until they became aware that Mrs. A. meant this to be a prolonged pattern. Some of them then became critical because she was giving Brenda a model that a mother should not work outside the home but should devote herself to being a housewife and a mother. When Brenda at age two still had her mother's breast freely offered, even though she was on a full regular diet, these friends shook their heads sadly. It was clear to them that Brenda had become excessively dependent on her mother and would have the greatest difficulty separating from her to become part of a peer play group.

But when Brenda was brought to a cooperative play group at age two and a half, she joined with the other children with great delight and scarcely noticed whether her mother was in the room or not. And at three, when morning nursery school was scheduled for every weekday without her mother, Brenda went off cheerfully. Moreover, each morning she asked in hopeful expectation, "School today?" and was disappointed on weekends when the answer was "not today."

Brad, on the other hand, was breast-fed for only a week. His mother's decision to breast-feed for at least a month was cut short because of pain due to cracked nipples. Also, Mrs. B. was in the early stages of a promising career in a competitive field and felt she had to show she was able to get back to work quickly. She began going back to work gradually, starting a month after Brad's birth, and was soon working full-time again. Her husband took a very active role in the baby's care, and she had an excellent, reliable baby-sitting arrangement, so that Brad was always in good hands, whether she was at home or not.

But some of Mrs. B.'s friends raised their eyebrows. They hinted to her, a few quite openly, that if she worked full-time outside the home Brad would suffer from the lack of emotional nourishment that only a mother can supply. He would be deficient in "attachment" to her, and she would fail to be "bonded" to him. For a while Mrs. B. did worry that she was actually a fifth wheel, that her infant son really didn't need her. Brad stayed cheerfully with his baby-sitter, a mature and affectionate woman, and preferred the roughhouse play his father gave him to the more gentle interplay with his mother. But Mrs. B. maintained her perspective, took care of him with loving care, and gave him the full, open expression of affection that her more reserved husband could not. And when her husband went away for ten days when Brad was two, the baby made it clear that he was perfectly happy to be with his mother alone.

The Insecure Parent

In sharp contrast to secure parents, there are the insecure ones. These are the parents who believe that everything they do with their child will influence his destiny. No matter what they do, their words, their acts, their attitudes will be graven on the infant's psyche and land him on the psychiatrist's couch years later. They are convinced—and many experts have preached this—that parenthood is a most difficult job, and their only options are between being a little bit wrong, if they are lucky, and being very wrong. Parenthood becomes an ordeal instead of a pleasure, and life with baby is a bit like constantly walking on eggshells. Reading books by the experts is no help, because their advice is so often contradictory. Any failure of the baby to live up to some ideal standard must mean a deficiency on the mother's or father's part as a parent.

Such couples are all too often afraid to have children for fear they will not be ideal parents. And even if they have a child who blossoms and shows no problems, they consider they were just lucky and are often afraid to test their luck again with a second baby.

Insecure parents can make a problem of any child care issue. For example, one mother had read how important breast-feeding was: The mother's milk provided the baby with passive immunity to the infectious diseases the mother had herself had, and breast-feeding was presumed to establish the closest contact between baby and mother, fostering the bonding and attachment that would be so important for their future relationship. The mother therefore decided she should make a total commitment to breast-feeding, with no substitute bottles at any time, at least not for the first six months. This meant that she had to be with her infant daughter, Winnie, all the time. Also, the father could not take over any of the night feedings. Furthermore, the mother's self-imposed rule was to give Winnie the breast whenever she fussed; otherwise, the baby would feel deprived and inse-cure. As could have been predicted, with this kind of response to her fussing, Winnie began to fuss more frequently, not less. Within a month she was on a two-hour feeding schedule, and the mother was a wreck from lack of sleep.

We knew the parents, and the mother finally consulted us informally in despair. What should she do? She knew she couldn't go on with this schedule much longer. On the other hand, she was afraid she would make Winnie insecure by ignoring her when she fussed. Actually, the mother was the insecure one, although this was not at all evident in her other activities and relationships, and her fears for her baby were reflections of her lack of self-confidence as a mother.

Fortunately, the mother was willing to listen to us when we said that it would do the baby no harm to fuss for fifteen minutes, even a half-hour, before she was nursed. This procedure would gradually lengthen Winnie's experience of a full versus an empty stomach, so that hunger would come at more widely spaced intervals. The mother was hesitant to follow through on this advice. Wouldn't she be harming Winnie, whose expressed desires should always take priority over theirs? After all, Winnie's future was at stake with every action of her parents. We pointed out that maybe this wasn't such an absolute truth and that in any case she had to take the chance with this breast-feeding problem. The mother followed our advice, and within a week Winnie was cheerfully nursing on a four-hour instead of a two-hour schedule. Whether this lesson changed the mother's overall view of her all-consuming responsibilities as a parent remains to be seen. But what if she doesn't change and continues to indulge her daughter? What can we predict from that? The mother's other activities will un-doubtedly be curtailed. Her relationship with her husband may be modified, perhaps not for the better. But as for Winnie, we really can predict very little. So many influences and so many variables affect the direction and nature of a child's psychological development that any pre-diction from one factor alone—the mother's functioning—is hazardous and speculative.

A parent who is insecure and has a temperamentally difficult child is all too likely to feel that it somehow must be her fault that the baby refuses to take new foods, is irregular in sleep schedules, and has outbursts of loud crying. In some cases, one parent's insecurity with such a child may be counterbalanced with good results if the spouse is self-confident and se-cure in the caregiving responsibilities. This pattern was dramatically illustrated by one set of NYLS parents, who had as their first child just such a temperamentally difficult infant. In our rating scheme, the youngster, Carl, scored as one of the most extreme examples of this pattern of temperament in our whole research sample. The mother was convinced that she was to blame for the extra difficulties in child care, and she became anxious and guilty. The father, on the other hand, was able to take a more objective view of Carl's behavior. On his own, without any help from us, he figured out that Carl's loud crying came primarily with the exposure to something or somebody new. He also recognized that if he and his wife were patient and consistent in their handling, Carl eventually adapted positively and was then cheerful and happy with whatever it was that previously had produced loud crying. Furthermore, the father, who was quiet and low-keyed in his expressiveness, was actually pleased at his infant son's high energy level. He would say with admiration, "Carl is certainly a lusty boy."

The father's positive view of their son greatly helped to calm the mother's anxieties. The mother did also undergo a course of psychotherapy, but it was clear that it was the father's self-confidence and insight into his son's behavior that created a positive family environment for Carl. As a result of his father's attitude, the boy's development throughout childhood and adolescence was smooth and happy. Carl did have a short period of stress and difficulty in functioning when he first went away to college and was suddenly confronted simultaneously with a whole series of different living and social arrangements and a new set of academic expectations. But he weathered this stress quickly and has functioned superbly since then.

Carl is now a lively, even ebullient young man of twenty-eight, at the beginning of a promising professional career and with an active social life and a number of special interests. His mother developed a progressive, lingering illness when he was an adolescent and finally died last year. Carl remembers her with deep affection, describes his parents' marriage as "very happy," and expresses great respect for his father. And well he should, for his father deserves it.

Some insecure parents are showing the same personality characteristics of self-doubt and lack of self-confidence that characterize their behavior in other life situations. Many others, however, show this insecurity only in their roles as parents. Why should an educated, knowledgeable young adult who has managed her social life with ease and fulfilled her school and work responsibilities competently and with self-confidence begin to act like a different person when she becomes a mother? It is true that she is now responsible for someone else's life and not only her own, but she usually shares this task with her husband. She also presumably knows that innumerable parents over thousands of years have managed this function successfully, so why shouldn't she? Perhaps at least a partial answer to these questions can be found in the blame-the-mother tendency that we examined in chapter 1.

The Intimidated Parent

There are some parents who are unable to say no firmly and quietly to a complaining or screaming child and stick to it. Some of these parents are among the insecure ones—afraid to trust their own judgment or afraid of the harm that will be done if their child is frustrated. Other parents have special guilt feelings; a father who spends very little time with his child, or who has neglected his children from a previous marriage, may try to appease his guilt by indulging this child. Other parents may be under severe stress for other reasons and give in to achieve some temporary peace and quiet. We are of course not recommending a rigid demand for instant obedience and an insensitivity to the child's needs, but the opposite extreme—the appeasement of the child irrespective of the reasonableness of his demands—can do no good either to the parents or to the child. A child tyrant is created, who may gain his whims and impulses at home but who then finds that the strategies that work there will boomerang in the outside world.

The results of such appeasement may appear self-evident and unnecessary to point up, but we have been struck over the years by how many parents slip gradually into this routine of appeasing an eight-year-old, or a five-year-old, or even a two-year-old. And in some cases, these parents were forceful and successfully assertive people in the outside world, leading figures in their professions. Yet they cringed before their young children's outbursts and learned only slowly and painfully to stand their ground.

The Overinterpretive Parent

Some parents become absorbed in trying to plumb the depths of their babies' psyches. They either apply their knowledge of theories like a blueprint or make up their own interpretations. For example, Margery's mother reported with pleasure that her baby, only two months old, was already jealous if her mother talked to other people and not to her. What was the evidence? When the mother talked to Margery, her daughter smiled and cooed. But if she held Margery and talked to another person, Margery began to wiggle and cry. The facts were correct, but the interpretation was another matter. When the mother talked to Margery, her voice was soft and low-pitched, appropriate to the short distance between them. When talking to someone who was farther away, the mother necessarily raised her voice. Margery, an infant with a low sensory threshold for sound, was not fussing because she was jealous but in response to her mother's sudden loud voice. We tested this explanation by talking across the room with the mother in soft tones, and Margery did not cry.

Parents who elaborate complex psychological explanations for their babies' behaviors are only following in the footsteps of many mental health professionals, who have been doing the same thing for years. It is probably in the main a harmless occupation and may even give some parents a sense of security to "know" what is going on in their baby's mind. It can be a different matter, however, if the parents interpret a normal characteristic, such as shyness with strangers, as evidence of some deep-seated anxiety. Then they may go off in the wrong direction, snatching at bits of evidence that seem to hint at anxiety and bedeviling the child so that he truly becomes confused and afraid. In fact, what is needed is to accept the child's slowness to warm up as a normal characteristic to be anticipated and tolerated. Visits, new activities, and new routines should not be expected to bring much overt enjoyment the first, second, or even fifth time. Only gradually will the shy child feel comfortable and behave in his spontaneous fashion. For him, this is a normal pattern of adaptation.

The Parent Who Feels Victimized

Some parents feel victimized by their young children. They plan to have a child and attend prenatal classes together. The father is present throughout the delivery. They follow to the letter the instructions that are presumed to guarantee a secure child who will be easy to take care of. The baby is breast-fed for a year, fed on demand, cuddled and caressed, and given visual, auditory, and tactical stimulation through devices appropriate to each succeeding developmental stage. Yet still there are problems.

Lila, at three years of age, refused to sleep in her own bed. Morning after morning she was found asleep in her parents' bed, having come there quietly during the night without waking them. She explained that she had awakened and became frightened: The shadow from the streetlight looked just like the goblin in the picture book. Her parents carefully explained the difference between story-book goblins and reality and told her firmly that she could not come into their room at night. As a result they now found her on the floor outside their bedroom in the morning instead of in their bed. They then decided that Lila must somehow be insecure, although in the daytime and evening she was a happy, well-functioning child. So they gave her extra treats, spent more time with her, and deferred their plans to have a second child, for fear this would increase Lila's "insecurity."

But all this made no difference in Lila's nighttime behavior. The parents then began to feel victimized. They had given their all to make Lila a secure and contented child; why should she show this "insecurity" at night? Somehow, they felt, it was not fair. Lila had not fulfilled her part of the bargain! With the sense of victimization, anger at Lila began to replace their affection.

Three-year-old Lewis also had parents who had devoted themselves to his care. But Lewis had loud tantrums in supermarkets and playgrounds when frustrated by a parental "No." These scenes, which didn't occur the same way at home, were most embarrassing to the parents. These parents too began to feel victimized by their child. Why should Lewis subject them to such public humiliation, when they were so attentive to his needs and had sacrificed so much for him?

Lila's parents and Lewis's parents finally came to seek help with their problems. It was a genuine shock to them to be told that they were acting like victims, stewing with suppressed anger and unable to focus on the meaning of their child's behavior. In Lila's case, perhaps insecurity was not the problem at all. Perhaps she was beginning, at her new maturational level, to struggle to make the distinction between what is real and what is make-believe. She may have been coping well with this issue in the daytime, but it may have been another matter to reassure herself at night, alone in the dark. She was becoming frightened, but not insecure. All she needed was reassurance at night—perhaps sleeping with a light on, perhaps permission to come into her parents' bed for several weeks, perhaps a more thoughtful response from her parents when she brought up her fears.

In Lewis's case, his parents had been handling his intense and prolonged outcries adequately at home by sitting by quietly until he finished his tantrum and was ready to accept their "No." In a public place, however, the parents were embarrassed and gave in to quiet him. This approach of course led to quieter outbursts at home and louder ones in public places. All the parents had to do was to remove Lewis gently from the public scene and tell him they would go back once he stopped fussing.

Lila's and Lewis's parents, like most others who come to feel victimized by their youngster, experienced a shamefaced relief when the issues became clear. They were no longer victims but still able to be effective parents for their children's welfare.

Unfortunately, not all parents who feel victimized by their young children are responsive to the counsel that they have lost their perspective and gone astray in struggling with their youngsters' difficulties. Some stick adamantly to their condemnation of the child and wave aside any evidence to the contrary. We always shudder when a father or mother, or both, make a pronouncement that their child is just "a rotten kid" or "lacking in self-discipline" or "out to make my life miserable." In such cases the prospects for a healthy parent-child relationship are indeed dim.

As we have followed such families in our longitudinal study, however, there has been a favorable outcome for some of the children, if not for their parents. Some of these youngsters, as they reached older adolescence, were able to achieve what we call an emotional distancing from the parent or parents with whom their relationship had been so antagonistic and unhealthy. Increasingly, they made their lives outside the home and recuperated from the stresses and frustrations of their earlier family life. The tragic outcome was for the parents, who lost the intimacy and friendship with their daughters and sons, for which they had invested so much over the years. Other youngsters caught up in the harmful consequences of a relationship with parents who felt victimized could not separate themselves from their parents in this way, and their psychological difficulties continued into adult life. One research question of interest on our own agenda is the analysis of our data to determine why and how some youngsters were able to achieve this emotional distancing and why others could not.

The Pathological Parent

Parenthood does not immunize a mother or father against mental illness, nor does it cure a parent's severe psychiatric problems. Serious mental illness in a parent does represent a liability, and often a severe one, to the creation of a healthy family environment. A mother who is chronically depressed or anxious will find it difficult to be alert to the child's signals and to respond to them positively. A father who is rigid, authoritarian, or paranoid will not give the youngster the flexible environment to explore and test out his special interests and individual style of functioning. Beyond this, the bizarre irrational behavior of some mentally ill parents can be truly frightening to a child. And it need hardly be added that physical or sexual abuse of a child by a parent can have far-reaching harmful physical and psychological consequences.

Some mentally ill parents, however, show a remarkable motivation and ability to mobilize themselves for the child's benefit. And in some cases the other mentally healthy parent or other close relatives take over and fill the gaps left by the sick parent. It should therefore not be assumed that a child brought up in a home with a mentally ill parent is doomed to a life of psychological disturbance. The professional studies are clear in documenting this variability of outcome for children of mentally ill parents (Anthony 1969a).

Parental Styles and Child Outcomes

Neat formulas are always tempting. It would be convenient if we could have a master blueprint or computer program to tell us exactly what kind of parent and what pattern of caregiving practices are best in bringing up a baby. But life is not that simple, certainly not when it comes to the interaction of parent and child. Most parents are not inflexible and can shape their behavior from the many cues the baby gives them. Infants, for their part, are most flexible and can adapt to many different approaches and environments.

Does this mean that all parental styles are equally effective in child-rearing? Not at all. First of all, a home full of tension because a parent is insecure, intimidated, overinterpretive, or feeling victimized is not a pleasant, relaxed environment for parent or child. It is not a family setting that provides a happy childhood, even though the youngster may cope successfully and go on to a full and healthy adult life.

Moreover, a certain parental style may make a highly significant difference with some children but not with others. This is our central thesis. The child's psychological development is not determined by the parents' style alone, or by the child's style alone, but by the match or mismatch between the two. We have called this match "goodness of fit," and we will elaborate it in detail in the next two chapters. Increasingly, the evidence from our own research findings and the studies from other research centers confirm the significance of this concept of goodness versus poorness of fit between child and parent, and between child and other family members, peers, teachers, and other adults in his life. With this concept in mind, we are free to sift over and retain the meaningful research findings from the past and discard their heavy overload of dogma and speculation as well as to incorporate new findings and insights as they develop.

4

Goodness of Fit: The Key to Healthy Development

I N the early and mid-1960s, we were faced with a new and crucial challenge. We had demonstrated that infants show individual differences in temperament from the first few months of life onward. We had devised a method for gathering detailed and systematic information from parents which enabled us to classify temperament into nine categories and three patterns that appeared to be functionally important for the child's psychological development. Furthermore, we had found that these temperamental traits could influence the parents' attitudes and caregiving practices, so that the relationship between parent and child was one of mutual, active influence, and not just a one-way process of writing the infant's future behavior on a *tabula rasa,* an empty mental slate. We had also worked out a practical scheme of identifying various types of "good" and "poor" parents, with regard to the way they handled and reacted to their young children.

It was also clear to us that as the children grew older, other influences would enter into and shape their lives: not only people, such as other family members, age-mates, and teachers, but forces such as the school environment, demands for academic achievement, and the moral and ethical values of the social environment, including its racist, sexist, and other prejudices. Special unexpected experiences such as the appearance and maturation of a special talent or an unpredictable yet important event might also occur in the life of a child. And the effect of these other factors, like that of the parents, would depend not only on the experience itself but on the child's reaction to it. The same life situation might have different effects on children with different temperaments, abilities, or motivations, and the child's characteristics might even affect the character or intensity of a specific life experience.

The Search for a Theory

To trace the influence of all these intertwining influences on the child's life, we needed a theoretical framework that would enable us to determine why some children pursued a smooth, healthy developmental course as they grew older but others were beset with all kinds of behavior problems. We were not concerned with the severe psychiatric disorders of childhood, such as autism, childhood schizophrenia, severe depression, or serious organic brain disease. These problems are of great concern, but our interest lay with the development of children whose lives were not crippled by such serious illnesses.

The dominant theories of the time were not useful to us. Temperament was certainly not the result of the presumed instinctual drives of traditional psychoanalytic theory, nor could it be derived from the formation of conditioned reflexes, at the heart of behaviorist theory. Moreover, both psychoanalysis and behaviorism tended to view a child's development as the direct consequence of a specific set of early childhood experiences, whether it was the conflict between drives and the real world, as the psychoanalysts would have it, or the persistence of conditioned reflexes as the behaviorists claimed. As we followed our subjects' lives, we found their psychological development too complex a process, with too many factors shaping its course at different ages, to make these or other simplistic one-dimensional theories acceptable.

An alternative approach had been suggested by a number of students of animal and human behavioral development, perhaps most definitely and comprehensively formulated in the early 1930s by the Russian psychologist Lev Vygotsky (1978). Vygotsky developed the concept of interactionism, which broadly defined views all behavioral attributes of an individual as interacting both with each other and with the opportunities, demands, and expectations provided by the environment. Vygotsky's ideas were not pursued by him in detail because of his early death. We have found his interactionist concept to be valuable in understanding children's lives and development and have applied it in our work. We also believe that the consequences of this process of interaction might in turn reinforce, modify, or change the person's behavior or the environmental influences, or both. This process of change and reinforcement is not limited to any one age period but is a lifelong process (Thomas & Chess 1980).

From the beginning of our longitudinal study in 1956, it was clear to us that such an interactionist view was necessary if we were to understand the influence of temperament, or any other attribute, on the child's behavioral course. This approach has now been accepted by leading developmental psychologists and psychiatrists. Various writers use different terms —interactionism, transactionism, the life-span perspective, biopsychosocial or systems theory—but all agree that the study of both normal and pathological psychological development must include multiple dimensions and influences that interact continuously over time (Chess & Thomas 1984).

But the interactionist approach, as essential as it is, is only a general theoretical concept. We also needed a principle that we could apply to the analysis of the development of any individual child. Why did the interaction of parent and child lead to a healthy outcome for one youngster and a disturbed development in another? What were the specific factors that could differ from one parent-child relationship to another and make for the differences in outcome?

The Goodness of Fit Concept

As we reviewed our subjects' lives, we identified a general principle that appeared to determine whether and why the child's development was proceeding smoothly or not. We also found that this principle could often provide the basis for quick and effective treatment of a child's behavior problems.

We have called this general principle "goodness or poorness of fit." Goodness of fit exists when the demands and expectations of the parents and other people important to the child's life are compatible with the child's temperament, abilities, and other characteristics. With such a fit, healthy development for the child can be expected.

Poorness of fit, on the other hand, exists when demands and expectations are excessive and not compatible with the child's temperament, abilities, and other characteristics. With such a fit, the child is likely to experience excessive stress, and healthy development is jeopardized.

A few simple examples will illustrate the difference between goodness and poorness of fit. A child with a slow-to-warm-up temperament requires time and a number of exposures to a new situation before she can become an active, comfortable participant. But it is essential for such a child, as for all children, to develop the social competence to adapt to all kinds of strange settings and experiences. If the parents and teachers recognize the child's temperament when the child first starts nursery school at four years, and if they do not pressure her into immediate involvement in the group but let her move at her own pace from the periphery of the group to full participation, there is a good fit. Parents and teachers have made a demand that is within the youngster's ability to fulfill. Nursery school, for this child, will become an enjoyable and stimulating experience.

This approach can become a model for introducing the child to all kinds of other new situations as she grows older. With repeated successes of this kind, she can move into adulthood having learned that she is capable of functioning effectively in new settings, even though her initial subjective reaction may be one of discomfort. A number of our subjects have told us just this in the early-adult interview. A typical comment has been, "When I go to a new job or a new social affair, on the surface I appear cool, calm, and collected. Actually, I am feeling tense and uncomfortable. However, I have learned that if I stick it out, my distress begins to disappear until finally I am in fact comfortable and relaxed."

If, on the other hand, parents and teachers expect the child to participate as quickly and fully in the new group as the other children are doing, and if they pressure her to an involvement that is incompatible with her temperamental pattern of initial quiet withdrawal and slow adaptation, there is a poor fit. The excessive demand will in all likelihood result in the child's pulling back, clinging to parent or teacher, and fussing to go home. This child, whether forced to stay in school or removed because she is "immature and not ready," will then have lost the positive social experience of adapting successfully to a new group of age-mates.

Goodness and poorness of fit may relate to characteristics other than temperament. Six-year-old Danny was referred to one of us (S.C.) because of his disturbed behavior in school. The teacher and the school psychologist described him as exhibiting bizarre behavior, disorganized language, and purposeless movements. These disturbances were not continuous, but they occurred frequently and without any cause that the teacher could identify. At other times, the boy's behavior appeared quite normal. Although they did not say so in so many words, it was clear that the teacher and the psychologist both felt that Danny was suffering from a severe psychiatric disorder, such as childhood schizophrenia.

When I saw the boy in my playroom his behavior, language, and use of various toys were all appropriate, without any sign of deviant functioning. Then, when he was holding a toy oven in his hand I asked him, "What is that?" He hesitated, then said, "Refrigerator." I pointed to a bunch of toy carrots and again asked, "What is that?" He blurted out, "Lettuce." I asked, "What do you do with the lettuce?" and he answered, "Put it in the oven," pointing to the refrigerator. I commented that it was unusual to put lettuce in an oven, and he immediately began to jump around, twist his face, and utter baby-talk syllables. He was clowning, and it was clear that this was the bizarre behavior his teacher had noted. I then persuaded him to try the dart game I had in the room, which he had played with when he first came in. He threw the first dart, scoring a bull's-eye, and immediately his behavior reverted to normal.

The diagnosis was clear. Danny was suffering from a form of development dysphasia—difficulty with language due to slow or distorted development of the brain areas controlling language. In his case, the dysphasia was limited to anomia, a difficulty in naming objects and people, and to poor spelling. He was extremely embarrassed by the anomia, which he tried to conceal from his teacher and schoolmates by clowning whenever he was called on to name something or somebody.

Danny's parents told me he had been a late talker, which is usual in such cases. They had noted his difficulty in naming objects but had not given it serious attention, because his use of language, even his discussion of complex abstract ideas, was on a superior level.

I discussed the problem with the parents and explained the defensive nature of his clowning behavior. The clowning was the real problem, for they had noted that his problem with names was improving. This made the outlook for his anomia optimistic, but the danger was that his defensive clowning behavior might become so fixed that it might continue even if the anomia got better.

Fortunately, Danny was attending a good private school. I spoke to his teacher, who understood the problem when I spelled it out. I suggested that whenever she saw him begin to clown she immediately draw him into some constructive activity that did not involve naming objects. This she did, and the clowning disappeared. The family then went to England for two years because of the father's business. I prepared a report for the parents to take to a British school. After several attempts, they found a school where the headmaster understood the issue and was prepared to carry through my recommendations. On their return to this country, Danny and his parents came to see me for a check-up. He had had two good years in the British school and was well advanced academically. There had been no return of any abnormal behavior. His anomia for objects had disappeared, though he still had difficulty in remembering the names of people, even friends. But he had developed various innocuous maneuvers to get around this problem, such as waiting until someone else in the group called the person by name or whispering to someone, "That boy's name slips my mind. Tell me his name." Whether this problem would improve with time was impossible to predict, but in any case Danny had learned how to deal with it in a reasonable manner. He was still a poor speller and probably always would be, but that represented only a minor issue in view of his superior academic achievements in general.

Unfortunately, not all cases of developmental dysphasia improve as Danny's did, and sometimes the problem remains a serious one for life. And if his case had been misdiagnosed, or if he had attended a school with unsympathetic teachers, his clowning could have continued until he became a class scapegoat. Instead of being a stimulating experience, school would have become a hellish environment for him, and he might very well have ended up in a class for "emotionally disturbed" children.

We conceptualized Danny's case as a special example of poorness of fit between the school's demands and his inability to meet them, which placed him under severe stress that he could not manage effectively. When the school's approach changed to minimize these demands, while still maintaining all its other academic and social expectations, the poor fit was transformed into a good fit, and his school functioning and inner sense of self-confidence blossomed.

The approach to toilet training sometimes provides a dramatic illustration of goodness or poorness of fit. An infant with regular biological functions may have a bowel movement at the same time each day—say, just after breakfast. If she also has a relatively low activity level temperamentally, she will be content to sit quietly on the potty-seat for five or ten minutes. Toilet training such a child will be a quick, easy matter, often accomplished well before two years of age, if that is desired. The child is pleased with her accomplishment and pleased that her parents are pleased with her. There has been a truly good fit between the parents' expectation and the child's ability to respond favorably. The child has achieved a milestone in social functioning, and that can only enhance a sense of self-confidence in meeting the demands of the world around her.

By contrast, another child may have a high activity level and be irregular in biological functions, so that the exact timing of bowel movements is unpredictable from day to day. Sitting her on the potty-seat will be an ordeal, because she will begin to squirm and fuss after a few minutes, no matter how much she is distracted or scolded. If the parents persist in this standard strategy for toilet training, it will be a fiasco, a poor fit between the parent's demand and the child's capacity. Of course, the child will eventually become toilet trained—say, by four or five years of age. In the meantime, however, she will have experienced her parents' disapproval, and she is likely to have been the butt of her age-mates' ridicule for still soiling herself when they are all toilet trained. Toilet training will have become a disturbing and unhappy experience, not one that will enhance her self-esteem and self-confidence.

But there are more ways than one of achieving a good fit with toilet training. If this child's parents recognize quickly that the approach that worked so easily with her older sister is getting nowhere with her because of her irregularity and high activity level, they can shift gears. They can first instruct the child to tell them as soon as she has had a bowel movement so she can be cleaned immediately. When this has been achieved and routinized, she can be asked to announce that she is feeling the movement starting to come so that she can be put on the potty. Finally, she can be told that she herself can recognize the sensation that a bowel movement is about to begin and put herself on the potty. With this sequence, she can feel a sense of achievement and parental approval each step of the way. For this child, too, toilet training can be a positive experience, an additional success in mastering her own functioning and in meeting the world's demands for social functioning.

Goodness of Fit Formulations by Other Investigators

The goodness of fit concept makes it possible to analyze the individual factors involved in the interaction between parent and child in a specific family unit. With this approach we are not hampered by an insistence that we look for the same causes in all cases in which a child is showing a behavior problem. Rather, there may be excessive demands of one type on one child, very different stressful expectations of a second child, and still another cause for poorness of fit in a third case.

As a result, an increasing number of investigators are finding the goodness of fit concept to be highly useful in understanding what is happening to the children and families they are studying. Some prefer the phrase *match and mismatch* or some similar term, but the meaning is the same. Brazelton puts it well in the epilogue to *Infants and Mothers* (1969):

In each of these infants, I have attempted to demonstrate the strong, inborn differences that predetermine their particular styles of development. In each case, certain reactions from the environment are more "appropriate" than others—that is, each infant can respond more easily to mothering which fits into his capacity to receive and respond. Each of the mothers I have portrayed is motivated by a desire to "understand her infant," and thus is able to find his particular style and fit herself into it. (p. 281)

Another leading child development researcher, Lois Murphy, of the Menninger Clinic, has conducted an intensive long-term study of the behavioral development of a relatively small sample of children. Her special interest has been in their coping mechanisms, and she has observed their ways of coping in a host of situations—at home, in school, at play, on special excursions, and so on. She too came to the formulation of goodness versus poorness of fit between mothers and babies, which she called *fit and misfit*. She gave typical examples from her study:

Mrs. Rogers was an energetic, intelligent devoted mother who did well with her energetic active baby, Malcolm, but with her next baby, Vernon, who was extremely sensitive and not as responsive, the fit was not as good. Tommy's mother, by contrast, was a sensitive little lady who was not up to the demands of her very vigorous, lively, energetic baby, (1981, p. 168)

Educational psychologist J. McVicker Hunt, of the University of Illinois, has described a study of cognitive functioning in schoolchildren in which the *problem of the match,* as he called it, was evident. If the demand for cognitive functioning was consonant with the child's ability (a good fit), the task was performed with interest and even joyful excitement. However, if the demand exceeded the child's cognitive level, the child typically showed a reaction of withdrawal and distress, and some even became tearful (1980).

Actually, the concept of goodness of fit has been used by a number of psychologists as far back as the 1940s as a theoretical model for various studies of the relationship between specific personality traits on the one hand and performance and satisfaction in performance on the other. A typical example is a study that found that students low on sociability performed better in lecture sections, whereas more sociable students performed better in leaderless discussion groups (Beach 1960). Lawrence Previn, of Princeton University, reviewed these studies in detail in 1968, commenting in his introduction that "for each individual there are environments (interpersonal and noninterpersonal) which more or less match the characteristics of his personality" (1968, p. 56). The research studies cited by Previn are limited in their scope, however. They tend to deal with global personality traits that are difficult to rate accurately, and they do not explore the possible significance of the individual study for a general theoretical model of child development. Previn himself, to our knowledge, has not carried out the positive formulation in his introduction with further studies of goodness of fit.

Finally, the concept of goodness of fit has been applied to physical as well as to psychological health. The eminent biologist René Dubos, of Rockefeller University, has said, "Health can be regarded as an expression of fitness to the environment, as a state of adaptedness. . . . The words health and disease are meaningful only when defined in terms of a given person functioning in a given physical and social environment" (1965, pp. 350–51).

Several investigators have begun to apply the goodness of fit concept as we have formulated it to experimental research study. Most noteworthy thus far is the project reported by Jacqueline Lerner, of Pennsylvania State University (1983). Lerner took forty-eight male and fifty-one female junior high school students and assessed their temperaments by means of a questionnaire devised for the adolescent age period. The teachers were asked to indicate the temperamental qualities they expected of their students, by completing sentences beginning "I expect my students to be . . ." Measures of pupil self-esteem, teacher judgments of pupil academic and social competence, and current academic achievement scores were then obtained for all students. Lerner found that the students whose temperament scores fit best with the teacher's expectations were more likely to have better scores on both self-rated and teacher-rated assessments of functioning. She concluded that the results provide some support for the view that the link between temperament and adaptation may lie in whether one's temperament provides goodness of fit with the demands of one's context.

What Goodness of Fit Is *Not*

The goodness of fit concept opens the way to an enlarged understanding of why some children's progress is smooth and positive, while others show disturbances and even clinical behavior problems. In our discussions of this concept at various research centers, a number of questions have been raised that require clarification.

Goodness of fit does not imply the desirability for parent and child to have similar temperaments. Sometimes the opposite is true. The child whose reactions to frustration are intensely negative will not be helped by a parent who responds to her tantrum with a similar outburst; the outcome then is a shouting match in which the original issue soon gets lost. Opposite temperaments may also clash. A quick-moving, expressive parent may get highly impatient with a slow-moving, low-keyed youngster. In such a situation the parent may also ignore the child's legitimate wishes, because they are expressed so quietly. The issue is not whether parent and child are similar, but what kinds of demands are made on a particular child and what reactions the child's behavior creates in the parent, irrespective of whether parent and child are similar or different in temperament.

Goodness of fit does not mean an absence of stress for the child. Quite the contrary. Stress and tension may accompany any demand upon an individual, adult or child, for a change in a habitual way of doing things or for the mastery of a new activity or task. Demands and stresses of this nature are an inevitable part of a child's increasing competence in social skills and task performance as she grows older. If there is goodness of fit and the new expectations are mastered successfully, developmental progress will have occurred, and the demands will have constituted a healthy stimulus for the child. If the new demand is beyond the child's capacity, however, and she cannot cope successfully with it, then a poor fit will develop. If the parents or others persist in their expectation that the child master this new demand quickly, the poor fit will lead to excessive stress. It is this excessive stress that can produce harmful consequences for the child—a sense of failure, symptoms of anxiety, and attempts to avoid the unachievable goal by evasions, excuses, or various forms of defensive denials.

Stress as such may be constructive in its consequences for the child's development if there is a good fit. To shield the child from such stresses is not helpful. For example, the parents of a very young child may be aware that she is shy and ill at ease with new children and adults in new settings. It is no service to the child to shield her from such situations; she will continue to lack the confidence that she can adapt to new age-mates, older children, and adults, because she has been denied the experience of such achievements. If, on the other hand, the parents expose her to new situations and new people slowly and gradually, and at most a few at a time, the results will be different. The child will be uncomfortable at first, even reluctant to enter a new situation, and will hold back and cling to her parents. The new situation will be stressful. But if she is encouraged to try, if the first encounters are brief and then gradually lengthened, she will eventually adapt and become an active, happy member of the new group. A good fit will have been achieved, but because the new demand has been shaped to the child's temperamental characteristics. Eventually such a child will be able to say, as one adolescent said to us, "I'm shy, but I'm not timid."

Some parents with a temperamentally difficult child attempt to avoid stress and turmoil by appeasement, giving in quickly to the child's every demand. Such parents only create a child tyrant, who learns to dominate the family by throwing tantrums. In such a case, the parents will have to learn to endure the stress on themselves as well as on their child by saying "No" quietly but firmly when appropriate and sticking to it until the child's tantrum subsides. It is stressful for a child with intense reactions to accept frustrations and rules she resents, but she must learn to do so if she is to be a decent, social human being. Through this process, though she may go through periods of turmoil she achieves a good fit with the reasonable expectations of other people.

Poorness of Fit and Defense Mechanisms

A major contribution of the psychoanalytic movement to developmental theory has been the identification and analysis of defense mechanisms. Such mechanisms can be defined operationally as behavioral strategies to cope with stress or conflict that a person cannot or will not master directly. This definition does not assume, as the psychoanalysts usually do, that defense mechanisms are necessarily unconscious. These mechanisms can take many forms, including among others the denial that a problem exists, avoidance of the stressful situation, and the attempt to excuse the difficulty with a pseudorational explanation that really avoids the issue.

A child under excessive stress because of poorness of fit is likely to adopt a defense mechanism to cope with such stress. The case of Danny, cited earlier in this chapter, is a dramatic example of the development of a defense mechanism, in this instance bizarre, clowning behavior to avoid the exposure of his problem. Because defense mechanisms constitute strategies to avoid rather than to master an environmental demand, they may intensify the unfavorable consequences of a poor fit. And all too often, as in Danny's case, the inappropriate or even bizarre behavior that the defense mechanism produces may in itself have additional harmful consequences, such as labeling a child as a misfit and making him a scapegoat for his age-mates.

The early detection of poorness of fit, therefore, becomes an important mental health issue in childhood, and sometimes even in adult life. Parents can often do a great deal to ameliorate a poor fit, as we will see in the next chapter. This issue should also be a major concern for mental health professionals, pediatricians, and educators.

Goodness of Fit May Change

Goodness of fit established between parents and child in early childhood makes for a good beginning for the youngster. But it does not by itself guarantee that this consonance between parental expectations and the child's capacities will last. Children change as they grow older, and so do parents. What was an easy simple goodness of fit in infancy may shift and become more complex in older childhood or adolescence. For example, an infant who has a low threshold to sensory stimuli may be awakened by a light being turned on in her room or by a noise, no matter how soft. Adult habits can easily be altered to avoid waking this infant. At a later age, a piece of clothing that is warm but itchy can be made tolerable by creating a soft lining for it. But this same low threshold may lengthen the time needed to complete homework, or cause the child to be inattentive during a teaching session. Reestablishment of goodness of fit may require parent and teacher to give the child regular systematic reminders to bring her attention back to the task at hand. The academic expectations on the youngster cannot be changed just because she has a low threshold; she does have to become educated. But to be effective, the manner of presentation of these demands has to be shaped by this temperamental quality of low threshold.

It is also possible for a poor fit to become transformed into a good fit. Nancy, one of the subjects in our longitudinal study, was a difficult child temperamentally from infancy onward. Her father was highly critical of her intense crying spells, her initial distress with most new situations, and the slowness with which she adapted to change. He had rigid standards of the way a child should behave, and Nancy's way of responding went opposite to his expectations. He demanded that she become easygoing, quiet, and able to adapt quickly to new situations and to any change in life routines. These were impossible demands for Nancy to meet, given her temperamental style, and her father became not only critical but punitive. The mother was intimidated by both husband and daughter, and she became inconsistent and uncertain in her handling of the girl. With such poorness of fit, by the age of six Nancy had developed explosive anger outbursts, fear of the dark, thumb-sucking, hair-pulling, and great difficulty in making friends. It was evident that she was suffering from a severe behavior disorder and that a drastic change in understanding and handling by the parents was essential. But a number of discussions with them were entirely unsuccessful. The father saw no reason why he should change. The problem, in his own words, was that Nancy was "just a rotten kid." The mother felt overwhelmed by what was happening and helpless to do anything. Psychotherapy was instituted for the child, with modest improvement—the best that could be expected under the circumstances. Nancy's future indeed appeared gloomy.

But then a dramatic change for the better did occur, unexpectedly and unpredictably. In the fourth and fifth grades Nancy showed evidence of musical and dramatic talent and became the star of the class plays. This brought increasingly favorable attention and praise from teachers and other parents. Previously, when the father had been stopped in the street by another parent, it had been to listen to yet another story of Nancy's misbehavior. Now he began to hear enthusiastic comments on his talented daughter. Fortunately for Nancy, these talents ranked high in her father's standards of desirable attributes. He now began to see his daughter's intense and explosive personality not as a sign of a "rotten kid" but as evidence of the temperament of a budding artist. He could be proud of her and made allowances for her "artistic personality." The mother was now also able to relax and relate positively to her daughter. Nancy was permitted to adapt at her own pace; the positive aspects of her temperament, her intelligence, and her talents came to the fore; and her self-image improved progressively. By adolescence, her symptoms had disappeared, she had many friends, and she was doing well in school. Both she and her parents agreed that she was still a "tempestuous" character but that this was no problem. Now, in her late twenties, Nancy is a poised, self-confident adult with clear goals that she is pursuing successfully. She has learned to control the intensity of her reactions when their open expression would be undesirable, but she can also let herself go when she has strong pleasurable feelings. She is still a little "cautious" with new situations, but she knows she can adapt and enjoy them.

Goodness of Fit and the Social Context

Goodness of fit is not an abstract concept, with a blueprint for what is desirable or undesirable that can be applied in the same way to all children and all situations. What is goodness of fit for one kind of child may become poorness of fit in a different environment. The social context in which the child lives always has a profound influence, but not always in the same way for all children. A striking example of the link between goodness of fit and the social environment became evident as we compared the temperamentally high-activity youngsters in our middle-class New York Longitudinal Study families with those in our sample of working-class Puerto Rican families. These children with high activity levels needed space and facilities in which to exercise their need for physical action and expend their high level of motor energy.

The middle-class families with high-activity children had no difficulty providing these youngsters with constructive outlets for their motor energy. They lived in private houses or large apartments, with adequate playground areas and safe streets. As a result, none of these high-activity children in the middle-class New York Longitudinal Study developed a behavior disorder related to constraints on their physical activities. The high-activity children of the working-class Puerto Rican families, by contrast, lived in public housing projects in the East Harlem area of Manhattan. Apartment space was limited, especially in relation to family size. Playground areas were absent or inadequate, and the streets were unsafe. If anything, these children were confined to their apartments more than the less active children, because of the mothers' legitimate fears that they would "run wild" in the streets. As a result, these high-activity children had inadequate opportunities for the physical activity they needed and became restless and tense. Several went through periods of disorganized and even destructive behavior, which relieved their physical tensions but wreaked havoc on the rest of the family.

A most dramatic example of the influence of the social environment on goodness of fit comes from a study reported by Marten deVries (1984). During the course of a fellowship in anthropology, deVries collected data on a group of infants in the Masai, a primitive tribe living in the sub-Sahara region of Kenya. DeVries obtained temperament ratings on forty-seven infants, aged two to four months, at a time when a severe drought was just beginning. With these ratings, he identified the ten infants with the easiest temperament and the ten with the most difficult temperament, using the criteria established in our studies. When he returned five months later, the drought had killed 97 percent of the cattle herd, and deVries was able to locate only seven of the families of the easy babies and six of the difficult ones; the families of the other infants had moved in an attempt to escape the drought. In our Western middle-class societies it is the temperamentally easy infants who usually thrive most favorably, and the temperamentally difficult infants whose development is usually more stressful. But in this tribal society, deVries found that of the seven "easy" babies, five had died, whereas all of the "difficult" infants had survived! Two speculations are possible. In this harsh and life-threatening environment it may have become goodness of fit to the point of actual survival if an infant could cry loudly and long and thereby receive more attention. Or it is possible that in that culture, in contrast to our own, a baby who cried often and loudly was more highly valued.

Special Parental Values

Parents sometimes have special value systems that are at odds with the expectations of their social community. Their child may adapt to the parental demands, so that there appears to be a good fit. When the child meets with a different and contradictory set of values in the outside world, however, she may not always be able to shift gears. She may find it too difficult to adapt one way at home and in a different way with her age-mates or teachers. What appears to have been goodness of fit turns out to be the opposite.

We have seen several such cases in our longitudinal study subjects. Kay had an easy temperament from infancy onward, but her mother was not pleased by Kay's ability to adapt easily and quietly. The mother felt that she herself had been that kind of child and had been easily pressured by her parents into doing what they wanted, which was not always in her own best interest. She was therefore determined that her daughter would not suffer a similar fate. She had decided to keep to a minimum any demands on Kay for task performance, so that the girl could develop "spontaneously." As a result, the youngster had increasing difficulties with any situation demanding specific task performance. A request to string beads in a specific pattern would lead to a social discussion of the "pretty beads"; when asked to name the capital of a state she might start an account of a camping vacation in that or any other state. She was a charming and socially vivacious youngster, who used these attributes, with her parents' approval, to sidestep demands on her. Life at home was pleasant and frictionless, and there appeared to be strong goodness of fit between parent and child.

In the preschool years, these social attributes also served Kay well with her playmates, and especially with older children and adults. Unfortunately, as she grew older, her ineptness with task performance made her more and more immature in her social functioning with her age-mates. Her problem was especially disastrous in school. Her difficulties in following instructions and focusing on academic achievement resulted in increasingly poor academic functioning. Unfortunately, her parents were unresponsive to guidance and counseling. As a result, Kay's development through the elementary school years was characterized by marginal academic achievement, a self-evaluation as "stupid," and increasing social difficulties and loneliness. Her parents were then willing to arrange psychotherapy for her, which proved very helpful. Now, as a young adult, Kay is motivated for a professional career and appears ready to come to grips with her remaining psychological difficulties.

It should be emphasized that our goodness of fit model does not imply that *all* environmental demands that appear consonant with the person's capacities are accepted as desirable. A subculture may expect its members to use alcohol or drugs, for example. This expectation may appear consonant with a person's capacities; she may suffer no apparent ill effects and even seem to thrive. However, in a larger sense, the drug use will interfere with the optimal use of her mental faculties and will therefore represent poorness of fit. A white male may accept the dominant racist and sexist attitudes of his group and take pleasure and comfort in the feelings of superiority they give him. But, again, this apparent consonance will mask a deeper impairment in the capacity for close human relationships.

Goodness of Fit and Other Attributes

Most of the examples given above of goodness or poorness of fit involve the child's temperamental characteristics. It is this relationship between temperament and goodness of fit that we have studied most intensively in our own research projects. Also, it does appear that in infancy and during the preschool and middle childhood years the problem of poorness of fit and its unfavorable consequences can be seen most often with demands and expectations that are incompatible with the child's temperament.

But this does not in any way mean that consideration of goodness of fit as the key to healthy psychological development should be focused only on temperament. The significance of the relationship between demands and expectations of the parents and the capacities of the child extends into many other areas. A common problem in middle-class families is an expectation for academic achievement beyond the youngster's intellectual capability. Some parents may have standards for other areas of accomplishment —athletics, music, or the social graces, for example—that their child cannot achieve.

In all such instances, the discrepancy between parental expectations and the child's characteristics does not necessarily produce a poor fit, with all its unfavorable consequences. Poorness of fit develops when the parents *insist* that the child meet their standards in their way and will not accept failure or even partial success on the youngster's part. This can only leave the child with a sense that she has let her parents down, that she is inferior, and that this specific inadequacy is an omen of future failures to come in other areas of life.

If the parents accept the child's inability to meet their specific expectations, however, even if they are disappointed in private, the story will be different. If they encourage her efforts, even clumsy ones; applaud her attempts to meet their goals, even though she may not follow their advice; modify and reshape their own expectations as they begin to appreciate their youngster's abilities and limitations; and compliment her on her success, no matter how partial, as long as it has represented her maximum potential; then the result will be a good fit rather than a poor fit. Such parental acceptance of the child's efforts and achievement will leave the child feeling a success rather than a failure, competent rather than inadequate, and will increase rather than diminish her confidence in meeting future challenges and demands.

5

Goodness of Fit: Practical Applications

I N the preceding chapter we have elaborated our formulation of goodness of fit as a valuable model for understanding why and how each individual child develops the way he does. Now we turn to the questions that parents and professionals have raised with us about the goodness of fit concept: Does it conflict with the parents' efforts to maintain their quality of life? Does it mean that parents have to give up their own moral and ethical standards? Does it mean that parents always have to give in if a child protests and is upset? How rigidly should the concept be applied in daily life? Does the concept help the parent and child to be on the same side, or does it tend to make them adversaries?

We will also spell out the guidelines for developing goodness of fit with each of the different temperamental characteristics at different age periods. And we will emphasize that not all parents can always figure out by themselves what changes are necessary to change poorness of fit to goodness of fit. In such cases, professional advice and parent guidance are usually very helpful.

Goodness of Fit and the Quality of Life

Becoming a parent necessarily brings many changes in activities, responsibilities, and daily routines of living. But individual parents vary tremendously in the way they make these changes. For one set of parents, certain alterations in life style are easily and cheerfully accepted, while others are irksome and even stressful. For another set of parents, there will be a very different pattern of changes in life style that are accomplished with little or no regret versus those that are carried through reluctantly.

Parents naturally tend to make insistent demands on the child in those areas that most affect their quality of life and are permissive in areas that interfere less with their life styles and preferences. This difference can be illustrated by the child's sleep schedule. Some parents can awaken quickly and easily when a child cries at night, bring him a bottle or otherwise comfort him, and get back to sleep immediately. The child's awakening once or twice a night involves a minimal loss of sleep, and the parent is still refreshed and alert in the morning. Such a parent will not be bothered if this night-awakening continues even into the child's middle childhood years. The parent's quality of life with regard to needs for sleep is maintained, so there is a good fit.

By contrast, another parent finds several interruptions of sleep during the night a real trial. She or he wakes up slowly, moves around groggily, and responds to the child's request slowly and even irritably. It then takes a long time to fall back to sleep and the parent arises in the morning still sleepy and unrefreshed. The rest of the day is hampered by a state of weariness. For such a parent, the child's night-awakening is significantly interfering with quality of life, and a change is legitimately in order. If one parent, whether it is the father or the mother, falls back to sleep with ease, this parent can assume all nighttime duties. Or, if each finds night awakening troublesome, they can alternate and share the burden. At a later age a night-light can be left on in the child's room and a bottle or glass of juice or other food item the child usually requests left on a bedside table. The child is informed that if she awakens at night she is not to awaken her parent. The child will in all likelihood protest, mildly or loudly depending on her temperament, and can be expected to keep calling for her parent on the following nights. But if the parent ignores the calls, they will gradually subside. Some children who are basically regular in their sleep patterns will even begin to sleep through the night; the ones with irregular patterns may still wake up during the night, but will have learned to take care of their own needs quietly. Goodness of fit will have been achieved, and the parent's quality of life with regard to sleep needs will have been preserved.

Of course, if a child awakens with a sudden pain or other symptom, a call for the parent is legitimate and deserves an immediate response. A parent can usually quickly differentiate when a child's call is one of genuine distress and when it is play-acting to get attention.

In another area of quality of life, some parents do not mind if their children engage in loud horseplay in the evening hours. They may even enjoy this background noise, and it does not interfere with their reading or other activities. Other parents, perhaps because of a low threshold to sound and high distractibility, find such horseplay so distracting that it interferes with their relaxation and concentration. In such cases, depending on the family setup, the children can be told that any loud prebedtime play has to be restricted to one room or distant area of the house or apartment. Again, the children will protest, but quiet, firm insistence on this rule may even teach them that life requires them to respect the needs of others.

Parental Standards and Goodness of Fit

Some parents have standards of courtesy that are an important part of a good quality of life in personal, social, and even work lives. They want their children to conform to these standards. We remember visiting one family and standing in the front yard chatting with the mother when her ten-year-old daughter burst in full of some exciting event she just had to tell her mother. She started in, "Mommy, guess what happened . . . ," and her mother turned to her and said, "You know you don't interrupt when grown-ups are talking. Just wait quietly until we are finished." The girl stood there abashed but unprotesting, and after a few minutes, in a lull in our conversation, the mother turned to her daughter and said, "Now, Kate, tell us all about it." Kate then launched into her story of her pet dog's latest exploit. We all listened, her mother expressed the proper interest and pleasure, and Kate went away satisfied. Fifteen years later Kate is a mature professional woman, not at all inhibited in her expressiveness, and with a warm, close relationship with her mother.

Other parents have a much more casual attitude toward the issue of proper manners for their children. Some might even be horrified at the behavior of Kate's mother. Yet there is no evidence that one standard of conduct is more desirable in a child's upbringing than the other approach. Each set of parents is entitled to make those demands on their children that will preserve their own quality of life, with two important cautions:

First, parents should not make demands that the child cannot meet because of his own characteristics. Doing so can only lead to poorness rather than goodness of fit. To insist that a youngster with a temperamentally high activity level engage only in quiet sedentary play in the evening hours so as not to disturb his parents is to invite trouble. Either he will be unable to obey and will be labeled "disobedient" and "selfish," or, if he is able to restrain his activity evening after evening, he will suffer in one way or another the consequences of such rigid restraints and inhibitions. Other solutions are possible, once the parents put their heads to it, that will satisfy both the child and the parents' needs.

Second, parents should not train or encourage their children to form patterns of behavior that will be at serious odds with the standards of the outside world. Two cases from our longitudinal study will illustrate this point.

Hal's parents gave great importance to the niceties of formal manners. They had no difficulty in training the boy, who was a temperamentally easy child, in this direction. But when he was four, his parents consulted us because Hal had become the scapegoat of his age-mates, who took his toys and teased him until he came home crying. The problem was apparent as soon as we saw Hal ourselves. His manners were polite and formalistic, and for his generation and community he stuck out as a caricature of a "stuffed shirt." There was goodness of fit at home, but severe poorness of fit in the outside world. We explained this to the parents, who understood and appreciated the need for change. They did try seriously to introduce more casual and appropriate standards for the boy, but they could do so only partially. Hal's behavior changed sufficiently so that he was no longer the neighborhood scapegoat, but he never overcame his stiff, formal manners, which interfered with his social relationships even into his college years.

At the other extreme, Stuart's parents, who were courteous and considerate people themselves, had casual standards of manners for their children. Stuart's speech development was precocious, and his observations of other people were quite acute. His comments and questions in his penetrating little boy's voice were so often incisive that his parents and even strangers would stop to express their amusement. However, as he grew older, these critical personal remarks in public places lost their cuteness and became more and more embarrassing to those who were the butt of his comments. His parents occasionally scolded him, but basically they enjoyed Stuart's verbal antics as an *enfant terrible,* and in effect they encouraged this behavior. As time went on, Stuart began to have trouble keeping friends, and his teachers complained that he was disrupting his classes with his comments, clever as they often were. His absorption in maintaining this behavioral posture also began to interfere more and more with his academic achievement, which took second place to his role as the class wit.

At this point the parents began to grasp the implications for Stuart's future if he continued ȯn this track. They took him seriously, and when he no longer found approval of his cuteness he began to take himself seriously. By the time he entered college he had the beginnings of mature, socially responsible goals, and as success brought success in college, he turned into a serious, thoughtful young man.

Dealing with a Child's Protests

The process of social and intellectual development necessarily brings demands for change as the child goes from one developmental stage to the next. What is appropriate behavior for an infant—say, a four-hour schedule of feeding and sleep—is no longer necessary or desirable for the toddler. The three-year-old may be only starting to try to dress himself; the six-year-old should be competent at this task. The two-year-old who is not toilet trained fits the common pattern; the five-year-old who is not has a problem. Parents have to be vigilant that a three- or four-year-old does not hurt himself; a ten-year-old is expected to know and observe rules of safety on his own.

All these and the many other developmental progressions require change and adaptation on the child's part. Some of these changes may be achieved spontaneously and without apparent effort, but others require alteration of established, comfortable habits. Depending on the child's temperament, he may respond to the demand for change with mild and brief protests or with loud and prolonged objections. Especially when the child protests vigorously, some parents become intimidated or guilty or both. They interpret the child's loud cries as a message of injury, a signal that they are imposing something harmful on the youngster, and they back off. Many are the parents who have told us they couldn't impose a reasonable bedtime or decent behavior at the dinner table because the child cried so bitterly that it must be doing him harm. In reply, we have asked, "Suppose your child had picked up a sharp knife, and you rushed to take it away from him, and he screamed to get it back. Would you worry about the harm this frustration was doing to him, and give him back the knife?" The answer is always "Of course not, it's too dangerous." In such a case the parent does not worry that the child's protest is doing him harm.

It is no different with a child's protest when a demand is made to achieve goodness of fit. A preschool child entering nursery school may have to adapt to going to bed earlier and getting up earlier and learn to eat what everyone else is eating instead of the special meals his mother has been making for him. Any child worth his salt will object mildly or loudly, depending on his temperament, at such assaults on his comfortable habits or rituals. We have the same reactions as adults, though they may be expressed by verbal protest or silent stewing, in contrast to the young child's shrieks. But harmful it is not; the youngster adapts and realizes that he is growing up and behaving more like his parents and older sisters and brothers. A new goodness of fit has been achieved appropriate to the child's new developmental stage.

If the child's resistance to change is prolonged and persistent, then it may be another matter. It may mean that even if the goal is appropriate, the parent is plunging in prematurely, demanding compliance overnight, or using punitive methods to enforce the change. In such a situation the parent should take stock, perhaps consult friends, family, or pediatrician, and start over again with a new strategy. Even when the goal and the demand are reasonable, the approach that will achieve the new goal constructively and effectively must depend on the child's temperament.

What Must Be, What May Be, and What Doesn't Matter

The goodness of fit concept should not be applied as a mechanical formula, stated and acted upon in the same way in all situations: "My child has this particular set of characteristics, and therefore I should expect him to react in this particular way and make my demands accordingly. Otherwise, there will not be goodness of fit, and all kinds of undesirable consequences will result." As a general statement, this principle is valid, but as with most general statements, there are exceptions. Some situations are *musts;* the child must adapt. In other situations the child's adaptation may be desirable, but it is not essential. And in still other situations disagreement between parent and child is insignificant. There is no need to insist that the child adapt, and an agreement to disagree actually represents goodness of fit.

The *musts* are numerous, and most of them are self-evident. A child must be toilet-trained. He must be trained to avoid dangerous objects. He must learn to dress himself. He must learn to respect the rights of others. And he must learn to function academically and socially in school.

There are other situations in which goodness of fit is desirable but not essential. For the three-year-old to sit down at the dinner table and eat the same meal as his parents, brothers, and sisters is a desirable social experience. It helps to cement the youngster's identity with his family and makes him feel he is growing up. And if the child has special food idiosyncrasies —if he won't eat green vegetables because his best friend told him they are full of bugs, or if he won't touch bread because he once had a bad stomachache after stuffing himself with bread—such special preferences can easily be honored. They may make him feel he is somehow different from the rest of the family and limit his goodness of fit with them, but there are all kinds of other positive give-and-takes with the family that can make up for them. Such food idiosyncracies become a problem only when the child wants to restrict his diet to a few items, such as hamburgers and french fries. In such cases, there is the danger not only of inadequate nutrition but of the child's becoming the autocrat of the dinner table, demanding his own special meal to be cooked separately. When this happens, the *may be* becomes a *must,* and the parents must insist that the child widen his food intake—but making the demand in a way that is consistent with the child's temperament.

Or, as another example, the child may develop special preferences in words and insist on playing word games. If his selections are reasonable, there is no issue: The parent's and child's preferences do not have to be identical. If the youngster picks up words or phrases that are impolite, unkind, or otherwise unacceptable to the family's mores, however, then the parent's judgment has to be honored, not his. The parent can give the child a choice, but only within certain limits. The *may be* with regard to words has become a *must,* at least for that particular situation.

The *don't matters* also cover a wide range of situations and choices. These are the issues in which the concept of goodness of fit does not apply. A parent and child may disagree—and inevitably do—with regard to style of dress, preferences in reading, movies, TV, and the choice of special interests and activities. The parent may be disappointed that such differences may interfere with the closeness and intimacy of the relationship, but goodness of fit is not involved. That is, the lack of consonance between parental expectations and desires and the child's functioning is not producing an unhealthy distortion of the child's development, with harmful consequences. To attempt to impose an artificial harmony when the differences really don't matter is all too likely to lead to future alienation and rebellion on the youngster's part.

When Parent and Child Become Adversaries

When a parent makes demands of a quality or in a form that are incompatible with the child's characteristics and persists in these demands, parent and child can become adversaries instead of friends. The parent interprets the child's inability to comply as "willful disobedience" or "lack of self-discipline," actual phrases used by parents in discussions with us. These can be parents who started out with a clear commitment to fulfill their responsibilities to their child and looked forward to a happy, intimate relationship with him. Yet they end up feeling victimized and somehow betrayed by their youngster. Other parents, faced with such poorness of fit, end up feeling guilty and inadequate; the problem is somehow their fault. They try appeasing the child, and that only makes matters worse. They may not blame the child directly, but there is an element of antagonism: "If somehow he were more cooperative, as other children are, then we wouldn't have the problems we are having." The child, on his part, either thinks that his parents are unfair and unreasonable in their expectations or worries that something must be wrong with him that he can't meet their demands.

Such a development between parent and child leads to an adversarial relationship, which can take many forms, none of them desirable. Sometimes the antagonism can become truly extreme. One father, a basically mild-mannered man, highly successful and esteemed in his profession, came to us with his wife for consultation over their ten-year-old son's problems. The father was in actual torment: "I wanted to be a good father, yet I realize that with Archie I've become a child abuser."

The story was not hard to piece together. Archie was a typical temperamentally difficult child from the beginning, and caring for him had not been at all easy. The parents had consulted several psychiatrists and received conflicting advice from each one. With all this professional confusion, and with their own bewilderment over what to do, the parents oscillated constantly. They tried giving their son special favors, they tried appeasing him, they tried making rigid rules calling for instant obedience. At the same time their two younger children, both temperamentally easy, were blossoming and responding cheerfully and cooperatively to the reasonable rules and requests which Archie was refusing to honor. At no time were the parents given the advice necessary for such a child as Archie—to set rules and limits quietly, consistently, and firmly, but to pick on only one or two at a time, outride the child's stormy protests, and then go on to the next issue. Instead Archie grew up knowing that his parents would give in if he made enough of a commotion. He became the tyrant of the family. Periodically, when his behavior became obnoxious enough, especially toward his mother, the father flew into a rage and tried to beat the boy into submission. His subsequent guilt over this punitive behavior was enormous but not helpful. A totally new treatment approach was necessary, based on the recognition of Archie's difficult temperamental characteristics and the strategies necessary to deal with them.

In another case, four-year-old David, a highly intelligent child, developed severe sleep disturbances and anxieties as he brooded over the death of his grandfather and its meaning. His parents had no appreciation of the depth of David's worries. They tried to brush them aside, and an escalating series of confrontations developed. When the parents came for consultation, the issues were identified, and the parents were immediately sympathetic to the boy's concerns. They realized that with all his superior intelligence David was still a four-year-old emotionally. In a follow-up letter some months later the parents reported a dramatic improvement and commented, "Where we went off the deep end was when we began to feel victimized by David's behavior. Once that happened we lost our perspective and could not help him. As soon as we understood this, we could be on his side."

We could add example after example. Once parents and child become adversaries because of poorness of fit, their relationship can only deteriorate with harmful consequences for the youngster. Parents who find themselves in the position of being their child's adversary must take this as a signal that they have gotten off the track. Sometimes they can rethink the issues themselves and right the situation, but sometimes they may need professional help before they can do so.

Goodness of Fit with Various Temperaments

We have emphasized that most parents can describe their child's temperament accurately. This is especially true if the parent is not entangled in a psychological theory that makes sweeping assumptions about the meaning of behavior: for example, that shyness always means anxiety, that intensity of emotional expressiveness always means hostility, or that slow adaptability always means a deliberate resistance to change.

We have also given examples of behavior typical for the various temperament attributes and patterns at different age periods in childhood. The parent's objective in identifying the child's temperament is, of course, not academic interest or curiosity. The issue for parents is the application of this knowledge to achieve goodness of fit between their expectations and the child's capacities. With this objective in mind, we offer a series of suggestions based on the information we have accumulated in the past thirty years in our longitudinal studies. Our suggestions for practical management will emphasize the extremes of each temperamental characteristic, inasmuch as these are the instances in which special management approaches may be desirable or even necessary. The child with an average level in all temperament attributes does not usually require unusual caregiving strategies, unless the parents misjudge the child because of their own special personal biases. For example, a father who expects the evening household to be quiet so he can concentrate on work brought home from the office may consider his son annoyingly "boisterous" and "loud," even though the boy is of average activity level and intensity of expression.

It should also be kept in mind that a child's temperament is very rarely completely consistent. Even a highly distractible child may be hard to distract in certain special situations; a child who tends to show initial withdrawal reactions to the new may plunge eagerly into a new situation that interests him greatly; a child who usually adapts quickly to change may be slow and cautious in certain situations that have special meaning; a young child with low intensity who usually expresses protests mildly may be capable of throwing a violent tantrum when frustrated over some special desire; and so on for any of the other temperamental patterns.

Finally, the demands of the infant, expressed by fussing, crying, or reaching, can always be considered reasonable. That is, the infant is expressing a need, whether hunger, sleepiness, skin irritation, or beginning discomfort from an acute illness, and satisfaction of that need is appropriate and desirable. His first clumsy attempts at turning over, standing, walking, and drinking from a cup should also be encouraged, even if these activities require vigilant attention to prevent harm or a mess. The older child, on the other hand, develops desires and preferences not always appropriate to the specific situation or to its long-range consequences. For example, a five-year-old going through the supermarket with his mother may be attracted to an expensive toy that is well beyond his developmental level. Or an eight-year-old who has fallen behind in his academic subjects and needs daily tutoring may strongly desire to go off on a four-day trip with friends. Denial of such requests becomes necessary, even though at another age or in another situation they might be reasonable.

Therefore, the following guidelines for promoting goodness of fit between parent and child should not be construed as absolute rules to be followed in all situations with a specific child with a particular set of temperamental characteristics. Rather, they are guidelines that will apply in most but not necessarily all conditions and all the behaviors shown by the child at all times. Flexibility in the child's behavior should go along with flexibility in the use of the guidelines.

Specific Guidelines for the Temperamental Attributes

Activity Level

In infancy the parent must always be sure to hold the high-activity baby firmly when he is lying on the bed or a changing table. All infants should be guarded against suddenly twisting or turning and falling to the ground, but this is a special risk for the high-activity infant. As such infants grow older more complex issues crystallize and require attention. The child can become restless, irritable, and fussy if taken on a long automobile ride without any breaks or forced to sit still for long periods, as at a religious observance or a concert, or if he is denied the opportunity to take part in his usual baseball game or other physical activity. Such plans may have to be carried through in spite of the child's fussiness, but they can usually be arranged to minimize the child's discomfort. An automobile trip can be broken up with periodic stops to allow the child to get out and move around; the parent and child can sit in the back of the concert hall and go out briefly several times so that the child can run around. If the sedentary restraint is unavoidable, such as in an airplane trip when everyone must be seated because of turbulent weather, the special circumstances and necessities should be explained patiently to the child. The explanation must include the clear statement that the child has no options, that he must sit where he is.

This type of normal temperamental high activity must be distinguished from the pathological condition of excess activity generally known as *hyperactivity.* In this condition, the very active movements are impulsive and accompanied by very short attention span and excessive distractability. Such a child finds it very hard to sustain his attention in any one direction. This kind of hyperactivity is usually easy to distinguish from the temperamentally high-activity child who does not show these symptoms of an attention disorder. Hyperactive children with attention deficits require active professional treatment, which sometimes includes the use of special medications.

The low-activity child presents no special issues in infancy. As he grows older, his slow movements may be interpreted as delays in development, subnormal intelligence, or an unwillingness to carry out a parent's request. Such a child may also become an irritant to the family if they are all ready for an outing and have to wait for him to get dressed at his slow pace. One first-grade teacher even recommended that one of our longitudinal subjects be left back, because his slowness in movement was to her a clear indication of mental slowness. Such a child, of course, should not be misjudged and penalized for a normal temperamental trait. Parental recognition of the reason for the child's slowness can make all the difference in the world. The child can be taught to plan ahead in many situations, such as laying out his school clothes the evening before. He can learn that he requires extra time to do his homework, but that this is no reflection on his intelligence. In emergencies, as in a sudden thunderstorm on a picnic, he will have to appreciate that everyone is hurrying and that if he does so and leaves a few unimportant possessions behind, no real harm is done. As he grows older, he can learn to use phrases such as, "Let me do my share, but I do it slowly. So let me start ahead of time."

Rhythmicity (Regularity)

The infant whose sleep-wake cycles, hunger patterns, and time of bowel evacuation are regular makes life easier for the parents. Schedules can be planned, substitute caregivers can be prepared to anticipate the timing of the infant's needs, and toilet training is usually easily accomplished. The same ease of management continues as the child grows older, and his capacity to adjust to the regular schedules of school, play activities, and work remains an asset.

The irregular child, by contrast, makes the daily routines of living harder for the parents. Naps, meal times, and night sleeping schedules are irregular and even unpredictable. The mother or other primary caregiver is never sure how to arrange her day-by-day or even hour-by-hour activities, including her own nap times. Toilet training is more arduous and complicated than for the regular child (see discussion in chapter 3).

This does not mean that such irregularity has to continue indefinitely. Training the child in regular bed habits and regular meal times is not difficult if the parent is consistent and patient in planning schedules and responding to the child's demands. For example, a toddler whose bedtime is irregular can be told he must go to his room at the same hour each night, dressed for bed, and close the door. This demand the child can follow, but not the one that he "go to sleep" at a certain hour. When he reaches school age and has to be awakened at the same time each morning, then the demand for a regular sleep time can be made. The child will by then usually be tired enough at night to be responsive to a schedule.

As the irregular child grows older, this temperamental quality usually becomes less important functionally. The regular schedules of school, the appointments for after-school or weekend games with his playmates, the regular timing of the family dinners of which he wants to be a part—all these serve to modify a basic tendency to biological irregularity. When we asked our young adult study subjects whether their sleep and mealtime patterns were regular, the usual response was "It all depends on whether I have to get up early for a class, or for my job, and when I have a break for lunch and dinner."

Approach or Withdrawal

The infant who responds positively to new situations, foods, and people also makes life easier for the parent. There is no fussing with the first bath, most new foods are taken easily, and a strange baby-sitter does not evoke a loud protest. The new situations that come along at succeeding age periods—new playmates, the first nursery school or kindergarten, change of school or neighborhood—are likely to evoke this same positive response. When the child experiences a special event or situation that creates anxiety and withdrawal, his atypical response should be a signal to the parents that something is wrong and that special investigation is required.

Quick positive responses are not always an asset. Especially if they are combined with intensity of reactions, they may lead the child to impulsive actions that are not always in his best interest. Here the traditional saying "Look before you leap" is a good one to teach the child.

A pattern of initial withdrawal reactions to new experiences requires special approaches on the part of the parent. Patient, quiet exposures, first brief and then longer, are usually needed before the baby begins to enjoy the bath, take to new foods, or accept a strange baby-sitter. For such a child, starting school requires a period of adjustment, and changes in school routines are likely to make him uncomfortable. With a new play group he is likely to stand apart, cling to his mother, and quickly ask to go home. But if he is brought back regularly, he will gradually warm up and eventually become an enthusiastic participant. As he grows older, a child usually has fewer new situations with which to cope, and his withdrawal tendencies may recede into the background. But he may remain cautious, if not actually inhibited with the new, and this is not always an undesirable trait. And such a youngster may even develop an enthusiastic interest in some hobby, so that he plunges into it in a way that is opposite to his usual tendencies.

For parents, the management of the child with withdrawal tendencies is not complicated, as long as they recognize that this is their child's normal temperamental quality and not some perverse intention to say "no" to everything new. The guiding principle is that one should not drop the attempt to have the youngster accept something new. That would result in a progressive restriction of the child's activities and deprive him of the experiences he needs in order to develop confidence that he is capable of mastering new things. Rather, the parents should persist in exposing their child to the new patiently and quietly but insistently, and beginning with small doses. The results of such an approach are uniformly gratifying. Discomfort changes to pleasure, and nonparticipation changes to active involvement.

Adaptability

The highly adaptable child is a pleasure to the parent, as compared with the child with low adaptability. The former takes to change easily and with little or no fuss, so that schedules and routines can be modified or altered without turmoil. With the child with low adaptability the story is different: Changes are accompanied by protest and struggle. In the early infancy period, the differences between the two types of children may not be dramatic. If the low-adaptability child refuses to take a new food, even after a number of trials, substitutes can usually be found. Changes in sleep routines or bedrooms can be accomplished if the parents persist quietly in spite of the child's protests.

As the children grow older, however, the differences in adaptability become more important. Playmates decide to play new games with new rules, school schedules and routines are always changing, and new people with different manners and personalities keep coming into the child's life. Because low adaptability is often accompanied by negative mood, an unpleasant first experience at a supermarket or a department store may constrain the parent from taking the protesting youngster shopping again.

As with the child with withdrawal tendencies (and withdrawal and low adaptability not infrequently go together), the parent who understands the meaning of this low adaptability can usually deal with it effectively. If the change is unimportant, there is no harm in giving it up. The child will even gain the sense that his parents do listen to what he wants. If the change is important, however, the parents must stick to their guns. Sometimes quiet reasoning is effective, especially if the youngster knows that the parent will be unmoved by his protests. (One ten-year-old whose mother finally gave in to the child's long and loud protests complained, "If she's going to do what I want anyway, why does she make me have to do all this crying and shrieking?") If reasoning doesn't work, the parents must be prepared to wait out the protests and wailing and then go on with the plan.

It may seem that high adaptability represents an ideal temperamental characteristic. It makes management of the infant easy, and as the child grows, it helps him to adjust successfully to the increasingly demanding and complex expectations of the outside world. To some extent high adaptability is desirable, but by no means completely so. Such a child may adapt quickly in a way that is undesirable to his parents or himself. One girl in our study suffered an upper respiratory infection when she was three. Previously she had slept through the night, but now she woke up several times nightly crying because of a stuffed nose. Her mother soothed her, gave her medication, and both went back to sleep. In a few days the infection disappeared, but the girl, with her quick adaptability, had learned to wake up several times a night and call her mother, who responded. This went on for several weeks until the mother came in to consult us, haggard from lack of sleep but feeling she had to respond to her daughter's calls. Questioning made it clear that the youngster was functioning well and showed no signs of anxiety. The mother was advised to ignore her daughter's night calls, even if she felt guilty. Within a few days the girl made another quick adaptation and was sleeping through the night again.

A youngster with easy adaptability also has to be careful not to be too easily swayed. His very ease of adjustment to change may at times make him give in too easily to the wishes of others, even when it is not in his own best interests. Here, the parents can be helpful in defining this issue, so that the child can learn when his quick adaptability is an asset and when he should stick firmly to his own position and refuse to change.

Sensory Threshold

High sensory threshold is rarely a problem, though it may make it difficult for an individual to appreciate nuances of color, music, or the texture of different fabrics. Low sensory threshold may sometimes create difficulties. William Carey, in his pediatric practice, has found that young children who awaken frequently at night are more likely to have a low threshold to sound and light than children who sleep through the night

(1974). And some mothers have complained of having a running battle with their child over clothes. The youngster claims that the clothes are either too tight or too rough and is satisfied with only a small number of the mother's choices. There are sometimes other causes for such a problem, but one reason can be that the child has a very low threshold to skin sensations. His clothes are truly irritating to his skin, even though they may not bother the great majority of other children. Here the remedy is clear. The child's skin sensitivity has to be accepted as normal for him, and clothing that is comfortable for his level of sensitivity must be provided.

Quality of Mood and Intensity of Expressiveness

We group quality of mood and intensity of expression together at this point, because the parent usually has to deal with them in combination. If a child makes an unreasonable request, the parent can stick to an initial "no" with greater serenity if the youngster responds with quiet fussing rather than loud crying. The child who is ebullient and openly expressive of delight at a gift or special treat is more likely to receive a cheerful parental response than the youngster who expresses his pleasure in a low-keyed, even deadpan, manner.

Parents usually get to know their child's typical mood quality and expression. It is the change from the typical that is most important. If a child is usually quietly pleasant and fusses only rarely, a loud and bitter complaint warrants immediate serious attention. But if a frequent loud complainer begins this kind of protest, the issue about which the child is complaining is likely to be a minor one, to be investigated in a different manner.

When the parents do not appreciate their child's mood pattern, poorness of fit is likely to be in the making. One set of parents in our longitudinal study consulted us because of their irritation and confusion over their daughter's behavior. They would take her to a special treat—say, the circus—and the girl would sit impassively throughout the performance and give no indication that she was enjoying it. Yet the next day the mother would hear her daughter describing the event to a friend with animated pleasure. On many occasions the parents could not figure out what the girl wanted or felt. They themselves were lively, cheerful, and expressive people, and so were their friends, and their daughter's temperamental style was completely alien to them. But they were able to listen and comprehend the issue during our discussion—their daughter was normal but just very different from them—and with this knowledge the parents were able to establish positive communication with this previously enigmatic girl.

Distractibility

The distractible infant is easy to manage. If he is resisting diapering, dressing, or being washed, his attention can be diverted by a toy or other object, and the routine care can proceed smoothly. When he begins to crawl and approach dangerous objects, such as electric outlets, he can also be drawn away easily. Feeding such a baby does have its nuisance aspects, however, as he keeps turning his head away to look at some new person who has suddenly appeared on the scene. The nondistractible infant, by contrast, may concentrate on feeding no matter what the diversions. His resistance to routine care is not as easily overcome as with the distractible baby, however. If he is resisting being dressed or bathed, no toy may divert him, and the procedure may have to be deferred or completed by main force.

For the older child, however, the ease of functioning for the distractible versus the nondistractible child may be completely reversed. This reversal happens as the youngster begins to take increasing responsibility for his own behavior at home, at school, and with his friends. Typically the highly distractible child forgets to carry out commitments, appointments, and assignments. He may start out cheerfully to carry through the responsibilities and even look forward eagerly to the enjoyment it will bring him. Along the way, however, some interesting scene or person distracts him and he gets actively involved with the new people and the exciting scene. Finally reaching home, he is reminded of his original goal and reproached for his irresponsible behavior, and he is typically overcome with remorse and confusion.

When such an event occurs, the behavior of the parents is critical. They may understand the problem, sit the child down, explain that he has to police himself against such distractions, and offer helpful suggestions, such as making up a written list of his commitments each morning and consulting the list frequently during the day. With such an approach, which may have to be repeated many times, there is goodness of fit between parent and child, and the outlook for the child's eventual self-control of his distractibility is favorable. If the parents take an adversarial position, however, and assume that the youngster's forgetting is deliberate, the outlook is changed. The child is charged with "disobedience," "laziness," "always wanting his own way," "rebelliousness," or some combination of these unworthy traits. By putting the issue in these terms, the parents raise questions that are not only irrelevant but that give the child no help in achieving more desirable behavior. The relationship then often goes from bad to worse, and a seriously poor fit may crystallize, with all its undesirable consequences.

The nondistractible child, by contrast, does not forget a responsibility once he has begun it. Parents say, "The house could burn down around him and he wouldn't notice it." The child's problem may be that he becomes *too* nondistractible, unable to notice peripheral stimuli and events once his mind is occupied with a project. This oblivion to what is happening around him may irritate his family, friends, or teachers, but he is usually forgiven because his conscientiousness and commitment are usually desirable assets. A parent will occasionally be irritated at having to call the child a number of times before he answers, but this rarely becomes more than a minor problem.

It is also worth pointing out that high distractibility can have its positive aspects. Such a child is quick to pick up nuances of behavior and feelings with his friends and his family. This quick understanding of others can prove to be a valuable asset in many situations.

Persistence and Attention Span

Persistence and a long attention span are highly valued in our society. While the parent of a young child may be annoyed by his persistent effort to obtain a forbidden object or to carry through a forbidden activity, the quality of persistence itself meets with approval. For the older child, persistence becomes an increasingly valued attribute in our work-oriented society.

By contrast, parents worry if their child gives up on a difficult task instead of seeing it through. They visualize all the unfavorable consequences this trait will bring in higher education and jobs and how it will prove a serious limitation to the child's achievements. They often fail to notice that this same nonpersistent child eventually returns to the task and completes it successfully. The combination of high distractibility and low persistence is especially distressing to parents and hard for them to understand as a normal temperamental characteristic. "I can stick to a job until I finish it, why can't he? He just doesn't have willpower and self-discipline." A parental demand that the child take on his parent's concentrative powers and persistence is doomed to failure. In one family in our study, the result was a boy without self-esteem and ambition, who said, "My father says I have no willpower, and he's right." Only if parents can focus on a child's eventual achievement, rather than on the behavioral style by which it was accomplished, is a positive outcome possible.

Occasionally, a highly persistent youngster may have difficulties, especially in school or with age-mates. At home, parents can easily make allowances for the youngster's temperament and take pride in his achievements. But in school or in play groups, rigid rules and routines may be set up that conflict with the youngster's own plan of activity. Coming up against a stone wall, without flexible arrangements, such a child may experience intense frustration and even blow up without explaining his reasons. If such episodes are repeated sufficiently, the child easily becomes a scapegoat and the butt of ridicule. One ten-year-old boy in our study with this problem finally said in despair, "Let's face it, I have some kind of a monster inside myself."

We now return to the question we raised in chapter 1: What made for the radical difference between Ricky and Eddie's development? We can give at least a partial answer.

Ricky's dominant temperamental qualities were high activity, quick and easy adaptation to new people and new situations, and moderate persistence. He lived in a suburban house with plenty of space to satisfy his needs for physical activity. His parents were permissive, but where need be, as in setting safety rules, they were quietly, patiently but firmly consistent in their demands. Ricky's quick adaptability made it easy for him to make friends and adjust to school easily. His moderate persistence and good intelligence helped to make his school career a successful one.

Eddie, by contrast, was a markedly difficult child temperamentally from early childhood on. The parents were bewildered by his loud persistent crying and slow adaptation, which was so contrary to their expectations. They vacillated between appeasement and angry responses with punishment, which only aggravated Eddie's difficult behavior. They consulted several child psychiatrists. The first told them that Eddie would "outgrow" this behavior, which did not happen. The second psychiatrist advised more "tender, loving care," a prescription the parents would have dearly loved to follow, but found ineffective when Eddie exhibited one of his frequent tantrums, or when he was in one of his less violent but still negative moods. The third psychiatrist told them that Eddie needed treatment five days a week. Inasmuch as the parents had only been able to bring eight-year-old Eddie to this psychiatrist by main force over his violent protests, such a treatment regime was clearly impractical. At no time was the issue of difficult temperament and an appropriate parental approach identified by these three physicians.

With the poor fit between parent and child, Eddie's difficult behavior only became worse, to the point where the household was in frequent turmoil, and Eddie's personal life was marked by social isolation and unhappiness. He was finally referred to one of us, and the sequence of unfavorable development became clearly evident from the parents' story. Remedial parent guidance was advised and instituted. The early results were promising, but the long-term outcome is still in doubt.

Achieving Goodness of Fit

The achievement of goodness of fit between the environmental demands and the child's capacities is an issue in all situations inside and outside the home. But it is the parents who usually have the greatest impact. They also have the most frequent opportunities to give the child insight into his own temperamental characteristics and the behavioral techniques that will minimize their unfavorable consequences.

Some parents can identify their child's special behavioral characteristics and figure out confidently the best approach to take. Such parents usually manage well on their own. Other parents may have similar insights but may be less confident of their validity, because their friend's or relative's baby behaves so differently. Here a simple evaluation by a mental health professional may be all that is necessary. Still other parents, however, find themselves confused and unable to understand their child's behavior. Such parents often end up in an adversarial position to the child, and perhaps to each other as well, whether out of guilt, a sense of inadequacy, or a derogatory judgment on the child. These are the situations of poorness of fit in which a behavior disorder in the child is a frequent outcome. Such parents need systematic counseling and advice from a mental health professional, a procedure we have called *parent guidance.*

The professional who provides parent guidance must first of all determine that there is no other cause for the problem, such as an unrecognized learning disability or brain damage. If the problem is identified as poorness of fit between parent and child, then the counselor should usually discuss with the parent the concept of temperament, the specific characteristics of the child's temperamental attributes, and the desirable versus the harmful ways of handling the child, given these temperamental characteristics. Several discussions, and sometimes more, are required to clarify these issues fully.

Such parent guidance is valuable not only for its effectiveness but also because it avoids the alternative approach of prolonged psychotherapy for child or parent, or both. In our longitudinal study we have found approximately 50 percent of the parents responsive to this line of discussion, with marked improvement or cure in the child. Some parents, however, could not be budged from their adversarial position to the child. This occurred not so much with the temperamentally difficult children but with boys with high distractibility and low persistence. The parents of the difficult children could be reassured that with proper management their children could prosper and meet their own and the community's standards. The parents of the distractible, nonpersistent boys, on the other hand, had to be told that proper management might mitigate these tendencies but their sons would basically not change. The parents interpreted this to mean that their sons would always do a job "sloppily" and would never "stick it out to the end." (It is of interest that all these objections came from the parents of sons, not daughters.) And with these character traits, how could their sons succeed in life?

A parent's resistance to parent guidance can occur for a number of reasons. A parent may have rigid standards of conduct that the child may not be able to attain. The parent may have a neurotic need for authoritarian control of the family or may want the child to live up to an ideal image that will make the parent shine as the perfect mother or father. Anything less than some a priori standard of perfection in the child may be a threat to some parents, who have some special neurotic need for success in all their undertakings.

In some cases of unsuccessful parent guidance, the parents were willing to consider long-term psychotherapy for the child. This had varying success—sometimes it was very helpful, sometimes not. Psychotherapy for the child was less likely to be successful if the parents persisted in the attitudes and demands that had contributed to poorness of fit in the first place. Some parents did recognize that their own psychological problems were contributing to the child's difficulties but could not change on their own and were willing to engage in treatment themselves, either in individual psychotherapy or in some form of group therapy. In these cases, the outlook for converting poorness of fit to goodness of fit, with a cure of the child's behavior problem, was much more favorable.

PART II

THE DEVELOPING CHILD: INFANT TO ADOLESCENT

6

Babies Are Human from the Start: The Beginnings of Social-Cognitive Development

A S WE DID our first parent interviews in our longitudinal study, when the babies were two to three months old, we came away with the vivid impression that the parents were describing *real human beings.* The infants were different, and that was the focus of our study, but the differences were human differences. If a baby didn't take to the first bath, her reaction was not just a passive withdrawal of some simple reflex nature. She kicked and squirmed and tried to get away, and her facial expression indicated definite displeasure. If her mother held her, smiled, and talked to her, she smiled, cooed, and babbled in return. These were complex responses to the stimulus from the outside, behavior very similar to that of an older child or adult in response to a pleasant or unpleasant situation. The infant's responses were simpler only in terms of the limits of her as yet immature brain development. And so it went with the baby's other behavior—the way she reacted to something new, the way she adapted to change, the way she became distracted by a sudden new person, object, or sound, the way she persisted in examining a toy or the movements of her hands. There were individual differences, but in all regards the behavior was complex and organized. In no way could the babies' behavior be described as a series of simple reflex actions. In addition, many of the observant parents gave us the same picture of their baby at the age of just one week—responding actively with complex behavioral patterns to the different stimuli coming from within herself (hunger, thirst, and sleepiness) and to all the new situations and experiences coming from the outside, and especially those from her caregivers.

This idea of the infant as a human being from the start was completely at variance with traditional views of the newborn baby, but it was in line with the research findings of a number of developmental psychologists and psychiatrists whose work over the past thirty years has transformed our views of the young infant and her capabilities. This issue is not only of interest to theoreticians interested in tracing the origins and sequences of a child's psychological development. It also bears on our concept of *infant bonding*, a term that has come into prominence in recent years. The way parents view their new baby can influence substantially their approach to this apparently mysterious person for whom they are now responsible.

Earlier Views of the Newborn

In past centuries, two contrasting views of the young infant vied with each other. Some considered the newborn infant to be a *homunculus*, literally an adult in miniature, who already possessed the physical and psychological attributes of the future adult. The *homunculus* concept, in which everything was hereditary, led to popular aphorisms like "The apple does not fall far from the tree," "He's a chip off the old block," and "the bad seed." In psychiatry, it led to such labels as "constitutionally inferior" and "constitutional psychopath," in which all kinds of abnormal behaviors were considered to be already present in the newborn infant. In the eighteenth century there was Rousseau's more idealized, romantic vision of the child as a "noble savage," endowed with an "innate moral sense," with "intuitive knowledge of what is right and wrong," but "thwarted by the restrictions of society" (quoted in Mussen, Conger, & Kagan 1979, p. 11).

Others held an opposite view. To them, the newborn was a *tabula rasa*, as the seventeenth-century British philosopher John Locke put it—a clean slate on which the environment would inscribe its influence until the adult personality was etched to completion. Essentially these two conflicting theories mirrored the debate in biology over the relative importance of heredity and environment, of nature versus nurture.

In this century, the mechanical view of the infant as a *homunculus* became increasingly discredited. The work of Freud and Pavlov demonstrated that much of the behavior that had been labeled as hereditary and predetermined actually arose out of the child's life experiences. A host of studies, continuing to this day, expanded and deepened our knowledge of the profound significance of the child's environment in shaping her physical and psychological development.

Unfortunately, as is so often the case, the pendulum swing went to the opposite extreme. By the 1950s, the newborn infant was no longer a *homunculus* but became a *tabula rasa*. The environment, especially the mother, became not only important but all-decisive in shaping the child's behavior and future mental health. All the psychological ills a child or adolescent could develop, from simple behavior problems to delinquency to serious psychiatric disorders, were laid at the mother's doorstep.

A more sophisticated variation of the *tabula rasa* came in the formulations of a number of psychologists. For them, the newborn's mind was not a completely empty slate, but her only mental capacity at birth was a series of simple reflexes or instincts. It was, then, the influences of the environment on these reflexes or instincts that shaped the development of the child's mind. In these formulations the newborn was a self-centered organism rather than a human being ready at birth to begin to enter into an active interchange with the environment, and especially with caregivers, on a number of levels.

The pioneering cognitive psychologist Jean Piaget held the view that the newborn's brain was a bundle of reflexes, of which grasping was the most important. As Piaget saw it, this grasp reflex, in which an infant tightened her muscles around any object she touched, was the foundation for the development of reaching for objects and manipulating them. It led to increasing skills, knowledge of the world, and finally the ability to form concepts and think abstractly (1952, 1954). With this view of the newborn's very limited ability to respond to the world around her, Piaget described her psychological state as one of "radical egocentrism."

In traditional psychoanalytic theory, the human infant came into the world with only a set of primitive instinctual drives, the "id." In Freud's words, "the id is a chaos, a cauldron of seething excitement . . . the id knows no values, no good or evil, no morality" (1933, pp. 104–105). It was only through the later development of the "ego" and the "superego" that, in this view, the asocial id impulses were repressed, controlled, and sub-limated, so that the infant gradually began to be a social human being. British psychoanalyst John Bowlby modified this view but still claimed that certain reflexes of the newborn were the basis of social development. The reflexes he emphasized were clinging, sucking, and crying, because they stimulated the mother's caregiving activities and thus provided the first step in the process of socialization (1969).

American psychoanalyst Margaret Mahler went even further. She and her co-workers visualized the newborn as completely self-centered ("nar-cissistic") and unable to integrate any stimuli from the outside or to be aware of other people, even the mother, as separate individuals. As Mahler defined it, "During the first few weeks of extrauterine life, a stage of absolute primary narcissism, marked by the infant's lack of awareness of a mothering agent, prevails. This is the stage we have termed *normal autism*" (Mahler, Pine, & Bergman 1975, p. 42). Mahler was thus comparing the newborn's state to autism, that very serious psychiatric illness, beginning in early childhood, in which the child is unable to relate socially with other human beings. She and her co-workers then postulated a second stage of development starting in the second month of life, "a phase of normal symbiosis, in which the infant behaves and functions as though he and his mother were an omnipotent system—a dual unity within one common boundary" (p. 44). Only at five or six months, in this theoretical structure, did the infant begin to "hatch out" as a separate individual from the mother (p. 54).

Mahler's ideas of the newborn and of the young infant's development have had a great influence within the psychoanalytic movement, and in-deed on many other psychiatrists and psychologists. She provided a de-tailed theoretical structure for formulating a sequence of development in the first months of life, which had been missing from previous psy-choanalytic concepts. She also buttressed her claims by the report of an extensive and elaborate research project that studied a group of young infants and their mothers at different ages and in a variety of settings (Mahler, Pine, & Bergman 1975). Her study, however, has very serious methodological problems that make it impossible to accept her conclu-sions. No objective behavioral criteria were established for the ratings of her categories of "narcissism," "symbiosis," or "autism." Rather, the ob-servers assumed the categories to be present and rated their "degree" from the infant's behavior. Mahler makes this approach clear in a number of statements regarding her research efforts: "The observers functioned more as sensitive clinicians than as cameras; we relied upon their experience to understand phenomena in spite of the potential subjectivity in this" (p. 239); "It was never our belief that we could, and never our intention that we should, codify all our observations to a standardized, let alone quantifiable, form" (p. 246); "We decided on the system described above with a priori observations of behavior possibilities (drawn from our past observations and clinical experiences) and with a direct rating of a child by a rater (by having a rater simply check off one of the a priori assumptions) rather than record the observed behavior in detail" (p. 255).

In other words, Mahler invented categories ahead of time, with no precise definitions of the child's behavior, and the observers assumed these categories were present and checked them off. With such a system, no one can go wrong! These inadequacies have come under sharp criticism even within the psychoanalytic movement. As John Bowlby has put it, "In brief, Mahler's theories of normal development, including her postulated normal phases of autism and symbiosis, are shown to rest not on observation but on preconceptions based on traditional psychoanalytic theory and, in doing so, to ignore almost entirely the remarkable body of new information about early infancy that has been built up over the past two decades" (1982, p. 673).

The analyst Emanuel Peterfreund has pointed out that Mahler's data cannot be taken as valid even if they are presumably based on observations of a baby, because they rest on a priori assumptions and because Mahler's concepts assume an equivalence between a baby's and an adult's behavior. As he notes, "The infant screams for his needs but the infant knows no other way, in contrast to adults who have other capabilities. The infant's apparently 'omnipotent' behavior has a totally different significance from that of an adult who acts similarly" (1978, p. 436). We can say only "Amen!" to this formulation.

Basically, these different views of the newborn—whether as a *homunculus,* a *tabula rasa,* a bundle of instincts or reflexes, radically egocentric, or autistic —stemmed from a common view of the extremely limited capacities of the normal newborn. As one leading British researcher, Rudolph Schaffer, put it,

> It was thought that in the early weeks of life a baby's senses were not yet capable of taking in any information from the outside world, so that to all intents he was blind and deaf. Unable to move much either, he seemed a picture of psychological incompetence, of confusion and disorganization. Only the regularity of his experience, provided principally by his parent, was thought to bring order to the baby's mind. Until that was achieved, all he could do was feed and sleep. (1977, p. 27)

Jerome Bruner, who has made far-reaching contributions to our knowledge of perception, cognition, and education, reports a visit by a pediatrician to Bruner's infant research laboratory at Harvard in the 1960s. The staff demonstrated one of their research procedures, in which a six-week-old, by sucking on a pacifier, sucked a blurred picture into focus. As Bruner reports it, "The visitor watched for a while, then blurted out almost in indignation, 'But babies of that age can't see' " (1983, p. 157).

What We Now Know

With such judgments of the newborn as blind and deaf, psychologically incompetent, and unable to communicate effectively, it is no surprise that scientific studies of early infancy behavior and mental functioning took so long to blossom. A few brave investigators, such as Arnold Gesell and Mary Shirley, did make the effort in the 1930s and 1940s. Useful as their work was, it was primarily restricted to descriptions of observable behavior, as they traced the process of maturation and time schedules in the evolution of skills and abilities. An occasional anecdotal report on the behavior of one or several infants appeared from time to time, frequently of the child of the reporter, but such single and superficial descriptions did not provide a basis for understanding the psychological characteristics of a young baby.

It was not until the 1950s and 1960s that a number of serious scientists began to observe and study the newborn and very young infant, with the idea that the prevailing notions might be all wrong. New techniques and procedures were developed that could yield inferences about the infant's mental processes: measurements of the time and quality of an infant's visual fixation on an object as a gauge of vision and preferential attention; the study of the infant's body movements in response to various types of stimuli; videotapes that could be analyzed frame by frame and even by computer; ingenious experiments such as Bruner's use of a pacifier to control the sharpness of a picture, making possible the measurement of the infant's perceptions and intentions; simple experiments to test the infant's ability to imitate; and careful, detailed descriptive accounts from parents and other caregivers regarding the patterns and sequences of infants' behavior. By now, a number of research centers in this country and abroad are devoted to the careful study of the young infant's capacities and functioning. The professional literature reporting these research activities has expanded tremendously.

With these research studies of the past twenty-five years, our view of the neonate has been turned completely around. Rather than "a picture of psychological incompetence" or, in William James's words, "one great blooming, buzzing confusion," it is now clear that the newborn begins life as an organism capable of perception, communication, imitation, and learning. The newborn infant not only recognizes visual patterns but gives preferential attention to such patterns and to complexity, movement, and three-dimensionality over plain visual stimuli. She is responsive to sound and can localize the direction from which a sound comes. Learning, as demonstrated by the formation of conditioned reflexes, starts actively at birth. Learning by imitation has also been demonstrated in the first days of life. As early as two weeks of age, the infant can differentiate between two live female faces, discriminate between voices, and begin to associate face with voice. It would take at least a volume to detail the careful, scientifically sound research studies that have identified the wide range of psychological capacities of the newborn. We can only give examples in the areas of perception, communication, learning by imitation, and behavioral integration.

Perception in the Neonate

A pioneer research student of visual perception in the newborn was Robert Fantz of Western Reserve University, who began this work in 1956 (Fantz 1956). Fantz devised a test in which the baby lay on her back in the crib and looked at a ceiling directly overhead. Various devices, such as movable shields and screen projections, were used to expose targets on the ceiling, then hide them and replace them with other targets. A small peephole in the chamber provided an observer with the opportunity to measure the time the infant fixed her gaze on any one target. This fixation of gaze was determined by the observer's ability to see, through the peephole, the centering of the corneal reflection of the target in the infant's pupillary opening. As long as the target was reflected in the infant's pupil, the observer knew the baby was gazing directly at it. The crux of the experiment was to determine whether newborns looked at targets of different patterns for the same length of time or for different lengths of time. If the length of gaze was different, it meant that the infant was distinguishing visually between the two targets. And, indeed, Fantz found that even the newborn could discriminate one-eighth-inch stripes from plain gray (1966).

This may seem like a very simple finding, but it has profound significance. In order for the newborn to discriminate between the patterned and the solidly colored object, as determined by difference in length of gaze, she has to do more than just see, just react visually to the two objects. She has to organize the innumerable visual stimuli coming simultaneously from the object into an integrated structure, or percept, as we call it. The brain's ability to organize stimuli into percepts is what enables us to recognize the differences and similarities between different faces or any other objects, or between different combinations of sounds or touch stimuli. This ability to form and differentiate percepts out of sensory stimuli is crucial to cognitive development. Percepts become organized into ideas and into the ability to recognize oral and written language, to understand the meaning of numbers, and so on. And the newborn, as Fantz discovered, comes into the world with the ability to form simple percepts, the beginning of perceptual-cognitive development. Fantz and his associates carried this work forward in a number of studies which demonstrated the increasing perceptual ability of young infants with each successive month and even week of life (Fantz & Nevis 1967).

Fantz's work on infant perception was extended in a series of experiments by Genevieve Carpenter, of St. Mary's Hospital Medical School in London. Under standardized conditions, in which the baby was calm, alert, and in a comfortable position (as in Fantz's studies), infants were exposed to the faces of different individuals. The discrimination among the different faces was measured by the length of time the infant looked directly at the face. As early as two weeks of age, the mother's face received significantly more attention than a stranger's face. Also, each face was looked at longer if it was accompanied by a voice, but the mother's face was a stronger positive stimulus even without voice than the stranger's face accompanied by voice. When the faces and voices were mismatched—that is, when the mother's face was presented with the stranger's voice, or the stranger's face with the mother's voice, there was a significant tendency for the infant to turn her gaze away (1975). Carpenter's experiments indicate that the neurobiological basis for perception, association of face and voice, and memory is so far developed at birth that in the first two weeks of life an infant is already able to make these perceptual distinctions and to make a clear association of face with the proper voice.

How quickly neonates begin this kind of learning is indicated by a recent study by Tiffany Field and her associates at the University of Miami. They showed that a group of forty-eight neonates averaging forty-five hours of age significantly differentiated between the mother's face and a stranger's face. The discrimination was measured by length of gaze, with both an observer and a videotape gathering the data. The strangers used were also mothers who had recently given birth, to rule out the possibility that the newborn's reactions were influenced by the odors associated with a woman who had just given birth or who was breast-feeding. At the time of the experiment the newborns had spent an average of only four discontinuous hours with their mothers (Field et al. 1984). This is truly a dramatic example of how quickly newborns begin to learn!

Active Social Communication in the Newborn

A striking capacity of the newborn is the ability to begin to enter into active social communication, that most basic element in the development of human relationships. Two investigators, William Condon and Louis Sander, of Boston University, used a refined technique of microanalysis of sound films of interaction between neonates and caregivers and found that "as early as the first day of life, the human neonate moves in precise and sustained segments of movement that are synchronous with the articulated structure of adult speech" (1974, p. 99). The precise synchrony occurred with both American and Chinese speech, but not with disconnected vowels or tapping sounds. This same kind of synchrony between newborn and caregiver has also been identified in sucking behavior (Kaye & Brazelton 1971). The infant's cry is an active and effective form of social communication from the moment of birth on and is powerfully reinforced with the development of the smile in the first weeks of life.

The Newborn's Imitation of Adult Gestures

A further exciting discovery is that the newborn can imitate certain adult facial gestures. This is indeed a complex activity. It means that the infant first forms a perception of the adult's gesture, then translates this perception into the image of an analogous action of her own, and finally is able to act on this image to reproduce it.

The major studies of newborn imitation have been done by Andrew Meltzoff, of the University of Washington. In a series of elegant experiments with forty healthy newborns ranging in age from forty-two minutes to seventy-one hours, the infants' responses to an adult who either protruded his tongue or opened his mouth were recorded by an infrared-sensitive camera. (The room was darkened and a spotlight directed to the adult experimenter.) Meltzoff was not satisfied to test the baby's imitation of only one adult gesture—say, the tongue-protrusion—for it might be argued that the newborn was aroused by watching an animated adult and that the increased movements of the baby's face might accidentally include movement of the tongue. This possibility of a randomly produced imitation was eliminated by the use of two test situations: tongue-protrusion and mouth-opening by the same adult. Meltzoff found that the newborns imitated both the mouth-opening and the tongue-protrusion to a significant degree. The frequency of infant mouth-opening was significantly greater in response to the experimenter's mouth-opening than to his tongue-protrusions, and the frequency of tongue-protrusion was greater to the experimenter's tongue-protrusion than to his mouth-opening. With this cross-experimental design, it was possible to conclude that the newborns were showing true imitation of the adult's facial gestures, and not just a general reaction to social stimulation by the adult (Meltzoff & Moore 1983; Meltzoff 1985).

Meltzoff concludes that this neonatal capacity for imitation of adults gives them "a mechanism by which to begin to identify with other human beings, to recognize them as 'like me' " (1985, p. 29).

Behavioral Integration in the Newborn

A baby is capable of responding to one or more stimuli in an organized or integrated fashion. For example, she is able not merely to hear a sound but also to turn her eyes (and in later weeks, her head as well) in the direction of the sound. This is behavioral integration.

T. Berry Brazelton has made extensive studies of newborns in naturalistic (rather than laboratory) settings and has demonstrated a wide range of behavioral integrative processes, variations in state behavior,* and responsiveness to various kinds of social stimuli. As a typical example, we watched him with a thirty-minute-old infant lying quietly awake in his nursery crib. Brazelton took a paper clip and stroked the sole of the baby's foot. The infant showed a sharp withdrawal reaction with his whole body. When Brazelton repeated the stimulus, the baby withdrew less sharply. With repeated stimulation with the paper clip, the baby first moved his leg, then only his foot, and then only his toes, and he finally fell asleep during the same stimulus that had originally caused a marked response. Brazelton explained, "See, the baby is able to protect himself against noxious stimuli." With these types of simple procedures, Brazelton has found significant evidence of cortical control and responsiveness with twenty-two behavioral items, which now constitute the widely used Brazelton Neonatal Behavioral Assessment Scale (1973). This is further evidence, from a different viewpoint, of the impressive level of behavioral capacities with which the newborn interacts with the surrounding world.

*One of the problems of infant studies is the great variability in very young infants' states of arousal, which determines their alertness. An infant who is falling off to sleep just after being fed will not attend to a stimulus. In contrast, an infant just awakening but not yet hungry will be quite alert. In reporting infant responses, it is essential that the state of arousal also be given. (The word "state" is frequently used to mean "state of arousal.")

The Infant as a Social Human Being

The infant thus comes into the world equipped biologically to enter immediately into give-and-take social relationships with her parents and other caregivers. And by no means is she a passive partner in these social activities; she is no *tabula rasa.* But neither is she a *homunculus.* She has the equipment to enter actively into social relationships, but the kind of relationships she develops and the kind of person she becomes is in no way preformed or predetermined. It is always the interaction between child and environment (parents, brothers and sisters, peers, teachers, and so on) that is decisive—and not just one or the other.

With the first fondling, the first feeding, the first perception of the human face and figure, the newborn responds to and integrates stimuli that have social and cultural significance. In turn, the active responses of the infant influence the character of the caretaker's attitudes and handling. From an evolutionary point of view, the perceptual, learning, and social competence of the human neonate is intimately linked to the long period of nurturance and dependency of infancy and childhood. These neonatal capacities make possible the maximum transmission of the cultural heritage of humanity, the adaptive mechanism that is so uniquely developed in human beings.

Early Interactions

Daniel Stern, a psychiatrist at the Cornell University Medical Center and a leading researcher in infant development, has thoughtfully studied the complexities and subtleties of the infant's first social relationship with the mother or other primary caregiver (1977). He has observed social interactions between caregivers and infants both in his laboratory and in the child's own environment. Many observations are videotaped and the tapes reviewed again and again; he notes that he has spent hours examining events that occur in seconds. At times a computer has been enlisted as an aid in looking for patterns and relationships.

From this extraordinary research study, Stern gives us a vivid picture of the mutual give-and-take and communication of two human beings—the infant and the mother. "The infant comes into the world bringing formidable capabilities to establish human relatedness. Immediately he is a partner in shaping his first and foremost relationship" (1977, p. 33). In this partnership, the infant is, of course, immature in relation to the mother. But, as Stern emphasizes,

The label "immature" cannot be a green light to dismiss a behavior until its more mature version arrives . . . ultimately any human being is simply what he is at the moment we find him. The behaviors of a three-month-old are totally mature and fully accomplished three-month-old behaviors. The same is true at two years, ten years, twenty-one years. (p. 33)

The parents who expect their baby to act like an adult in miniature or ignore her behavior because it is immature will lose the spontaneity, responsiveness, and pleasure that the relationship with the infant should bring.

Stern develops the thesis that throughout the first months of life, starting at birth, there is an optimal level of stimulation of the infant that the mother provides in the course of the routines of daily life—feeding, dressing, nursing—as well as in spontaneous play. When the mother's stimulation is optimal, the infant smiles and coos and gazes at the mother alertly. The mother in turn is gratified, and her behavior is reinforced by the baby's response. What Stern calls a "mutual feedback system" is set up.

If the stimuli are too weak or too repetitive, however, the infant is not adequately stimulated; if they are too strong or too complex, the infant cannot absorb them and integrate them productively. But Stern emphasizes that the mother does not have to walk a tight and narrow path to make sure she provides exactly the right amount of stimulation for the baby, and not too much or too little. Quite the opposite: The range of optimal stimulation is wide. Further—and this is a crucial aspect of Stern's findings—the mother-child relationship has the all-important characteristics of fluidity and flexibility. By his careful study of the sequences of interaction in mother-infant pairs, Stern has definitively found that both mother and child can regulate the amount of stimulation the infant receives. If the level goes too high or too low, both partners have behaviors with which they can return the level of stimulation to the optimal range. Moreover, the mother's "mistakes" in occasionally overstimulating or understimulating the baby—and no mother is ideally sensitive to her infant at all times—may actually be important in a positive sense. Stern points out that the infant requires constant practice in these adaptive behaviors under slightly different conditions.

We heartily agree with Stern's judgment of the importance of spontaneity in a caregiver's social behavior. The parents who worry about whether they are stimulating their baby just enough, too much, or too little, and who keep looking for signs in the baby's reactions to reassure themselves, will lose this spontaneity and the pleasure that comes with it. Their stiffness and self-consciousness is then all too likely to stifle the normal give-and-take with the infant, with all the natural communication and self-correcting feedback that are so desirable for both parent and child.

Infant Competence and the Social Interaction

How much does it matter that, as we now know, the human newborn is a competent human being, and not some bundle of instincts who also holds in her brain such complex ideas as narcissism and omnipotence? Does it matter that she begins to be a separate individual at birth, rather than "hatching out" psychologically at four months?

To the research worker in child development the facts matter a great deal. They shape the researcher's theories, and they point to the directions for further research. If the investigations are based on solid facts, the work is likely to be fruitful. If the theories are fanciful, the researcher will end up in a blind alley.

But does it matter to the parents? Indeed it does. The parents who see their new baby as some primitive animal organism who has to be fed, cleaned, and kept warm are likely to view these tasks as boring and even annoying chores they have to endure until the infant becomes a human being. The parents who see their new baby as already a responsive, actively communicating human being will find meaning, interest, and pleasure in the baby's movements and vocal sounds.

It is very important to have the feeling that one is caring for a real person, that a social interaction is taking place, that one's baby is already a competent person. But infantile competence should not be equated with adult competence. When one says that an infant is competent to see, this means that she sees best at a certain distance, and can distinguish patterns of a certain complexity and not beyond this. She is not ready to see as an adult can; that takes practice. But she is practicing by interacting as a social being with the caregiver. Her visual acuity is best at just that distance at which a caretaker's arms hold her comfortably, and it is not a mistake when mother, father, grandparents, and delighted brothers and sisters feel that this new member of the family is really looking at their faces and studying them for future recognition. Because that is indeed what she is doing.

The baby's hearing is also set to go. She hears a range of vocal sounds; in fact she hears the female voice a bit better than the male voice. If her mother talks to her on one side and her father on the other, she will turn preferentially to the side on which her mother is standing. One up for Mother! But given Father and a strange male voice, after a few weeks she turns preferentially toward the familiar male voice. One up for Father!

True, she doesn't make sense out of words, and she cannot yet distinguish small sound differences. But she is working at it in a social way, responding to being talked to by movement, by facial expression that becomes gradually clearer as her control of facial muscles increases and as she learns through repetition to associate with actions. Her hearing is competent—but again, competent for the needs of an infant.

Moreover, the infant responds to touch and to the way she is held. How often have you seen a mother or father take a crying infant from someone else and seen the child's crying stop as soon as she is held, talked to, perhaps rocked? These parents are important to the baby; she already knows them, knows them as a competent infant can. And as her senses and muscle coordination improve, her signals of sociability become more translatable, not because she is finally becoming an individual but because she has from the beginning been an individual who is maturing.

The infant even shapes her environment through her own behavior. Some of the things the parents do are done simply because they evoke pleasure in her, and this gives pleasure to them. Other things are done because the baby makes them happen. It may be that she won't accept being fed until she is clean and dry; it may be that her pattern of sleeping and waking make it necessary to do certain things at certain times—such as taking a shower when she has just fallen asleep instead of one's usual time, when she is awake and hungry. Who, then, has taken the lead? Just as with babbling when it becomes established, sometimes it is the baby who takes the lead, sometimes it is the parents, and sometimes there is clear turn-taking, a dialogue of sounds and actions—a social interaction.

Exactly what the baby can do to demonstrate her social individuality will change with development. Certainly she gets better with practice and with maturation. She is learning all the time, and so are her parents. To say that a newborn is already a social human being is not to say that, at day one, she is as competent as at day sixty. Her human nature keeps taking new forms.

The ways of knowing what she wants change as the infant matures and can do more and take in more. Just a simple action like the bath demonstrates the social side of an infant. At first she is cleaned with a washcloth, until her cord has dried and healed. But then she goes into a little tub. It takes her time to get used to it—five minutes or two weeks, depending on her individual style, but she does get used to it and shows that she likes it. She looks at the person bathing her and kicks and moves her arms. When she is dried and lotioned, she moves in a way that makes the bather say, "She loves being bathed and toweled" or perhaps, "She likes one part and dislikes the other." Her whole body moves with joy, or she cries and thrashes with displeasure. Whichever it is, or something in between, her body movements and vocalizations communicate her reactions.

And, in response to the baby's signals, the caregivers modify their handling. If she likes the bath but dislikes the drying and dressing, then she tends to be left in the bath longer, and the dressing is done quickly to get it over with. If she likes both aspects, then the daily bath may become the high spot of the day for both the baby and her parents. There is action and interaction. Sometimes the parents do the initiating; after all, the baby is bathed regularly, like it or not. Sometimes she does the initiating, as when she smiles as she is wrapped and cuddled in the towel, bringing about an extension of the routine. The interaction is there from the first, and both parents and baby engage in it. Why do adults talk to babies? Even during the period when psychologically sophisticated parents believed that infants were merely bundles of biologic matter, needing food, cleanliness, and little more, parents talked to their babies. It is the natural thing to do; friends do not just sit in silence.

Parents and babies are friends from the beginning. And, as in any good friendship, sometimes signals are missed or mistaken. But in any good friendship errors are recognized and made up for, and on the next occasion the signal is read more accurately. No harm has been done. Perhaps the caregivers will modify their handling. But at times it is the baby who modifies her behavior. Infants are adaptable, accommodating. After all, parental personalities come in many individual styles, and cultures have many different ways of handling their babies. Infants come into this world with remarkable abilities to adjust to so many differing caregiving styles and cultural habits.

Infant Plasticity

The plasticity of infants is an important feature of their human nature. Not only are the habits and rules of cultures very different, one from the other, but households and the parents who shape them have their own individualities. If infants came with only one way of responding to the outside world, they would have quite a time surviving in such different environments. But the human infant has the built-in protection of plasticity, the ability to adapt to an extraordinary range of living conditions and psychological climates. It is indeed the unadaptable infant, the one for whom just one set of circumstances will do, who is in trouble. For the most part, infants and children have the plasticity that allows them to adapt to an extraordinarily wide range of circumstances. They thrive under nomadic life; they thrive under life lived in one place throughout childhood.

They are content strapped to the mother's back as she goes about her work, bending and standing again, subjecting the baby to constant changes of posture; they thrive held in the father's or mother's backpack or nestled in a snug carrier in front of the parent's body; they lie contentedly in a baby carriage or on the sofa. They adapt to being swaddled and, once adapted to this manner of existence, cry when their limbs are left free; they kick contentedly if left unencumbered from day one.

All these ways of handling a baby have been used by various cultures, and the babies have adapted to the necessities and conveniences of that culture. Babies have been brought up for centuries in situations of multiple mothering, of being cared for by sisters, of having nannies and wet nurses; they are also brought up with a single nurturing figure, one caregiver who is responsible for all care. Fathers have been distant figures, fathers have shared equally in routine care, and fathers have had circumscribed but definite responsibilities. Foods available differ widely from place to place, class to class, cultural habit to cultural habit. With all these differing circumstances in which babies have grown up generation after generation, how can one can be so foolish as to dictate any single way of child care that is "correct" for all children in all families and all cultures?

Communication Between Infant and Parent

The infant communicates from birth on, with ever-increasing powers of differentiated activity. As the weeks and months go on, she can vary her cry, kick, flail her arms, arch her body. Gaze becomes more capable of being fixed on faces, eyes, and objects. The head can be turned toward an object with the smile of pleasure or the open mouth of eating or of exploration. She can push away the bottle, the spoon, the cup, the offered finger food, or she can move away from the first taste, only to open her mouth in eager acceptance after the actual taste has been discriminated. She can giggle with pleasure at being held high in the air, kicking her legs in glee; she can cuddle and smile at gentle play—a whisper in the ear, fingers stepping up her cheeks and pouncing on her nose, a cloth placed over her face for her to remove and see her companion. Or she can howl in negation of participating in any or all of these games.

Is true communication only the increasing skill of the parent to read the precise signals of the baby? Does the baby in fact always have precise signals? When she is hungry and is given milk that she drinks with pleasure, one might think so. But had she been offered solids—baby food from a jar, a preparation of small morsels of table food, a piece of cracker—and accepted these with pleasure, might the adult equally have believed himself or herself to have cleverly read the baby's signals correctly? And if the baby continues to cry, does that mean that the caregiver is a dolt, oblivious to the baby's attempt to communicate?

Communication builds up gradually. It takes several weeks for a parent to learn to distinguish between the cry of hunger, the complaint of wanting company, and the anguish that means some body discomfort—bellyache, earache, malaise. It may require time for a parent to learn that certain fussing at a particular time of day is best handled by putting the baby to bed to fuss herself to sleep to get the rest she needs, or for the baby to learn that crying longer during the night will not get her into the parents' bed, thus ensuring future full nights' sleep for both child and parent.

Why all this comment—don't we know it all already? Yes and no. Communication between infant and caregiver is all too often presented as if the match requires that the adult learn to read all the child's signals immediately and accurately and fill the indicated need. That would be a wondrous achievement indeed. Adults are themselves often full of vague longings, of discomforts and despairs they cannot specify. How can one expect an infant always to give precise signals that have only one satisfying response? The baby is moving in her capricious way toward developing likes and dislikes. One day a food is a favorite and another day it is pushed aside. One afternoon her father plays with her with mutual pleasure while mother departs, and on another occasion, this same scenario results in seemingly endless screaming.

Should the parents feel incompetent if they cannot always read their baby instantly and accurately? By no means. There will always be times when they are at sea about what their baby really wants at a particular moment. And the child care expert—whether pediatrician, nurse, or mental health professional—may not be any wiser at such times. (We remember the occasion when we were driving with one of our daughters-in-law and her six-month-old daughter. The baby started to cry and couldn't be consoled. She was not hungry or wet or sleepy, and she usually enjoyed a car ride. Our daughter-in-law turned to us and said, half-seriously but without real worry, "Now, you experts, tell me why is she crying." All we could say was, "We don't know, any more than you do.")

A good fit between infant and parent is not the same as perfect communication and instant gratification of the baby's needs at all times. The social system between parent and infant has enough flexibility and adaptability built into it that there is plenty of room for miscalculation, misjudgment, and trial and error.

Parents can be and should be spontaneous with their infants and trust their ability to become gradually acquainted with the special individual characteristics of their babies. This parental spontaneity and confidence that time is on their side with their babies are the best assurances for the growth of a healthy parent-infant social relationship.

Two Questionable Concepts

Infant Bonding

We have emphasized the concept that a human relationship between parents and infant begins to be established at birth and that the newborn has the capacities to enter into this relationship as an active partner. This attachment of parent to child and child to parent develops and expands as the baby grows and depends on the multitude of events and interactions that occur between them in daily life as the weeks, months, and years go by. Our emphasis on this concept of the gradual and progressive development of the parent-child attachment grew out of our observations in our own studies, as well as from the research studies of others, as summarized above in this chapter.

In 1976, however, two respected pediatricians at Western Reserve University, Marshall Klaus and John Kennell, published a volume, *Maternal-Infant Bonding,* with a different thesis. They stated categorically, "We strongly believe that an essential principle of attachment is that there is a *sensitive period* in the first minutes and hours after an infant's birth which is optimal for the parent-infant attachment" (pp. 65–66). If the child is separated from the mother during these first hours after birth, so their thesis went, optimal development would not occur. To ensure this positive "bonding" of mother to infant, Klaus and Kennell recommended that all newly delivered mothers have immediate skin-to-skin contact with the newly born baby in the delivery room for a brief period of time, perhaps up to thirty minutes. They also advocated that mothers should have free access to their babies, either in the hospital nurseries or by rooming-in. Such free contact between mother and baby was limited or even forbidden by hospitals at that time, for fear of transmission of bacteria and viruses from the mother to the vulnerable newborn infant. Klaus and Kennell marshaled impressive evidence, especially from studies in Guatemala and at Stanford University, that free contact of mother and infant after delivery did not increase the risk of infection in the baby. This conclusion has not been challenged by any contradictory studies and is now generally accepted as valid.

The psychological importance of this immediate mother-infant contact, however, is an entirely different story. Klaus and Kennell reported a number of studies that presumed to show positive effects, such as greater affectionate behavior and less child abuse and neglect, in those mothers who had this immediate skin contact with their babies.

Klaus and Kennell's claims of the psychological benefits stimulated a host of studies by a number of investigators. Most of these studies could not confirm Klaus and Kennell's reports of the value of immediate infancy bonding (Chess & Thomas 1982). In 1983 Susan Goldberg, of The Hospital for Sick Children in Toronto, published a detailed critical analysis of the reported studies—both favorable and unfavorable—and came to the following conclusions: (1) There has been no really systematic study of the possibility that a sensitive period for the beginning of maternal behavior exists. (2) Studies that have reported short-term effects have mostly not related these findings to later maternal behavior. (3) There has been no convincing demonstration of consistent effects of extra contact opportunities in the delivery room. Another review by Barbara Myers, of Virginia Commonwealth University, also criticized the positive reports as having a number of methodological problems: performing many statistical tests but reporting only the positive ones, artificially combining different ratings to create composite scores whose measuring is questionable, and using single outcome measures that had uncertain relevance to bonding (1984). There are a host of other studies that add up to powerful doubts as to the validity of the infant bonding concept (Svejda, Pannabecker, & Emde 1982), though a number may be methodologically flawed.

Klaus and Kennell's writings have had two important effects, one positive and the other negative. On the positive side, they have been a major influence in opening up newborn nurseries to the mothers, instead of banning such contacts. Whether or not this increases "bonding," it has been a humanizing change in hospital practice, so that mothers can get to know and enjoy their babies without delay. On the negative side, innumerable mothers have been made anxious and guilty because they have missed this initial skin contact with the baby for one of a number of reasons—hospital rules, a Caesarian operation under general anesthesia, or a physical problem that necessitated rushing the baby to an intensive-care unit, possibly in another hospital. Such mothers all too often felt that they could never love their baby as they should, because they had missed this initial bonding experience.

With all these criticisms and negative reports, Klaus and Kennell have softened their position in the 1982 revision of their volume. They now state that it "seems unlikely that such a life-sustaining relationship would be dependent on a single process" (p. 70) and that "each parent does not react in a standard or predictable fashion to the multiple environmental influences that occur" (pp. 56–57). As humane clinicians, they are also genuinely distressed that mothers who missed this early experience should feel guilty and cheated. They state, "Sadly, some parents who missed the bonding experience have felt that all was lost for their future relationship. This was (and is) completely incorrect" (p. 55).

The present consensus is best summed up in a recent paper by an experienced and respected team of investigators from the University of Colorado (Svejda, Pannabecker, & Emde 1982). They review a number of negative aspects of the bonding concept: the lack of satisfactory research support for the idea; the questionable formulation of a biologically based sensitive period; the overemphasis on the newborn period; the oversimplified model that ignores the multiple factors in the family network; the elevation of the term "bonding" to a reified theory in itself; and the harm done to parents who cannot be with their babies immediately after delivery. From this summation they conclude "that the bonding model . . . is no longer useful" (p. 91).

We agree with their conclusion and fervently hope that this negative judgment will not affect the more humane atmosphere that has developed in many newborn nurseries. The justification for such an atmosphere can stand on its own merits and does not need the support of a doubtful and questionable theory.

Infant Psychiatry

An outgrowth of the new studies of infant development and mother-infant relationships is the burgeoning in recent years of a self-styled specialty of "infant psychiatry." To us, this movement represents an extreme swing of the pendulum from the time when we knew very little about the capacities of the very young infant for perception, communication, imitation, or behavioral integration.

As we and others have emphasized, our new and increasing knowledge of the infant's abilities should give us a view of the flexibility and plasticity of the infant's functioning, the various parent-child combinations that can lead to healthy outcomes, and the many self-righting tendencies that both infant and caregivers possess if their relationship goes off the track temporarily. But the "infant psychiatrists," on the contrary, have taken the research findings of recent years and used them to propose a new kind of Procrustean bed for infants and their mothers. They have postulated a series of stages at different age periods in infancy to correspond to the increasing maturity and competence of the growing infant. Stages are given to cover the first two years of life. For each stage, they list a series of infant behaviors that are "adaptive" or "maladaptive" and a series of tasks for the caregiver that are "adaptive" or "maladaptive" and change with each new change in the baby's developmental stage. If the infant's or caregiver's behavior is "maladaptive," then the psychiatrist or other mental health professional should intervene. A summary of these infant psychiatry theses is given in a recent article by two leaders of this movement, Stanley Greenspan and Reginald Lourie, of the National Institute of Mental Health (1981).

Our concerns over this movement are several. On the theoretical side, we question the validity of forcing all infants into specified developmental stages at succeeding short age periods. The first stage, from birth to three months, is called "homeostasis" or "balance interest in the world," and the second stage, from two to seven months, is called "attachment." But all our new knowledge emphasizes that babies begin to form attachments to caregivers actively from birth and that "balanced interest in the world" is in no way a special phenomenon of the two-month-old infant but a lifelong process. Babies are just too different in their speed and quality of maturation and in their individual differences in behavior to be fitted into such fixed developmental schemes.

On the practical side, we are concerned that this approach will make unrealistic and even impossible demands on mothers. The adaptive caregiver for the child from birth to three months is told to be "invested, dedicated, protective, comforting, predictable, engaging, and interesting," and for the two- to seven-month-old she is "in love and woos the infant to 'fall in love'"; she is to have "effective, multimodality, pleasurable involvement" (Greenspan and Lourie 1981, p. 727). What real mother in the real world could live up to these prescriptions? Mothers get cranky, overtired, overwhelmed by the chores of baby care, even bored at times by diaper-changing, washing clothes, and preparing the baby's food. Babies, too, can be fussy and cranky. They can cry at night for no obvious reason and give their caregivers an occasional hard time. Yet in real life caregiver and infant thrive with such routine "maladaptations."

The danger is that the infant psychiatrists tend to pressure mothers to be constantly on the alert for any sign that they or their babies are deviating from the prescribed ideal and to take "preventive" action. Thus Greenspan and Lourie state that "the infant who only puts his hand forth very slowly in order to make contact can initially be met by the mother three-fourths of the way. Slowly, by finding novel stimuli she can encourage him to begin meeting her halfway" (1981, p. 730). So now the mother is supposed to measure the infant's hand movement toward her and decide if it is too slow. (What if it is three-fifths? Is that also a danger sign because it is not exactly halfway?) Multiple new tasks and responsibilities are imposed on the mother, without clear evidence that they make a difference in the long run.

It is certainly true that therapeutic intervention may be important in infancy when clear-cut evidence of pathological behavior or retarded development exists. And some parents may need professional help if they are depressed, confused about their babies' behavior, overwhelmed by their caregiving responsibilities, or exhibiting serious unhealthy attitudes regarding their parental roles. But there is a real danger that the infant psychiatrists will try to extend their prescriptions and interventions to more parent-infant pairs simply because they are not measuring up in one way or another to some "ideal" standard. As Daniel Stern points out (1977) and as we would emphatically agree, we should be very cautious about such interventions. A parent-child interaction that appears undesirable may be self-correcting as time goes by. And even if it persists for some months, our ability to predict its long-range consequences is far from exact. To sacrifice the parents' spontaneity with their baby for such uncertain usefulness would indeed be a case of the cure being worse than the disease. Stern himself cites an instance with one of the mother-infant pairs in his research study in which a pessimistic prediction at first seemed justified. The mother was blatantly intrusive and overstimulating with her young infant, who was reacting by avoiding eye contact with her mother. This situation grew worse, and by four months Stern felt he would have to intervene. But then the interchange between mother and child began to improve and continued to do so. Stern was never sure why this happened, but no intervention was required. He comments, "The journey I traveled with them engendered much restraint about predicting outcomes and evaluating the need and timing of intervention—a restraint that remains still" (1977). We and others who have followed children and their families over time have also learned this same restraint.

7

Children Are Learning
All the Time

> "A coral reef which just comes short
> of the ocean surface is no more to the
> horizon than if it had never begun,
> and the mere finishing stroke is what
> often appears to create an event
> which has long been potentially an
> accomplished thing."
> —THOMAS HARDY,
> *Far From the Madding Crowd*

IN the preceding chapter we detailed the complex capacities of the newborn's mind, capacities undreamed of before the research of recent decades. We indicated how these abilities for perception, communication, imitation, and behavioral integration enable the infant to start life as a social human being, engaged in an ever-expanding social relationship with his caregivers and with a multitude of other human beings as he grows older. In the most profound sense, the human being is a social being from birth onward.

At the same time, these same characteristics with which the newborn is biologically endowed enable him to begin to *learn* as soon as he is born. And it is this learning in a social context that leads to language and the ability to symbolize and form abstract thoughts. These abilities are present to a greater or lesser degree in certain other species, but their extraordinary development in human beings has produced a unique ability to control and exploit our environment (and the ominous present potential for destroying ourselves and all life on this planet).

All species pass on their characteristics to the next generation by the genetic mechanism of inheritance. Human beings pass on their physical characteristics and the capacities for social and cognitive functioning that are already evident in the newborn. (The linguist Noam Chomsky has also postulated, as the result of his studies, that the human being also inherits a preprogrammed mechanism for the processing of language [1957].)

But humans possess a second, unique *nongenetic* mode of inheritance. The special endowment of the human being to form social relationships, to learn, and to use language has made it possible to inherit *culture*. The achievements and life experiences of one generation are not forgotten but passed on to succeeding generations. Other species, such as primate societies, possess this capacity in a very primitive form, but only humans can transmit a cumulative, highly developed cultural inheritance—in science, the arts, philosophy, technology, and athletics. And this capacity to inherit culture comes from our special genetic endowment, which makes us sensitive to experience. As a leading geneticist, Theodosius Dobzhansky, has put it,

We do not inherit culture biologically. We inherit genes which make us capable of acquiring culture by training, learning, imitation of our parents, playmates, teachers, newspapers, books, advertisements, propaganda, plus our own choices, decisions and the products of reflection and speculation. Our genes enable us to learn and to deliberate. What we learn comes not from the genes but from the associations, direct and indirect, with other men. (1966, p. 14)

How Babies Learn

Mrs. B., while changing the diaper of her three-week-old daughter, noticed that Sharon's eyes seemed to be focusing on the blue powder box. She mentioned this to her husband, asking, "Don't you think we ought to buy some toys to give her stimulation?" Consulting friends whose child was now thirteen months old, they were advised to subscribe to a toy series, the proper toys for each age period would be sent at the appropriate time. In this way they would be sure that proper stimulation would be provided for optimal development of the baby's vision, hearing, movement, and coordination.

Mrs. A., as a conscientious new mother, faithfully attended a mother's group. When her son was eight months old, she was told by the group leader that it was time to play peek-a-boo with the baby, so that her infant would learn that when she went away, she would always return; otherwise he would feel abandoned.

What about such advice? Is it necessary to supply specially designed educational toys and play prescribed games? Without such toys will a baby fail to develop properly? Without such specific activities, will the infant be harmed?

Three-week-old Sharon focused on the blue box because it was there and because she was capable of noticing the colorful object. Clearly, such ordinary objects of her world were stimulating and interesting, and her home was full of things that had color, shape, size, and texture. As she became capable of more discrimination and control of her muscles (eye, neck, limbs, torso) her gaze would gradually become selective and linger longer, and familiarity and recognition would emerge.

There is no harm in manufactured toys, which do, for the most part, capture the growing capacities of babies. If a toy is meant for an older child, the baby doesn't care—he simply uses it as it fits. Give a stacking toy with graduated rings of differing colors to a baby seven months of age. Although the rings are "supposed" to be stacked on the pole in order of size, this baby puts one in his mouth, takes it out, looks at it, and replaces it in his mouth or tries another. He has, in fact, used the toy quite correctly —for his developmental level. The toy is indeed being explored, its use is contributing to his growing ability to discriminate color, size, texture; to help him locate it in space, to grasp what he sees with his fingers, to train the muscles of his arms, fingers, and wrists to move as needed, to provide in the joints the sensations of coordinate actions between muscle groups and of eyes with muscles.

So, too, will a host of ordinary household objects provide these stimulating possibilities. Often, out of an array of toys, the infant's favorite turns out to be a colorful pot holder, an egg carton, a plastic box lid. Unless a household is devoid of objects, an infant can easily be provided with stimulating things that he can play with and learn from at his particular developmental level. Many a parent has eagerly brought home an expensive toy with the assurance that it will stimulate an eighteen-month-old's "cognitive development." To the parent's chagrin and even confusion, the infant ignores the toy and concentrates instead on the kitchen pots, pans, and other utensils. The toy would have been fine if the child had become interested in it. But his use of the kitchen objects represented no deprivation. By manipulating them, stacking them, inventing games to use them with his own toys, he was being just as stimulated cognitively as he would have been with the new educational toy.

What about peek-a-boo? Are there in fact specific games that are unique, that provide sequential events that are needed in order for a baby to learn essential concepts and social assurances?

Sometime during the latter part of the first year, if the infant is shown an attractive object and it is then hidden, he will try to find it. In other words, he knows the object has constancy, that it has not vanished, and that it should be possible for it to reappear. Before this time, if an object disappears from sight, the infant behaves as if it no longer exists. The development of object constancy is an important step in the infant's growth of understanding of the outside world. But there is no evidence that games such as peek-a-boo will stimulate the concept of object constancy. The infant will reach this stage when his brain maturity and life experiences make it possible. Peek-a-boo and other games between child and caregiver are fine. They can be fun for both and increase the pleasantness of their relationship. But they are not necessary to stimulate cognitive development.

Similarly, there is no evidence that games such as peek-a-boo will prevent separation anxiety, the distress that an infant of six or eight months begins to exhibit when the primary caregiver leaves the room. After all, in the course of daily activities, mother, father, and other caregivers come and go. They are not at all times within the infant's sight or hearing. With daily life providing lessons to the baby that a departure is not forever, a formal game to teach this is not essential. The failure to play peek-a-boo or other similarly constructed games does not doom a child to insecurity.

Toys and games are, in fact, an imitation of reality. All cultures provide children with toys that are replicas of things important in the social world the child is to inhabit. Games provide a rehearsal for participation in that society and reflect events and interactions of that world. They are fun for adults and children, and they are useful. But they are a reflection of reality and should not be made into a mystique of some greater reality than reality itself.

Babies' Learning: Myth and Reality

To say that babies are learning all the time from the ordinary objects and experiences of their daily life may seem obvious to an experienced parent. To say further that this kind of learning goes on throughout childhood and, for that matter, throughout life is also not new. Unfortunately, there are many professionals these days making a mystique out of infant learning and preaching the advisability, even the necessity, of special games, objects, and procedures to ensure the baby's best intellectual and social development.

Why has this mystique developed? There are several reasons. First, there is the tendency of the pendulum to swing from one extreme to the other. A quarter-century ago, in the heyday of the influence of psychoanalysis, all the emphasis was put on the emotional development of the infant. Parents were told that their babies needed large doses of TLC (tender loving care) throughout the day and night. If they followed this prescription, all would go well with their child, including his intellectual development. This was also the era when it was still widely believed in professional circles that the young infant's ability to see, to hear, and to communicate socially was at best very primitive, so he could learn little, if anything.

Then came the gradual recognition and acceptance of the monumental studies of Jean Piaget on the stages of cognitive development, or the child's ability to think. Piaget demonstrated that the ability of the older child and adult to think abstractly and reason logically did not arise suddenly and spontaneously. Rather, like Thomas Hardy's coral reef, this ability was the "finishing stroke," the culmination of a progressive and systematic process of intellectual development that started in early infancy. In this same period, the research studies of the developmental psychologists brought to light the impressive abilities of even the newborn infant to perceive, to communicate, and to learn (as we have discussed in chapter 6). It also became increasingly evident to parents that their children's chances for a successful career in our technologically advanced society might depend more on their intellectual abilities than on any other factor.

Thus the pendulum has swung from extreme concern for the emotional life of the infant to extreme concern for his intellectual development. Tender loving care is no longer enough to ensure the baby's future happiness. What he needs even more is "cognitive stimulation" so he can learn to learn, expertly and fast, and get into one of the best medical, law, or business schools. Piaget himself once commented, in a meeting we attended, that Americans were not satisfied to understand the stages of a child's intellectual development; they wanted to speed up the process.

This new spotlight on the baby's learning was then intensified by several assertions, presumably based on actual research, that if the baby does not learn the right things in the right way at the right time, he will not have a second chance. Two of the statements came from certain studies of animal behavior, primarily from the group known as ethologists, led by

Konrad Lorenz. The ethologists have postulated the existence of two important influences on early learning, which they have labeled "imprinting" (Lorenz 1952) and "the critical period" (Scott 1958). Imprinting is described as a unique form of early learning from one single experience that has irreversible and permanent effects. The critical period hypothesis asserts that the young organism must be exposed to a given learning opportunity within a specific time period or suffer a deficit that later learning cannot remedy.

If human infants were actually to learn by imprinting and in critical periods, we would indeed have cause for worry. If a baby were "imprinted" accidentally with the wrong learning experience, the damage would be permanent. And if he somehow missed learning something essential during its "critical period," he could not make it up later. Fortunately, this is not the case. Even with regard to animal behavior, the concepts of imprinting and critical periods have been increasingly questioned by researchers such as Robert Hinde (1966), of Cambridge University, one of the most distinguished students of animal behavior in the world. For human infants, no evidence even suggestive of imprinting has ever been reported. As for critical periods, the findings are so contradictory and indefinite that two reviews of the subject conclude that the concept and term should be abandoned (Wolff 1970; Connolly 1972).

Two other attempts to invest infant learning with a special mystique should be mentioned because, although generally now discredited, they received respectful attention from many professionals when first reported, one in 1964, the other in 1976. They are still quoted by some experts who should know better and still create unnecessary worry among some parents about how much their child learns in the early childhood years.

In the first of these, Benjamin Bloom, of the University of Chicago, claimed as the result of a series of statistical analyses that fully 50 percent of a child's intelligence is developed by the age of four years (1964). This report has been widely quoted and has been used by many educators to explain away their failure to educate underprivileged children. But the study had a fatal flaw, exposed by Robert McCall (1977), of the Center for the Study of Youth Development at Boystown, Nebraska, one of our most sophisticated experts in statistical methods in child research and a creative, challenging figure in the field. McCall pointed out that Bloom reached his conclusion by calculating the statistical correlation between IQ scores at four and seventeen years of age. But this correlation is a measure only of the *stability* of the IQ over time, and not the actual level of the child's intelligence. (For purposes of this discussion, we are assuming that the IQ is an adequate measure of intelligence, an assumption that is actually quite shaky [see chapter 14].) In fact, Bloom's analysis of the correlations ignores the fact that the child's mental age—that is, his level of intellectual functioning—will increase by four and a half times during this four-to-seventeen age period (McCall 1977). The IQ test takes this into account by requiring higher standards of performance each succeeding year. Therefore, a child may maintain the same IQ as he grows older, as measured by his mental age divided by his chronological age. But this stability of IQ is maintained only because both the mental and chronological ages increase over time. In other words, the IQ stability may reach a 50 percent level by four years—that is, the four-year-old will have a 50 percent chance of having the same IQ score at seventeen years. But if he does, his actual intelligence level will have increased by 450 percent over the same thirteen-year period.

The second formulation goes even further. Burton White, of Harvard, as a result of one study of an early childhood group in the 1970s, made the most sweeping generalization of it (1976). To the questions "Is it all over by the time we are three years old? Are the limits of our capacity for future achievement irrevocably fixed during the first thirty-six months of our lives?" White gives an emphatic answer: "To some extent, I do believe that it is all over by three." He further asserts that the child's own family is obviously central to the child's developmental outcome, and that if the family does a poor job in the first years of life "there may be little the professional can do to save the child from mediocrity" (p. 4). We are back to scapegoating the parent with a vengeance!

But White's sweeping and alarming judgment was based on data accumulated in the first three years of life, *with no reports of follow-up into later life.* No other study has confirmed these pronouncements. On the contrary, we now have an impressive body of evidence to the contrary from leading research workers. Stephen Richardson of the Albert Einstein Medical Center has shown that even children with deprived, understimulated, and malnourished early lives can respond to enrichment programs with dramatic improvement in both their physical and intellectual functioning (1976). Myron Winick of Columbia University and his co-workers have reported on a group of adopted Korean children who suffered early malnutrition and a generally deprived environment (Winick, Meyer, & Harris 1975). The authors found that the effects of this early deprivation could be overcome by the environmental enrichment resulting from adoption. The successful rehabilitation was documented by measures of significant improvement in physical growth, school achievement, and IQ.

Beyond these reports on malnourished and severely deprived children, there are several impressive, carefully done studies, with adequate follow-up, of the long-term effectiveness of preschool enrichment programs for underprivileged children. These were children who were about three years when they were enrolled in the programs, an age when, according to Burton White, they were already intellectually doomed. One collaborative study in the 1970s observed the long-term effects of preschool programs in twelve different centers that were run or closely supervised by the investigative teams and were of carefully documented quality (Lazar & Darlington 1982). The findings clearly showed that early education programs for children from low-income families had longlasting positive effects in school competence, developed abilities, children's attitudes and values, and impact on the family. Another study of an early intervention program started in Ypsilanti, Michigan in the 1960s demonstrated higher rates for high school graduation and continuing education, better employment records, less use of welfare, less adolescent pregnancy, and fewer violations of law than a control group at age nineteen, fifteen years after the intervention (Berruetta-Clement et al. 1984).

The explanation of these dramatic and longlasting effects of good early intervention programs is not hard to find. The disadvantaged child has typically arrived at school age inadequately nourished and has not acquired many of the facts that kindergarten and first grade teachers assume have already been learned. Such children may also arrive at school hungry.

Poor and disadvantaged are not interchangeable terms. Many poor families have clear expectations of their children and have taught them good learning habits and a good fund of basic knowledge. The disadvantaged child who begins school ill prepared for formal learning, who has a home environment that makes study and homework difficult, and who attends a poor, overcrowded school is not likely to find school attendance and learning stimulating and exciting. Poor achievement discourages him, and school failure lowers self-esteem. There is a cumulative snowballing effect that carries him further and further in an unfavorable direction over the years. On the other hand, the disadvantaged child who has had the benefit of an effective preschool program (which usually includes meals) starts formal schooling well prepared, is responsive to the learning experience even in an overcrowded school, and gets the teacher's approval for his interest and efforts. With this positive reinforcement of his preschool experience, a positive snowballing effect takes place.

Can We Produce Intellectual "Superbabies"?

We've seen that the intellectual level of underprivileged children can be raised, but is the same thing possible for middle-class families? Indeed many parents are bent on this enterprise. They shower their infants with educational toys, they have them watching "Sesame Street" before they are two, and they start them on the alphabet and counting at the same age or even earlier. By three or four years of age the child is being pressured to learn to read and even to write. Some parents even drill their three-year-old children on IQ questions so they will pass with flying colors into the nursery schools that require such tests, with the hope that if they start out in the best nursery school, they will end up in an Ivy League college.

Does such a program make sense? It does not. There is a difference between a program that raises an underprivileged child to his intellectual capacity, which an unstimulating home environment and a poor day-care center cannot do, and an effort to stimulate and pressure a middle-class child to reach an intellectual level that is actually beyond his capacities. The middle-class parent may think that the latter is happening if the child learns to read, write, and do simple arithmetic at an early age. But the long-term effects are another matter. The child will reach his level—sub-normal, average, or superior—in spite of the early push at home. *No study has shown that a program of cognitive stimulation of a preschool child from an affluent home will permanently raise his intellectual level.*

Let us take an example from athletic skills. If a child has not had the opportunity for athletic coaching and practice, such a program will raise the level of his skill to its potential, whether it be modest, average, or superior. But if a child is from a home with all kinds of opportunities to manipulate objects, throw and catch a ball, or even practice swinging a tennis racket or golf club, he will learn various athletic skills at his own level in the course of daily life. Of course, if he shows talent and interest in one athletic area, the parents can help him achieve his maximum level of competence. But that does not mean he will become an Olympic star, and pushing him hard will not achieve that goal if he does not have the potential ability.

In the same way, parents cannot make intellectual giants out of their children. They can encourage the child's interests and open up opportunities for him, so that he can reach his potential, but this potential may turn out to be a modest or average one. Pushing and pressuring will not raise his IQ permanently and may produce stress that will make learning distasteful instead of pleasurable.

How Children Learn

What, then, do we know about how young children learn? Actually we know a great deal.

As we saw in the preceding chapter, the baby comes into the world biologically endowed with a level of brain development that enables him to start learning immediately and quickly. One of our most eminent child psychologists, Jerome Kagan, of Harvard University, has summarized succinctly what we know.

The newborn is ready to experience most, if not all, of the basic sensations given our species from the moment of birth. The baby can see, hear, and smell and is sensitive to pain, touch, and changes in bodily position. Although the sensitivity of these modalities is not yet at its maximum . . . the infant is responsive to information from all of the senses. The infant can detect the differences between a pattern composed of stripes only one-eighth of an inch wide and a completely gray patch, between vertical and oblique gratings, between linear and curved lines, and between richly contoured, in contrast to minimally contoured, designs. In the auditory mode, the young infant can discriminate between the musical notes C and C sharp and between the spoken syllables "pa" and "ba," and is acutely sensitive to rate of change in sound energy during the first half-second of an auditory event . . . New knowledge is most often acquired when the infant's attention is focused on an event, and change is one of the central qualities governing the alertness and maintenance of the infant's attention . . . Particular changes in the pattern or arrangement of elements also have the ability to hold the infant's attention, at least during the first year of life. (1984, pp. 31–34)

We also have seen that very young infants can imitate the actions of adults, engage in active communication with them, and move in precise and sustained synchrony of movement with adult speech. Conditioned reflexes, that elementary form of learning in which a stimulus from the outside becomes linked to an inborn reflex, begin to be formed at birth. Recent research has indicated, however, that the speed or even immediacy with which conditioned reflexes are formed in the young infant may vary with the adaptive value of the stimuli. That is, the brain may be "prepared" to organize certain combinations of stimuli, responses, or reinforcers immediately, others slowly, and still others not at all (Sameroff 1979).

Granted that the young infant can respond to a wide variety of sensory stimuli, recognize patterns of different shapes and designs, link stimuli from the outside world to his own system, begin to imitate others, and communicate in an active give-and-take with his caregivers. How does he organize all these stimuli, perceptions, and other experiences into permanent, accurate patterns in his brain, ready to be recalled as necessary, ready to shape his behavior when indicated, and ready to be modified and even transformed by subsequent inputs from the environment? In other words, what are the mechanisms by which the infant learns?

This question is an extraordinary challenge that has faced the budding science of child development. The infant cannot verbalize and tell us what he is thinking. He cannot answer our questions or pose questions of his own. But we can infer a great deal from careful objective studies of his behavior, of his responses to special stimuli. We can employ special techniques and equipment, such as observations of visual fixation time, the use of video cameras, and laboratory techniques such as attaching a sensor to a pacifier, as described in the previous chapter. From all these methods, and the analysis of the data they provide, we can put together a picture of how the infant thinks. And when language begins, the verbalizations of children add enormously to our information of how their minds work.

Jean Piaget: How Children Learn to Think

Foremost among the pioneer students of cognitive development was Jean Piaget, the Swiss scientist whose contribution to our knowledge of how children learn to think has been monumental. Piaget was not a professional psychologist but an epistemologist, interested in the study of the mechanisms by which children acquire bodies of knowledge. He closely observed children of different ages, starting with early infancy. He devised simple but ingenious experiments, such as showing children of different ages two similar glasses filled with water, pouring the water from one glass into a tall thin glass, and asking the child which glass had more water in it. Or he asked questions such as "What makes the clouds move?" From their answers he traced the evolution of children's concepts of the world and the objects in them into an accurate image of the world. He hypothesized that the child's actions are the raw materials out of which knowledge and thought are generated. He further postulated a motivational force that impels the child to integrate and organize more and more complex stimuli into his level of cognition, allowing him to grasp and comprehend more and more about the world around him.

Piaget, like all creative thinkers, made bold leaps in his concepts and formulations, not all of which have stood the test of time. But as Bruner has put it, "He made a tremendous contribution to our understanding of the mind of the child and how it grows, and indeed to our understanding of mind in general. . . . Piaget could be completely wrong in every detail but he would still have to be reckoned one of the great pioneers" (1983).

Lev Vygotsky: The Complexity of the Learning Process

Another creative pioneer in the study of thinking and learning in children was the Russian psychologist Lev Vygotsky, who died prematurely
at the age of thirty-seven in 1934 (a recent reviewer aptly called him "the
Mozart of psychology"). Hardly known in this country until the transla-
tions of two of his volumes in 1962 and 1978, his work and ideas have had
an increasing influence in recent years. He was one of the first to formulate
clearly the concept of a child's development as not a simple step-by-step
transition from one set stage to the next but as a complex process characterized by unevenness in the development of different functions, qualitative transformation of one form into another, and continuous intertwining
of external and internal forces. He also challenged the conventional, static,
and narrow view of the measurement of abilities, as in the standard IQ test,
and instead emphasized the identification of the child's potential intellectual development as determined through his problem-solving capacity
with adult guidance or in cooperation with more capable peers.

Jerome Bruner: The Social Context of Learning

In this country, a leading figure in turning academic psychology around
to pay attention to cognition, the mental processes in the supposedly
unknowable "black box" of the human mind, was the psychologist Jerome
Bruner, who with his colleague George Miller established the Center for
Cognitive Studies at Harvard in 1960. As Bruner described the timing years
later, "In 1960 we used 'cognitive' in our name defiantly. Most respectable
psychologists at the time still thought cognition was too mentalistic for
objective scientists. But we nailed it to the door and defended it until
eventually we carried the day. And now there are Cognitive Centers every-
where" (1983, p. 124).

Under Bruner's leadership the Center became a magnet, drawing able
students and researchers from all over the world. The Center's contribution to our knowledge of how children learn has been of tremendous value.
Bruner's concern has always been on the social context in which learning
takes place, an emphasis missing from Piaget but not from Vygotsky. Thus
he states as a basic theme,

> We take the view that cognitive growth in all its manifestations occurs as
> much from the outside in as from the inside out. Much of it consists in a human
> being's becoming linked with culturally transmitted "amplifiers" of motoric, sen-
> sory, and reflective capacities. One need not expect the course of cognitive growth
> to run parallel in different cultures, for there are bound to be different emphases,

different deformations. But many of the universals of growth are also attributable to uniformities in human culture. . . . Cognitive growth, whether divergent or uniform across cultures, is inconceivable without participation in a culture and its linguistic community. (1973, p. 2)

Some of Bruner's experiments linking culture with perception and cognition are rather complex, but one of his early ones is ingeniously simple. He contrasted a group of Boston children from poor families with an affluent group. Each child was given a half-dollar to finger and then asked to compare its size with an array of circular objects of different sizes. The poor children consistently rated the half-dollar larger than did the affluent ones. Different life experiences had influenced their judgment of the size of the coin (1983).

In his studies of early infancy, Bruner emphasizes how much the child achieves his growing competence through play activity. A six-month-old learns to hold on to an object and get it into his mouth and then begins a number of play variations: He shakes the object, bangs it on his high chair, drops it over the edge, and so on. It is through such activities that the child achieves what Bruner calls "mastery play" (Bruner et al. 1966). For the older child, Bruner emphasizes the importance of modeling adult behavior in the growth of cognition. This ability in fact begins with the newborn's capacity to imitate the facial gestures of adults.

Bruner gives a fascinating example of the influence of culture on the learning process of the young. In an African study, the play of baboon juveniles and Bushman children in a similar habitat was observed. The baboon juveniles' play was virtually all with their age-mates, and they learned from each other in this play. The adults did no "instructing" and interfered only to place general limits on the juveniles. Among the Bushmen there was also very little explicit teaching, but in contrast to the baboons there was a great deal of joint activity between the children and the adults. The child learned from direct interaction with the adults, but the teaching was implicit, in that it was in the context of action to teach the child a particular thing (Bruner et al. 1966). Bruner then comments that in a complex technological society this kind of direct, implicit teaching changes. "The knowledge and skill within the culture comes increasingly to exceed the amount that any one individual can know. . . . Increasingly, then, there develops a new and moderately effective technique of instructing the young based on *telling* out of context, rather than *showing* in context" (p. 62). The school becomes the main instrument in this new technique, but, as Bruner emphasizes, there is also a great deal of telling by parents, also out of the context of action, for there are relatively few situations in which practicing *in situ,* as the Bushmen do, can be done by parent and child. Bruner postulates that this development explains the importance of the "why" question in the child's response to his environment.

For all his emphasis on the roles of life experience and culture in the growth of the child's mind, Bruner by no means considers the newborn as a *tabula rasa.* He points out, very correctly, that

> the infant comes early to solve problems of high complexity and does so on the basis of encounters with the environment that are too few in number, too unrepresentative, or too erratic in consequence to be accounted for either on the basis of concept attainment or by the shaping effects of reinforcement. Initial "learning" has a large element of preadaptation that reflects species-typical genetic instructions. But it is a highly flexible preadaptation. (1973, p. 2)

Jerome Kagan: The Discrepancy Principle

Jerome Kagan has also made extensive and careful studies of the process of learning in infants. He has concentrated on the characteristics of the memory trace in the infant's brain after specific stimuli and experiences. That such a trace, or residue, must exist is clear; otherwise the infant could not differentiate a familiar from an unfamiliar object or imitate an action he has previously observed. Kagan has called this memory trace in the brain a *schema,* "a representation of experience that bears a relation to an original event. . . . Infants create schematic representations that originate in what they see, hear, smell, taste and touch. Schemata permit recognition of the past" (1984, p. 35), which exists even during the first days of life. Succeeding exposures to an event are never identical, so the schema created by the mind is a *schematic prototype,* a composite of all the experiences. Kagan also indicates that there is some evidence that even in infancy a schematic prototype may represent abstract qualities, independent of any concrete experience. The young infant is indeed able to think!

Kagan's studies have led him to formulate the discrepancy principle: "Events that are a partial transformation of existing schemata begin to dominate the infant's attention. . . . An event that can be assimilated produces excitement, but one that cannot be assimilated produces uncertainty" (1984, p. 39). Kagan has formulated this principle on the basis of a series of experiments with infants. For example, there is a positive relation between degree of contact between mother and infant and the occurrence of a distress reaction to strangers during the second half of the first year. The closer the contact between the infant and a single caregiver, the more likely the infant will show distress to a stranger (1971).

An example of the discrepancy principle in infancy is seen when a baby sees his mother with a new hair-do and dress. Her appearance is a partial transformation of an existing schema and attracts the infant's positive attention. On the other hand, the appearance of a stranger who does not resemble a family member and who attempts to hold or dress the baby is too discrepant and will produce uncertainty and distress.

Kagan elaborates this discrepancy principle into a general conception of the learning process. He suggests that the new ideas and knowledge that we learn best are those that are slight modifications of our current beliefs. On the other hand, new ideas that are very different from those we already hold are either ignored or rejected outright. While this formulation may appear too simple to encompass all the complexities of the learning process, it certainly corresponds to many of the reactions of both children and adults to the slightly new versus the markedly new.

Why Children Learn: Social Competence and Task Mastery

We have seen that the newborn enters life ready to learn and to form social relationships and immediately begins to pursue these goals with vigor and effective actions. But *why* do infants learn and continue to learn as they grow older? This seems like an all too obvious question, but it can have a number of answers. On one level we can say that babies have to learn so that they can walk, talk, take care of themselves, and find a place for themselves in the society into which they are born. On another level, the biologists could say that by natural selection in the evolution of the human species, learning has been developed as the attribute that above all has secured the survival of the human race.

As students of child behavior, however, we would like a more specific answer to this question. We would like to have an answer that would give us a basis for generalizing the multitude of different activities the infant and older child carry through every day. Many of these activities can appear unrelated and can be identified differently: "He is playing," "he is playing out his fantasies," "he is curious about all these objects in his environment," or "he is imitating his parents or his older brother." We would like to be able to generalize in a way that would bring these separate activities together under one or several categories and purposes and would give us an understanding of these separate behaviors in greater depth. That in turn would help guide us in formulating further ideas and studies of the child's development.

As we and others have thought about the different kinds of capabilities of the newborn and watched infants go about their daily activities at different ages, it has become possible to answer this question of why children learn on a new level. Our suggestion is that they learn to achieve *social competence* and *task mastery*. Consider the basic questions we ask about any new person we meet, child or adult: Is he comfortable and interesting to be with? Does he make friends easily, and does he know how to keep his friends? That is, is he socially competent? Also, we want to know if he is responsible, competent, and efficient in carrying out a task he assumes. That is, what is his level of task mastery? Of course, we may be interested in other information—his special interests and talents, his ethical values, his ambitions, his health, and so on—but a prime issue is always his social competence and task mastery ability.

Watch a young infant, and these social and task issues are always there to be noted. If you smile at him, he smiles back. If you ignore him and he wants your attention, he cries or tugs at you or both. Here is social competence at an early stage. If he spies a new object, he reaches for it, grabs it, puts it in his mouth, takes it out, feels it all over, throws it, and then tries to retrieve it. Here, also, is task mastery at an early stage. In the traditional psychoanalytic scheme, if a baby puts an object into his mouth, this is a manifestation of an "oral instinct." In our formulation, which does not require such a system of instinctual drives, the infant puts the object into his mouth as part of his effort to gauge its contour, smoothness, hardness, and taste—that is, as part of his effort to master the use of the object.

The older child practices social competence and task mastery in many ways, mostly in play. We do not have to look for hypothetical unconscious meanings for the child's play, once we see it as a pleasurable activity with both social and task mastery purposes. The two-year-old who sits in his high chair and pretends to eat his plate, fork, and napkin, all the while giggling for his parents' attention, is mastering the task of distinguishing inedible from edible objects and doing it in a manner that promotes his positive social interchange with his parents. The four-year-old who places dolls on little chairs around a little table, gives them plates and plastic tableware, and pretends to go through a meal with them is practicing the social rules of table manners, again a social and task activity. The five-year-old who learns the rules of a group game in kindergarten is mastering the task posed by the game and simultaneously learning how to be an accepted member of his age-group.

And so it goes with the increasingly complex demands and life experiences with increasing age—they can all be conceptualized as expectations for social competence or task mastery, appropriate to the child's developmental level. It is the same for the adult. A new job tests his ability to master the tasks he faces and also calls on his competence in his new social relationships. The same issues come up in marriage, parenthood, or a vacation trip. It is of interest that Freud himself emphasized these same goals for the healthy adult, in his terms of "work and love."

Why does the infant have these drives for social competence and task mastery? We assume they have evolutionary significance, inasmuch as the newborn comes into the world already set with the substantial capacities to achieve these goals. The biologists are right in their explanation that these abilities have been developed by natural selection in the evolution of the human species. Social competence and task mastery are clearly decisive assets for the human being in mastering the environment, not as an isolated individual but as part of an organized social group. With this concept, we do not need hypotheses regarding presumed instinctual drives that have to be mastered by repression or other devices. In science, the principle of parsimony holds that that theory is preferable which requires the fewest number of unproven hypotheses. The newer generation of psychoanalysts have recognized this and postulate that learning is not the result of the effort to master unacceptable instinctual drives. Rather they link learning with what they call the "autonomous ego" (Hartman 1958), which really comprises those capabilities of the infant we have been describing.

We were certainly not the first or the only developmental psychiatrists or psychologists to arrive at this formulation of social competence and task mastery. Bruner puts this concept neatly: "For convenience, the forms of early competence can be divided into those which regulate interaction with other members of the species and those involved in mastery over objects, tools, spatially and temporally ordered sequences of events. Obviously, the two cannot be separated, as witness the importance of imitation and modeling in the mastery of 'thing skills' " (1973, p. 1).

We have found it helpful for parents to have this concept of social competence and task mastery as the child's goals. It gives them a better understanding of the significance of the child's play activities, as well as the importance of his struggles to master a new task. With this understanding, the parents can much more easily figure out when to encourage the child, how to participate in his play fantasies, when to stand by and let him struggle by himself, and when to step in and help if the child is attempting a task well beyond his developmental level.

The Plasticity of Human Development

As Bruner suggests in the passage quoted earlier in this chapter, the genetic endowment of the newborn "is a highly flexible preadaptation" (1973, p. 2). Actually, this flexibility and plasticity of the human brain from the beginning is an attribute of great developmental significance. Normal children show a wide range of variability in their perceptual, conceptual, and cognitive attributes. Individual differences in temperament are striking and functionally significant. The time of emergence of motor capacities and skills and the effective use of language varies widely from one normal child to another. Children from different social classes and cultural backgrounds can show conspicuous differences in norms of behavior, speech, and values.

This individual variability and flexibility in response to the environment has vital advantages for humankind. The parents who worry that their infant shows more changes in behavior than other babies, even though no problems are evident, should be heartened by the observation of the research psychiatrist Robert Emde, of the University of Colorado:

> Is it not likely that what is especially adaptive is *a variability and range of behavior?* In other words, would not these features provide selective advantage during evolution and therefore be preprogrammed in our species? I would think that an individual newborn characterized by sufficient variability of behavior would be favored, with more opportunities for matching or synchronizing such behavior with a caretaking environment—an environment which to a considerable extent would be unpredictable. Indeed, the vulnerable infant may be one who is consistently "modal" or who otherwise has a narrow range of behavioral variability over time. (1978, p. 136)

Actually a prominent and disabling symptom in children suffering from certain severe psychiatric disorders, such as autism, organic brain damage, or severe neuroses, is the loss of this variability and range of behavior.

The potential and the value of this capacity of the brain for flexibility and plasticity is dramatically illustrated in the development of deaf children, blind children, and children born with severe motor handicaps. We have had the opportunity to study the development of a large group of children who suffered one or another of these handicaps because of the mother's infection with rubella (German measles) in their prenatal lives.

Deaf children can see the world but cannot hear it. There is no delay in motor skill acquisition. But deaf children whose parents do not know sign language cannot ask questions and cannot hear the answers. Explanations cannot be given, at least not in oral language, and restrictions of activity are necessarily greater for safety reasons than for hearing children. In all these ways, deaf babies are limited in their experiences and their opportunities to learn. Yet the deaf children in our rubella sample as a group showed a significant improvement in intellectual test performance between the preschool and middle childhood years (Chess 1978). How do we explain the rising adaptation of these deaf children? Originally they are deprived of the possibility of learning through the spoken word, and their early intellectual functioning is retarded. But then they develop their system of communication and learning through visual cues such as gestures, sign language, and lip reading, and they make up their lag in development. Their brains have found an alternative and effective form of functioning.

Blind infants, by contrast to the deaf, show delays in motor development. They raise their heads later, sit, stand, and walk later than sighted or deaf babies. Blind children cannot see the objects in their environments that would stimulate them to the movements that would enable them to see better or to try to grasp these objects. As they mature, however, these children catch up to sighted babies, often by the age of three to five years (Fraiberg 1977a). Their brains have learned to use sound and touch cues as powerful stimuli, again a testimonial to the plasticity of the human brain.

The infants with motor handicaps suffer from diminished sensorimotor experience and a limitation on their ability to explore the world around them. In Piaget's theory of cognitive development, the infant first learns to coordinate sensory stimuli and motor experiences. This step provides the basis for the first stage of learning, what Piaget called sensorimotor intelligence. For an infant with a severe motor handicap who is deprived of these active sensorimotor experiences, a deficiency in learning and cognitive development would appear inevitable. Yet the many such people who attain an average and even superior intellectual level that they use productively and creatively are again a vivid testimonial to the inherent capacity of the human brain for plasticity of development.

The deaf child, the blind child, the motor-handicapped child—each can find a developmental pathway in keeping with his capacities and limitations, thanks to the plasticity of the brain. By the same token, the environmentally handicapped child is not inevitably doomed to an inferior and abnormal psychological course. Whether the handicap comes from social prejudice, poverty, a pathological family environment, or stressful life experiences, the plastic potential of the brain offers the promise for positive and corrective change. We know this is possible from the studies cited earlier in this chapter—the adoption program with Korean children, the twelve-center preschool project, and the Ypsilanti, Michigan studies.

But this promise is not a guarantee. The professional and political authorities who formulate educational, remedial, and therapeutic programs for these youngsters can translate this promise into a reality. But they will do so only if the people of our country are committed to this social goal and demand that its implementation be given high priority in the budget decisions of city, state, and federal governmental agencies. Here, mental health professionals have a special responsibility, because of their knowledge and status in the community. Edward Zigler, of Yale University, the former director of Head Start and an outstanding active advocate for the rights and needs of children, has put it forcefully: "We must remember that in Washington, knowledge is power, and as psychologists we have a great deal of knowledge. We must be willing to share that knowledge outside of the University. . . . We must rid ourselves of a mystique held by too many, namely, that impacting social policy is too far afield, too Byzantine, and too self-defiling to be engaged in by self-respecting psychologists" (Zigler & Muenchow 1984, p. 420).

There are cases in which damage to or disordered maturation of the brain limits or destroys its capacity for flexibility. Even if we cannot expect significant positive changes with treatment in these children, they do remain the responsibilities of society and deserve the special care they require.

8

Cognitive and Emotional Development

I N the previous chapter we discussed the general topic of learning in children. We emphasized that the newborn's capacities for perception, communication, imitation, and behavioral integration enable her to start learning about herself and the world around her from the moment of birth. In fact, a few investigators now even suggest that learning may start in the womb. They seem to have demonstrated that newborns can remember sounds they heard prenatally, such as the mother's heartbeat or even a particular story that the mother read many times. The newborn infant shows a memory for the sound by changing the way she sucks to elicit the recording of the sound. The findings are intriguing, but their importance is still unclear.

We can now consider the question of the sequences or stages that children go through as they learn about themselves and the world around them, and also as they learn to think. Put most generally, what they learn is both cognitive and emotional. In the modern Western world, thought and emotions appear to be contradictory attributes of the mind. Rational thought has been most highly prized, even if not always followed in daily life, and philosophers like Kant and Spinoza have viewed strong emotions as a danger to the intellect. The passions of the creative artist may be tolerated and excused as "artistic temperament" but not admired as models for others to emulate.

Thought and reason appear as unique human characteristics, flowering
with the individual's maturation and life experiences from childhood into
adult life. Other animal species at best show only a rudimentary capacity
for thought. Emotions, or at least some of them, appear to be shared with
other species and are already evident for the most part in childhood. Unlike
cognition, whose development involves expansion and elaboration, emotional maturation appears to involve learning control and inhibition; we
often reproach an adult's expression of passionate feelings with the injunction "Don't behave like a child." And while objective research studies of
cognitive processes are being constantly refined, quantified, and extended
into new areas, the study of emotions has in the main been much more
impressionistic and even speculative.

To debate the relative importance of emotion and thought in psychological development, however, is as fruitless and irrelevant as the argument
over heredity and environment. Emotion and thought are basic mental
attributes that are intimately meshed in a process of mutual influence. As
a leading scholar in the field of educational psychology, Edmund Gordon,
of Yale University, has put it, "Unfortunately, our tendency has been to
separate the affective [emotional] and cognitive domains from each other.
Yet, we cannot separate the two, whether for study, or emphasis, or in-
structional purposes. They are so integrally related that it makes no sense
to talk about one independent of the other" (1975, p. 11). Empathy and
scorn, altruism and selfishness, benevolence and aggression, love and hate,
cooperativeness and competitiveness—all involve definite emotions toward another person or persons and simultaneous thoughts about those
persons. The feelings reinforce the ideas, and the ideas reinforce the
feelings.

The intimate relationship between emotion and thought is strikingly
evident in cyclical manic-depressive illness. This condition is primarily a
disturbance of mood; the person swings through moods of great elation
(the manic phase) and feelings of melancholy (the depressed phase), as
well as variable lengths of time in which the emotions are more normal—
neither highly elated nor melancholy. During the manic mood, the person
develops ideas of grandiosity and expectation of great achievement. In the
depressed phase, ideas of guilt and self-derogation develop and then serve
to deepen the depressed mood. Thus, whether manic or depressed, the
special emotional state stimulates specific ideas, which in turn influence
the mood and its expression.

We will explore in this chapter a number of questions regarding cognition and emotion. How can we define them? Do they go through specific
developmental stages? If so, what determines the sequence of these stages?

What significant individual differences does each one show? And finally, what practical value does our information have for parents in their caregiving role with their children?

Although we have emphasized the intimate relationship between cognition and emotion, these issues will be clearer if we look at intelligence and emotion separately.*

The Nature of Intelligence

We are not concerned here with the measurement of intelligence, which will be considered in chapter 14, but rather with its definition. An excellent review of this issue has been recently published by a leading cognitive psychologist, Robert Sternberg, of Yale University. For Sternberg, "intelligence consists of those mental functions purposively employed for purposes of adaptation to and shaping and selection of real-world environments" (1985, p. 1111). A similar definition of intelligence is given by another prominent cognitive psychologist, Howard Gardner, of Harvard and Boston Universities: "An intelligence is the ability to solve problems, or to create products, that are valued within one or more cultural settings" (1985, p. x). Both definitions indicate that intelligence cannot be defined in the abstract but only in relationship to the individual's environment and that it involves action in that environment.

Sternberg surveys the many, varied views of intelligence, which seem as numerous as researchers in the field, and places them into five groups, according to the model and theory used. The first is the *geographic model:* intelligence as a map of the mind. This model goes back to the naive phrenologists of the past century, who measured intelligence by the number, shapes, and locations of bumps on the skull. In recent years, it has been utilized by sophisticated researchers using special statistical techniques such as factor analysis of intelligence test ratings to determine how many factors involving intelligence presumably reside within the brain. (Factor analysis is a statistical method for identifying the levels of relationship

---

*The terms *cognition* and *intelligence* are used loosely by most psychologists in discussions of thought and knowledge. We personally canvassed a number of prominent psychologists, asking each the difference between the two terms. Each one gave us a different answer. Some said the two terms were really synonymous or that there were only very minor differences between them. Others said there were differences, but each one who said so had a different formulation for those differences. Given this lack of agreement, we have decided that the simplest and least confusing approach is to use the terms *cognition* and *intelligence* interchangeably.

among a set of ratings and measurements that have been obtained independently of one another.)

The psychologists who focused on this geographic model came to differ on how many factors constituted intelligence and what these factors were. Some opted for one single general factor, labeled g, which pervaded and determined the results of any specific test of mental ability. Others claimed that there were only two factors, and others that there were even more; one worker in the field proposed as many as 120 factors (Guilford 1967). This approach has gradually lost favor for several reasons. First, two people can get the same score on an intelligence test by getting completely different items correct. Clearly, such test results could not be measuring the same factors. Secondly, different methods of factor analysis may yield different results with the same data. It proved very difficult to determine that one method of factor analysis, which produced one set of intelligence factors, was superior or inferior to another, which came out with a different set of factors.

For these reasons, most psychologists have abandoned the search for a model of the brain that consists of separate distinct intelligences. The one notable exception is Howard Gardner (1985), who has proposed a theory of seven multiple intelligences: linguistic, musical, logical-mathematical, spatial, bodily kinesthetic, interpersonal, and intrapersonal. (For an exposition of the meaning of these seven "intelligences" and their significance, the reader is referred to Gardner's erudite and stimulating volume, *Frames of Mind.*) Unlike other psychologists who searched for evidence of different intelligence factors in the brain, Gardner has not relied on factor analysis but on information gathered from a number of sources: prodigies, gifted individuals, brain-damaged patients, experts in different lines of work, individuals from diverse cultures, normal children and adults, and so-called *idiot savants* (mentally retarded individuals who possess an extraordinary talent in one specific area, such as arithmetical calculation). Sternberg is skeptical of the validity of Gardner's formulations, and it remains to be seen whether Gardner's ideas hold up or not.

The second model identified by Sternberg is the *computational model:* intelligence as a computer program. This has become the fashionable model in the past decade, as computers have been constructed that can perform more and more of the tasks that had been considered uniquely human, such as playing a superior game of chess. This model has many variations as it is applied by various psychologists. Sternberg is critical of this approach, questioning whether the laboratory procedures used to explore this model are relevant to what real people can do in real-life situations. This is a criticism that has been justly applied to much psychological research—that it relies on the results of artificial tests in artificial situations, rather than on the behavior of children and adults in real life (McCall 1977). The laboratory approach is clean and neat, and the procedures can be easily duplicated by other researchers, but how much does it relate to how people actually behave?

Sternberg calls the third model the *anthropological model:* intelligence as a cultural invention, "the notion that the nature of intelligence is wholly or partly determined by the nature of the environment in which one lives" (p. 1115). The radical extreme of this position denies any common element to intelligence across cultures; it can be criticized for its one-sided approach and its failure to consider similarities in brain functioning across cultures. But Sternberg is also critical of the more moderate versions of this model, including those of the so-called life-span psychologists. He agrees that these so-called contextual positions "have the appeal of taking into account the fact that not all cultures view intelligence in the same way" but feels that they tend to ignore even the underlying cognitive processes within particular cultures. He also objects, however, that if one has to analyze intelligence in its cultural context one would have to study each individual separately, because "each individual does, in fact, live in at least a slightly different subculture or intermeshing of subcultures" (p. 1116). This interpretation appears to us to be something of a caricature of the position of the cultural theorists. From our reading of their literature and also from personal discussions with several of them, it seems clear that they recognize the importance of biological as well as cultural factors.

Sternberg's other models are the *biological model,* as exemplified by Piaget, and the *sociological model,* as proposed by Vygotsky. Finally Sternberg proposes his own theory, which he calls a *political model:* intelligence as mental self-government. "As is the case with a government, understanding of intelligence requires an examination of internal affairs (relation of intelligence to the internal world of the individual), external affairs (relation of intelligence to the external world of the individual), and the processes of government as they evolve over time (relation of intelligence to experience)" (1985, p. 1117). This model does attempt a comprehensive view of intelligence as related simultaneously to the internal world of the brain, the external world, and the individual's life experiences. As such, it appears conceptually to be not far different from the life-span model. Sternberg ends by pointing out that intelligence evolves over time and that components of intelligence must be examined as "they are applied to the everyday world at varying levels of experience" (p. 1117). True indeed, and the same formulation is apt for other psychological characteristics—temperament, motivations, talents, and personality structure.

Cognitive Development: Piaget's Model

As we have indicated in the previous chapter, the issue of cognition in children has been studied intensively by many leading psychologists. When it comes to the question of the sequences of cognitive development, it is the Swiss scientist Jean Piaget who has formulated a systematic model to explain how the child goes successively from one stage or level of cognitive ability to another as she grows older.

In organizing the data he obtained from children, Piaget was critical of the one-sided approach that viewed the child as a passive organism whose mind was shaped by her cumulative life experiences. He also rejected the notion that the infant was endowed with an innate intellectual capacity that unfolded and matured with age. Rather, he conceived intelligence as the outcome of the child's adaptation to the world in successive stages, which he considered to have an invariant sequence. It was the child's action on the environment, starting with the innate ability to respond to sensory and motor stimuli with which she is born, that Piaget considered crucial to her intellectual development (1954; 1963).

Piaget called the first stage *sensorimotor intelligence,* encompassing the infancy period (up to two years). In his formulation, the neonate begins life with a set of motor and sensory reflexes that are the foundation for her interaction with the environment. Out of this interaction the infant learns to coordinate the sensory and motor experiences into an awareness of the external world as a permanent place with objects that are independent of her own perceptions. As one example, the neonate starts with a grasping reflex, which is elicited by stimulating the palm of her hand. As she grasps various objects, the infant learns to experience different shapes, textures, weights, and temperatures.

The second cognitive stage in Piaget's system is the period of *preoperational representation,* which extends approximately from age two to age seven. In this stage the child internalizes her sensorimotor experiences and their imprints in her brain into symbolic representations. Language development during this period is one example of this symbolic transformation; words become symbols of objects, people, categories, and activities. In the next stage, that of *concrete operations,* extending from age seven to age twelve, the child begins to structure and integrate her thoughts into a coherent system, to make classifications of objects and their properties, and to abstract concepts such as length, width, volume, and time. These mental operations are applied to concrete objects, hence the term *concrete operations* for this stage.

Finally, after age twelve, the child becomes capable of *formal operations,* which Piaget viewed as the most advanced form of cognitive activity; some people may not reach this stage in some or even in any areas of thought. In this style of formal operations the child or adult is no longer bound by concrete objects and relationships but is able to grasp abstract concepts, potential realities, and the implications of various assumptions and ideas.

Piaget's work has had an enormous influence on thinking and research in cognitive psychology. His basic formulations have been the basis of innumerable studies, in which they have been applied fruitfully to different groups of children and adolescents under various experimental and natural situations. Not surprisingly, however, such a pioneering effort could not come up with all the answers for all time. Many studies have indicated that children do not necessarily move smoothly from one stage to another in the way Piaget thought. Children, and even adults, can perform some tasks at a higher level of development and other tasks only at a lower level (Gardner 1985). This has become so evident that psychologists have begun to question the notion of a period or a stage, and some have abandoned the notion (Sternberg 1985). Furthermore, Piaget concentrated his studies on the development of logical thinking and ignored such issues as fantasy, the role of special talents, and the role of emotion and motivation in relation to thought. Also, Piaget developed an abstract theoretical scheme to describe how the child absorbs and integrates new experiences, a scheme which depends on concepts, such as "schemas," "assimilation," and "accommodation," that are so general and vague that they have been of little use as guidelines to other researchers.

But with all these limitations, Piaget has remained a pioneer in opening up systematic and objective methods of tracing the development of thought in children. Without the stimulus that his work and ideas provided, the advances in cognitive psychology would have come much more slowly and painfully.

Individual Differences in Cognitive Development

Implicit in the theories and findings of Piaget and Vygotsky, as well as of others such as Bruner, Kagan, and Sternberg, is that intelligence depends on both maturation and life experience. Since children mature in different ways and at different rates (a fact easy to observe in the differences in language development in normal children), and since they have many differences in their life experiences, we can expect significant differences in their cognitive development. This issue is the subject of a recent comprehensive review by Kurt Fischer, of the University of Denver, and Louise Silvern, of the University of Colorado (1985). They note that "in general, research on development over long periods in children and adults [demonstrates] big differences between age-groups as well as substantial differences between individuals within age-groups" (p. 617). These differences are even more marked in older children than in younger children.

Fischer and Silvern document the various factors that can influence differences in intellectual level, even within the same child. Environmental factors include task difficulty, differences in task content, and the amount of support and assistance the child receives from others. Internal influences include the state of arousal and alertness, the ability to integrate (internalize) information from the environment into their own skills, and a wide variety of personality factors, such as motivation and various emotions. The authors emphasize that "a framework that conjoins organism and environment holds that people move through different developmental sequences, different series of specific skills. There is neither a fixed organism nor a fixed environment to produce a single, fixed developmental sequence" (p. 641). They also point out that when behavior is analyzed in highly abstract terms (perhaps as by Piaget), then all individuals may appear to develop in similar ways. However, when analysis of behavior takes into account each individual's internal state and environmental context, then the various developmental sequences can be seen to differ significantly. Fischer and Silvern conclude that studies of cognition must be based on the conjoined influences of organism and environment. "To move toward such an approach, research designs should routinely incorporate variations in both important organismic variables, such as age, ability, and emotional state, and important environmental variables, such as task, practice, and environmental support" (p. 643). We agree emphatically with this approach. It is perhaps a central theme of our book that this kind of research reveals the range and richness of individual differences in human beings. It is in stark contrast to the approach of most psychologists, which is glaringly exemplified in IQ testing and evaluation (to be discussed in chapter 14).

Cognition and Metacognition

In the past decade a new and exciting approach to the study of thought processes, metacognition, has developed, spearheaded by the eminent cognitive psychologist John Flavell, of Stanford University (1976). Stated simply, cognition refers to what a person knows and how she uses that knowledge. Metacognition refers to the self-regulation of the thinking process, the person's knowledge of how she goes about, or should go about, performing a task or solving a problem. A homely example can illustrate the difference between the two forms of thought. A person may be a skilled cook and consistently produce appetizing and elegant-looking dishes. But when asked for a recipe, she may say, "I can't give it to you. I just do it. If you want to do what I do, you will have to watch me cook and take notes." Such a person has expert cognition but does not have metacognition. She knows how to cook (cognition), but she does not know how she plans and executes this knowledge (metacognition). Or we can take the reverse. A person buys a set of parts to put a crib together for the first time. She knows how to plan this task: She will study the diagram, identify the parts, and follow the instruction sheet. But she does not succeed because she does not fully understand one or more crucial parts of the diagram or instruction sheet. Such a person has metacognition for this task (she knows how to plan and organize the solution of the task), but she does not have cognition (she does not have the knowledge to follow through on her strategy of solving the task).

The importance of metacognition is recognized by a number of cognitive psychologists. Sternberg refers to "metacomponents or executive processes, through which one plans what to do, monitors it while it is being done, and evaluates it after it is completed" (1985, p. 1117). Lauren Resnick, of the Learning Research and Development Center of the University of Pittsburgh, speaks of "higher order thinking," which tends to be complex, often yields multiple solutions, and involves nuanced judgments and the application of multiple criteria (in press). Such thinking, Resnick adds, also means self-regulation of the thinking process and involves imposing meaning—that is, finding structure in apparent disorder.

Kagan demonstrated the importance of metacognition through strategies to aid memory: rehearsing the information, making up associations, looking for patterns of organization in the information, counting and clustering items that belong to the same category. When given a memory task, the children taught these strategies showed a significant memory gain on all tasks. Another group of children who had been highly motivated to learn but not taught these strategies did almost as well, because they spontaneously invented some of the effective strategies. The children who were neither highly motivated nor taught the strategies showed the least improvement (1984).

A key question arises. Children can be taught specific information and intellectual skills and thus their cognitive level can be improved, but can they also be taught this higher order of thinking, metacognition? If this were possible, the implications for education would be enormous. Resnick gives a review of the current state of research on this question. She has no doubt that the average normal child can learn this type of thinking, which in the past was reserved for an elite group. She is cautiously optimistic but concludes that present research has reported varying results and that many projects have not been properly evaluated, so that no clear answer can be given.

Resnick does make several important points. The attempt to teach metacognitive skills should not be done in the abstract but has to be embedded within the traditional school disciplines, which provide the knowledge base from which higher order thinking skills can be taught. For example, in writing a book report, a student could be taught to analyze the major and minor themes of the volume, the strategies the author uses to elaborate and document these ideas, and the methods used to relate them to one another. The student could then learn to apply the same type of reasoning to a report of a scientific experiment. Also, the evidence is clear that teaching such skills should rely on a social setting and social interaction, such as a study group. She points out that the social setting provides occasions for modeling effective thinking processes and encouraging the new learner's initial tentative efforts. Resnick also emphasizes that it is not enough to teach a child new cognitive processes; she also has to be taught and motivated to use these processes extensively. Higher order thinking is different from ordinary cognition and as such "may involve some social risk—of disagreeing with others perceived to be more powerful, of not arriving at the expected answers, above all of not always responding immediately" because one is weighing multiple alternatives. In this last statement, Resnick implies, though she does not say so, that the attempt to introduce the teaching of metacognitive skills in schools may meet with great resistance from the educational establishment.

The Significance of Emotions

The difficulty that psychologists and psychiatrists have in establishing a consensus on the definition of intelligence pales by comparison with the problem of defining emotions (or affects, as they are often called). Cognitive phenomena can at least be studied through a variety of objective tests, as Piaget has demonstrated. Different cognitive capacities can also be inferred from information obtained from persons with special talents or various types of damage to the brain, as Gardner has suggested.

Emotions, on the other hand, are private, subjective feeling-states that are very difficult to evaluate objectively. Facial expressions may give us clues, but they do not provide definite answers. A certain smile may show that a child is enjoying a game she is playing, or that she is anticipating some happy event scheduled for the next day, or that she is indulging in some private daydream. With adults, who have learned to control and conceal their feelings, emotional expressions are an even less reliable guide to a person's actual emotional state. A man may smile at meeting another person while actually feeling anger or anxiety. He suppresses his feelings because of social conventions regarding correct public behavior or because their open expression might create difficulties for him.

Parents are well aware that children learn to control the public expression of their feelings early in life. One mother was watching her three-year-old from the window as he played in the yard. The boy tripped and fell, without causing any real damage to himself. He got up, rubbed his knee, and started to cry. Nobody paid attention so he stopped crying after a few minutes. Then, apparently deciding that he merited sympathy, the boy headed for the house door and as he approached it again began to cry and rub his knee.

In addition to the private feeling-state and the public expression, there are also various physiological reactions that accompany emotion. These vary tremendously from person to person and are hardly specific in their meaning. A rapid heart rate may accompany a highly enjoyable experience or a frightening one. In the face of acute danger, one person may vomit, another may have diarrhea, a third may feel an urgent need to urinate, a fourth may sweat profusely, and a fifth may experience no physiological evidence of the tension and fear.

Above all, emotional states are influenced by cognitive factors, the meaning attached to a specific situation or experience. Thus, a person with strong convictions regarding the pernicious effects of racial prejudice is likely to react with intense anger at the use of derogatory racial epithets, while another person who does not share these convictions may respond to the epithets with equanimity or even enjoyment. A child who judges a barking dog to be a menace will retreat in fear, while another child will interpret the bark as a friendly sound and run forward to pat the dog. These different judgments, by child or adult, reflect past experiences that become internalized as a part of the person's system of cognition.

On the other hand, emotions may influence cognition. A child who has had a series of pleasurable, playful experiences with a certain adult may take on many of that person's ideas. Another child who has by chance had a number of unpleasant encounters with children of a specific nationality, color, or religion may easily adopt derogatory stereotypical ideas regarding all people of that ethnic group.

A major problem in discussing emotions is that we use similar terms to designate emotions in children and in adults, yet the anger, joy, or sadness of a young child is not the same as that of an adult. They have different meanings and consequences, and often even different origins.

Definitions of Emotion

Given these complex features that make up emotional states, it is not surprising to find so little consensus on the definition of emotion. Some theorists emphasize the biological component, while others contend that social influences shape emotions. Some suggest that emotions are intimately linked with and even secondary to cognition, while others insist that they are independent mental characteristics (Izard 1977). Psychoanalysts have concentrated on theories of emotional states as derivatives of the individual course of presumed instinctual drives in the infant and young child. But their methods of analysis of the retrospective early memories of adults and their highly inferential interpretations of the meaning of childhood play activity have not enabled them to lay the basis for an objective, systematic study of emotions in children. Behaviorists, for their part, have simply proclaimed that emotions are just not worth studying and cannot even be studied scientifically because of their subjective nature. For some years developmental psychologists were primarily interested in cognition, on which they could obtain reliable quantitative data not possible in the study of emotions.

In recent years this situation has changed, and a number of capable developmental psychologists and psychiatrists have undertaken serious studies of emotion and struggled, in the process, to elaborate satisfactory definitions of emotion. Especially impressive has been the work of one of the country's leading developmental psychologists, Michael Lewis, and his co-worker, Linda Michalson, both of Rutgers University. In *Children's Emotions and Moods* (1983) they present a comprehensive definition of emotion, examine the issue of emotional development, and report on their own methods for studying children's emotions systematically and objectively.

Lewis and Michalson define and analyze emotion in terms of five components: elicitors, receptors, states, expressions, and experiences. Although others have made some distinctions among several of these elements, no one else has discussed all five in detail.

Elicitors are defined as the trigger events that set off change in the internal physiological state of the individual. External elicitors may be nonsocial, such as an irritating bright light or loud noise, or social, such as a brutal attack or a reunion with a loved one. Internal elicitors range widely, from a drop in blood sugar level to a daydream or absorption in a difficult cognitive task. They are harder to identify, and for this reason most research deals with external stimuli. Researchers also attempt to determine precisely what elements of the elicitor have activated the emotion. Not all stimuli that produce a physiological change can act as an emotional elicitor. For example, a blast of cold air may cause shivering, but it is not an emotional elicitor unless the shivering person blames the sudden cold on some other person's carelessness or deliberate intent.

Emotional receptors may be either specific areas or pathways in the central nervous system or nonspecific general systems in the body related to arousal, and through arousal to particular emotional states. Information about emotional receptors is meager; it is a very difficult area for research studies, and much of its discussion is speculative.

An *emotional state* is defined by Lewis and Michalson as "a particular constellation of changes in somatic and/or neurophysiological activity that accompanies the activation of emotional receptors" (p. 105). This definition corresponds roughly to the definition offered by a number of other investigators (Izard 1977). A person can have emotional states without being aware of them. It is the study of those emotional states that lie outside of conscious awareness that has been a major element in psychoanalytic theory and practice.

Emotional expressions are those manifestations in the face, voice, body, and activity level that are potentially observable by another person. These expressions have been the subject of much study, measurement, and classification, with each investigator usually concentrating on one area—facial expression, body, posture, and so on—but the relationships among them have received almost no attention.

Emotional experience is "the interpretation and evaluation by individuals of this perceived emotional state and expression . . . Emotional experience occurs through the interpretation and evaluation of states and expressions. Thus, emotional experience is dependent on cognitive processes" (Lewis & Michalson 1983, pp. 118–19). Emotional experience involves a complex of evaluations—the internal state, the context in which the emotion has occurred, and the identification of the immediate eliciting stimulus.

Lewis and Michalson go into a detailed discussion of these five aspects of emotion, citing many examples from real-life situations and tying in their concepts with the work of other investigators. They relate their five components to each other and put forward a developmental view of emotion. Their breakdown of emotion into these five components is a persuasive model and emphasizes the complexities of emotion, which on the surface appears simple compared with cognitive processes.

Emotional Development

Because of the complexity of the factors that shape emotional states and the lack of reliable methods of investigation and data-gathering, the study of the development of emotions over the life-span is indeed a difficult task. The evidence we do have suggests that children may develop the beginnings of complex emotions at a remarkably early age. For example, there is empathy, the concern for and even sharing of feelings that one observes in another. Dunn and Kendrick's landmark study on siblings (1982) found that thirteen out of sixteen children between two and three years of age showed definite evidence of empathic behavior toward their younger eight-month-old siblings. These behaviors included such items as helping the younger child with a toy when she was frustrated by it or offering toys or food when the infant was crying. This early onset of empathy is confirmed by Lewis and Michalson's review of the literature (1983, p. 180), as well as by Kagan (1984, p. 126).

A thoughtful attempt to organize our knowledge of the development of emotions is presented by Jerome Kagan in *The Nature of the Child* (1984). Very few psychologists are as well qualified to suggest such a schema as Kagan, with his own wealth of studies of child development and his command of the research literature. His discussion of emotion is necessarily brief, given the sparseness of our knowledge, even though he covers the ages from infancy through adolescence. But his formulations make a valuable contribution. He emphasizes throughout that developmental changes in emotional states "are due, at least in part, to the maturation of new cognitive functions and to new knowledge" (p. 183). Thus, for example, "the appearance of guilt is delayed because its cognitive base takes time to mature. The cognitive talent in question is the ability to recognize that one has a choice" (p. 175). The two-year-old does not have this ability, but the four-year-old does and therefore becomes capable of experiencing the emotion we call guilt.

The systematic study of emotional development is in its infancy, but it represents an important challenge to researchers. Lewis and Michalson put forward a generalization that should be a useful guide to research in this field:

> More than one model may also be necessary to explain emotions at different developmental levels in children's lives. . . . Maturation, biological processes, and socialization forces all play key roles in the developmental sequences that start with a relatively undifferentiated organism and result in a highly differentiated, cognitively aware individual capable of engaging in a rich affective life. (p. 139)

Individual Differences in Emotion

Given the complexity and variability of the factors that appear to shape emotional states, it is no surprise that there are great individual differences. This fact is a matter of common observation: Some children (and some adults) are highly expressive in their feelings, and others are much less so or even poker-faced. Different experiences evoke different emotions in different children, and differences in the expression of their emotions. Here temperament plays an important role. The easy child, with her predominantly positive mood and quick adaptability to new situations, will show a cheerfulness most of the time, while the temperamentally difficult child, with opposite characteristics, will typically show a great deal of negative feeling-states by fussing and crying and other evidences of frustration or distress. The persistent nondistractible child who is forcibly pulled away from an activity in which she is absorbed will typically react with anger or distress or both, while the distractible child can usually be induced to shift activities easily and even cheerfully.

Other obscure factors also play a part. Some children are cheerful and playful when they awaken, others are fussy and grouchy for some minutes or even longer. At the other end of the day, some children become cranky and irritable when they are sleepy, while others tuck themselves into bed on schedule without any fuss.

It is worth repeating the theme of earlier chapters that these individual differences represent variations on the normal, and one pattern is not "more normal" than another. When a child with one type of emotional expressiveness suddenly changes, however, either overall or in some specific situation, the change requires investigation.

Implications for Parents

Some parents may ask, "All this information about cognition and emotion is interesting, but how do I apply it concretely with my child in everyday living?" This is a legitimate question, and a number of practical points can be made.

Parents can usually recognize the individual cognitive and emotional patterns of their children and shape their own behavior to achieve a good fit. One child may want to know how a bicycle operates and how to maintain equilibrium on a bicycle before being willing to try riding one. Another child will be impatient with such discussion and learns by getting right on it. One child will reflect silently before answering a question, and that does not mean that she is avoiding it in any way. Another child may answer quickly, sometimes accurately, sometimes not.

Similarly, cognitive abilities and emotions mature at different rates in different children, and different ones at different rates within the same child. Some children talk earlier or learn the concepts of numbers or reading sooner than others. Some children develop the ability to empathize earlier than others. Pressuring a child for a level of cognitive ability or emotional expressiveness that the child has not yet attained can only have negative effects. Each child's developmental course has to be respected, even if it differs from those of her age-mates, unless there is definite evidence of excessive deviation. This is usually easy to identify: In the case of a three-year-old who still cannot talk or a five-year-old who has fears or distress without any apparent cause, or in other cases where the parent is in real doubt, professional consultation is advisable.

Above all, the child's interest in thinking and learning must be cultivated. Kagan's study of metacognition in a memory task cited earlier in this chapter emphasizes how important motivation is in stimulating children to develop their own strategies of mastering the task. Resnick, in her discussion of higher order thinking, points up the importance of motivation: "Through encouragement to try new, more active approaches, and social support even for partially successful efforts, students may come to think of themselves as capable of engaging in independent thinking, of exercising control over their learning processes" (in press).

Parents can do a great deal to encourage motivation for learning. As we have said, this does not mean using gimmicks of one kind or another to increase the child's IQ. Such efforts are futile, even if the immediate results may appear to be an impressive increase in the child's knowledge. This is rote knowledge, and if the child is pressured in such a manner, learning may cease to be an interesting and stimulating process for her. But parents can have many opportunities to do what Resnick suggests. We can illustrate this by examples from our own family. One evening at the dinner table, one of our sons, then about four years of age, lapsed into a silence that lasted for some minutes. He then announced, "I know why fish swim so well. They practice all day." We could have laughed and made a family joke of this incident, embarrassing him and discouraging him from this kind of thinking. Instead, we took his remark seriously and complimented him on his thoughtful analysis. We then went on immediately and on subsequent occasions to discuss the anatomy of fishes that made them capable of swimming, as well as the differences between animals that lived in the sea and those that lived on land. On another occasion, he was absorbed in putting a model airplane together when it was time for a family excursion. He clearly preferred to stay and finish his task rather than go with us. Inasmuch as there was someone remaining in the house who could keep an eye on him, we indicated our approval of his commitment to his problem-solving interest and went off without him. When we returned, he triumphantly showed us the final product and received our praise. If we had insisted that he drop his task and come with us, he would have lost an important experience in demonstrating to himself his ability at problem-solving.

One final caveat for parents is in order. The research activities in metacognition promise to lead to evidence that training in the process of thinking may succeed in raising a child's ability to do higher order thinking. If so, individuals or groups will undoubtedly appear, as they have for the IQ and other issues, with claims that they have simple, guaranteed methods for teaching metacognition. When this happens, parents should be very wary of such claims, investigate them thoroughly, and get the judgment of competent professionals before pushing their child into such programs. Metacognitive training, if it becomes possible, will undoubtedly not translate into some very simple procedure but will require a number of carefully planned and executed strategies by true experts.

9

The Child's Self-Esteem

So FAR we have focused on what the recent research has taught us about the capacities of the newborn and young child, the impressive array of abilities with which the baby enters the world. These abilities are not like the elaborate system of instincts with which newly hatched insects are born and which enable them to float away or fly away on their own, ready within a few days to duplicate the lives of their ancestors. The human baby, by contrast, is helpless to operate on his own. But he has unique capacities that insects and other organisms do not possess. He can perceive and quickly differentiate the human face, he can enter into communication with his caregivers, and he can begin to imitate adults, the beginning of learning by communication. He can also actively explore objects in his environment and soon learns to feel them with his mouth and fingers and to manipulate them in all kinds of ways. And all these activities he does with his own individual temperamental style.

In all these ways the human infant is set to learn what his culture expects and demands of him and to develop, as he grows older, any special talents and abilities he may possess. He is also set to make social connections and relationships, first with his caregivers and then with an ever-widening circle of other people.

These insights into the young infant as a competent human being interacting with his environment and constantly learning bring us to a central issue in child development: When and how does the child develop a sense of *self?*

The sense of self is one of those terms that we all experience subjectively and yet find hard to define. It is related to a number of attributes that we recognize as important, even decisive, elements in a child's development and behavior and an adult's functioning: self-respect, self-esteem, and self-confidence.

A simple and useful definition of the self is that it is made up of the identity, character, and essential qualities of a person, which tend to be enduring in nature. In essence, the self is one's own person or being, as distinct and apart from all others.

Experimental evidence suggests that other higher animals, such as chimpanzees, may have at least crude self-awareness (Goodall & Hamburg 1975). But it is in the human being that the sense of self is highly developed, the sense of being a person who simultaneously remains the same and yet changes over time, who is similar to yet different from other people. We change as we cope with one life experience after another, yet a central core of our psychological being appears to us to remain the same and to endure. The sixty-year-old knows he is vastly different from the young adult he was at twenty; at the same time he feels deeply that he is the same person he was at twenty.

The Importance of Self-Esteem

As the sense of self develops in the child, it takes shape in a positive or negative direction. The child either develops a sense of self-esteem and self-confidence or forms a low opinion of himself and his abilities to function socially and master challenging tasks. There are also mixtures, children and adults who have high self-confidence in certain areas, perhaps where they have special skills and talents, and yet feel they cannot function successfully in other areas.

Self-esteem can be considered central to psychological functioning, both for the child and for the adult. With a healthy self-esteem the child can meet the challenges of life with confidence in his ability to master them successfully. With a poor or uncertain estimate of his abilities—in other words, with inadequate self-esteem—the child doubts his capacity to master new demands and new expectations as he meets them. He even worries that his current and past achievements are below par when compared with those of his age-mates, whether in play, in school, or in jobs that he undertakes.

Once a sense of high or low self-esteem begins to crystallize in a person's mind, it often becomes a self-fulfilling prophecy. The child, adolescent, or adult with a strong and accurate sense of his abilities is likely to mobilize himself effectively for a new task, cope with it directly, and thus assure a level of success that will reinforce his self-confidence. A youngster who is unsure of himself and afraid of failure is all too likely to approach a new challenge with apprehension and self-doubts and even to avoid the task with one flimsy excuse or another, guaranteeing failure and confirming his poor opinion of himself. Sometimes his self-doubts are hidden behind a facade of bravado or boasting, which does nothing to help him and usually only adds another worry—that others will not be fooled by the front he is putting up and will think even less of him.

It is sad how often mental health professionals are consulted by people with serious self-doubts, when their actual abilities and personalities should have insured them a healthy self-esteem that would have made an enormous difference in their lives. The importance of self-esteem is recognized in the vast professional literature on the subject by psychiatrists and psychologists, as well as in the attention given to it over the ages by novelists and playwrights. Only the traditional behaviorists have ignored the study of self-esteem, placing it in the subjective "black box" of the mind, which they claim cannot be studied scientifically. The rest of us disagree strongly. To ignore the issue of self-esteem in the study of the child's psychological development is like performing *Hamlet* without Hamlet.

The Origins of the Self

Self-esteem is such a central issue that its origins and development have become critical areas for theory and research in child development. What we learn can make a big difference for parents and others in knowing how to stimulate and nurture the growth of a strong and healthy self-esteem in children.

In order for a sense of self to begin to develop, the infant must be able to perceive himself as an individual, separate from his caregivers and other objects. He must be able to differentiate himself and his own behavior from stimuli and actions coming from the outside world. The infant's experiences must also leave memory traces or schemas in his brain (see Kagan's definition and description of the schema in chapter 7) so that he can recognize others as different from himself.

Traditional Views

Traditionally, the very young infant was not thought capable of the differentiated responses to the environment that are required for the beginning of a sense of self. To Piaget and Bowlby the newborn's brain was composed of only bundles of reflexes, and to Freud it was made up of a system of instinctual drives. These theories labeled the newborn as undifferentiated, egocentric, narcissistic (preoccupied with his own needs regardless of the environment), or in Mahler's terms, in a state of "normal autism."

Anna Freud's views on the young infant's egocentricity were similar to Mahler's, though she did not develop an elaborate scheme such as Mahler's "symbiosis" and "separation-individuation." Anna Freud's formulation of early infancy egocentricity appears to have been based on the idea that the infant can relate independently to the outside world only in the latter part of the first year, when he has reached the stage of "object constancy"—that stage at which an infant realizes that if an object disappears from sight it is not gone forever. In her formulation, "Before the phase of object constancy has been reached, the object, i.e. the mothering person, is not perceived by the child as having an existence of her own; she is perceived only in terms of the role assigned to her within the framework of the child's needs and wishes" (1965, p. 58). In other words, she viewed the young infant as so egocentric that he could not perceive even his primary caretaker as an independent person. She considered the newborn undifferentiated and therefore incapable of a sense of separate self. Only later, usually around four to six months, would the infant's interaction with the world make him capable of beginning the process of self-differentiation.

Anna Freud's reasoning was basically a speculation built on the fact of object constancy, and she offered no objective evidence to support it. Other psychoanalysts have challenged these views of Freud and Mahler. Erik Erikson places the beginning of self and identity in the first few months of life, in the first of his scheme of developmental stages. This stage, which Erikson designates as *trust versus mistrust,* includes "a rudimentary sense of ego identity" (1950, p. 58). Like Anna Freud, however, Erikson gives no objective research evidence to support this intriguing and different view.

More recently, the Chicago psychoanalyst Heinz Kohut impressed many analysts with his challenge to the traditional psychoanalytic view of the Oedipus complex and its resolution as the central issue in early child development. (The Oedipus complex is considered to involve a conflict between the three- to five-year-old boy's sexual attraction to his mother and the fear that his father will castrate him as a result.) Kohut and his followers instead emphasize the earlier infancy period, in which the development of the self is seen as both the first and most complex task (ultimately a lifelong task) of the child (Kohut 1977). But again, Kohut's formulations have not been subjected to scrutiny in the light of our increasing empirical knowledge of the young infant's capacities and his active communication with his caregiver. These ideas of Erikson and Kohut, as attractive as they may appear compared with the formulations of Sigmund and Anna Freud and Margaret Mahler, have stimulated lively speculative debate among psychoanalysts, which in the absence of empirical evidence has generated more heat than light.

In general, these various psychoanalytic concepts of the development of the self suffer from two difficulties. First, the primary evidence is obtained from retrospective memories of older children or adults in psychoanalytic treatment. Aside from the special nature of such cases, as compared with normal people, such retrospective memories are highly unreliable, as Freud himself discovered and others have documented (Robbins 1963; Wenar 1963). Second, the newborn's behavior is evaluated as if he were a miniature adult or even an older child afflicted with an illness such as autism. Endowing the newborn with such labels as *egocentricity* and *omnipotence*, which would be pertinent for an adult with similar behavior, ignores the fact that the young infant's cerebral functioning cannot possibly even approximate the level where such ideation is possible. As Emanuel Peterfreund points out (1978), if an infant cries loudly until his needs are satisfied, this is not the "omnipotence" or narcissism of the adult who insistently demands immediate satisfaction of his desires. The infant has no other way of signaling that he is hungry, soiled, or in pain. The adult has many other alternatives. To equate the two is to commit the adultomorphic fallacy.

Objective Studies of the Development of the Sense of Self

To these theoretical speculations, we would counterpose the implications to be clearly derived from the recent objective empirical studies of the newborn and young infant. Our own view (Thomas & Chess 1980) is that the perceptual, communicative, and learning capacities of the newborn make possible individuation and self-differentiation starting at birth and growing as the infant engages in increasingly diverse and complex interactions with his caregivers, other people, and even inanimate objects. This development is analogous to the sequential evolution of language development, in which the first spoken words at nine or twelve or eighteen months are not the beginning of language function but a new stage that has evolved from the preceding period of babbling and nonverbal gestures that began at birth.

By the third month, or even earlier, infants spend many minutes at a time gazing at their hands, twisting the wrists and looking intently at the hands as they do so. At the same age, or perhaps a few weeks later, many infants when alone in a crib not only babble for long periods but at times keep repeating the same sound. As that astute observer, Judy Dunn, has pointed out, "We know that by the third month of life babies are delighted by events that follow from their own acts (this is shown by some of the research on smiling, for instance), and are upset if their own behavior with other people fails to produce the reaction they expect" (1977, p. 32).

In all these instances, the young infant is initiating behavior that has consequences of which he clearly appears aware (movement of his hand, a sound, a smile, the responsive actions of other people). This is certainly the beginning of that basic constituent of positive self-concept, the awareness that "I" can produce changes in the external world. "I" must be a separate entity from the outside world if "I" can accomplish this.

In a recent important paper, Daniel Stern, a psychoanalyst as well as a researcher, has elaborated the thesis of the newborn and young infant as a differentiated organism capable of a sense of self. From his knowledge of recent research findings about infants' perceptual organization, action tendencies, and cognitive competencies, findings based largely on experimental and observational approaches to the infant, Stern draws the emphatic conclusion that "infants probably never experience an undifferentiated phase of life—that is, the infant is predesigned to discriminate and to begin to form distinct schemas of self and others from the earliest months of life" (1983, p. 50). He is critical of Mahler's concepts, arguing with persuasive research data against her ideas of "symbiosis," infantile confusion between the infant's self and the caregiver. According to Stern, "the experiences and schemas of self and others never were systematically or pervasively fused or confused by the infant in the course of early development, but rather formed separately, as emergent sensori-motor and cognitive constructs" (p. 51).

In a recent book, *The Interpersonal World of the Infant* (1985), Stern draws on his own studies and the substantial research of others to propose a systematic progress in the infant's sense of self. The first stage he calls the sense of an *emergent self*, which forms in the first two months from birth. During this period, infants have separate unrelated experiences, but also begin to integrate and organize these separate experiences. It is from this process of beginning organization that the infant develops the basis for an emergent sense of self. The second stage Stern calls the sense of a *core self*, which forms between two and six months. It is during this period, the research evidence indicates, that the infant forms a sense that he has control over his own actions (your arm and leg move when you want them to) and that these actions have consequences (if you hit a mobile toy it moves). The third stage Stern labels the sense of a *subjective self*, which develops between seven to fifteen months. Stern puts it that in this age period "infants gradually come upon the momentous realization that inner subjective experiences, the 'subject matter' of the mind, are potentially shareable with someone else" (p. 124). This sharing can take many forms, such as asking for something or focusing someone else's attention on a toy. The fourth stage is that of a sense of *verbal self*, which forms after fifteen months. The development of language makes possible the formation of verbal signs and symbols, and the capacity to engage in symbolic action such as play.

Stern emphasizes that these four senses of self are not successive phases that replace one another. "Once formed, each sense of self remains fully functioning and active throughout life" (p. 11). Stern's formulations represent the first systematic attempt based on solid research findings to trace the evolution of the sense of self through the infancy period. Some of his concepts are necessarily speculative, as are all attempts to understand what an infant, who cannot as yet communicate to others through language, is thinking and feeling. But Stern's work and formulations do promise to expand and deepen our understanding of the child's early psychological development most significantly.

In his earlier paper (1983), Stern makes a very important point pertaining to much of the psychoanalytic and other psychiatric theorizing and speculation, which is all too often presented as if it were proven fact. He says, "We have too long put ourselves at a disadvantage by viewing normal stages in terms of later pathological mistakes or delusions about the nature of reality" (p. 80).

Lawrence Kolb, a leading psychiatric clinician and teacher at Columbia University, has made the same point with regard to adults. He suggests, in contrast to usual psychodynamic formulations, that the positive aspects of personality "undoubtedly derive from developmental processes quite different in origin and action from those productive of psychopathology. In the ill, those processes concerned with the mastery of the environment are either inhibited or have failed in their evolution" (1978).*

---

*This emphasis on what is normal and healthy as well as what is pathological sounds obvious. Yet in our teaching of psychiatric residents, we have found that this is usually their greatest blind spot. They can identify and describe a child's or an adult's pathological behavior, but when asked, "What are his strengths and assets? What is healthy about him?" they either look blank or hem and haw and indicate that this question has never come up with their other instructors. Aside from its other implications for developing a proper treatment

The rapid development of the self-concept in the early months of life is illustrated by several ingenious experiments by two developmental psychologists, Michael Lewis and Jeanne Brooks, of the Educational Testing Service. They found that starting at about nine months of age, infants responded positively to strange children but negatively to strange female adults. They further observed infants' responses when, through the use of mirrors, it appeared that the baby was being approached by himself. The infant showed as much pleasure with the mirror image as he did to the real approach of the mother (1974). If the infant's negative reaction to a stranger reflects differentiation from the mother, as is often assumed, then the response to the strange child and the infant's own image in the mirror should be even more negative than to an adult female stranger, who is much less different than the image of the mother. The positive response suggests that an infant compares faces not only with his mother's but also with his own, requiring at least the beginning of an organized sense of self.

In another ingenious experiment (1975), Lewis and Brooks had mothers of children nine to twenty-four months of age unobtrusively rub a little rouge on the child's nose. The child was then brought in front of a mirror. If the child touched his rouged nose on viewing his image in the mirror, that indicated an ability to identify the image with his own self. Only a small number of the nine-month-olds did so, but the percentage of infants who did so increased progressively through the second year.

Implications of an Early Sense of Self

Does it matter whether the sense of self begins to develop at birth and in the first few weeks of life, or not until later, whether in the fourth, the sixth, or the eighth month? It does matter greatly, for several reasons.

First, the study of early child development is a scientific field, and we want that study to be as accurate as possible. That is one of the basic principles of science. The study of the origins of the sense of self may also, however, have practical applications. A better knowledge of the causes of the origin might help us to devise methods of stimulating the growth of positive self-esteem. Also, a number of the serious psychiatric disorders of early childhood, such as autism, mental retardation, and the consequences of severe brain damage, cause distortions in the sense of a separate in-

---

approach, this emphasis on the pathological has had serious consequences for the advice experts give to parents. As Stern indicates, if normal stages are viewed in terms of "pathological mistakes," then how can a presumed expert who follows this dictum properly advise the parents of healthy children?

dividuality that relates with other people. A finer insight into the mechanisms and timing of the growth of the sense of self might give valuable clues for the treatment of these early psychiatric disturbances.

Moreover, if the emergence of a sense of self is pushed toward the middle or later months of the first year of life, then as we have seen the younger infant and newborn are necessarily described by terms that have negative and even pathological implications: egocentricity, symbiosis and fusion with the mother, narcissism, and omnipotence. Inevitably, such terms are carried over to descriptions of older infants and older children, so that a ten-month-old child may be labeled as still egocentric, narcissistic, or having failed to "hatch out" as a separate self from his symbiotic identity with his mother. Such labels then lead to judgments that a child is suffering a psychiatric problem, when in fact he is basically normal and is only maturing slowly. To correct the presumed problems, treatment procedures may be prescribed that are bound to be inappropriate and even harmful.

For the parent, as we have pointed out, it can make a great difference to know that they are nurturing a real human being and not just feeding, bathing, cleaning, and dressing a tiny scrawny object who will someday become a human being. The routine and sometimes irksome chores of caregiving similarly take on a different significance when they are viewed as part of the process by which the newborn develops a sense of self. Baby and parent are then two separate selves interacting with each other in a way that is beneficial to both.

Finally, Stern, in his recent book (1985) offers an intriguing speculation. "Once parents see a different infant, that infant starts to become transformed by their new 'sight' and ultimately becomes a different adult. . . . Seeing the infant as different begins to make the children, adolescents, and adults different a generation later" (p. 276). In other words, the parents' view of their infant influences their behavior and attitudes toward the child and affects significantly his psychological development. This new kind of parental understanding and its consequences for the child, once psychiatrists become aware of it, will modify their theories of the origin and evolution of many psychiatric disorders.

The Growth of Self-Awareness in the Second Year

By the second year of life it is clear that the sense of self has blossomed into a strong sense of identity and self-awareness. With the acquisition of language, the older infant can verbalize "I" and "me" as contrasted to "you" or "he" and show that he is well aware of himself as a separate person in a world of many different kinds of people.

The most careful and thorough studies of self-awareness have come from the work of Jerome Kagan (1982). He was concerned with identifying the various manifestations of self-aware behavior in the last half of the second year of life and in making cross-cultural comparisons of these behaviors in three sets of children—twenty-six middle-class Caucasian American children, sixty-seven Fijian children, and seven Vietnamese children who had recently arrived in this country. Kagan was also interested in determining the implications of his findings for the biological as well as the social basis of these behaviors.

Kagan started with the use of abstract constructs like passivity, sociability, hostility, achievement, reflectivity, and identification, most of which came at least partly from psychoanalytic theory. He tried to accommodate his observations to these personality attributes, and although they seemed useful in studying older children, he became aware that they were inappropriate for observations of young children. He shifted his strategy to an empirical one in which he noted the surface behaviors of the children and then made inferences that did not go beyond his data. (We have also found that this is the key method for the study of behavior in young children.) Kagan also observed, most appropriately, that "Young children are uncertain in most experimental situations, and this state is often a major cause of their reactions" (1982, p. 364). (A number of other investigators would do well to heed this injunction. All too often, studies of young children in experimental situations fail to take this factor of the child's uncertainty into account.) Kagan therefore conducted the major part of his studies by observing the child's behavior in the familiar home setting with the mothers present. His findings can be summarized briefly:

The appearance of standards. At around seventeen to twenty months of age, children display an obvious concern with objects and events that deviate in some way from what adults consider normal. For example, they point with trepidation to small holes in clothing, tiny spots on furniture, and missing bristles on a broom and utter phrases like "Oh-oh" in a distressed tone. These many events share no common physical quality but do share a variation from the normal, for which the parents have presumably indicated disapproval.

Also, between nineteen and twenty-six months the speech of every child indicated references to standards that were being violated ("broken," "boo-boo," "dirty," "wash hands," "can't," "hard do"). Kagan points out that it is unlikely that all twenty-four-month-old children have formed these standards on their own and identified their violations. It is most likely, he suggests, that the child has learned these standards from direct or subtle parental communications.

Empathy.   Like Dunn & Kendrick (1982), Kagan describes the ability to appreciate the psychological state of another as maturing in the second year. For example, two-year-olds begin to react to the distress of another child by hugging him, giving him a toy or food, and requesting aid from an adult.

Anxiety over potential failure.   After a period of free play, the examiner modeled several difficult tasks, such as making a doll talk on the telephone, with the child watching and then invited the child to play. The examiner did not ask the child to imitate these actions. Expressions of distress were evident in the children, appearing first around fifteen months and increasing with age until a peak was reached around the second birthday. Kagan infers that "the child experiences an obligation to implement the acts of the model, and . . . has some awareness of her inability to do so. As a result, the child becomes uncertain and begins to cry or stop playing. If the child has no uncertainty over meeting the standard and believes she can be successful, she makes the attempt" (p. 369).

Smiles of mastery.   Another phenomenon of this age period is the occurrence of a smile after the child has attained a goal through effort, a smile unaccompanied by a glance to an adult for confirmation. Kagan interprets these smiles as "private, not social" and as "signifying that the child has generated a goal . . . , persisted in attempts to gain that goal, and smiled upon attainment" (p. 370). If this assumption is correct, then the two-year-old not only has the ability to generate goals but is also able to know when he has achieved that goal.

Directives to adults.   Behaviors emerge in the two-year-olds that indicate a wish to influence the behavior of adults through requests. Kagan suggests that "the child would not have begun to direct the behavior of an adult if she did not have an expectation that the request would be met. . . . The child expects he can influence the behavior of others" (p. 371). Kagan differentiates these desires from the pointing and whining of an eight-month-old at an object out of reach. He presumes, and this appears reasonable, that the younger infant does not have a conscious conception that the cry or gesture will change the adult's behavior, as does the two-year-old, but that it represents simple frustration at seeing the object that is out of reach.

Self-descriptive utterances.   Words and phrases referring to the child himself are not at all evident when speech first begins. In Kagan's study, self-descriptive utterances were absent at seventeen, eighteen, and nineteen months, increased markedly around the second birthday, and were quite elaborate by twenty-seven months, including phrases like "I do it myself." The child now becomes aware of what he himself is doing.

Kagan describes several other behavioral changes in the second year that he also relates to the development of a sense of self: *the replacement of self in symbolic play* (putting a telephone to a doll's head rather than his own) and an increased *memory for locations,* which Kagan interprets as an increase in the motivation to meet a standard of competence.

What emerges from Kagan's careful, sophisticated studies is the dramatic extent to which the sense of self has developed by two years and the sensitivity of the two-year-old as a separate person to the objects and people around him. The appearance of standards, the ability to show empathy, the anxiety over potential failure, the positive awareness and response to mastery, the directives to adults, and the use of self-descriptions in speech—all these attest to the remarkable development of the sense of self that has taken place by a child's second birthday.

Like the research data we now have on the first year of life, Kagan's findings represent a radical departure from psychoanalytic approaches and theories. The psychoanalysts, with some exceptions such as Daniel Stern, start with a prior assumption of the nature of child development, mostly derived from clinical work with adults suffering from various psychiatric disorders. These hypotheses also presume certain subjective states in the infant (egocentricity, narcissism, identity with the mother), as we have seen. Using such assumptions, most psychoanalytic studies have attempted to probe directly or at least to speculate on the infant's subjective state, looking especially for conflicts between "id" and "ego," the development of conflict related to the presumed oral and anal instincts and the Oedipus conflict, and fantasies related to these conflicts. (The self-psychology of Kohut, while it has challenged a number of traditional psychoanalytic concepts, is also committed to a search for the infant's subjective experiences and fantasies.) But many of us, even some psychoanalysts, have found such a subjective approach unrewarding. As Stern puts it, "Has classical libido theory, in assuming one or two basic drives that shift developmentally from one erotogenic zone to another and have a variety of vicissitudes during development, been helpful in viewing an actual infant? The answer is no" (1985, p. 238).

The explosion of knowledge of the infant in recent years has instead rested on empirical descriptive studies, done as much as possible with techniques and situations that correspond closely to the child's natural environment. That does not mean that theory plays no part in such research. New theoretical concepts have emerged, as we have seen in this chapter and the two preceding ones. The infant comes into the world with a number of biological endowments, but these are not mere reflexes or hypothetical instincts. Rather, they are capacities, such as perception, communication, and imitation, that enable the newborn to begin to respond to and act on his environment as a social human being. Kagan, in his study

of the two-year-olds from three different cultures and from the information we now have on the maturation of the higher brain centers, feels that
"the last half-century has awarded too little influence to biological maturation" (1984, p. 277). He in no way downgrades the social influences on the
child: there is an interaction of the social and the biological. He postulates
specifically that the psychological advances in the two-year-old, and their
similarities in different cultures, indicate that these changes "are inevitable, psychological consequences of maturational events in the central nervous system, as long as the child lives in a world of objects and people"
(1982, p. 376).

The Formation of Self-Esteem

With the crystallization of a definitive sense of self in the first two years
of life, the stage is set for the development of self-esteem. The recognition
of standards set by parents, the self-judgments on potential failure or
mastery, the awareness that one's own behavior can influence others—all
these make for sequences of achievement and recognition of one's competence or for successive failures and self-doubts. And this self-evaluation
is at all times a social judgment within a social context. As Erikson has
put it,

> The growing child must, at every step, derive a vitalizing sense of reality from
> the awareness that his individual way of mastering experience (his ego synthesis)
> is a successful variant of a group experience. . . . Ego identity gains real strength
> only from wholehearted and consistent recognition of real accomplishment—i.e.,
> of achievement that has meaning in the culture. (1950, p. 208)

The Role of Weaning and Toilet Training in Self-Esteem

Within this context of "wholehearted and consistent recognition of real
accomplishment" as a basis for strong "ego identity" (that is, self-esteem),
something must be said about weaning and toilet training. These two
landmark accomplishments of infancy have been turned on their head by
traditional psychoanalytic theory, which makes them fearful experiences
rather than positive achievements.

The theory of development as elaborated by Freud assumed the existence of basic instinctual drives appearing in sequence in the young child
—first the oral drive, then the anal, then the genital. The process of so-

cialization involved the repression of these instinctual drives through the demands of the parents and the larger society. As Freud put it, "Civilization is the fruit of the renunciation of instinctual satisfaction" (1924, p. 297). Improper management of weaning and toilet training—either too early or too late, too harsh or too permissive—could have permanent effects on the child's personality. The psychoanalytic literature described personality types that were presumed to result from early mismanagement of weaning or toilet training, "the oral personality" and "the anal personality." These terms have been fading from the literature in recent years, as the lack of empirical evidence to sustain them has become more and more evident.

Even Erikson, with his broad modifications of traditional Freudian theory, remained committed to these views. Of weaning, he asserted that "even under the most favorable circumstances, this stage leaves a residue of a primary sense of evil and doom and of a universal nostalgia for a lost paradise" (1950, p. 75). As to toilet training, he observed that "bowel and bladder training has become the most obviously disturbing item of child training in wide circles of our society" (p. 77).

Concepts such as these die hard, even in the face of contradictory facts. In 1948 a group of investigators tried to validate the theory that every infant first experienced an oral instinctual drive, which required a certain amount of sucking for the infant to be satisfied. (Margaret Ribble, a prominent child care expert of the time, even stipulated that every infant required a minimum sucking time of two hours a day [1943].) The investigators took sixty babies and divided them into three groups of twenty each. In the first ten days of life, one group was breast-fed, another fed by bottle, and the third fed by cup alone. The strength of the sucking reflex was measured in each infant, and detailed observations were made of each child's spontaneous oral activity, amount of crying, and level of general body activity. According to traditional psychoanalytic theory, the cup-fed infants, being deprived of their presumed oral instinctual needs, should have shown stronger sucking activity and various indications of discomfort and distress. On the contrary, the investigators found no significant differences between the groups with respect to spontaneous oral activity or crying. The breast-fed babies, rather than the cup-fed ones, developed a stronger sucking reflex, and the other two groups did not differ from each other. The findings with regard to general body activity were inconclusive (Davis et al. 1948). In other words, there was no evidence that deprivation of the sucking experience of the cup-fed babies had affected them unfavorably. And strength of sucking was influenced by experience and not deprivation; the breast-fed babies spent more time sucking than the other two groups.

Yet so great is the influence of an ingrained theory that a senior member of this group of investigators, in spite of its study challenging the idea of an oral drive, wrote some ten years later, "The weaning process, except under the most fortunate circumstances, is bound to be frustrating to the child" (Sears, Maccoby, & Levin 1957, p. 83). One is reminded of the cynical comment that makes the rounds of scientific circles: "Never let the facts interfere with your theories."

It may be argued that this cup-feeding experiment was inconclusive. Although there may not have been any *immediate* observable harmful effects, the "lack of gratification of oral instinctual need" might have a deep-seated unconscious effect that would show up in later life in one undesirable form or another. (This argument of course ignores all the evidence that there is no simple direct correlation between early child care practices and later personality.)

In this case, however, we do have evidence of later outcomes with children cup-fed from birth. In the early 1960s a Kansas City psychiatrist, Richard Davis, heard of a fourteen-year-old youngster (not a psychiatric case) who had been the patient of a pediatrician who had advocated cup-feeding from birth. This pediatrician had been concerned at how many of the mothers in his practice bottle-fed their infants by propping up the bottle in the crib so that they would not have to hold the baby during a feeding. The pediatrician felt that this lack of contact during feeding was not desirable for either infant or mother. He therefore advocated cup-feeding for all his families.

As was to be expected, some of the mothers followed his advice, and others did not. Through the boy's mother, Davis was able to locate twenty former patients of this pediatrician, all of whom had been cup-fed from birth. This group, now adolescents, were paired with twenty classmates of similar cultural and economic background, who had been breast- or bottle-fed in infancy. All the adolescents were then interviewed and also given psychological tests by psychologists who did not know which ones had been cup-fed from birth. When the interviews and tests were analyzed, no statistical difference could be found between the two groups. Bottle- or breast-feeding in contrast to cup-feeding did not appear to make any difference in terms of emotional development and overall adjustment (Davis & Ruiz 1965).

We investigated the issue of early weaning and early toilet training by analyzing the information available in our New York Longitudinal Study. Detailed accounts from the parents were available on each child's behavior preceding, during, and following weaning and toilet training. Analysis of the data for the first fifty children in the study showed evidence of disturbance associated with weaning in only one child. In this one case, the disturbance appeared to reflect overall rigid and inconsistent parental practices. In some of the families, weaning was accomplished by the child's spontaneous rejection of the bottle. In some of these instances the mothers persisted in their efforts to continue with bottle-feeding and stopped only when they found their efforts to be of no avail. These attempts to delay weaning were due to the mothers' fears, which they expressed openly in the interviews, that early weaning or toilet training might be harmful to the child. (This was in the late 1950s, when many presumed authorities were warning of the dangers of such early weaning and toilet training.) Some of the mothers even confessed to feeling uneasy about the early weaning accomplished by the child, for fear their friends would assume they were using rigid, outdated, and harmful child care practices. The findings with toilet training were very similar. Training was not only accomplished without disturbance, except for one case, but in a number of instances the children themselves initiated the training, usually in imitation of an older brother or sister.

The myths of past years regarding the potentially harmful effects of weaning and toilet training may not be as prevalent today. But they still come up in new forms. One of our acquaintances, a first mother with an eighteen-month-old son, was cautioned strictly by a friend who was keeping up on the newest wrinkles in child care advice, "When you toilet train Sandy, make sure he doesn't see you flush his bowel movement down the toilet. Otherwise, he will see this precious possession of his disappear and be lost to him." What did this woman, or her child care expert, think of all of Sandy's experiences in watching his soiled diaper being thrown into the garbage?

Let us take a different view of weaning and toilet training. Instead of being the frustrating experiences visualized by theories of oral and anal instinctual drives, weaning and toilet training can be considered sources of achievement, satisfaction, and enhancement of social relationships. The use of a cup gives the child a control over the flow of liquid intake and swallowing that he does not have when sucking at a nipple, whether breast or bottle. Toilet training gives him control over the time and place of bowel and bladder evacuation and the comfort of always being clean and dry. With weaning and toilet training the child takes further important steps in his social integration into the family group. These ideas are not mere speculations. One who observes young children will have many youngsters run to greet him or another visitor with the proud announcement, "I'm a big boy (or big girl) now. I don't need diapers anymore when I go to school. And I drink from a cup just like Mommy and Daddy."

Toilet training may be quick and easy or more prolonged and difficult, depending on the child's temperamental characteristics. But if it is accomplished peacefully, without threats or turmoil, it becomes a positive achievement for the child, another step in the mastery of his own functions and a successful response to the expectations of his world. As such, it represents an important step in the development of self-esteem and self-confidence. The same can be said for weaning, though here there are fewer children for whom the process is difficult, as compared with toilet training.

And so it goes with all the many achievements of the young child—dressing and undressing, feeding himself, playing as an equal with his age-mates. All these represent successes in task mastery, and the approval of his elders and the acceptance by his peers bring an increasing sense of social competence. And these are the events that promote self-esteem and self-confidence. For the older child, the tasks become more complex, as he faces the external demands for learning, which become more and more abstract. He may also develop, through one set of events or another, special fears and fantasies within himself. But with continued maturation of the brain and sufficient self-confidence born out of previous life experiences, older children become quite capable of coping successfully with abstract learning and special fears or fantasies.

Goodness of Fit and Self-Esteem

Goodness of fit, as we have discussed it in chapters 4 and 5, is also highly significant in shaping the course of a child's self-esteem. Goodness of fit and self-esteem are profoundly linked in a give-and-take relationship; each affects the other.

To repeat Erikson's formulation, "Ego identity gains real strength only from wholehearted and consistent recognition of real accomplishment—i.e., of achievement that has meaning in the culture" (1950, p. 208). "Ego identity" and "real strength" add up to genuine self-esteem. And "achievement that has meaning in the culture" results from goodness of fit between the child's abilities and characteristics and the demands and expectations of the environment. The child who is self-confident and has had the consistent experience of coping successfully with successive expectations will face a new challenge with the conviction that here again he will master the new demand. Even if some tasks turn out to be too difficult for his developmental level, an occasional failure will not undermine his basic self-confidence.

Success through goodness of fit nurtures self-esteem. Self-esteem makes a child struggle with a task that at first may seem impossible and if necessary seek help without embarrassment. By contrast, repeated failures through poorness of fit diminish and even destroy self-esteem. Lack of self-esteem makes a child avoid new challenges that he could master successfully. It also makes it difficult for him to seek help, which will only expose his presumed inadequacy further. Another failure is thus added to his list, and his self-esteem sinks even lower.

Erikson uses the significant phrase "consistent recognition of real achievement." That is, self-esteem is built not by the achievements them-selves, but by their "consistent recognition." One boy in our longitudinal study took the highly competitive entrance examination for a prestigious high school. Warren studied long and hard for the examination and passed. The school decided that Warren should repeat his last year of junior high school, however, because he was one of the youngest in his class and because his present school had not prepared him adequately in certain subjects for the new school. This was a perfectly appropriate recommenda-tion, but although the boy's examination grade represented an impressive achievement, his father considered it a failure because of the school's decision that he should repeat the year. The boy accepted his father's verdict and stayed in his old school. This was not the only occasion when the father made excessive demands on his son, but this incident, when the youngster had worked so hard to succeed and had actually done so, left him with a fixed conviction that he was a failure, no matter how hard he might try.

On the other hand, there is the child, or adult, who nurses a deep sense of inferiority and who tries to cover it over with a facade of excuses, boasting, and bravado. "I could beat any one of you if I wanted to. But why should I bother." Or "The teachers are against me and that's why I don't get A's." Sometimes it is easy to detect the hollowness of these boasts and the falsehood of the excuses. At other times, however, such a young-ster may maintain a facade that is clever and convincing enough to deceive others. But the devil usually comes home to roost, and the exposure of such self-debasing feelings may be devastating. The youngster may then need strong support from family, friends, and professionals to create the good-ness of fit that will improve his self-esteem.

The Evaluation of Self-Esteem

Most of us think that we know ourselves, that we have an accurate sense of self and self-esteem. As one investigator has put it, "Everyone knows what the self is," yet "despite the seeming clarity of the concept, people do not seem to agree by what they mean by it" (Becker 1968, p. 194).

One dilemma in evaluating self-esteem is whether to base it on the person's statements about himself or on his actual behavior. The sense of self is a highly subjective attribute, and maybe only the person himself can tell us how he feels about himself. On the other hand, objective information about the person's goals and efforts to attain these goals will give us clues to what is motivating his actions, and these motivations may give us insight into how he feels about himself, specifically what he feels capable of achieving—certainly a basic element in self-esteem. We have had a number of instances in the New York Longitudinal Study in which the subjective and objective appraisals were in direct contradiction. Here is one such vignette.

Richard's striking temperamental characteristic was extreme persistence. This tenacity of effort usually did not make for problems but rather brought approval from family and teachers. If Richard was interrupted or otherwise frustrated in an endeavor in which he was deeply absorbed, however, all too often the result was a violent, prolonged tantrum that brought all kinds of unfortunate consequences. One day in the first grade he insisted on continuing his complicated block building when it was time to move to another activity. He could not be budged, and the exasperated teacher finally swept away his carefully constructed edifice. Richard responded with loud, prolonged crying and kicking. Immediately he became the class scapegoat, the "cry baby" and the butt of teasing. The situation went from bad to worse until he was finally transferred to another school. Here Richard made a fresh start, and his persistent efforts in the school activities brought him the approval of his teachers and the friendship of his classmates.

Almost inevitably, another disruptive incident occurred several years later. For Brotherhood Week a poster contest was arranged, and three students from his class, not including Richard, were chosen for the contest. Richard, however, was fired with the idea and labored long and hard to make his own poster, which he proudly brought to school. His teacher construed this behavior as gross disobedience, scolded him, and tore up his poster. Predictably, Richard had a massive blow-up that included throwing a book at the teacher. He was now labeled not only a disobedient child but a violent one. Again he became the school scapegoat. His self-esteem hit bottom, and he told us, "I just have a monster inside of me, and every once in a while it gets out. I don't want to talk about it."

School life for Richard continued on this see-saw course. He would do well, but every few years some crisis recurred at school. Usually it began with some idea or behavior that involved intelligence and thoughtfulness but one that a teacher refused to acknowledge. Richard would pound away, and even if he proved himself right, the classroom was by that time in turmoil and the teacher in no mood to acknowledge Richard's valid ideas. Instead, he was left back in several courses because of the antagonism he had created.

Fortunately, as Richard went through the upper high school years and college, his independent thinking and challenges to various teachers' authority began to be respected for the thoughtful ideas based on hard academic work that they actually were. He settled on a career in business and entered graduate school at twenty-one.

It was at this point that we saw him as part of our scheduled early-adult-age follow-up. In this interview he was depressed and self-deprecating, and he took a pessimistic view of himself and his future possibilities. From his subjective self-evaluation we had to grade his self-esteem as very low. Yet as we reviewed the objective facts of his development, we found them studded with incidents in which he had shown confidence in his own thinking and battled for his own ideas. He had even committed himself to a local political campaign that he knew would be difficult and worked hard and effectively at it. Putting this record together, we could only conclude that a youngster who showed this kind of confidence in his thinking and in his abilities must have high self-confidence and self-esteem.

Which was correct, the subjective or the objective evaluation? Or was this a case of a contradictory mixture and confusion of a person's sense of self—a phenomenon that is not unusual? In Richard's case his further development was favorable, and the contradiction in his sense of self was resolved in a positive direction. When he was interviewed at age twenty-eight, his depressed mood had vanished, and his self-estimation blossomed. He had completed his graduate courses successfully and had found a job in a field and with an organization that attracted him. To his employers his persistence and thoughtfulness were highly valued assets, and he was being rapidly promoted. He appeared happily married, with three children for whom he expressed deep affection.

Why did Richard change so dramatically for the better in his mid- and late twenties? As we looked back over his life history, one attribute was evident. No matter how unfavorable a reception one of his activities or ideas met, he fought long and hard for it. Sometimes this resulted in turmoil, disapproval, and scapegoating, but sometimes it met with final success and approval. He stuck to his guns because of his temperamental quality of intense persistence. But he was also an intelligent youngster, and his battles were almost always over issues in which he was right. Together with his occasional successes and positive responses from others, his intelligence and persistence were sufficient to give him a sense of self-esteem, no matter how discouraged and unsure of his future he was at times. Two life experiences then made for a dramatic change for the better. He made a good marriage and felt strongly positive about his active involvement with his children. And he obtained a position with a company that recognized the value of his ideas, which were implemented with good results, and he was getting ahead in the company.

It was certainly not ordained that Richard's life course would evolve so favorably. Chance played a part. Enough teachers and employers recognized his positive qualities, were not bothered by his "stubbornness," and gave him the chance to prove himself. This has not always been the case with our study subjects, several of whom have shown characteristics opposite to Richard's. Their objective functioning was dismal, usually the result of some drastic poorness of fit between their capacities and their parents' demands. Yet when interviewed they spoke with apparent conviction of their unusual talents, which they believed were beginning to be appreciated, and their rosy futures. Follow-up with these cases has shown a mixture of results; several have done well, and others continue to do badly. In other youngsters, perhaps the majority, the subjective and objective evaluation of self-esteem were consistent. Those who thought highly of themselves were doing well functionally; those who thought poorly of themselves were functioning inadequately and even marginally.

Our experience leads us to suggest that self-esteem is a complicated attribute that should be evaluated both subjectively (the person's self-report) and objectively (the evidence from the level of his functioning and the kinds of commitments he makes and carries through). This is an issue well worth emphasizing, for many judgments of self-esteem, whether in research studies or in the evaluation of applicants for academic or work positions, tend to rely primarily on the person's subjective self-evaluation in a questionnaire or an interview.

Self-esteem is also not a global quality. Some persons can esteem themselves highly and function well in some areas, such as academic courses, athletics, scientific projects, the arts, or social skills. At the same time they may downgrade their capacities severely in other areas, a self-derogation

that often becomes a self-fulfilling prophecy. Good teachers and psychotherapists recognize the ways in which self-esteem may be split in such
ways. The positive areas of self-confidence and actual functioning can then
be used as the mobilizing forces and assets in the struggle to change the
negative, self-defeating areas of self-devaluation.

What Parents Can Do

Parents are a vital factor in shaping the growing child's sense of self and
determining the kind of self-esteem the youngster develops. This influence
shows itself in the daily routine activities of the household, as well as in
the handling of special events and experiences.

As we have shown, goodness of fit and the development of a healthy
self-esteem are intimately related. Any parental attitude, reaction, or behavior with the child that promotes goodness of fit will stimulate the
blossoming of a strong sense of self in the child. Any pattern of parental
functioning that leads to a poor fit between parent and child is all too likely
to undermine the child's self-confidence and self-esteem.

It is the parents who are in the best position to give their child the
recognition of achievement that is so fundamental to the growth of healthy
self-esteem. Real achievement is not limited to unusual, spectacular accomplishments. Rather, the more important achievements for parents to
recognize and praise are the developmental landmarks—task masteries and
social competencies that all normal children achieve, such as walking,
talking, toilet training, self-feeding, self-dressing, and keeping up with
peers socially and academically. These are the important accomplishments
to appreciate, just because they occur sequentially in the course of normal
development. Parental recognition and appreciation provide the child with
the affirmation that he is growing up the way he should be and that he is
capable of mastering the new challenges that life is always bringing.

Some parents, however, go overboard in their expressions of delight and
praise for their child's routine developmental progress and achievements.
Knowing that such praise is important, they make too much of a good
thing. Or they may be so pleased at the magic of their child's development
(and the child's maturation is truly magical) that they spontaneously exclaim with delight and excitement at every new accomplishment of their
child. Whatever the reason, such excessive praise by the parents will not
foster the child's self-esteem. The child knows he is taking important steps

forward, but he also knows that they are not extraordinary; he sees other children following the same course of development. The parents' unbounded enthusiasm then has a false ring and is likely to confuse the child rather than serve to reinforce a positive sense of self.

Other parents may hesitate to correct, criticize, or frustrate their child, for fear that such "negative" actions will hinder the youngster's growth of self-esteem. But as we will discuss in chapter 15, the parent is the first and best teacher the child has. The parent can communicate criticisms as a friend who cares and who wants the child to learn the lessons he needs to thrive in the outside world. If the parent holds back, the child is all too likely to be a tyrant in the home, a role that does not foster the development of a healthy sense of self. When the child finally has to learn these lessons in the outside world, the experience may be harsh and unfriendly, not conducive to a sense of self-esteem.

Unfortunately, there are some parents who find it difficult or impossible to give their children the praise they deserve. A parent may have unrealistic standards of accomplishment. Many a youngster has been crushed when he brought home an impressive school report card, only to have the parent say, "Not good enough. You have one B+, and you should have all A's." Or a parent may become competitive with the child and downgrade his achievements. A parent may be disappointed in the child, failing to understand and appreciate the special interests that absorb him. Some parents may have serious psychological problems of their own which prevent them from making a positive emotional contact with their children or other people. In this case, even if the parent does offer praise for a child's accomplishments, it is likely to have a cold or perfunctory character that does not help the child's self-esteem. A severe psychiatric problem in a parent can certainly damage the child's ability to grow in self-confidence, but this is not always the case. If the child receives sufficient positive feedback from other members of the family, from friends, and from teachers, the one parent's negative or even hostile judgments can be more than balanced by the opposite responses he receives from other people.

Parents of younger children should be especially alert to the issue of self-esteem. A younger child's accomplishments may seem to him meager and unimpressive compared with the more advanced and exciting things his older brother or sister is able to do. The parents are the ones who can put the younger child's abilities, successes, and achievements in perspective, assuring him that they are important and that when he reaches his older brother or sister's age he will be able to duplicate their accomplishments in his own way and in his own style.

Parents should always remember that the process of development is uneven from one normal child to another. Some blossom early and gain recognition easily. Others are "late bloomers," and the parents may easily fail to recognize the early positive signs of the potential of such children. For example, the best and the worst class athletes may both have walked at the same time. The late talker may blossom into the star of the debating team.

Parents do play this vital role in influencing their child's sense of self and self-esteem. But, as in other areas of child development, the family does not operate in a social vacuum. Outside factors, such as racism, sexism, and religious or class prejudice, may harm a child's self-esteem, sometimes drastically. Parents can often do a great deal to overcome the effects of such social prejudices, but they cannot always cancel out the effects of such noxious social forces. There may also be an unexpected, unpredictable event in an older child or adolescent's life that has a profound effect on his self-esteem, for good or for bad.

Everything is not settled in the first few years of life. Parents are also not omnipotent; their influence is vital, but it does not decide everything in the child's future. And, finally, their mistakes with a child are not fatal. They can misjudge their child's behavior, praise too much or too little, but they and their child always have many chances to recover from such an error.

10

Sex Differences and Gender Identity

T HERE HAVE BEEN many dramatic developments in the field of child development, and we have documented a number of them. Ideas about the newborn and her psychological capacities and readiness for human social relationships have been revolutionized. Old concepts that viewed the newborn as inept, undifferentiated, and incapable of functioning as a human being have been swept away.

Another area of fruitful research that has challenged traditional shibboleths is that of sex differences. How do girls and boys differ from each other, and why? These studies have decisively challenged the prevalent ideas of the past that females are intellectually inferior to males, passive and clinging where males are assertive and active, and controlled by impulsive subjective states in place of the calm rationality of the male sex.

Traditional Views of Sex Differences

Many reasons have been given with glib assurance, though without evidence, to justify these sexist judgments, just as similar unverified pronouncements have been given to justify prejudices against blacks or other racial or ethnic groups. The best-known and most influential professional formulation of sexism came from Freud. According to Freud, the young girl notices that she lacks the penis that boys possess, becomes jealous and envious, and even fears that she has been castrated. This "penis envy," as he called it, was thought to have profound permanent effects on a girl's psychological development. Freud charged,

> Character traits which critics of every epoch have brought up against women —that they show less sense of justice than men, that they are less ready to submit to the great necessities of life, that they are more often influenced in their judgments by feelings of affection or hostility—all these would be amply accounted for by the modification of the super-ego which we have already inferred. We must not allow ourselves to be deflected from such conclusions by the denial of the feminists, who are anxious to force us to regard the two sexes as completely equal in position and worth. (1950, p. 197)

Freud assumes that the way in which men make moral judgments is the standard, and if women use different rules, then they are modifying what is the correct position. It is pertinent to note that the paper in which he made this sweeping sexist formulation was titled "Some psychological consequences of the anatomical distinction between the sexes." And women could not change this formulation, for his dictum was that "biology determines destiny."

Freud was the master, and his dictates were sacred to his followers. As late as 1944, with all the activity and struggle in the feminist movement, one of Freud's most prominent followers, Helene Deutsch, a Boston psychoanalyst, faithfully repeated Freud's prejudices. Women were narcissistic, passive, and masochistic; these were fixed, unchangeable characteristics. Women who entered fields of work previously closed to them were becoming "masculinized," and they should give up these attempts and return to the home (1944). Lest this seem to the younger generation as some kind of caricature, we can testify that we remember clearly how Deutsch's book was taken seriously and quoted by all too many mental health professionals (few of whom bothered to note that while writing her book Deutsch was not "staying at home" but working as a psychoanalyst, a field certainly dominated by men at that time). Girls and women were not just different from men; they were inferior in a host of qualities prized by our society—assertiveness, concern for others, a sense of moral judgment, and rational control of one's emotions.

Challenges to the Traditional Views

It was not until the 1930s and early 1940s that a group of psychoanalysts in the New York area openly and directly challenged this Freudian shibboleth within the psychoanalytic movement. This group, which included among others Karen Horney, Clara Thompson, Judd Marmor, and Bernard Robbins, questioned a number of Freud's formulations that relied on an unproven theory of biologically determined instincts and ignored the crucial role of social and cultural factors. Most emphatically, they pointed out that the sexist prejudices and discrimination of society could well account for the special psychological problems suffered by many women. There was no need to invoke a fatalistic "penis envy" explanation.

Furthermore, these analysts pointed out that the behavioral characteristics that society, including psychoanalysts, ranked as desirable happened to be those most evident in white males. The same attribute would be given a positive label in a male and a negative label in a female. For example, assertiveness in a male was "initiative" and "praiseworthy ambition," but in a female it became "aggressiveness" and "hostility," further "proof" of penis envy. And if a woman asserted herself with a man, she was labeled as a "castrating" female, intent on depriving him of his masculinity.

It took a great deal of professional courage, a half-century ago, for psychoanalysts to challenge openly certain of Freud's basic theoretical concepts, especially one so firmly entrenched as penis envy. The authors of such deviations risked ostracism from the orthodox psychoanalytic establishment (the equivalent of excommunication). In fact, this group suffered that fate, but it left them free to explore new ideas and treatments without concern over whether they were orthodox or some kind of heretic.

Theories of the presumed inferiority of female children were further undermined by the recent succession of careful research studies on normal infants and children. These studies were compiled and analyzed in 1974 in a monumental volume, *The Psychology of Sex Differences*, by Eleanor Maccoby and Carol Jacklin, two psychologists from Stanford University (1974). These authors reviewed over 1,400 studies of subjects ranging in age from birth to maturity. They could find evidence for only four behavioral differences between the sexes: (1) girls have greater verbal ability than boys; (2) boys excel in visual-spatial behavior; (3) boys excel in mathematical ability; and (4) males are more aggressive. As to the basis for even these few differences, Maccoby and Jacklin concluded that "there are probably not very many initial biologically based behavioral differences" (p. 343).

Several studies typical of the many hundreds tabulated by Maccoby and Jacklin can be cited. One study measured the relative variability of intelligence of 10,070 subjects, aged eight to thirteen, on a National Intelligence Test. No sex differences were found (Rigg 1940). In another study of 152 college students, the subjects initially completed two self-esteem measures and an intelligence test. At a second session, the subjects were informed either that they had done extremely well or that they had done extremely poorly on the intelligence test. The subjects then completed both self-esteem measures again. No sex differences were found in the changes that occurred between the first and second self-esteem ratings, either in the subjects who were told they did very well or in those who were told they had done very badly (Nisbett & Gordon 1967). In another study, measures of vocabulary and grammatical skills were given to 127 subjects, aged three to five. No sex differences were found (Mehrabian 1970).

Our own findings in the New York Longitudinal Study have been similar to those of other researchers. We made a number of comparisons between the girls and the boys in the total group of 133 subjects, including temperament in the first five years and in early adult life, adjustment at three years, adjustment at five years, and adjustment in early adult life. No striking sex differences were found. Out of seventy-nine comparisons of sex difference, only nineteen were statistically significant, and these were scattered in random fashion throughout the different ratings. With the statistical methods used, these few differences are most likely due to chance and without any functional meaning. The only consistent significant finding was a higher activity level for boys, found in years one and three and in early adult life (Chess & Thomas 1984). Several other studies of sex differences in temperament in infancy have been reported from Sweden, Taiwan, and Quebec. In all instances, the sex differences found were scattered and in general inconsistent (p. 93).

In a recent review, Jacklin and Maccoby emphasize the smallness of the differences that exist between boys and girls. They make the basic point that "there is very little to explain. . . . Despite the biological importance of sex, many aspects of human functioning are not dimorphic with regard to sex" (1983, p. 176).

So much for Freud's assertion that "biology determines destiny."

A few studies have tended to exaggerate the importance of certain small sex differences in the newborn infant by speculating on their influence on later development. For example, one investigator reported that the female newborn is "orally sensitized" (itself a dubious generalization from the evidence). She then related this presumed sex difference in the newborn to certain forms of psychiatric disturbances more frequently found among adult women than among adult men (Korner 1973). Considering all the many factors that influence the course of psychological development from one age period to another, to make such a conceptual leap from the newborn to the adult—and without any evidence to boot—is certainly without merit.

The most decisive blow to sexist ideas, prejudices, and practices came from the women's liberation movement. Its struggles have gone far to destroy the stereotypes that have served to keep women in an inferior position, as women have successfully assumed professional, administrative, and executive roles. In the realm of psychological theory, the feminist writers have been especially effective in exposing the fallacious nature of theories of female inferiority, whether they derive from Freud's "penis envy" or from other pseudoscientific concepts. No respected psychiatrist or psychologist, no matter what some of them might think privately, would now attempt to advocate a theory of child development that labeled female children as inherently inferior to males.

The battle for equal rights for women has had many successes in recent years, but many hard struggles still remain to be fought out. It is distressing, for example, how many well-intentioned men will still comment, "Oh, well, it doesn't matter if we don't encourage our daughter academically. She's going to get married and be busy raising children." The issues of sex differences in child development and the differential attitudes of parents and others to girls versus boys not only are important questions in their own right but may also shed light on some of the debates over the origin and nature of sex differences in later life.

Actual Differences and Their Possible Causes

There is, of course, no question that females and males differ profoundly biologically. The differences on the physical, endocrinologic, and neurophysiological level are areas of extensive current research by many investigators. An ironic comment is in order at this point. With all the stereotyped ideologies and prejudices concerning the superiority of males, it turns out that male infants and boys are actually physiologically more vulnerable than girls. More males are conceived than females, perhaps 20 percent more. But death of the fetus and deaths at birth are more common among males, so that the number of live full-term male infants is only slightly larger than that of female infants (Jacklin & Maccoby 1983). Girls usually begin to speak earlier than boys, and their language development is more rapid. Girls most often also reach puberty and full adult height earlier than do boys. On the other hand the average newborn boy weighs more than the average newborn girl, and during childhood boys are taller and have a greater proportion of muscle mass.

Finally, the life expectancy of women is significantly longer than that of men. The phrase "the weaker sex" should not be applied to either sex, but certainly when it comes to speed of maturation and life expectancy, there is nothing weaker about the female sex. Our concern in this chapter is with the psychological: what differences exist in young girls and boys in behavior, thinking, and emotional patterns; the origins of such differences; the influence these differences have on the course of psychological development; and how parents can provide a positive healthy force in areas where sex differences appear to be important. Of special interest is the fact, confirmed by one study after another, including our own longitudinal studies, that boys are significantly more susceptible to a number of psychological and psychiatric disorders, including behavior problems in general, hyperactivity, dyslexia (difficulty in learning to read), and even autism. By adolescence, this sex difference tends to level off (Chess & Thomas 1984).

The Influence of Biological Factors

Aside from the specific vulnerabilities of boys to certain psychiatric disorders, there is no evidence for any significant biological differences in the behavioral attributes and styles of girls versus boys in the newborn or in infancy. As we saw earlier in this chapter, Maccoby and Jacklin did find sex differences in four areas with older children, although they emphasize the relative unimportance of these differences next to the marked preponderance of sex similarities. Two of the differences—superior verbal ability in girls and superior visual-spatial ability in boys—may very well have a biological basis, but it is plausible that they are not innate differences in brain functioning fixed for life, inasmuch as no substantial evidence exists for the persistence of these differences in adult life. Rather, they appear to be the result of differences in the speed of maturation of various physiological and psychological functions. Thus, girls usually reach puberty earlier than boys, but then boys catch up. The same sequence is probably true for the childhood sex differences in verbal and visual-spatial abilities.

The differences in mathematical ability could be the result of biological factors or environmental influences from inside and outside the family, or both. We do not have the facts at hand to decide definitively among these alternatives. In any case, the differences found between the sexes in mathematical ability show considerable overlapping. In other words, a substantial number of girls are above average and some even highly superior in this talent, even if the average for all girls may not match that for boys. It would be entirely wrong, therefore, to discourage a girl who shows an interest in mathematics. She should be given the same opportunities as any boy to develop this interest and have the same career opportunities to use her mathematical abilities.

The significance of the fourth sex difference found by Maccoby and Jacklin—aggressiveness—is especially controversial. Some authorities, including Freud, have assumed that wars and other evidences of violent behavior in so many societies must be due to an innate biological aggressive instinct (Lorenz 1966). But such an assumption would be a retrogressive step in our concepts of human psychological development. All our research and knowledge has pointed to the conclusion that complex human personality characteristics are not based on predetermined fixed instincts. They may have a biological basis in some instances, but essentially they are the result of what we *learn* from our family and from society as we grow up. Concerning human aggressiveness and wars, the psychiatrist Judd Marmor has pointed out:

> Other widespread social institutions of man's past, like slavery, dueling, ritual human sacrifice and cannibalism, which in their times and milieus seemed equally rooted in human nature and destiny, have been, in the course of history, almost entirely eliminated. It is also a fact that various societies have existed without recourse to war for many generations. (1974, pp. 374–75)

But in our society, the aggressive male, ready to give battle and inflict violence, continues to be the role model for boys in a host of popular movies and television shows. This alone would be sufficient to account for findings of a greater tendency for boys to be aggressive as compared to girls. It is our own firm conviction, therefore, even if the scientific evidence is still incomplete, that sex differences in aggression are the result of learning and not due to any biological "instinct."*

*In a recent article in the *New York Times Magazine* (4 August 1985), two Harvard professors, Richard Herrnstein and James Wilson, assert that the evidence from a number of studies indicates a biological genetic factor in the causation of criminal behavior. They cite evidence to this effect from projects that have used the standard research methods for studying genetic differences in individuals and groups. In these studies crime is also found to occur much more frequently in males than in females. The authors agree that this sex difference can be explained purely on the basis of social factors, but they assert that the accumulated evidence indicates a biological factor as well. They do not opt for a discredited instinct theory but propose that crime, especially with the repeat offender, is caused by a "combination of predisposing biological traits channeled by social circumstances into criminal behavior" (p. 30). They speculate that the biological factors may involve intelligence and temperament, but the evidence they present to support this view is weak. Herrnstein and Wilson's overall thesis

Girls and Boys Are Treated Differently

Although there is evidence for only modest biological sex differences, there is an impressive body of research demonstrating the great range and depth of the differences in social attitudes, biases, expectations, and judgments of girls versus boys as they grow up. A systematic and thorough review of this research by Beverly Birns, a psychologist at the State University of New York at Stony Brook, concluded that "it seems evident that the environment in which all American children mature clearly projects sex-role stereotypes. These stereotypic expectations and the differential responses they elicit are sufficiently clear and unambiguous to account for the cognitive and personality differences in children that ultimately lead to the different roles they fulfill" (1976, p. 252).

Two studies out of a multitude of others can be cited in support of this conclusion. John and Sandra Condry enlisted 204 young adults to rate the same infant's emotional responses. Four different stimuli were used, such as pushing a teddy bear toward the child and then pulling it back. The adults were asked to rate the emotional responses of the infant to these stimuli. Half the raters were told they were observing a boy and the other half that they were observing a girl. The researchers found that the response of the same infant in the same particular situation were rated differently depending on the sex attributed to the infant, the sex of the rater, and the rater's experience with young children (1976).

In our New York Longitudinal Study, for those children with behavior problems, we emphasized the treatment procedure of parent guidance, described in chapter 5. Parent guidance was at least somewhat successful and sometimes very successful in the majority of cases in each temperamental pattern group with the exception of the distractible, nonpersistent youngsters. There were four cases of behavior disorder in the distractible, nonpersistent children, and these were all boys. In all four cases, parent guidance was a failure. For the parents of these youngsters—and this was true for the longitudinal study families as a whole—persistence and low distractibility were considered essential to success in professional careers or business. They did attach great importance to academic achievement for their daughters as well as their sons. But they showed little concern if their daughters were nonpersistent temperamentally. A successful career for the girls was not of great importance to them. The opposite was true in their attitude toward their boys. A distractible, nonpersistent boy was labeled

---

certainly cannot be rejected out of hand, given the studies they cite. On the other hand, neither can it be considered as proven. Further detailed studies are required, which the authors themselves recommend.

as "weak willed," "lacking in stick-to-it-iveness," and not likely to succeed in his work. The demands for change that the parents made on these
boys were unattainable and only resulted in problem development. In no
way could we convince the parents to accept their sons' temperament as
normal, and all our counseling was unsuccessful. The difference in parental
standards and expectations for their sons as contrasted to their daughters
was indeed sharply highlighted through these four cases.

Differences in Moral Judgment

In the past few years, a new dimension to the debate over sex differences
and their psychological significance has been introduced by the work and
writings of the Harvard psychologist Carol Gilligan. The arena for this
dispute lies in the proposition of the psychologist Lawrence Kohlberg that
moral judgment develops through a sequence of six invariant stages (1976).
Through his research studies on adolescent males, Kohlberg defined these
six stages and ranked them in order from the most immature to the most
mature level.

The earliest stage consists of an obedience and punishment orientation:
In the second stage, rules are followed when they are in the immediate
interest of the child or another person. The youngster then progresses
through stages in which goodness is equated with helping and pleasing
others, then a stage when relationships are subordinated to social values
and rules. In the sixth and most mature stage, moral judgments are based
on self-accepted universal principles of justice. According to Kohlberg,
only a small minority of adults ever reach this sixth highest level of moral
development. He further claims that "the stage sequence in moral development is universal; the same sequence is found in all cultures, subcultures
or social class structures" (1978, p. 210). Kohlberg's thesis has stimulated
a great deal of interest and research in developmental psychology. Its
similarity to the cognitive stage sequence proposed by Piaget has also made
the concept more persuasive to some investigators. Kohlberg's scheme has
also received severe criticism from a number of sources, however. Its claim
to cultural universality has been challenged, and moral development has
been found to be "far more reversible than in Kohlberg's model" (Vaillant
1977, p. 343). A leading methodologist's analysis of Kohlberg's data leads
him to doubt whether "there is any systematic interrelationship between
the responses to his set of moral judgment items that would warrant the
use of the stage concept with regard to them" (Wohlwill 1973, p. 198).

Gilligan's challenge to Kohlberg's thesis is on another level. She has
pointed out that his studies were conducted entirely with males and has

noted that "in the research from which Kohlberg derives his theory, females simply do not exist" (1982b, p. 18). Furthermore, Kohlberg speculates that mature women not working outside the home will reach only his third stage of development. These deficiencies imply, in Gilligan's words, "that only if women enter the traditional arena of male activity will they recognize the inadequacy of this moral perspective (helping and pleasing others) and progress like men toward higher stages" (p. 18).

In her major work, *In a Different Voice,* and in her other writings, Gilligan has proposed an alternative concept. Her thesis is that because the social attitudes and relationships females experience as they grow up are different from those of males, the development of their moral judgment differs fundamentally from Kohlberg's six stages. One example from her studies can be cited to illustrate her findings. Kohlberg's basic method in testing levels of moral judgment is to present the subject with a series of dilemmas and then explore the logic of the subject's resolution of each dilemma. In one of his well-known items, a poor man, Heinz, needs a drug to save his wife's life but cannot afford to buy it. The subject is asked, "Should Heinz steal the drug?" and is then questioned further to get at the reasoning behind the answer.

Gilligan posed this question separately to two eleven-year-olds, Jake and Amy (1982a). The children, both highly intelligent, were in the same grade in school and had similar social backgrounds. Amy was interested in science, while Jake preferred math. Jake was clear that Heinz should steal the drug, because a human life is worth more than money, and that the judge should give Heinz the lightest possible sentence. Amy, by contrast, gave what appeared an evasive answer. Heinz should not steal; "I think there might be other ways, like if he could borrow the money or make a loan or something, but he shouldn't steal the drug, but his wife shouldn't die either." Also, Amy was worried over the long-term consequences if Heinz had to go to jail. "His wife might get sicker again . . . so, they should really talk it out and find some other way to make the money."

Gilligan points out that Jake would deal with the dilemma through systems of logic and law, while Amy would deal with it personally, through communication. According to Kohlberg's system, Amy, although she was as thoughtful and mature as Jake, would score a full stage lower in "moral maturity" than the boy. Gilligan has pursued this issue with several research groups and concludes,

Women's construction of the moral problem as a problem of care and responsibility in relationships rather than as one of rights and rules ties the development of their moral thinking to changes in their understanding of responsibility and relationships just as the conception of morality as justice ties development to the logic of equality and reciprocity. Thus the logic underlying an ethic of care is a psychological logic of relationships, which contrasts with the formal logic of fairness that informs the justice approach [as in men]. (1982a, p. 73)

Gilligan's reports and ideas have produced intense controversy in the field of developmental psychology. Many agree with her concepts and consider them a major contribution to our understanding of sex differences and their significance. Others have been sharply critical of her methodology and broad generalizations. It is also claimed that when men and women of similar education and occupation are compared, the sex differences disappear (Colby & Damon 1983).

Whatever the final judgment may be on Gilligan's work, in our opinion it has already made important contributions. She has exposed the sex bias in a number of psychological studies; unfortunately it is not restricted to Kohlberg's work. She has highlighted the fact that a number of psychological reports and theories have been based on investigations of exclusively male samples and the findings have then been generalized to include women as well. We remember attending a meeting on psychological research shortly after Gilligan's book was published. In the course of the discussion, someone in the audience raised the question of the pertinence of Gilligan's work to the discussion then under way. One of the male speakers, up to then the model of a calm, objective scientist, jumped up and blurted out, "I'm sick and tired of hearing about Gilligan." A scientific training and career unfortunately does not immunize one against sexist ideas.

Gilligan's work also suggests that whether or not Kohlberg's system is valid, the differential life experiences of girls and boys can result in profound differences in the moral values they develop. Of course, the differences will not always be clear-cut: some males may treasure moral principles more typical of females, and some females may hold moral beliefs like those of most men.

Finally, Gilligan has not attempted to make a value judgment on the differences between females and males, as Kohlberg and others have done. Males and females may differ as a rule in their moral judgments, but both types have their values. They are different, but one is not necessarily superior to the other. This view corresponds to our own thesis that children may differ in temperament, but all these differences are normal. Beyond this, it is consonant with the age-long battle to establish that differences in race, religion, color, nationality, or socioeconomic class do not make one person inherently superior and another inherently inferior.

Homosexuality

While parents' concerns that their son's or daughter's interests and behavior may be signs of homosexuality are often unfounded, many parents do eventually learn that their adolescent or adult daughter or son is homosexual. The discovery is always a blow. Even sophisticated parents who accept the growing consensus on the rights of homosexuals will wish it were otherwise with their own child, for homosexuals usually have to cope with special problems and conflicts in our society, which may complicate their careers and personal relationships. The less liberal-minded parents, bound to the traditional derogatory and hostile stereotypes regarding homosexuality, are likely to respond to their homosexual son or daughter with varying mixtures of anger, confusion, condemnation, contempt, and disbelief. Such parents may finally accept the situation, though often with the secret or outspoken attitude that "if he only had enough determination, he could change." Others may in effect disown their child.

It is of interest that hostile condemnatory attitudes toward homosexuals are generally much more intense toward male than toward female homosexuals. Many people seem to find it an outrage, and perhaps even a challenge, that a man should be ready to sacrifice the masculine attributes which give him such advantages in our society over "inferior" women. It has also been speculated that this hostility stems from men's unconscious fears of their possible latent homosexuality. There is no firm evidence to substantiate or refute this speculation. In any case, it would not explain the hostile attitudes of many women toward male homosexuals.

Added to the distress of parents with a homosexual offspring are the haunting questions "Was it our fault? If we had treated her differently when she was a child, would it have been different?" And these are by no means academic questions. A great deal of the psychiatric writing on the subject, especially in the past, has asserted that homosexuality is indeed the result of the parents' characteristics and their upbringing of the child. Homosexuality, in this view, is not due to biological, biochemical differences but is rather learned by the child who grows up in an unhealthy family environment. A comprehensive review of the subject in 1975 by Judd Marmor concluded that "the most prevalent theory concerning the course of homosexuality is that which attributes it to a pathogenic family background" (p. 1513). As an example, one widely quoted study (Bieber et al. 1962) concluded that male homosexuality is caused by a detached, hostile father and a close-binding, seductive mother who dominates and minimizes her husband. But, as Marmor points out, many boys grow up with such parents and do not become homosexuals. This study, and other similar ones, are also seriously faulted by methodological weaknesses. The conclusions are drawn from patients undergoing treatment for various symptoms, the psychiatrists treating them are biased in favor of finding the cause in early childhood, and there are no adequate control groups of similar men but without symptoms or homosexuality for comparison.

This does not mean that psychological factors, such as fear of or hostility toward members of the opposite sex, may not be important in individual cases. But such reactions may develop during a child's upbringing for many reasons not necessarily related to the personalities of the parents and their behavior toward each other and the child.

Biological factors also have been investigated as possible causes of homosexuality. While there have been some suggestive findings, none have been conclusive (Marmor 1975, p. 512).

Social environmental influences do seem significant. The great variability in the frequency of homosexuality in different societies, depending on the favor or disfavor with which it is viewed, attests to this. The frequency of male homosexuality in ancient Greece comes to mind. Other external situational factors can also make a difference, as witness the increase in homosexual practices in men or women living in groups isolated from the opposite sex. Even economic factors may play a part. Marmor reports that homosexuality is frequent among the Chukchee people of northern Siberia, apparently as the result of the high purchase price of a wife, which few men can meet (1975).

A comprehensive study of homosexuality done with careful attention to methods has finally come recently from the Kinsey Institute (Bell et al. 1981), which is famous for its careful and large-scale studies of human sexual behavior. Three- to five-hour interviews were conducted by specially trained interviewers with 575 white and 111 black male homosexuals and 229 white and 64 black female homosexuals. An adequate sample of heterosexual men and women matched for race, sex, age, and educational level were also interviewed. Most of the subjects had never received psychiatric treatment. A specialized, powerful statistical method called path analysis was used to analyze the data. The major weakness of the study is that it had to rely on retrospective recall—that is, the memory of earlier life events recalled years later. Such recall, we know from longitudinal studies such as our New York Longitudinal Study, is subject to gaps, biases, and distortions. Other studies of homosexuality have also relied on retrospective recall to obtain their data, however. To eliminate the problem by doing a longitudinal study would be a complicated and expensive undertaking, considering the thousands of families who would have to participate to obtain a substantial number of children who become homosexual, and the complexity of the data that would have to be collected.

The Kinsey Institute study found that neither closeness to the mother nor a negative or seductive mother-son relationship was a causative factor in male homosexual preference. About half the male homosexuals had less favorable relationships with their fathers than did their male heterosexual counterparts. However, the statistical path analysis of the data showed that the bad relationship was a *consequence* and not a *cause* of the son's homosexuality.

Among the females, whether homosexual or heterosexual, most reported having had good relationships with their mothers, although a larger percentage of the homosexual women did describe unsatisfactory relationships with their mothers. A more common finding was a poor relationship with the father among the homosexual women, while very close relationships with the father were rare.

Homosexual preference in both boys and girls was usually determined before adolescence by the emergence of homosexual feelings, though actual sexual activity may not have begun for several years or more.

Gender nonconformity in childhood was not strongly predictive of later homosexual development. Thus, while half of the homosexual men reported interests and activities in the traditionally masculine direction as boys, nearly a quarter of the heterosexual men were interested as boys in the traditionally feminine interests. Similarly, both the homosexual and heterosexual women reported a high incidence in "tomboy" activities in their early years.

The Kinsey Institute study concludes that there is no one causal model that explains all cases of homosexuality. The researchers lean cautiously and tentatively toward the concept of a deep-seated biological predisposition, though they concede that their findings might be due to some type or types of "early learning experience." It is clear from their findings that no single pattern of family relationships exists for all homosexuals. As Marmor puts it in his review of this study, "Efforts to 'explain' homosexuality in terms of a single type of interpersonal model or family constellation are both simplistic and reductionistic" (1982, p. 960).

Our own findings from the New York Longitudinal Study confirm Marmor's judgment. Thus far, three of the subjects, one male and two females, have become fixed homosexuals by early adult life. Our detailed information on the parents and on these three subjects from early childhood onward does not reveal any consistent pattern in the parents, their relationships to each other or their relationships to the child. In none of the cases could we say, "If the parents had done this or that differently, the sexual outcome in the youngster would have been different."

One of us (S.C.), in the course of a private child psychiatry practice over many years, has seen in follow-up seven homosexual adolescents who had been treated for a behavior disorder in earlier childhood. In reviewing their records, we found that in no case could we have predicted the sexual outcome. Nor was there any single pattern in the family relationships; they were all different.

The complexity of this issue of the origins of homosexuality is illustrated in a remarkable study by John Money and Jean Dalery, of Johns Hopkins University (1976). They identified seven individuals who were biologically female on the basis of chromosome studies but who had been born with a penis as the result of excessive fetal excretion of adrenal hormones before birth. Four had had surgical removal of the penis in early childhood, were being reared as girls, and considered themselves females. They played with dolls only rarely, however, and preferred traditional boys' toys such as cars, trucks, and guns. They were too young at the time of this report to make appropriate statements on their romantic interest in boys. The other three individuals, who were older, were reared as boys, considered themselves to be males, and performed sexually as men with women partners.

From this review of the subject, we concur with Marmor's statement that homosexuality is "multiply determined by psychodynamic, socio-cultural, biological and situational factors" (1975, p. 513). The evidence is also clear that homosexuality as such is not a psychiatric illness and can be associated with normal psychological functioning in all other areas. And when homosexuals do show psychological disturbances such as anxiety, guilt, or depression, these symptoms appear to be the result of the stress created by the condemnation of society. A poll of American psychiatrists taken by the American Psychiatric Association in 1974 showed that a majority had come to the conclusion that homosexuality should not be labeled as a mental illness. (Credit should be given to the campaign waged by militant gay groups in challenging psychiatrists to prove that homosexuals were psychiatrically ill.)

Guidelines for the Parent with a Homosexual
Son or Daughter

We offer several suggestions to parents who discover that their son or daughter is homosexual.

First, no matter what your own feelings or prejudices, take the attitude that this discovery does not change your love or respect for the youngster. Homosexuality does not mean—and this is the truth—that the boy or girl is abnormal or a pervert. Do not allow this issue to disrupt your relationship with each other.

Second, if your son or daughter wants professional help to deal with problems created by being homosexual, or if he or she wants to try to change the sexual orientation, by all means encourage this. (It is true, however, that psychiatric and hormonal treatment for homosexuality has been generally unsuccessful.) If the youngster insists that homosexuality is normal and is satisfied with this sexual functioning, do not advise psychiatric treatment. The advice will only fall on deaf ears and communicate the message that you really consider your youngster emotionally ill.

Above all, do not blame yourself. As we have documented above, there is no real evidence that parents are the cause of homosexuality in their children. The causes of homosexuality are still obscure, and they are likely to be multiple, and to vary among different individuals. Much research is required before we will have any definitive answers.

Sexual Stereotypes and the Parent

Some parents today are determined to treat their daughters and sons in exactly the same way. By doing so they hope to avoid the effects of sexist prejudice on both daughter and son. Other parents, at the other extreme, will insist that no matter how social attitudes may have changed, their daughters will be brought up to be "perfect ladies" and their sons "real men," in the traditional sense of these labels.

Our view is that parents should avoid stereotyped goals for their children. The idea that females and males should have identical personalities and value judgments is just as much of a stereotype as the Victorian distinction between a lady and a gentleman. The issue is the same one that we have been making throughout this book: Different children have different interests, talents, and goals. Whenever possible, parents should encourage these individual abilities and interests of their children. They can do so effectively only if they do not confuse these goals with stereotyped judgments about sex difference. Two examples come vividly to our minds.

Some years ago, a father consulted one of us (S.C.) because of his distress at his eleven-year-old son's behavior. The boy had little interest in athletics, especially for the rough-and-tumble varieties. On the other hand, he was developing a passionate interest in the study and collection of insects. The father had no complaints about his behavior otherwise. The boy had friends, was cooperative at home, and did well in school. What was the father's concern? "Well," he asked, "if my son is not interested in manly activities and has such an unusual hobby, doesn't that show that he is becoming a homosexual?" I assured him that the boy's functioning was in no way predictive of his future as far as sex was concerned. As further reassurance, I interviewed the youngster and found no evidence of any abnormalities. I gave the father my positive judgment that he had no basis for his worries and advised him to stop pushing the boy into athletic activities but rather to show that he respected his son's ability to pursue his special interests so diligently. The father followed this advice, but clearly he was not really reassured. He was only convinced when another boy of his son's age and with a similar hobby moved into the neighborhood. This boy was a good and active athlete. The two boys became fast friends, and the example of this other youngster finally convinced the father that a "nonmanly" hobby did not mean anything to his son's future sex life. The succeeding years confirmed this judgment, as the boy developed clear heterosexual interests in adolescence.

The other case concerned another father who consulted one of us (A.T.) because of his concerns over his twelve-year-old daughter. She was a bright, friendly girl who showed no evidence of any behavior disturbance. What, then, was the problem? The father was a surgeon, and he and his family lived in a middle-class suburb in which high academic achievement was greatly prized and emphasized for both daughters and sons. The father's daughter was doing adequate work in school, but in his judgment —with which her teachers agreed—she was capable of doing much better. But the girl made it clear that her real interests did not lie in academic accomplishment but in traditional feminine activities, such as cooking and sewing. The father felt strongly that his daughter had reverted to an outdated period when young women had no choice but to follow such an "inferior" feminine role. I interviewed the girl and found her to be perfectly normal. She confirmed her father's report regarding her interests but felt that they were right for her. I told the father that in his own way he was still reacting according to the age-old prejudices of what was "superior" and what was "inferior" in the behavior of the sexes. Sexual equality did not mean that girls *had to* pursue the same goals as boys. It meant rather that they should have all the same options open to them. And it did not mean that she should be denied a traditional female goal, if that represented a genuine interest. In the same way, if a boy wanted to become a nursery school teacher, or a cook, or a dancer, the fact that so many females were involved in these vocations did not make them "inferior" choices.

The father accepted my professional judgment, but reluctantly. He was startled at my direct implication that he had been acting out of sexist prejudice, when he had prided himself on his liberal attitudes. The girl continued on her way, decided on nursing as a profession, went through her training with zest, and then functioned happily and successfully in this traditional female profession.

Occasionally, a different problem may arise when a boy's personality and interests do not fit the usual masculine stereotype. The parents may be appreciative and supportive of their son's activities and there may be no problem within the home, but outside the home the boy may be labeled "sissy" and scapegoated by his peer group. (It is of interest that girls who used to be criticized and scapegoated as "tomboys" because of their forceful personalities and athletic interests now meet this judgment much less commonly.)

With the boy who is being bedeviled as a "sissy," there are a number of things parents can do. They can reaffirm their support of their son and emphasize that the problem comes from the other boys' prejudices. They can encourage him to stick to his guns, and if he does, in time his age-mates may change their opinion. They can look for a special group or club with activities similar to their son's and arrange for him to participate. They can discuss the problem with the boy's teacher. A good teacher can then work up a project around the life of some famous man who made great contributions in the field of this boy's interests.

The rule for parents is simple: Do not apply sex stereotypes to your children's behavior, activities, and interests. This statement may appear self-evident. As in the cases cited just above, however, sex stereotypes may take many different forms and may be subtle rather than obvious. But parents can always reorient themselves if they catch themselves pressuring a daughter or son to be more "feminine" or more "masculine."

11

The Child Goes Off to School

IN our technologically advanced society a solid education has become a necessity if a youngster hopes to look forward to a good life. It may not be sufficient by itself, but without it, the child who is not born into the small ranks of the upper class is often doomed to a dreary existence in the public welfare system or as a marginal unskilled or semiskilled worker. And the unskilled and semiskilled jobs keep disappearing, together with all kinds of white-collar positions, as their tasks are taken over by automatic machines, computers, and robots. The time of the Horatio Alger dream is gone, when the determined and ambitious young immigrant or farm boy with minimal education could come to the big city carrying his belongings in a small suitcase and a few dollars in his pocket and make his way up the ladder of success step by step.

Just as important, without a good education the child loses the opportunity to enjoy his heritage in the arts and sciences and to apply his knowledge as a responsible citizen and as a guardian of the environment. He is denied the possibility of a quality of life that should be the birthright of every human being.

But, tragically, just as society requires a decent education as a prerequisite for a good life, it does not make the commitment to give every young boy and girl the opportunity to achieve this goal. As it stands now, only the affluent upper-middle classes and the upper classes can guarantee their children a first-rate education. They can utilize the expensive private schools or move to suburbs where the public school system is still highly adequate. If one of their children requires special training in reading or arithmetic, or tutoring in some subject, they can arrange it. They can offer a family and community structure in which all kinds of educational materials and projects are available to supplement the school's curriculum. Teachers find it satisfying and rewarding to work in such settings and with such families.

At the other extreme, the underprivileged children of the inner cities and the poor rural areas face an entirely different prospect. The public school system is deteriorating, federal and local budgets are being cut, many classes are overcrowded, and only a minority of schools have the skilled professional staff to identify children with special learning problems, let alone the resources to provide remedial training for such youngsters. Teachers often have to function with inadequate educational materials and in many areas their salaries are shockingly low; excessive paperwork takes time away from teaching. Under these conditions it is the unusual teacher who can maintain a high morale and a zest for teaching over the years. Demoralization and apathy are the more likely consequences, and again it is the children who are the victims of such a system.

Skilled working-class and lower-middle-class families are caught between these two extremes. They cannot afford the private schools, and they shouldn't have to. Their neighborhood schools are rarely at the optimal level that their children deserve. They can only hope that their children do not develop any special educational problems and are sufficiently ambitious and motivated to transcend the school's limitations and end up as educated adults. On the other hand, whether schools are well or ill endowed, it has been demonstrated that positive leadership of principals and high teacher expectations have a strong relationship to the success of pupils (Lightfoot 1983; Rutter 1980). Fortunately there have been recent indications of rising reading levels across the nation, which we hope is more than a transient phenomenon.

It is not an exaggeration to say that at present one of the most serious failures, if not the greatest failure, of the democratic ideal of our country is in the educational system. Instead of equal opportunity for all, we have huge gaps between the opportunities of the children from affluent families and the deprivations suffered by poor children. And the consequences of these differential educational possibilities are lifelong.

Ironically, our biological inheritance is more democratic than our social structure. As we have detailed in previous chapters, all physically healthy and nonhandicapped children are born with the biological endowment for learning quickly and on a broad scale. Furthermore, cognitive development proceeds systematically and effectively as children's brains mature and as they interact actively with the stimuli and experiences of their everyday life. Biology does set limits; not everybody, no matter how intensively trained, can become a Shakespeare, Picasso, or Einstein. Some children's intellectual development will be within average limits and others will go on to superior levels, even given similar opportunities. But within these limitations, the brain does not discriminate for and against groups of individuals, as society does.

Against this background, we can ask a series of questions for which a number of research studies have given us at least the beginnings of answers. What are the specific factors that distinguish a good from a bad school? What part does temperament play in a child's adaptation to school? What can we expect from "cognitive stimulation"? What are some of the specific problems that children may show in the school setting? What kinds of programs can raise the educational level of underprivileged children? What role can parents play?

Nursery Schools

Private nursery schools for three- and four-year-old children are licensed institutions that have to meet local and state requirements, primarily with regard to adequacy of space and safety and health factors. They take many forms, from small cooperatives formed and run by parent groups to formal institutions associated with private schools. Their quality and curricula vary widely, and no systematic studies have been made of differences in the social or educational effectiveness of different types of nursery schools. In addition to being a social and a beginning learning experience for preschool children, the nursery school may also be a valuable caregiving resource for the mother working outside the home.

Nursery schools provide the three- and four-year-old child with opportunities for group play and goal-directed activities, such as painting, block building, and riding a tricycle. The youngster also learns to take turns, to engage in cooperative play activities, and to follow rules that have social meaning, such as clean-up routines.

These first school experiences can be valuable in introducing the child of any class background—working, middle, or upper class—to the social expectations of the world outside his home. The mastery of the tasks he meets in adapting to nursery school can be important in enhancing his self-esteem and giving him confidence in his ability to adjust successfully to his next school experience.

Now that kindergarten is available to the vast majority of American children, there has been an increasing trend to begin schooling in the earlier years. The Bureau of Census has reported that the number of three- and four-year-olds enrolled in formal preschool programs increased from 1.5 million, or 21 percent of this age group, in 1970 to 2.6 million, or 38 percent, in 1983. The figures for 1984 showed a further increase to 2.7 million. Nearly two-thirds of these children were enrolled in private facilities. The programs vary from sophisticated private nursery schools to the federally subsidized Head Start program to small, informal settings in private homes (Fiske 1986). This wide expansion of early schooling has prompted many educators to recommend dropping the entering school age from six or five years to four years. In New York City, a mayoral commission has recently recommended that a half-day of formal education be made available to all the city's four-year-olds. A fundamental issue still remains to be resolved: Should preschool education concentrate primarily on the development of social skills, which it clearly can do, or should it also emphasize intellectual training, whose value for middle-class preschools has yet to be demonstrated (Fiske 1986)?

A special type of nursery school that attracts parents in many communities is the Montessori school. Maria Montessori was the first woman physician in Italy, receiving her medical degree from the University of Rome in 1894. She became interested in the education of mentally retarded children and utilized specially prepared teaching materials for stimulating their perceptual and motor skills. When her approach led to impressive gains for these children, she turned her attention to her mentally normal child patients who came from underprivileged families. She noted that these children often showed retardation in their perceptual, cognitive, and motor levels as compared with the children from affluent families. Montessori inferred that this relative backwardness resulted from their impoverished, unstimulating environment and that the methods she had used to stimulate the development of retarded children would be useful for these children as well. She established a school for poor preschool children and found that they indeed responded positively to the approach. Her methods —organized techniques of giving children active experiences with shapes, textures, densities, designs, and uses, and linking these experiences with their daily lives at home—were simple and easy to apply. Her success led to the establishment of similar schools in other European countries and the United States. (In her own native country, her schools were closed by Mussolini in 1934 because of her opposition to his fascist regime.)

Montessori schools can be found in many communities in the United States. They have a more structured (though flexible) curriculum than most other nursery schools. Ironically, because these are private schools, they are utilized primarily by middle-class children, rather than by impoverished children, as Montessori intended. They are almost uniformly well-run nursery schools, but whether they provide any special long-term benefits for middle-class children is a question on which there are no reliable data.

Maria Montessori herself is a historical figure to be greatly admired. She was a pioneer in developing concepts and practical methods for the education of underprivileged children. In a sense she can be considered the spiritual parent of such programs as Head Start, Sesame Street, and others that we will consider later in this chapter. Her devotion to the needs of handicapped and underprivileged children was unstinting and lifelong. And it took considerable courage to defy the fascist Italian regime at a time when it was firmly entrenched.

Elementary and High Schools

It might seem self-evident that the resources of a school and the quality of its teachers should make a difference in the kind of education its students receive. The better schools, we would think, should produce graduates with higher academic achievement levels. But sometimes it is hard to prove what is obvious, and sometimes what appears obvious may not actually be true.

Thus until recently the educational research was widely interpreted as showing that the character of a school made very little difference. This view was largely based on an extensive study in the 1960s of some 645,000 students in 4,000 elementary and high schools in this country. The investigators, James Coleman of the University of Chicago, and his associates, concluded that educational achievement was largely unrelated to the kind of school a child attended (1966). The presumption was that it was not the school but the nature of the child's family that was most important in the level of his scholastic success.

The Coleman report, with the impressive size of its sample and its array of statistics, had a wide impact in educational and political circles. Teachers and principals in schools where pupils were doing badly could shrug off any responsibility for such failures by pointing to Coleman's conclusions. Political figures personally opposed to spending more money to help the poor could quote Coleman to justify their opposition to special school programs for underprivileged children. Coleman himself had no intention of letting incompetent or indifferent school authorities off the hook—to say that the family was more important in no way meant that the school made *no* difference—but it was all too easy to use his conclusions to point the finger of responsibility for a child's lack of school achievement at the family rather than the school.

Furthermore, Coleman's findings were based on methods of questionable validity. The data suffered from great unevenness, for they relied heavily on questionnaires filled out by school administrators, teachers, and others whose educational understanding and knowledge of their school's functioning varied widely. The rate of return of the questionnaires was uneven, and in many categories there was a return of less than 50 percent. One cannot know whether the results would have been different if the other 50 percent had also responded. For their direct interviews, Coleman sometimes relied on untrained interviewers with limited knowledge of the issues on which they were gathering information (Deutsch 1969).

The Coleman report was followed in 1972 by a further study along the same lines by Christopher Jencks, of Harvard, and his associates. Using a mass of statistical data from the Coleman report and other studies, Jencks concluded that equalizing the quality of high schools would have an insignificant effect on equalizing cognitive differences. He claimed that "additional school expenditures are unlikely to increase achievement, and redistributing resources will not reduce test score inequality" (1972).

This pessimistic conclusion served to reinforce the stance of many inner-city school principals and teachers that there was little they could do to give their students an adequate education. But here again, the Jencks study had serious weaknesses. These were catalogued by Michael Rutter and his associates at the University of London (1979). To summarize these criticisms briefly: (1) The studies cited by Jencks relied mainly on a single measure of verbal ability. This measure bears little relationship to the subject matter most schools aim to teach. (2) The studies evaluated only a very narrow range of school variables, primarily various aspects of the school's resources. They failed to examine the internal life of the school: its attitudes and values, and its qualities as a social organization. (3) Jencks's analyses were primarily concerned with the question of how far an improvement in the equality of schooling would reduce inequalities in academic achievement. That, however, is not the issue. Individual children show a wide range of differences in their educational potential, so that raising the quality of education cannot result in making all students the same. The issue is rather whether raising the quality of education will affect the group's overall level of achievement, even if individual differences in attainment persist.

Finally, we now have a school study that has avoided the weaknesses and methodological errors of the Coleman and Jencks report. This is a comprehensive and meticulous study of inner-city secondary schools in London, conducted by Rutter and his associates. Their report, published in 1979, is titled *Fifteen Thousand Hours,* the average number of hours a youngster spends in primary and secondary schools. Rutter has a well-deserved international reputation for conducting research studies that are carefully planned, carried out meticulously, and concluded with comprehensive and sophisticated analysis of the data obtained. All these qualities are impressively in evidence in this school study, and *Fifteen Thousand Hours* has been consistently hailed in professional reviews as a definitive and authoritative report, destined to become a classic—a judgment with which we emphatically agree.

The Rutter study involved 1,500 children in one borough in inner-city London who went to twelve different secondary schools. They were assessed at age ten years, just before entering secondary school, and again at fourteen and sixteen years, by means of tests of reading and intelligence and teacher questionnaires on student behavior. The assessment at age sixteen also included their scores on a national examination. A detailed study was also made of the twelve schools, including a wide range of aspects of school life, organization, and functioning. More than two hundred teachers were interviewed in detail; questionnaires were obtained from more than 2,700 students on their school experiences; over five hundred school lessons were observed and rated; a series of observations was made in school corridors and on school playgrounds; and the physical condition of the classrooms and buildings was systematically rated.

The data were coded in a form that permitted detailed quantitative analyses comparing characteristics of the schools with student behavior and academic achievement. These analyses showed large and significant differences among the twelve secondary schools in every measure of student behavior and achievement. As one example, the school results on the national examination scores ranged from more than 70 percent better than the national average level to more than 55 percent below this level. These differences were evident even after due allowances were made for variations among the geographical areas served by the schools and in the proportions of students admitted with behavioral difficulties, social disadvantage, or low achievement in elementary school. Therefore, these striking differences had to be due to differences within the schools themselves. The findings with regard to the schools can be summarized as follows:

1. The differences were not due to differences in financial resources, class size, or overall pupil-teacher ratio. These findings are similar to those of Coleman and Jencks. Rutter does point out that these twelve schools were relatively well funded and that there is likely to be a threshold of funding below which

schools and their students will suffer. Rutter suggests, in line with his findings, that above this threshold, if extra funds are available, cutting the size of each class by a few students is not very helpful. The money would be much more usefully spent, he feels, for expanding special programs such as remedial programs.

2. There were no differences in outcome according to the extent to which children were placed in different tracks according to levels of ability.

3. Good discipline had a crucial effect. But good discipline did not mean more punishment. Punishment was ineffective, and frequent disciplinary interventions in the classroom and constant checking by the teacher or physical punishment made for worse and not better student behavior. On the other hand, praise and approval when the students' work was done well did make a difference. Students behaved better and achieved more when their teachers emphasized their successes and positive potential rather than emphasizing their failings and shortcomings.

4. Students did better in schools that provided a pleasant and comfortable environment and were concerned with the care and decoration of the classrooms and the school generally. Rutter cities other studies that indicate that people work and behave better when they feel that those in charge understand and respond to their personal needs.

5. The social and ethnic mix of the classes did not matter, but a reasonable balance of intellectually able and less able children did make a difference. Rutter points out that this conclusion applies to the London schools he and his colleagues studied, which drew less on ghettos of the kind found in various cities in the United States. In the latter situation, the issue of ethnic and social mix may be more important.

6. Students did better in schools that placed an appropriate emphasis on academic subjects and homework and in schools that gave students opportunities to participate in the running of the school by being form captains or homework monitors or by taking similar responsibilities.

7. The models provided by the teachers were important. For example, student behavior, attendance, and achievement were worse in schools where teachers frequently started lessons late or ended them early. Students also did better if the teachers were prepared for the lesson when the students entered the classroom. Children's behavior was better when teachers spent most of their time with the class as a whole, rather than focusing on particular students.

8. Finally, students did better in schools when curriculum and approaches to discipline were decided and supported by the staff acting together, rather than left to the individual teachers to work out for themselves.

Rutter has commented in a summary lecture on his study,

It is scarcely surprising that children benefit from attending schools that set good standards, where the teachers provide good models of behavior, where they are praised and given responsibility, where the general conditions are good and where the lessons are well conducted. Indeed this is obvious, but of course it might have been equally obvious if we had found that the most important factors were attending a small school in modern purpose-built premises on one site, with a particularly favorable teacher-child ratio, a year-based system of pastoral care, continuity of individual teachers, and firm discipline by which unacceptable behavior was severely punished. In fact *none* of these items was significantly associated with good outcomes, however measured. (1980, p. 218)

The striking differences between the Rutter study on the one hand and those by Coleman and Jencks on the other provides an important lesson for research workers in general, and especially for those whose project can affect public social policies, about drawing conclusions that go beyond the data. Rutter, Coleman, and Jencks came to similar conclusions from their research data regarding the relative unimportance of the school's financial resources in determining the students' educational achievement. Coleman and Jencks went on to draw sweeping conclusions that it mattered little what kind of school a child attended. Rutter, on the other hand, saw that Coleman and Jencks had investigated only *one* aspect of the school's characteristics and had jumped to conclusions based on this narrow view. He recognized that there are many other ways in which the school, as a social institution, could affect students' behavior and academic achievement. Rutter's study included these other factors, which were much more complex and challenging for the researcher to investigate. By doing so, he identified clearly and definitively a number of vitally important ways in which the characteristics of a school can influence the functioning and achievement of its students.

We have presented the Rutter study in detail for several reasons. It is a model of how meaningful research in a complex psychosocial area should be conducted. It reminds us that good research requires that the questions to be investigated should be clearly defined, that the procedures of the study should be adequate to deal with the questions under investigation, that the data should be analyzed with all the meticulous detail required, and that the conclusions reached should rest on a solid foundation of findings and should refrain from judgments not justified by the data of the study.

In addition, the Rutter study is an important social document. It provides parents, educators, and concerned citizens with a report that spells out the requirements for raising the quality of our schools. It is a rebuttal to those who claim that nothing can be done. It gives guidelines to those who want to do something about the education of our children, but who have gone off in directions that have only led to blind alleys.

Temperament, Goodness of Fit, and the School

The school makes a number of new demands on the child. The child must not only master increasingly complex cognitive tasks but at the same time adapt to a new geographic setting, to strange adults in unfamiliar roles, and to a host of new rules and regulations. Peer group activities become more elaborate and challenging, even to the child with previous nursery school experience. A child's adaptation to school, as to his earlier life situations, is determined by goodness of fit, in this case between the child's own characteristics and the demands and expectations of the school.

Children vary tremendously in the ease or difficulty with which they settle into school life. Some breeze along happily from the beginning without turning a hair; others struggle with tension and even distress until they finally achieve a sense of success. And a relatively small minority are overwhelmed by the social or the cognitive demands of school, or both. These are the children who become school problems, sometimes temporarily and sometimes throughout their school life.

The earlier chapters of this book have discussed the issues of temperament and goodness of fit, the capacity for task mastery and social competence, the sense of self-esteem, and the sequences of cognitive development in the young child. All these factors now come to the fore separately and together and interact with the significant characteristics of the school to determine the course of the child's academic and social functioning in school.

A number of specific issues relating to temperament in the school setting are worth further emphasis. Occasionally, a teacher will underevaluate a slow-to-warm-up child's intelligence because of his slow adaptability. (This does not happen with the temperamentally difficult children, probably because their intensity of expressiveness compensates in the teacher's mind for the slowness of adjustment.) An example of this kind of underevaluation of a slow-to-warm-up child occurred with Jane, one of the children in our study. Jane was of superior intelligence, did very well academically in the first grade, and was accelerated to the third grade, skipping the second grade. When our staff member interviewed Jane's third grade teacher during the spring term, the teacher reported that at first, in the fall months, the girl had done badly. She hadn't caught on to the school work and didn't even appear to be paying attention. When the teacher had conferred with Jane's mother at that time, she had suggested that the acceleration was probably a mistake, that Jane was perhaps not intellectually up to this special demand, and that she would be better off going back to the second grade. The mother, who knew and appreciated her daughter's temperament, had told the teacher that this slow beginning was typical of Jane, that the acceleration had confronted her with new classmates and new academic subjects, and that if the teacher were patient Jane would soon begin to improve. The teacher concluded the story by commenting to our interviewer, "I thought this mother was just making excuses for her daughter, as so many do, but I decided to wait. And you know, the mother was right. Jane has now caught up to the rest of the class, is alert, interested, and involved with the other pupils."

This kind of teacher reaction to the slow-to-warm-up child intrigued us, so we did a special study in a suburban kindergarten with the school psychologist, Edward Gordon (Gordon & Thomas 1967). We relabeled our temperamental patterns *quick-* and *slow-to-warm-up* to make them more vivid to the teachers. We defined four groups of children for them along these lines: (1) the plunger, the child who plunges into new activities quickly and positively; (2) the go-alonger, the child who goes along in a positive manner but does not plunge right in; (3) the sideliner, the child who stands on the sidelines waiting, then slowly and gradually gets involved in the new activity; and (4) the nonparticipator, the child who remains a nonparticipator in a new situation for many weeks or months. The plunger corresponded to a quick-to-warm-up child, the sideliner to a slow-to-warm-up youngster. The go-alonger was intermediate, between quick and slow, and the "nonparticipator" was probably a child with some kind of behavior problem.

We asked two experienced kindergarten teachers in this school to rate their ninety-three children on this scale. We also asked them to estimate each child's general intelligence on a scale ranging from very inferior to very superior. The children had as yet not been given IQ tests, so the teachers had nothing to go on but their own impressions.

The children were given an IQ test the following year, and we compared the results with the kindergarten teachers' ratings of the children's behavior and intelligence the year before. We found that, to a significant extent, the teachers *overestimated* the intelligence of the plungers and *underestimated* the intelligence of the sideliners. (Only one child had been rated as a nonparticipator, and this child had moved out of the school district before an IQ was obtained.)

Underestimation of a child's intelligence by a teacher may not be a trivial issue. Teacher judgments can easily be communicated to a student, either openly or subtly (Rosenthal & Jacobson 1969). A youngster who senses that his teacher thinks he is of low intelligence may be easily convinced that this is true, especially if he has a shaky self-image to begin with. Once he believes it, his ability to learn may be affected, and the teacher's judgment then becomes a self-fulfilling prophecy.

Another temperamental attribute that can lead a teacher to underestimate a child's intelligence is low activity level. The child's slowness of movement, and often speech as well, can appear to reflect slowness on an intellectual level. We had several such children in our longitudinal study, and communication with the teacher was necessary to correct this misjudgment. Such a child may also become the class scapegoat, the butt of the other children's ridicule as a "slowpoke." Intervention by the teacher, in consultation with the parents, may be necessary to prevent such a harmful development. It is also important for both teachers and parents to keep emphasizing to such a child that his slowness in movement or speech is not an evidence of anything wrong, that he is perfectly normal, and that he can keep up with his age-mates, even if at a slower pace.

The high-activity child may have difficulties in the classroom because of his restlessness and the stress produced by the demand to sit quietly in his seat for hours at a time. Experienced and sensitive teachers can usually spot such a child easily and give him periodic relief by sending him on errands and asking him to clean the blackboard or distribute books or papers to the rest of the class. Otherwise, such a child may become the class nuisance to the teacher, though less so to the other pupils.

Finally, the temperamental traits of distractibility and persistence may influence significantly the child's school functioning. Teachers may have greater demands for concentration and persistence than the parents' expectations at home. Meeting this demand is easy for the highly persistent child with low distractibility, but difficult for the child with the opposite temperamental constellation of low persistence and high distractibility. This does not mean that the latter child necessarily learns less effectively. He may have to study and do homework in short spurts with frequent breaks, but if the issue is recognized and evaluated correctly by parents and teachers, the youngster can progress as effectively as his more persistent agemates. Tragic consequences can ensue, however, if a demand is made on such a child for a level of concentration and persistence that is impossible for him to meet.

We have had one such case in our longitudinal study. The boy was intellectually bright and highly motivated to learn. His father was a highly persistent worker in his own profession and hard to distract. His son was at the opposite extreme of both these temperamental traits. The father refused to accept this difference as normal, in spite of our numerous discussions with him. He kept insisting that it was an issue of "self-discipline" and "willpower" and that his son was a weakling who lacked these vital characteristics. The boy tried to meet his father's standards but found it impossible. In the face of the continual barrage of criticism by his father, his school performance, which had been high to begin with, and his self-respect deteriorated progressively. By age seventeen he had dropped out of school and was dejected and extraordinarily self-derogatory. "Let's face it," he told us, "my father doesn't respect me, and why should he?" As to the father, he reproached us by saying, "You told me to leave him alone" (a complete distortion of our counseling over the years) "and look at the result." Several courses of psychotherapy failed to change this boy's self-image, and as a young adult he was leading a listless, parasitic life.

Occasionally, high persistence, which is usually an asset in the school situation, can create problems if there is a poorness of fit with the school's expectations. This happens typically if the teacher demands that the youngster immediately drop an activity in which he is absorbed. Some highly persistent children can cope with such a demand even if distressed, but others with a low frustration tolerance may explode violently, with unfortunate consequences for them. This latter sequence happened frequently to one of the boys in our longitudinal study (Richard, whose story is detailed in chapter 9). He finally overcame this problem and is now functioning very well in his late twenties, but the outcome could easily have been different. He could also have been saved the anguish of an unhappy childhood if various teachers had recognized the temperamental issue correctly and had consistently given him advance notice to terminate an activity by a certain time, instead of demanding abrupt and immediate compliance.

Sometimes teachers and parents become concerned at the superior academic achievement of a persistent child who is highly motivated to study and learn. Such a child is called an "overachiever," a label that presumably indicates that the child is doing better academically than would be predicted from his IQ score. He is not behaving according to the statistical tables, so something must be wrong—with him, but not with the statistical tables. But the IQ score is only one predictor of school achievement, and not always an accurate one. Temperamental traits such as persistence and other factors such as motivation for achievement are just as important. We suggest that the term "overachiever" be dropped and a positive designation such as "high achiever" be substituted.

Other Temperament Studies

Barbara Keogh and her associates at the University of California at Los Angeles have done a number of studies using a short form of a temperament questionnaire we have developed for teachers to rate their pupils' temperamental characteristics (Keogh 1982; Pullis & Cadwell 1982). From the ratings obtained from thirty-five teachers, they identified three primary temperamental patterns that appear significant in the school setting. The first pattern, which they call task orientation, is made up of a combination of persistence, distractibility, and activity level. The second, called personal social flexibility, includes approach/withdrawal, quality of mood, and adaptability. The third, called reactivity, is made up of sensory threshold, quality of mood, and intensity. The investigators found a strong and consistent relationship between the pupils' temperamental patterns, as organized in this school-related fashion (especially in the area of task orientation) and various of the teachers' classroom decisions, such as classroom management, work assignments, and class placement recommendations. They also found that the teachers' estimates of their pupils' ability related significantly to their ratings of task orientation and social flexibility.

Keogh summarizes these research findings as showing that "these variations in [temperamental] patterns are clear contributors to teachers' views of pupils' teachability, to the estimates they make of pupils' abilities, and to the kinds of expectations they have for pupils' educational performance" (p. 278). There is the danger that these evaluations may become self-fulfilling prophecies. A teacher's judgment based on the child's temperament rather than on his actual abilities and teachability can easily affect both the teaching approach and the pupil's actual school performance.

Roy Martin and his associates at the University of Georgia, using a revised form of our teacher temperament questionnaire, have also found significant correlations between the child's temperament and teacher attitudes (Martin, Nagle, & Paget 1983).

All these studies make clear how important it is for teachers to be aware that their pupils have individual differences in temperament that are important in the classroom. Keogh notes, "Teachers who have participated in our research have reported that consideration of pupils' temperament has made them more sensitive to their own perception of individual children" (p. 277). This has also been our own experience. We have discussed our research studies with teachers from many different schools over the years. They have consistently told us that learning to shape their classroom decisions to the needs of students with different temperaments, and not to confuse temperament with ability, makes their teaching activities easier as well as more effective.

Cognitive Stimulation

These days parents, and middle-class parents especially, are besieged by advocates of one special program or another that claims to raise the preschool child's IQ and give him a competitive edge over his classmates when he begins his academic studies. Are such special projects of "cognitive stimulation" necessary or desirable? As we have noted earlier, in a middle-class home, as well as in stable working-class families, the child as an infant and a preschooler is exposed to a host of objects and activities that give him sufficient stimulation to ensure adequate cognitive development. The handling of household objects, the imitation of parents' activities and those of any older brothers or sisters, the verbal and nonverbal communication with family members and visitors (as opposed to orders and directives), shopping trips to the supermarket and other stores with their array of fascinating new objects, visits to other homes where he can observe and even participate in different family life style activities, play experiences with age-mates in which he gradually learns all kinds of new rules about social relationships—all these and the many other natural experiences of daily life provide constant stimulation for the young child to learn and to expand his cognitive level.

Playing with educational toys, being read to, and watching TV programs such as "Sesame Street" are useful adjuncts to the child's intellectual development, but there is no evidence that they make an essential difference to the child who is being actively and continuously stimulated in the routines of his daily life. Special programs of "cognitive stimulation" may succeed in raising a child's IQ score temporarily, but not because the program actually raises the child's intellectual potential. Rather, the elevated score is a practice effect; the program teaches the child how to answer the kinds of questions that make up an IQ test. There is no evidence from research studies that such programs have any permanent beneficial cognitive effect on children who are not socially and economically deprived. An analogy can be made to the nutritional needs of a child. If his routine diet is adequate nutritionally, supplying extra vitamins, minerals, or other food supplements will be unnecessary and of no value in increasing physical health. Only if his diet is deficient in some essential element will he need supplementation of his usual food intake.

On the other hand, it is desirable to encourage and assist a preschool child who is eager to learn to read and do simple arithmetic. A generation ago, some experts believed that such early learning could be premature and injurious. A number of private schools in that period also held the same view and refused to start formal instruction in reading until the second grade, when the child was biologically "ready." Again, there is no evidence for such a thesis, and the idea is by now out of fashion. What is true is that children mature at different rates. One child may be ready to learn to read at four years, and another not until he is six. But that does not mean that the slow starter is necessarily intellectually inferior to the early reader, just as early walking and talking are not significantly correlated with later intellectual capacity.

Cognitive stimulation may sometimes be an issue for the truly intellectually gifted child. Such a youngster, who learns very quickly, may easily become bored, restless, and dissatisfied if restricted to a routine academic curriculum. He may even be turned off from learning, which should be an especially exciting adventure for such a gifted youngster. The remedy here is obvious. The school may be able to provide the advanced cognitive stimulation such a child needs, but if not, the parents will have to take the initiative and work out special extracurricular programs to satisfy the youngster's cognitive needs.

The very recent studies in metacognition, described in chapter 8, for the first time offer the possibility of genuine programs of cognitive stimulation even for advantaged children. The discovery that children can begin at an early age to understand how they think and how they gain knowledge opens exciting possibilities for stimulating cognitive development. If children can be trained to comprehend this metacognitive ability, then an increase in learning capacity might be possible. The research in this area is still too recent to be able to make any definitive statements in this regard. And if the studies continue to be promising, we must hope that "metacognitive stimulation" does not become the province of entrepreneurs who exploit it for their own ends and discredit it in the process.

Head Start and Other Programs for
Disadvantaged Children

It is for the socially and economically deprived child that programs of cognitive stimulation as we now know them are important and even vital. Such children all too often suffer from excessively stressful but cognitively unstimulating home environments and attend schools that are likely to be deficient in resources, discipline, and teacher morale. As a result, studies have shown that such deprived children exhibit a cumulative disadvantage over the years on tests of academic achievement (Eisenberg & Earls 1975). The tragic consequences of this deficiency are enormous in terms of school failure, difficulties in job functioning, and antisocial behavior.

As we have seen, the great promise that programs of cognitive stimulation could offer to disadvantaged children was first demonstrated by Maria Montessori in Italy. In this country, pioneering projects in the same direction were conducted by Martin Deutsch and his associates at New York University's Institute for Developmental Studies in the 1950s and 1960s (1967). In a series of carefully planned and executed studies, including comparisons with matched groups who were not given special attention, they showed that continuous intervention procedures with disadvantaged preschool children could have a substantial positive influence on the performance of these children and avoid the cumulative academic failure that otherwise was all too frequent. The programs consisted of a variety of techniques in perceptual and language training, and the positive effects could be measured in both the nursery school and kindergarten years.

The work of Deutsch and several other investigators provided a major impetus for the development of the Head Start program as an important component of the "war on poverty" of the Johnson administration. Other aspects of that program languished and vanished as their usefulness became dubious. Head Start, however, remains a viable and important national program for disadvantaged preschool children, in spite of the onslaughts over the years of many powerful political figures who opposed such a special service for poor children.

The accomplishments of Head Start over the past twenty years have very recently been evaluated by Edward Zigler of Yale University, who was a member of the original planning committee and a former director of Head Start (1985). He points out that one of the basic decisions that faced the planning committee involved the choice between a centralized, uniform, professionally run program and a decentralized set of community projects, conducted equally by parents and professionals. Head Start chose the second option and has stuck to it—wisely, in Zigler's opinion. The rigidity and inertia that are always the dangers with a centralized bureaucracy were avoided, innovation and flexibility were possible, and parents were actively drawn into the programs as advocates for their children. Through participating in the programs, hosts of parents also learned a great deal about normal child development and its application to their own children. This decentralized approach had its price, however. The centers varied widely in the quality of their programs, and no uniform method of monitoring was possible. In many centers, power struggles developed among different community cliques, each laying claim to authority over their particular Head Start unit. Overall, however, as Zigler states, "Head Start has been a place where members of different ethnic and socioeconomic groups learned to cooperate to achieve common goals. While still imperfect with regard to racial mix, Head Start continues to represent the best our nation has been able to do" (pp. 605–6).

A number of the criticisms leveled against Head Start (Jensen 1969) are the result of what Zigler correctly calls "the initial grandiose and unrealistic expectations for the Head Start program. The error of thinking that we could solve the problem of poverty in America with an eight-week intervention for preschoolers . . . is now obvious" (p. 606). That would be like taking an undernourished three-year-old child, giving him an adequate diet for eight weeks, and then sending him back to his original, unhealthy environment and expecting him to maintain his nutritional gains intact. Every year Head Start continues to service more than 100,000 children, who gain valuable health and nutritional services as well as programs of educational stimulation. It is hoped that these benefits do give many of these children a head start that is not lost in their subsequent lives. Head Start has also been a model for the development of myriad medical and social programs intended to improve the lives of disadvantaged children. Zigler is concerned that there is evidence of a falling off in the quality of a number of Head Start programs, that Head Start still reaches only about 20 percent of eligible families nationally, and that it has not been able to develop programs for even younger children. Given the present political climate, our hope of expanding Head Start into a year-long quality program for all disadvantaged preschool children remains a dream—but a dream to fight for, no matter how long it takes.

Other Early Intervention Programs

Head Start, because of the great variability in the nature and quality of its decentralized programs, cannot provide solid evidence of the effectiveness of early intervention programs for disadvantaged children. A number of other carefully conducted early intervention programs, however, each limited to one area and to a few groups of children at most, have been carried through in various parts of the country. Each of these programs has been able to establish uniform procedures for data collection and analysis and to provide information on the long-term effects of the programs. Three of these studies are cited in chapter 7: the Korean adoption center, the collaborative twelve-center study, and the Perry Preschool Project in Ypsilanti, Michigan.

These studies and a number of other early intervention programs, including the Yale Child Welfare Programs, are reviewed in a recent article by Sally Provence, of the Yale University Child Study Center (1985). Overall, the evidence is consistent and impressive. Early intervention projects that combine educational, health, and social services for disadvantaged children and also involve their parents in the program produce substantial and even impressive improvement in academic and social functioning. The Yale Project provided a coordinated set of pediatric, educational, and social services to a group of children from birth to age thirty months and a variety of support measures for the parents in their parental roles. Five years later, at follow-up, the project children had higher IQ scores, better social achievement, and markedly better school attendance than a comparison group who had not received these special services. The beneficial effects were still present in a ten-year follow-up. Provence concludes that the evidence shows that "long-term benefits of early intervention programs appear to be closely linked to the inclusion of parents as active participants in efforts to bring about change and facilitate development" (p. 366).

The evidence is clear. It has been amply demonstrated that early intervention programs can have important positive consequences for poor children. But on a practical level the issue is far from solved. There is no governmental commitment to providing the resources to maintain the quality of existing programs and expand them to include all children who need them. The problem of reaching all parents for active involvement in these programs is formidable, given the never-ending struggles of so many of these parents just to cope with the pressures and problems of their day-to-day existence. And even if effective programs do have long-term effects, these cannot approach the levels possible for middle-class children unless the schools in poor neighborhoods are adequately upgraded. Finally, a youngster's motivation for academic achievement is closely related to the rewards such achievement will bring. Unless adequate jobs are available, schools in the inner cities will all too often appear as dead ends to the children who attend them.

Children with School Problems

Many children show problems at school in their social or academic functioning or both. These can arise from many causes: poorness of fit between the child's temperament and the school's demands, a behavior disorder from some other cause, brain damage, mental illness, or a developmental lag in language development or in the ability to learn to read and do arithmetic. This last group, generally labeled learning disability, has received special attention recently in a number of research studies. In the past, such learning difficulties were assumed by most mental health professionals to be the result of an emotional disturbance, and psychotherapy for the child or the family was routinely recommended. We now know that many of these learning disabilities have a biological basis in lag or other disturbance in maturation of the neurophysiological structures required for learning to read and do arithmetic. In such cases, remedial training of one type or another becomes the treatment of choice.

A special comment is in order with regard to the condition known as *hyperactivity*, because the diagnosis is so often misused, especially in the school setting. The hyperactive child is suffering from a pathological condition, in contrast to the temperamentally high activity child, who is at one normal extreme of the temperamental attribute of activity level, and it is important to distinguish between these two types of children. They may appear similar in some respects: both the hyperactive and high-activity child may show a high level of motor activity. Both may become fidgety and restless if their movements are restricted—if, for example, they have to sit quietly in their seats in school for several hours at a time. There are, however, crucial differences between them. The hyperactive child tends to shift from one uncompleted activity to another, has difficulty in sustaining attention to tasks and activities, and is easily distracted. The temperamentally high-activity child, by contrast, does not have these difficulties in organizing, sustaining, and completing his activities. Because of these symptoms of the hyperactive child, the official psychiatric diagnostic manual has suggested the label *attention deficit disorder,* on the presumption that the highly disorganized activity results from a problem of sustaining attention. The cause of this condition is unknown, although a biological basis is likely.

Paradoxically, these hyperactive children's symptoms often respond favorably to medication of the amphetamine series, such as ritalin, which typically are stimulants and not depressants of brain activity. The reason for the effectiveness of these drugs is not clear. The medication must be used cautiously and carefully monitored, because it can have undesirable side effects.

What has unfortunately happened in many school systems is that the label of "hyperactivity" has been applied carelessly, even promiscuously, to all children who are restless and fidgety in the classroom. A child may be restless for many reasons: he may be bored by a dull, unstimulating teacher; he may have anxiety in school for other reasons; or he may have a high activity level temperamentally. All too many children have been incorrectly labeled as "hyperactive" by a teacher who finds such a child a nuisance. The parents are then told to take the child to their pediatrician and get a prescription for a drug. The pediatrician, faced with an exaggerated report from the teacher, may go along with the recommendation. In such cases, the drug is useless and may even be harmful, and the true diagnosis is missed.

A child with a significant school problem deserves immediate expert attention so that early intervention and treatment procedures can be instituted promptly if they prove to be called for. Such early treatment can prevent the many disastrous consequences that can result over the years from the cumulative effect of a child's difficulties in school. The parent and teacher should work together in arranging for adequate professional evaluation and treatment. The parent should be wary, however, of any professional advice that is given without a thorough evaluation of the possible causes, which should include issues of temperament and brain functioning, as well as those that may be primarily emotional.

12

Middle Childhood and Adolescence

MIDDLE CHILDHOOD is generally considered to be the age-period from approximately six to twelve years. It is of interest that many different cultures have identified the child of six or seven as competent to assume a new level of functioning (Shapiro & Perry 1976). During the Middle Ages, children became pages at court at this age, and in a later period children were apprenticed away from home at seven years. In modern society formal academic schooling usually begins at six or seven years.

For the average child, especially in middle-class families, the middle childhood years bring fewer new environmental demands and expectations than the infancy and preschool periods, and the speed of physical growth and neurobiological maturation diminishes. The demands for established routines and socialization—regular sleep and feeding patterns, toilet training, adaptation to the rules of family life and play relationships with age-mates, learning to feed and dress oneself—have been made in the earlier age-periods and successfully accomplished by most children. Most children have attended nursery school or kindergarten, or both, so that the need to adapt to a new and different environment outside the home, to a new structured schedule of activities, to more formal play situations with other children, and to educational work has already been mastered by age six. With this background, the beginning of formal academic education, usually in the first grade, therefore, presents few if any significant problems to most children.

The Transition to Middle Childhood

For the psychoanalysts, middle childhood begins with the "resolution of the Oedipus complex" (see chapter 9 for a definition of the Oedipus complex). In this formulation, the five- or six-year-old child is able to repress the sexual attraction for the parent of the opposite sex into the "unconscious" and replace it with an interest in school and age-mate activities. This theory is based on the hypothetical system of instinct drive development in early childhood. Needless to say, no serious objective evidence for this concept has been found, and its usefulness and validity have been questioned even by a number of prominent psychoanalysts (Marmor 1974; Stern 1985).

Translated into nonpsychoanalytic terms, the Oedipus complex would appear to be a label for the conflicts that can occur in the preschool years between parent and child. These are the years when the young child is learning the rules of safety and social living, the do's and don'ts of daily living. All kinds of prescriptions and proscriptions are demanded by the parents: "Don't touch the electric light outlets"; "Don't come to dinner until you have washed your hands"; "I'm trying to read and you're making too much noise. Go play in your own room"; "Say 'thank you' if someone gives you a present." By age six, most children have learned that the parents' demands and expectations do make sense. And even if some of the demands still appear unreasonable, they are no longer so important, as the child becomes involved more and more with individuals and activities outside the home. There are extreme cases, either where the parent's demands are outrageously unreasonable or the child remains excessively emotionally attached to the parent for her age-level, where this harmony between child and parent has not been attained by age six years. In psychoanalytic terms, this would represent a "failure to resolve the Oedipus complex." For the rest of us, it would be termed a problem of psychological development that will lead to a behavior disorder if it continues.

In other words, if one is not committed to the psychoanalytic concepts of instinctual drives and their special significance at different ages in childhood, no special theory of the transition to middle childhood is necessary. Instead of the psychoanalytic formulations of early childhood as a series of transitions from the "oral stage" to the "anal stage," then to the "genital stage" with its "Oedipus complex," and finally to the "post-Oedipal stage," we can substitute the objective, descriptive stages of development and transition as "infancy," "toddler stage," "preschool age," and "middle childhood."

Stability and Development in Middle Childhood

For most children, the middle childhood years represent a period of relative stability, with fewer demands for new adaptations. This stability is also reflected in our tabulation of the age of onset of childhood behavior disorders in our New York Longitudinal Study. These disorders were caused, with very few exceptions, by environmental changes and expectations with which certain children could not cope successfully because of their own characteristics—in other words, poorness of fit. Of the forty-five childhood cases of behavior disorder (over half were mild), thirty-two, or 71 percent, began by the age of five. Twelve, or 27 percent, began between the ages of six and eight, and only one, or 2 percent, between nine and twelve years.

Stability, however, does not mean lack of change or development. As the child progresses through the middle childhood years, very important changes occur in her cognitive abilities and psychological characteristics. Piaget considered that in this age-period children develop concrete concepts, such as the notions of conservation and invariance, which then lead to the later acquisition of complex reasoning (1952).

On the psychological side, Erik Erikson calls this age-period the "age of industry" and "socially a most decisive stage" (1950). Theodore Lidz of Yale speaks of the beginning of "a sense of belonging" and "a sense of responsibility" in this period of life (1968).

These descriptions by Erikson and Lidz reflect a consensus among psychologists and psychiatrists that for most middle-class children in our culture the middle childhood period is one of stability and healthy development. The struggles and challenges of the earlier childhood years have been mastered. The child's sense of self has crystallized, her life experiences have given her confidence in her task-mastery abilities and social competence, and her language and cognitive development have matured so that she can face the demands of formal learning with confidence. Given at least a fair degree of stability in her environment, the six-year-old youngster begins to use her psychological assets in the succeeding years of childhood as her horizon of interests and activities widens. She learns academically, she becomes more competent socially, her cognitive development advances, a sense of responsibility to herself and to others begins to crystallize, specific personality characteristics begin to take shape and definite interests, goals, and ambitions may begin to emerge.

Middle childhood is, then, a most active developmental stage, a passage from early childhood to the end of childhood with the onset of adoles-

cence. It may not show the rapid changes that are evident in early childhood and adolescence, but it is no less important as a developmental stage.
Edward Zigler has put it wisely: "My own predeliction is that we cease this
pointless search for magic periods and adopt instead the view that the
developmental process is a continuous one, in which every segmer; of the
life cycle from conception to maturity is of crucial importance and requires
certain environmental nutrients" (1975).

We do not mean to paint an idyllic picture of the middle childhood
period. While most youngsters proceed smoothly through middle childhood, this is certainly not true of all children. As we saw in the previous
chapter, school difficulties of one kind or another may make this period
highly stressful for some. Behavior disorders or severe mental illness,
either persisting from earlier childhood or originating in middle childhood,
can also make this age-period difficult and even result in deterioration in
behavioral functioning. Tragic or catastrophic events, such as incest, death
of a parent, divorce of the parents, or a serious illness or accident, may
make for a highly stressful period for the child and sometimes even cause
long-lasting psychological damage. Michael Rutter (1966) has reported a
study of the reaction of children to the death of a parent. Although the
immediate grief reaction was more short-lived in the younger children, the
delayed consequences in terms of psychiatric disorder was sometimes
greater for them. These long-term effects were probably the results of
consequences of the death, such as the breakup of the home, financial
stresses, and the effect of the bereavement on the surviving parent.

Leonore Terr, of the University of California, has made a study of the
long-term psychological effects of the Chowchilla school-bus kidnapping
(1983). In July 1976, three young kidnappers, who never explained their
motives, kidnapped twenty-six schoolchildren and their bus driver at gun-
point in the town of Chowchilla, California, drove them around for eleven
hours in two darkened vans, and buried them alive for sixteen hours in a
truck-trailer. Two of the kidnapped boys finally dug the group out. Terr
did a careful four-year psychiatric follow-up of twenty-five of the group;
the twenty-sixth victim could not be traced. She found that four years
after the traumatic event, *every* child still suffered from symptoms, including pessimism about the future, belief in omens and predictions, shame,
fear of experiencing anxiety, various other fears, repeated nightmares, and
dreams of their own death. The symptoms were strikingly similar despite
the fact that the children ranged from six years to adolescence. Some had
had brief psychiatric treatment five to thirteen months after the kidnapping, but that did not prevent symptoms four years later. There were
evident relationships between the severity of symptoms and the stability

and health of the family and any preexisting psychological vulnerabilities in the children. Thus, an overwhelming single catastrophic event, even if short-lived, can have long-lasting effects in children, as they can in adults.

Similar long-term psychological damage occurred in almost all the survivors, children and adults, of a terrible flood that tore through several coal-mining villages in Appalachia in 1972. The sociologist Kai Erikson, who headed the study, made a pertinent observation that applies as well to the Chowchilla children. He pointed out, "It is a standard article of psychiatric wisdom that the symptoms of trauma ought to disappear over a period of time." If they don't, the theory goes, "then it follows that the symptoms themselves must have been the result of a mental disorder predating the event itself" (1976, p. 184). But this logic requires the assumption that all the victims of the flood or of the Chowchilla kidnapping had suffered from significant degrees of psychological disorder before the disaster struck. Erikson further suggests that the dynamics of chronic symptom production may apply also to individuals living under conditions of "chronic disaster," such as chronic poverty and unemployment without hope for the future.

These reports by Leonore Terr and Kai Erikson make it clear that the smooth developmental course of most middle-class children in our society reflects the benign environments in which they live. For the children of the same age living in impoverished areas, especially inner-city ghettos, the story may be quite different. Even before reaching adolescence, many of these children are caught up in a life of drug abuse, delinquency, and school truancy, manifestations of what Erikson calls living under conditions of "chronic disaster."

Cross-Cultural Variations

Sociocultural factors may also play a part in shaping the developmental course in middle childhood. Not all cultural groups necessarily follow the usual middle-class sequence of diminished environmental demands in middle childhood as compared to the infancy and preschool years. For example, in our longitudinal studies the incidence of behavior disorders in children from unskilled working-class Puerto Rican families was relatively lower during the preschool years than in the children of native-born middle-class families. By contrast, the incidence of behavior disorders in the middle childhood years was higher in the Puerto Rican group than in the middle-class children (Thomas et al. 1974). This difference appeared to be clearly related to the fact that the Puerto Rican parents were very permissive with their preschool children. They did not pressure the children to modify sleep or feeding irregularities or other types of mild behavioral disturbances. Their typical attitude was "He's a baby—he'll outgrow it." Few of these children attended nursery school. Environmental demands and pressures on these children in infancy and the preschool years were therefore significantly less than on the middle-class children. This difference was reflected in the difference in the incidence of behavior disorders.

With the start of school at age five or six, however, there was a sudden increase in the number of new demands made on the Puerto Rican children. Getting to school on time meant that sleep schedules had to be regularized, and demands for discipline, learning, and obedience to safety regulations were made by the school. These were issues that the middle-class children had faced in the preschool years. For the Puerto Rican children they were deferred until the beginning of the middle childhood years, so that the behavior disorders of the children in this group who could not cope successfully with them began in this period, rather than in the earlier years.

Irving Berlin, of the University of New Mexico, has made a study of the emotional problems of American Indian children (1982). As part of his project, he visited a number of boarding schools attended by Indian children. In most of these schools he found the youngsters to be depressed, anxious, and failing to learn. The causes were evident. The schools were unrelated to the tribes from which the children came, and the children felt alienated and lonely. The school staff made no attempt to deal with this problem. On the contrary, the children were harshly treated and disciplined. Berlin found one exception, a boarding school in which the dormitory supervisors were concerned young adults who had been carefully selected to represent each of the tribes in the school. The teachers and counselors were alert to any signs of problems in living and learning, and the children flourished in this atmosphere. In the majority of the boarding schools, however, middle childhood was a highly stressful period because of the isolation and alienation of the children from their own culture.

We will cite one other cultural setting in which middle childhood is also a difficult period, but for a different reason. On a trip to Japan several years ago, we met a number of child psychiatrists in Tokyo and several other cities. Among other questions, we always asked them, "What is the most common childhood behavior problem in Japan?" We were taken aback by the answer, which was always "school refusal among boys." In our country, we use the term "school phobia." Both mean the same—the child develops anxiety symptoms each morning and tries by every means to avoid going to school. In the United States this is not a rare condition, but it is far from being the frequent disorder that it is in Japan. In our country there are many reasons why a child may develop school refusal, but in Japan the cause appears to be almost always the same. The Japanese school system is so structured that each phase determines the next. The child's record in elementary school determines the kind of high school he will be accepted into, and it in turn determines the prestige of the college he can attend. In turn, the college from which he graduates largely determines the status of the corporation or professional school that will accept him. It is a stepladder system, with each rung determining the next. And the focus for job attainment is on sons rather than on daughters. The elementary school boy is therefore under severe pressure by his family—and within himself—to achieve a high level of performance from the first grade onward. Most of the children cope with this pressure, but a significant number are overwhelmed by it and become school refusers. Some become so anxious that they require hospitalization, and we saw a number of such children when we visited several Japanese psychiatric hospitals. It would indeed be rare to find such a case in an American hospital.

The Concept of the Latency Period

A popular idea among many psychiatrists is to call middle childhood "the latency period." This concept derives from psychoanalytic theory, in which this age-period was considered a period of latency between the passage of the "Oedipal stage" and the beginning of adolescence. During this period, so the concept goes, the energy of the hypothetical infantile sexuality is diverted or repressed from sexual goals and directed toward other aims. In Erik Erikson's words, the term implies a kind of "psychosexual moratorium in human development" (1968). With the onset of puberty and adolescence, sexuality reawakens and the latency period disappears.

The concept of the latency period is dubious on a number of counts. It rests on a sequence of innate psychosexual drives and goals as the prime force in childhood development—itself a simplistic theory, devoid of any objective scientific proof, and an idea that has been challenged by many leading contemporary psychiatrists (Lidz 1968; Marmor 1983). Furthermore, the idea that sexual interests and activities disappear during middle childhood is a myth, at least in contemporary society. As a leading student of child development at Columbia University, Arthur Jersild put it, "When viewed in the light of empirical studies of children's interest and actions during this period, 'latency' cannot be taken literally. For many children, interest in sex is not latent or inactive or held in abeyance, but is distinctly manifest and active. In normal development, sex never takes a holiday" (1968). This was confirmed by the reports of the parents in our longitudinal study. The middle childhood children were described as showing active sexual curiosity, most masturbated at least occasionally, and many played variations of the game "Playing Doctor," with its sexual overtones.

The concept of latency is also easily capable of misinterpretation. While Freud used the term specifically for psychosexual development (dubious enough), the word itself can suggest that nothing really changes during this period. As one child psychiatrist in his textbook has pointed out, latency is "an unfortunate term since it suggests that nothing really important is happening and that the child is simply waiting for puberty to begin" (Shaw 1966). Actually, the middle childhood period is a period of continuous psychological growth, cognitively and emotionally, even though it is relatively nonstressful for most youngsters. It is also a new developmental stage, in which specific personality characteristics begin to crystallize definitively, and in which the youngster becomes progressively capable of assuming new responsibilities and goals.

To call such a period "latent" is a misnomer. Together with an increasing number of other psychiatrists, we prefer the term "middle childhood," which is purely descriptive and has no unproven implications about its character or development.

The Transition to Adolescence

As much as middle childhood is considered by parents and mental health professionals to be a relatively smooth, conflict-free developmental stage for most youngsters, the same cannot be said for adolescence. Traditionally, adolescence has been viewed as a period of turmoil, sexual conflict, and rebelliousness toward family and society, in which a difficult "generational gap" develops between the adolescent and her parents. Many parents actually anticipate the onset of adolescence in their sons or daughters with apprehension, fearing the worst. Are these fears justified? Does the well-behaved and cooperative ten-year-old child suddenly turn into a self-centered, selfish monster with the onset of puberty, making life miserable for her family and even herself?

Like infancy, adolescence is an age-period in which rapid biological changes and maturation are combined with new environmental demands and expectations. For those youngsters who have suffered from a behavior disorder in childhood that continues into adolescence, the new demands of adolescence may increase the stresses with which they struggle and exacerbate their behavior problems. Other youngsters who have made rather shaky and fragile adjustments in childhood may be overwhelmed by the extensive changes and expectations of adolescence and develop behavior disorders. But there are still others who have had a healthy childhood and have developed a solid sense of self-confidence and self-esteem; for these boys and girls, adolescence might be an expansive and stimulating period of psychological growth.

What are the facts? How many adolescents fall into these different psychological categories? How many find adolescence a difficult and stressful period? How many, to the contrary, find adolescence a positive, happy, and relaxed developmental period?

A substantial body of careful, detailed, and objective research now exists, so that we can supply satisfactory answers to these questions. The most extensive and carefully done epidemiological study of the frequency of mental disturbances among adolescents has been the very recent study by Daniel Offer and his associates at the Michael Reese Medical Center in Chicago (Offer, Ostrov, & Howard, in press). Offer has been one of the leading and most respected investigators of mental health issues among adolescents in this country for many years. Using the appropriate methods for obtaining a random sample representative of the community as a whole, he and his associates selected 260 students in a Chicago suburban township. They chose additional students from two Roman Catholic parochial schools in Chicago itself, to obtain as diverse a sample as possible from different socioeconomic, racial, and religious groups.

Each student was given the Offer questionnaire (a self-rating psychological survey that has been standardized on many thousands of adolescents), a checklist for evidences of delinquent behavior, and a personal interview with one of the research staff members.

The information obtained was rated quantitatively and analyzed statistically. The findings indicated that about 20 percent of the adolescents studied were emotionally disturbed to a meaningful degree. The disturbed adolescents were subdivided into those who were "quietly disturbed"—that is, those who had not been seen by a mental health professional more than once, had never been arrested, had never been involved with the courts, had never been held in a detention center, had never run away from home, and had never abused drugs or alcohol—and those who did not meet these criteria, who were considered "active." The sex distribution was quite striking. Thirty-five percent of the disturbed males were quietly disturbed and 65 percent actively so, but for the females the figures were almost exactly reversed: 62 percent were quietly disturbed and only 38 percent actively so.

Offer's figures correspond to those of other studies. A series of studies by Philip Graham and Michael Rutter conducted on the Isle of Wight, off the coast of England, found the prevalence rate for psychiatric disorder in fourteen- to fifteen-year-old youngsters to be 21 percent (1973). In our New York Longitudinal Study, twenty cases of psychiatric disorder in childhood persisted into adolescence. Twelve new cases developed in adolescence, making a total of thirty-two adolescents with psychiatric problems, or 25 percent of our total sample. (We included two cases with organic brain disorder, who are often eliminated from other studies. Discounting them would bring our percentage down to 22 percent.) Whether we use the figure of 22 percent or 25 percent, our figures approximate those of Offer's and Rutter's studies.

From their findings, Offer and his associates conclude, "As has been true whenever research has been conducted with representative groups of adolescents, the results demonstrate that the vast majority of adolescents in this study are happy and well-adjusted" (in press). This finding is very much in line with our own.

The 20 percent who are disturbed cannot be ignored, however. They represent approximately 3.5 million people nationally. Furthermore, the Offer study indicates that about half these adolescents have not received any mental health care. This is a public health problem of serious magnitude, and one that has received little attention nationally.

The Facts about Adolescent Turmoil

Traditionally, in both popular and professional writings, adolescence has been viewed as a period of marked emotional upheaval and turmoil arising from rapid physical changes, the onset of adult sexuality, and the expectation for increased responsibility within the family combined with increased identification with age-mates outside the home. This view of the adolescent was expressed vividly at the beginning of this century by G. Stanley Hall, at that time the leading academic authority on adolescence: "The teens are emotionally unstable and pathic. It is a natural impulse to experience hot and perfervid psychic states, and it is characterized by emotionalism" (1904, p. 74).

This view of adolescent turmoil has been further developed in the psychoanalytic movement. Leading psychoanalysts have viewed adolescence as a period of emotional instability in which the maintenance of a steady psychological equilibrium would in itself be abnormal (Blos 1979; Eissler 1958; A. Freud 1958). This psychoanalytic thesis has been summarized succinctly and accurately by Daniel Offer and Judith Offer:

> Psychoanalytic theory describes adolescence as a time of psychologic imbalance, when the functioning of the ego and superego are severely strained. Instinctual impulses disrupt the homeostatic equilibrium achieved during latency, and inner turmoil results, manifesting itself by rebellious or deviant behavior, mood swings, or affective lability. Unresolved preoedipal or oedipal conflicts are revived; the repressions characteristic of latency are no longer sufficient to restore a psychologic equilibrium. (1975, p. 161)

The psychoanalytic jargon may be confusing, but the meaning is clear. A further distressing view for the adolescent and her parents is added by Erikson's influential concept of adolescence as a period of "identity crisis" (1959).

Fortunately, this grim picture of the normal adolescent now stands completely contradicted by a series of studies by a number of investigators. All agree that this picture of adolescent turmoil and disturbance is grossly exaggerated. Daniel Offer and Judith Offer, in their longitudinal study of seventy-three middle-class, midwestern adolescent males (1975), found that 23 percent were characterized by smooth continuous progress and 35 percent by alternating periods of spurts and leveling-off in their development, though the latter were functioning as well as the smoothly progressing group. They could label only 21 percent of the group as having substantial turmoil that interfered significantly with their functioning. Another 21 percent could not be classified because of mixed scores. (This 21 percent with difficulties comes very close to the finding of the recent study, cited above, that 20 percent of adolescents showed significant psychological disturbances.)

Our findings from the New York Longitudinal Study confirm the Offers' report of the two types of healthy adolescent development: the smooth course free of turmoil and the more turbulent course but with healthy functioning. The two groups together made up about 75 percent of the total sample, with the remaining 25 percent having significant psychological problems due to various causes (Chess & Thomas 1984). We have not as yet tabulated the percentages of the smoothly functioning versus the more turbulent but healthy group, although it is our impression that a greater number fall into the smoothly functioning group.

Two reviews of the extensive literature on adolescence are also worth citing. John Coleman, of the University of London, reviewing the large-scale empirical studies, concluded that "the teenage years are very much more stable and peaceful than had previously been concluded" (1978, p. 2). Rutter's comprehensive and systematic review of the professional literature came to a similar judgment:

> It is also evident that normal adolescence is *not* characterized by storm, stress, and disturbance. Most young people go through their teenage years without significant emotional or behavioral problems. It is true that there are challenges to be met, adaptations to be met, and stresses to be coped with. However, these do not all arise at the same time and most adolescents deal with these issues without undue disturbance. (1979, p. 86)

Given this unanimity of judgment on the normal adolescent from the wealth of empirical studies available in recent years, how does one account for the distorted, unhealthy picture of the adolescent drawn by so many prominent psychoanalysts? The most likely explanation is that these psychoanalysts have taken their findings with disturbed adolescents and young adults and generalized their conclusions to the normal adolescent, without making studies of normal groups to check the validity of their speculations. They simply assume that the psychological characteristics of a sick patient population must also be true of normal healthy individuals. This tendency has plagued many psychiatric theories. Lawrence Kolb, a leading psychiatric teacher and clinician, has pointed out that psychiatric training always tends to emphasize people's liabilities and the unhealthy side of their psychological make-up, rather than their healthy assets (1978). The Offers have made this point cogently in their criticism of Erikson's concepts of adolescence:

> Erikson does not present examples of healthy and adaptive adolescence. Surely, examples of true "normative" crises ought to come from others than patients, exceptional individuals, and fictional or biographical profiles. These are the adolescents with whom Erikson has had contact, and they then circularly support the theory that he has spun based on his experience with them. (1975, p. 163)

The Myth of the Generation Gap

The popular and professional literature has made much of the "generation gap," the idea that adolescents develop such different values, goals, and life styles from those of their parents that positive communication between the two generations is lost and a gap develops that cannot be bridged.

As we have followed the youngsters in the New York Longitudinal Study from early infancy to early adult life, we have not been impressed with the frequency or seriousness of the generation gap between the parents and their sons and daughters. It is true that in those families in which the parents' demands and expectations were excessively stressful for their children (what we have called poorness of fit), with the result that behavior problems developed in the children, the parent-child relationship was usually either cold and distant or openly antagonistic. But this alienation of parent and child almost always started in childhood, even in early childhood.

Outside of these behavior problem cases, those of our subjects with strong positive ties to their parents in childhood—indeed, a healthy majority of the total sample—maintained these positive relationships even as they strove in adolescence to develop their independence and freedom of functioning in the outside world. In a few instances, conflict and rebellion were evident; one older adolescent, for example, left home because he could not accept the rigid moralistic standards of his father. In several other instances, youngsters experienced a lack of closeness with their parents, which they correctly felt to be a great deprivation. One young woman of twenty-six wept openly in the interview with us as she described her inability ever to get close to her mother, whom she described as a heavy drinker and emotionally distant. Her father didn't drink, but emotionally he was as aloof as the mother. In a few other instances, adolescents or young adults regretted a lack of closeness with their parents but had made their peace with a casual, superficial friendliness.

Such cases of a generation gap were distinctly in the minority in our longitudinal study. The same conclusion has been reached by both Rutter and the Offers in their studies of adolescent groups whose sociocultural backgrounds were different from our sample's. Rutter, from his Isle of Wight study, states, "The evidence suggests that there has *not* been a widening of the supposed 'generation gap' " (1979, p. 143), and the Offers report that "in the social as well as the psychological realm, we have seen the continuity between generations. . . . Most [adolescents] cherished the values of their elders" (1975, p. 197).

Sex and the Adolescent

The past few decades have witnessed a dramatic change in the frankness with which sexual activity is portrayed and discussed in all the popular media. For an unmarried couple, living together openly, which would have been a scandal in the past, is now acceptable and commonplace in most communities. This "sexual revolution" has been clearly reflected in our subjects in their adolescent and early adult interviews with us. With few exceptions, they talked about their sexual activity with open, guilt-free and conflict-free attitudes. There was also a notable absence of the concerns of earlier generations with masturbation or the possibilities of unplanned pregnancy or venereal disease. This was also true in the group who had special interviews because of a psychological problem.

By age eighteen, 61 percent of the males and 64 percent of the females had had sexual intercourse at least once, with an additional 14 percent of the males and 12 percent of the females starting between age nineteen and twenty. At the early adult interviews, about 9 percent of both males and females who had still not experienced sexual intercourse were judged to be sexually inhibited. Another 16 percent of both sexes expressed definite religious or other moral scruples against sexual intercourse before marriage. The majority of these sexually inhibited young adults had been or still suffered from a behavior disorder.

Thus, taking this longitudinal study group as a whole, the majority began an active sexual life in adolescence. Sexual problems appeared to be present only in a relatively small minority of the group. Sex as such was not a problem for most of these youngsters. What did concern them more in adolescence and early adult life was the challenge of combining physical with emotional intimacy in a sexual relationship. Sex was not viewed with anxiety and conflict, but with a few exceptions neither was it embraced as a casual, impersonal source of pleasure.

It was of interest that sex was one area where intimate communication between most of the parents and their adolescent sons and daughters was minimal. Paradoxically, most of the parents had a fairly accurate idea of the extent of their adolescent youngsters' sexual activity, but it came mostly from inference and not from direct communication. In addition, there was little discussion between most parents and their adolescent sons and daughters about such matters as birth control, pregnancy, abortion, and venereal disease. This was true even in families where parents and their youngsters communicated openly and freely on other topics. The adolescents clearly preferred to obtain their knowledge about the technical aspects of sex through the school, the library, or friends, where the information was freely available. Our overall impression was that by the time these youngsters were sixteen, in most cases sex was a closed topic between themselves and their parents. The adolescents guarded their privacy in this area quite carefully, and for the most part parents respected that privacy. Sex was the one area in which a generation gap appeared to exist, although it did not become a source of conflict and antagonism between parent and child.

This lack of intergenerational discussion of sex did not appear to extend beyond the family. In the interviews at age sixteen, most of the youngsters were quite comfortable and open in talking about sex with our middle-aged interviewers. It was our impression that the avoidance of the discussion of sex with their parents was a manifestation of the adolescents' wish to establish independence. In some cases it also appeared to be the way the youngster avoided the family tensions and conflicts that such discussion might have provoked.

Drug Abuse and Alcohol Use

As a group, the New York Longitudinal Study subjects came into adolescence after the period of greatest drug experimentation and abuse among middle-class adolescents which peaked in the late 1960s. Whether our data reflected the general decline of drug use or whether other factors were also operating, overall these adolescents reported to us that their use of alcohol was modest, the majority were nonsmokers, and only a minority had experimented with cocaine, LSD, and/or stimulant or depressive drugs. All denied the use of heroin. The majority of the group had tried marijuana, and a substantial number used it regularly, but only a few used it more than once or twice a week. In our current follow-up, for which we have already interviewed over 50 percent of the sample at ages twenty-five through thirty, there has been no evidence of any addiction to the potent form of cocaine known as "crack." The recent explosive use of crack in the U.S. population has apparently not affected this group of young adults.

About 25 percent of the group could be rated as moderate to fairly heavy users of alcohol or marijuana or both. In this group, however, there were no cases of alcohol or other drug addiction. No psychotic reactions to LSD or the amphetamines had occurred, although several of the adolescents reported "bad trips" with LSD. A number had tried cocaine once or twice but shrugged it off as "too expensive and not worthwhile." Our figures on cocaine use correspond to a study of 16,000 high school seniors done in 1985 by the University of Michigan (*New York Times,* 18 January 1986). Of this group 17.3 percent reported that they had used cocaine at least once. This figure was 1.2 percent higher than in a similar survey in 1984. The greater increase in cocaine use, however, has occurred among affluent adults rather than adolescents (William Frosch, personal communication, 1986).

It became clear as we interviewed our NYLS subjects during their adolescence that there was a definite tendency by some of the subjects to underreport their current drug use. This was to be expected in an area so heavily loaded with value judgments. In their early adult interviews a number of subjects reported a greater degree of drug and alcohol use during their adolescent years than they had described in their adolescent interviews. They were in effect saying, "Now that I'm no longer doing it, I can be honest about how much I did it in the past." Perhaps 10 percent admitted to rather heavy use of alcohol or marijuana in their early adult period, but we could find no evidence from them or from their parents of any cases of actual addiction. Infrequent use of marijuana continued to be reported by perhaps half the group at this later age-period.

The underreporting of drug and alcohol use in the adolescent years occurred even in interviews with us, after a long relationship with them and with their families in which the subjects could be confident that any information they gave us would be kept strictly confidential. This finding underlines the difficulty of obtaining accurate information on drug use by adolescents, especially when impersonal questionnaires are administered by strangers.

It should be emphasized that these findings on drug and alcohol use came from adolescents brought up in affluent families, who could view with confidence their opportunities for the future in the mainstream of society. As we know, the figures on drug use are much higher among underprivileged and undereducated youths whose current reality is bleak and whose future offers little hope. For them, the escape from their reality through drugs and alcohol can be very tempting.

Suicidal Behavior in Adolescence

Suicidal behavior among adolescents has become an issue of great concern. Though rare in previous generations, the rate appears to have at least doubled in the past thirty years (Holinger 1979), and suicide is now the third leading cause of death among adolescents (Robbins 1985). Many more girls than boys attempt suicide, but fatal outcomes are more frequent among boys (Chess & Hassibi 1978, p. 143). Suicides are very rare under ten years of age, with a progressive several-hundredfold increase between ten and twenty years (Rutter & Sandberg 1985).

A number of studies of adolescent suicides and attempted suicides have been made, and it is clear that there is no single cause for this tragic event. The presence of a depressive disorder, which is probably biological in origin and which can begin in adolescence, is certainly the basis for suicide in some adolescents, as it is in adults (Robbins 1985). Various other causes have been suggested in specific cases, such as a disturbed family background, some precipitating event associated with shame and humiliation, such as sexual abuse, a serious quarrel with a parent or lover, or an impulsive act while under the influence of alcohol or other drugs (Brooksbank 1985). In rare cases, unintentional death due to self-strangulation may occur as the result of a pathological autoerotic act. Occasionally, an apparently healthy and happy youngster will commit suicide without any identifiable precipitating event. In such cases, it is most likely that a depressive illness has begun but been undetected by the family or friends.

From all these surveys, it is evident that signs of depression in an adolescent should be taken seriously. These symptoms can include expressions of unhappiness, unworthiness, or hopelessness; unreasonable feelings of guilt or shame; the onset of sleep difficulties; or loss of interest in activities that the adolescent formerly enjoyed. Threats of suicide should also not be taken lightly, even if they seem to be impulsive statements made during a quarrel. An adolescent who has been through a shocking, humiliating experience such as rape should also be considered as a suicidal risk. In all such cases, the parents should seek competent professional consultation quickly.

The Adolescent and Society

Even some of those who agree that "the past portrayal of adolescence carried too heavy an emphasis on turmoil and maladaptation" still view the adolescent period as "difficult" because this is "a period of extraordinary change, multiple conflicts, and marked societal demands upon the individual" (Fishman 1982, p. 39). Yet early infancy is a time of even greater change and greater societal demands than is adolescence, but it is not labeled a difficult period, except perhaps for the small minority of children with difficult temperament. The preschool years, with their demands for peer play relationships, and the early school years, with their demands for formal learning, are also periods of great change and new expectations. Yet we expect them to go smoothly for most youngsters. The childhood years may be especially stressful for some children, such as those with difficult temperament or learning problems, but we do not generalize from these particular cases and designate these periods as "stressful" for all.

What is different about adolescence is not the extent or intensity of change but its quality and its implications in our society. Parents take unqualified pleasure as they watch each new step in their child's physical and psychological development. But they are likely to have mixed reactions to the process of development in adolescence. They may be pleased at their son or daughter's sexual maturation but at the same time worry whether the adolescent will use this new ability wisely. They may be impressed by their teenaged son's muscular development but be concerned at the havoc he can wreak if he gets angry or frustrated. At the same time, the adolescent's assumption of more mature responsibility and an independent role in the family, as positive as these may be, are also coupled with the loss of the absolute parental and teacher control that existed in the childhood years. The adolescent now brings into her life from her peer group a new set of standards and values that may conflict with the parents' value system. Even when they do not conflict, the adolescent's way of expressing these values and following these standards may be quite different from her parents' style. And even in areas where the parents have adopted a permissive and flexible position and encouraged open communication on a subject such as sex, they may be disconcerted to discover that their adolescent son or daughter prefers to seek education and guidance outside the home.

The adolescent encounters the ills and problems of the outside world, as well as its exciting opportunities, as she begins to move actively into this world on her own. She responds with a fresh view, and her sharp and critical responses, when they occur, may reflect not some inner identity crisis but rather the faults of this world, faults to which most adults have become inured. It may be, as one psychiatrist has put it wisely, that each "society gets the type of adolescent it expects and deserves" (Anthony 1969b).

Implications for Parents

If goodness of fit between the parents' expectations and the child's characteristics has been achieved in infancy and the preschool years, and if the child has made a positive adjustment to school, then the parents can expect the middle childhood years to progress easily and smoothly. A special event, such as the death of a close family member, the move of the family to a new and strange environment, or a problem with a difficult teacher or classmate in school, may be a source of special stress to the youngster. But usually, with the support and advice of the parents, the child will be able to master the problems and tensions produced by such a specific situation. If not, professional counseling will be advisable.

With increasing intellectual and emotional development, the middle childhood youngster may begin to display special interests and talents. If the parents rank these high in their own value system, they will offer their child encouragement and try to supply her with the additional resources she may need. Occasionally, however, parents may worry that their child is becoming too intensively involved in some special interest. We have had many consultations over the years with such parents, especially when the child's interest, such as in some special area of reading, involved her in a great deal of solitary activity. The parents then became concerned that their child was becoming "socially isolated" and that her solitary functioning might be a way of avoiding some problem with social activities with her age-mates. Occasionally this was true, but more often a detailed history of the youngster's functioning indicated clearly that she had friends with whom she was at ease and that she was quite competent socially. There was no problem except the unnecessary worry of the parents.

In other cases, a child's special interests may not conform to her parents' value system. She may become absorbed in athletics when they would like to see her pursue intellectual activities, or vice versa. The parents may be disappointed, but they have to respect the child's choice, as long as she pursues it constructively and does not neglect her other responsibilities.

A parent's knowledge of the child's temperament or other characteristics may be very useful with respect to a child's special interests. For example, one of the boys in our longitudinal study subjects had a markedly difficult temperament. Throughout his early years, his first reaction to any new situation was a stormy refusal, followed by slow adaptation. The parents handled these situations with quiet and persistent understanding, and with this goodness of fit the boy's development flourished. In middle childhood very few new situations arose, and he was not aware of his pattern of response to new demands. But his mother remembered. When he was about ten, he became interested in music and asked if he could take piano lessons. His mother agreed, with one condition: No matter how he felt, he had to stick to the lessons for six months. Then, if he wanted to, he could give them up. He agreed, started lessons, and began by hating them. But he stuck to the bargain, and six months later his mother asked if he wanted to quit. His answer was, "Are you crazy? I love it!" and he continued his lessons with enthusiasm into his college years.

The adolescent years for many youngsters may also be smooth sailing, as shown by the research studies cited earlier in this chapter. In many instances parents may be startled to find that their formerly conforming youngster suddenly as an adolescent begins to adopt weird manners of dress, hairstyle, or speech. Before jumping to any conclusions about "adolescent turmoil" or "identity crisis," the parents should check up with a friend or teacher familiar with adolescent fashions. They may discover that what appears bizarre to them is simply a current, harmless adolescent fad. It may be distasteful to them, but it should not become the basis of a conflict or confrontation. Given this tolerance, the parents will usually discover that their adolescent son or daughter is still the same youngster they have respected and loved.

If the adolescent begins to challenge her parents' values and life style, it behooves the parents to listen seriously. Their youngster may have a valid argument based on her fresh viewpoint. If the parents disagree, they can agree to disagree amicably. The old chestnut about the young man of twenty who marveled at how much his parents had "learned" in the past five years carries a lot of truth in it. Patient tolerance on the parents' part usually pays off in the end.

But there are times when the parents have to take a firm stand if they are convinced their adolescent youngster is embarked on a course of behavior that is immoral, dangerous, or both. At the same time the parents have to realize that they no longer have the control and leverage over their child's behavior that they did when she was three or ten years of age. Sometimes they can still act effectively—refusing to let their adolescent youngster use the family car because of her reckless driving, for example —but in other instances their stand may be ineffective. If the parents insist that the youngster always be home by a certain hour at night, and the son or daughter refuses to stick to this rule, there may not be much the parents can do to enforce their demand. Punishment may work, but more often it only sets off an escalating series of conflicts and confrontations.

The fact is that parents must accept the reality that their child is changing into an adult. The process may go very smoothly, or it may have its turbulent periods. Whether smooth or turbulent, it requires a significant change in the parents' orientation and relationship toward their youngster. But if the relationship has been positive and close in the earlier years, such a change in viewpoint not only is possible but is the first step in the transformation of the relationship to one of mutual respect and closeness among adults.

PART III

SPECIAL FAMILY
ISSUES

13

Special Children with Special Needs

WE ARE primarily concerned in this book with the psychological development of the physically healthy child who does not suffer from a serious psychiatric disorder. It is not possible in a book such as this to discuss as well the many different kinds of physical and psychiatric disabilities that children can suffer, or to cover adequately their psychological consequences and problems of management. Fortunately there are now a number of manuals available to parents that spell out the details of both the physical and psychological handling of the various specific kinds of handicaps.

We do feel, however, that a brief discussion of certain important general psychological issues that may arise with handicapped children would be useful. The value of this discussion should not be restricted to parents with a handicapped youngster. Many other parents may at one time or another have to contend with one or another of these issues. A close friend or a member of the extended family group may have a handicapped child. How do friends and relatives relate to such a child on visits back and forth? Or a child may strike up a friendship with a handicapped child in the neighborhood and bring him home for after-school visits. Again, how should the parents respond to such a special visitor to their home? And finally, some of the psychological issues that apply with special force to handicapped children may also be applicable, perhaps in modified form, to special situations that may arise at times with normal children.

The Handicapped Child and Normal Development

Is the handicapped child normal? How we answer this question depends on our definition of what is normal. This is not just an academic or theoretical issue; the definition has profound practical implications for the training and education of handicapped children. If we believe that there is only one standard of normality—the way children without handicaps behave and speak—then the handicapped child is normal only if he can duplicate not simply the level but also the manner of achievement of a nonhandicapped youngster. If, on the other hand, we broaden the concept of what is normal in terms of achievement and functioning, then the handicapped child does not have to be a carbon copy of his nonhandicapped age-mate to be considered normal.

The difference between these two approaches can be illustrated dramatically by the example of how language and communication skills are taught to deaf children. Until recent years, the vast majority of the schools for the deaf in the United States used only oral training—that is, lipreading and voicing of words. This approach rested on the firm conviction that there was only one normal road to the development of language and thought— that taken by the child with normal hearing. Sign language, which had been developed as an effective method of communication for the deaf, was labeled by professional teachers of the deaf as inferior and incapable of stimulating normal intellectual development. Parents were instructed in the most authoritative terms to eliminate all gestures of any kind in communicating with their deaf children, in order to insure the success of oral training.

Evidence from a number of studies in the past fifteen years has challenged this viewpoint decisively, however, and exposed the inadequacy of pure oral training to meet the needs of deaf children, especially those with severe or profound hearing loss. Hilde Schlesinger, of the University of California, and Kathryn Meadow, of Gallaudet College for the Deaf, showed that deaf children of deaf parents, who communicated with each other from infancy onward, showed greater academic and language achievement than did deaf children of hearing parents who were not skillful in sign language (1972). An extensive British study tested 468 adolescents, deaf from infancy onward but with no additional handicap, who were graduating from schools for the deaf. All the schools used only the oral method of language training. The study found that the more severe the child's loss of hearing, irrespective of intelligence, the less language skill he had developed (Conrad 1979). In our own longitudinal study of children born deaf because of congenital rubella, we found that oral speech training significantly increased speaking ability in only a small percentage of the children. In line with other reports, we found that the use of sentences in the orally trained children varied inversely with the severity of hearing loss. Even at the nine-year-old age level, fewer than 15 percent with profound deafness used any kind of sentences. These youngsters, if trained only orally, were unable to learn effectively or communicate socially. On the other hand, once total communication was introduced (the combined use of lipreading, sign language, facial expression, and gestures), academic achievement and social functioning quickly accelerated. A number of other studies have reported the same conclusion: Oral training alone is completely inadequate for severely or profoundly deaf children. Sign language is a true language that can stimulate intellectual development, just as normal speech does in children who are not deaf. By now, all the major schools for the deaf of which we are aware have accepted these findings and made a commitment to the use of total communication.

We have detailed this history of the education of the deaf because it illustrates a basic thesis so clearly: The brain is so flexible that there is no single road to normal development. If a handicap prevents normal development in the usual way, there are alternative pathways in the brain that can be utilized to achieve similar normal emotional, social, and intellectual development. By the use of total communication, the deaf child's visual and motor abilities can be harnessed to compensate for his auditory handicap. He can argue, push limits, understand why and when safety rules are necessary, learn social necessities, express emotions clearly, explore ideas, and master abstraction and symbolization.

This same principle holds for the blind child or the child with cerebral palsy or other problems of smooth motor functioning. Most of us know people who have found ways of overcoming one handicap or another and gone on to reach impressive levels of functioning. We know of one talented professional violinist with marked cerebral palsy. This condition has affected the hand he uses for bowing the violin, but by using the flexible alternative brain pathways he has mastered, he has extraordinarily effective control of the violin.

There is also the case of Jerome Bruner, one of this country's most distinguished and productive psychologists. In his autobiographical essay *In Search of Mind* (1983), Bruner relates that he was born blind because of congenital cataracts that could not be removed until he was two years old. Then, although he was no longer blind, he could see only by the use of thick, heavy glasses. The removal of the natural lenses of his eyes, required by the operation, also meant that his visual field was restricted. He had no peripheral vision and could see only what was directly in front of him. In effect, he went through his childhood years as though he was wearing blinders. As he reports it, "It was not until I was fitted with contact lenses as an adult that I realized what I had missed by way of peripheral vision as a child" (p. 16). But these handicaps did not stunt his intellectual growth, nor did they prevent him from becoming an expert swimmer and sailor and a man of social charm who made and kept many friends.

The clarification to a family that their handicapped child is still basically a normal human being can at times be the crucial factor that sets the course of the child's further development. We remember vividly a boy of eight whose arm had been crushed in a bizarre accident and required amputation. The boy was a patient on the rehabilitation service of our medical center, where he was being fitted for an artificial arm. The psychiatric resident on that service was called in because the boy was depressed and so overwhelmed by his tragic accident that he could barely cooperate with the hospital staff. The boy's father, who was partially responsible for the accident, was shattered not only by his guilt feelings but by the loss, as he put it, "of all my dreams of teaching my son to play baseball, and all the fun we were going to have together as he grew up in all kinds of sports and outings. Now all that is gone." With this reaction, the father was actually becoming distant from his son and could not give the boy the support and encouragement the youngster needed so desperately. The stage was set for a self-fulfilling prophecy—the boy would become a cripple, dependent on his family, feeling he could no longer be a part of his normal age-mate groups, and isolated from his father, whose feelings of helplessness would only make him more guilty and more distant as he watched his son become more and more handicapped.

The psychiatric resident consulted with one of us (S.C.), and we formulated a strategy of intervention. The resident, a mature and thoughtful person, felt that it was crucial to work with the father to change his perspective, and he was absolutely right. The resident was able to make a strong positive contact with the father and discussed with him in detail the many steps that the father could take to help his son learn athletic and social skills in spite of his handicap. These ideas were a revelation to the father. He now began to see his son not as doomed to be a hopeless cripple but as the normal boy he had always been, a boy quite capable of leading a normal life. The father came out of his shell and began to plan with his son how they would work and play together to minimize the boy's handicap. The resident made the same points to the boy, but it was the father's turnabout that made the difference. The youngster's depression lifted, and he plunged into the hospital program, now determined that he could and would learn to lead a normal life again.

Unfortunately, such positive outcomes for the handicapped child are not always possible. If there are multiple handicaps, such as brain damage combined with cerebral palsy, deafness, or blindness, or if the handicap is extreme, as with severe and profound mental retardation or very serious muscular or neurological defects, the goal of basically normal development may be unattainable. But even in many of these cases, proper professional guidance and treatment may make a big difference in the youngster's life, as limited as it may be.

Stress on the Family

The presence of a handicapped child inevitably leads to an increase in the stresses, problems, and worries of the family. If the handicap is temporary, as with a premature infant without complications, the family difficulties will be brief and relatively mild. If the problem is correctible surgically, as with certain forms of congenital heart disease, the family stresses may be more severe and prolonged, but the outcome will also be a happy one. If the handicap is chronic and noncorrectible but relatively mild, as with mild mental retardation or the less severe forms of cerebral palsy or other motor difficulties, then the strains on the family and the child may be continuous but manageable. If, however, the child has a severe chronic handicap, such as disabling cerebral palsy, profound deafness, or blindness, the special training and other resources that will have to be devoted to such a child's safety and education can put a heavy burden on a family's functioning. And if the child's problems are even more serious, as in the case of severe mental retardation or autism, the family may face the anguish of deciding that it cannot cope with the child at home and that some kind of institutional care is required.

Finally, there are the healthy children, developing normally in every way, who are suddenly stricken with a malignant tumor or become the victim of a crippling illness or accident. Even if treatment is successful, the child's life and the family's responsibilities for the youngster may be drastically and tragically transformed.

Denial and Overprotection

Parents of a handicapped child often go through an initial period of shock and bewilderment when faced with the fact that their child will not develop and function in the fully normal way they had hoped and expected. We witnessed these parental reactions in our study of children with congenital rubella, who had all kinds of handicaps—deafness, blindness, mental retardation, neurological problems, and cardiac defects—and sometimes more than one handicap. We were impressed, however, by how most of the parents, once they understood the nature of the handicap and the special attention and training their child would need, faced up realistically to their responsibilities for the child's welfare. This has also been true of many parents of other handicapped children who have consulted us in hospital clinics or privately over the years.

Other parents of a handicapped child, however, try to deal with their shock and stress by the use of one of two psychological mechanisms. They may try to shut their eyes to the magnitude of the problem and even deny that their child's handicap needs any special attention. Or they may go to the opposite extreme and become so concerned and anxious over their child's special problems that they try to insulate him from difficult and stressful situations. Either attitude—denial or overprotection—can be disastrous for the youngster.

When the parents deny the problem, the child is put in a hopeless double bind: He is expected to be as competent as the nonhandicapped child, and at the same time he is deprived of the special services and training that could minimize the effects of his handicap. Furthermore, with certain handicaps such as deafness and blindness, there is the danger that he will lose the opportunity to learn the special rules of safety he will need to navigate on his own in the outside world.

On the other hand, the excessively sheltered handicapped child is denied many opportunities to discover the extent of his positive assets and abilities as well as his limitations. He misses the many experiences he can master that can give him confidence in his capacities to cope with the outside world as well as sharpen his judgments about what he can or cannot do. The overprotected handicapped child often grows up with a self-fulfilling prophecy. His parents' attitude that he must be protected from all the stresses and demands of normal living results in his becoming incompetent and helpless, when these effects could have been minimized by a different, more constructive approach. The handicapped child should be given every opportunity to test his positive capacities and should be cheered on, especially for all his difficult accomplishments. Failures should not be the occasion for helpless disappointment by parent and child but opportunities for testing other approaches that will convert failures into success. Sometimes the solutions are very simple. A child with unstable control over his fine muscle movements may not be able to grasp a pencil and write with it, but if a thick band such as an eraser with a hole in it is slipped around the middle of the pencil, the child will be able to grasp the pencil firmly and use it effectively. Such strategies create the golden road to the handicapped child's achievement of a healthy self-esteem and self-confidence. Most communities have competent, trained rehabilitation experts who can work with parents in developing alternatives for the child in mastering the difficult tasks imposed by his handicap.

We can illustrate the sad consequences of overprotection and denial with two case examples. One involved a blind girl overprotected by her parents, and the other a deaf boy whose parents tried to deny his handicap.

Marie developed a rare tumor of both eyes in infancy, which required the removal of both eyes. She was expertly fitted with false eyes and was quite attractive in her general appearance, and it was not at all evident to a casual observer that she was blind. She went to a community public school with a special resource teacher who taught her to read Braille, and she was able to make academic progress, though slowly, through her successive school years.

Marie's parents, however, refused to take any initiative or responsibility for the special training a blind child needs to become functionally independent. They would not enroll her in a mobility-training program in which she could learn, as other blind children do, to navigate on her own with the use of a cane. Instead, her mother held her by the hand wherever they went. The parents also serviced all her needs and whims and made minimal demands on her for any kind of independent functioning. By age fourteen, Marie had become a petulant youngster, utterly dependent on her parents and prone to loud tantrums if thwarted in any of her desires. In school, however, where such behavior was not tolerated, she behaved rather reasonably. It was at this time that her mother brought her for psychiatric consultation because of her difficult behavior at home. Treatment for both Marie and her parents was focused on the goal of making her more independent and not indulging her demands, which perpetuated her dependency and helplessness. Discussions with Marie and her mother, sometimes separately and sometimes together, spelled out the many specific ways in which this goal could be achieved and the difference it would make in the girl's life. The suggestions made no impact on Marie. The mother gave lip-service to the discussions but always had some excuse why she could not carry through any of the recommendations. After some months of treatment, with no progress evident, the family moved to the West Coast, and we never heard from them again. Our unhappy judgment was that Marie was doomed to a life of dependency and helplessness and would not attain the level of positive functioning so many blind persons do achieve.

The other case was Jeremy, who was profoundly deaf as the result of congenital rubella. His affluent middle-class parents absolutely refused to allow their deaf child to learn sign language, even though it was clear that he could never become proficient in lipreading and vocal speech. He had none of the other handicaps that frequently result from congenital rubella, so that the ability to use sign language would have made him a competent member of the deaf community.

The boy's parents, however, tried in every way possible to disguise and hide Jeremy's handicap. It was not just a question of fooling other people; much more it was an issue of trying to fool themselves. As long as he tried to lipread and to talk, no matter how minimal his accomplishments were, they could persuade themselves that his handicap was slight and that he could learn to conceal the fact that he was deaf. But if he began to use sign language, they could not shut their eyes to the fact that he was permanently and profoundly deaf and could not communicate as normal children do. They refused to enroll him in a school for the deaf, instead placing him in a private school with a program for deaf children. This program included a special resource teacher who would explain the scheduled lessons to the deaf children in sign language, but again the parents refused to allow Jeremy to be taught sign language, so the special resource teacher could be of little help to him. The poor boy sat in class, unable to participate, and unable to learn effectively.

Our discussions with the parents could not budge them. The boy himself told us, in his few barely understandable words, that his aim in life was to be the manager of a fast-food restaurant. We suspect that he will in appearance achieve this goal. His parents will buy him a franchise for the restaurant, he will be the nominal manager while someone else actually runs it, and they will have their "proof" that his handicap was really minimal. But the youngster himself will have been denied the opportunity to learn to communicate effectively in the deaf community and to link this achievement to relationships and activities in the nondeaf world.

Mainstreaming

During the 1960s and early 1970s, many parents of handicapped children became progressively more dissatisfied with the traditional separate educational facilities available to their children. They questioned whether their children could grow up and function in the wider society if they were so restricted in their social and educational experiences. Parents, special educators, and a few physicians teamed up to form advocacy groups that worked to bring about the passage by Congress of Public Law 94–142, The Education for All Handicapped Children Act. This law, enacted in 1975, guarantees the right of a handicapped child to a free, appropriate public education in "the least restrictive environment." This provision requires that wherever possible school-aged handicapped children be educated together with nonhandicapped children; in other words, they should be educated in the mainstream of their community's life. Handicapped children are to be assigned to special schools only if the nature or severity of the handicap is such that education in regular classes is not feasible.

The mandate of P.L. 94–142 was clear. Public school districts would have to provide the special personnel and the space required to accept responsibility for this new group of previously excluded children. Steps would have to be taken to identify the handicapped children in the community, so those who would benefit by mainstreaming could be accepted into the public school system. Each handicapped student would have to be provided with an individualized educational plan, for the special needs of children with different handicaps vary greatly.

The concept of mainstreaming, as expressed in P.L. 94–142, marks a milestone in the education of handicapped children. Unfortunately, as is so often the case, the implementation of the concept has varied greatly in different schools and different communities. Some schools have taken this mandate seriously. They have welcomed the handicapped children into their classrooms, devised all kinds of imaginative plans to make them feel at home, involved the other students positively with their new classmates, and carried through the special educational programs the children needed. At the other extreme, all too many schools have given only lip-service to the concept of mainstreaming. They have given little attention to the special needs of these handicapped children, and the children are again segregated, but now in a regular schoolroom instead of a special school.

The failure of the responsible educational authorities to monitor adequately the implementation of the congressional mainstreaming mandate is shocking. The federal government itself, although it passed P.L. 94–142, has failed to provide the funds required for its implementation (Zigler & Muenchow 1979). Many, if not most, local school boards have been unwilling or unable to provide the funds required for mainstreaming to be successful. And with the federal government progressively cutting back on funds for local and state community services, the outlook is for further shrinkage in the number of adequately funded mainstreaming programs. A cut in a school budget may mean the elimination of the special resource teachers who had made a good mainstreaming program possible.

Nor have adequate funds for research into the effectiveness of different types of mainstreaming programs been provided. We are unable to answer certain basic questions: Which handicapped children benefit from attending a regular community school, and which children profit more from attendance at a special school? What types of special resources are necessary for various kinds of handicaps, and how should these special resources be applied? Edward Zigler pointed out in 1979 that "much more work is needed to determine . . . just which children, with which handicaps, can benefit from mainstreaming" (p. 995). Almost ten years later, this work still remains to be done, and given the present political climate, we are pessimistic that it will be accomplished in the near future. In the meantime, parents with a handicapped child can only solicit empirical advice from knowledgeable educators about which type of school seems best for their child. Trial and error may be also required, to test out where the child will do best. It is indeed a tragedy that a decade after the passage of the mainstreaming law, this is still the best advice we can offer parents.

Parent Support Groups

Support groups for parents of handicapped children can help in a number of ways. The guilt feelings that many mothers have—"I must have done something wrong during my pregnancy"—can be expressed openly and fully to a sympathetic audience. The audience is reassuring, and there is generally at least one mother in the group whose child has the same handicap and can say, "Look, I managed my pregnancy differently from the way you did, and yet my child has the same handicap as yours." The mothers of children with congenital rubella need special reassurance with regard to their guilt feelings, because it was their infection with this virus during pregnancy that was transmitted to the unborn child. In most cases, the disease was not diagnosed, because the mother suffered only a brief mild rash, and emphasis on this fact can be very helpful in relieving guilt. Parents whose children have suffered permanent damage from some serious accident also are likely to have strong guilt feelings, and supportive reassurance is often more helpful from other parents than from the impersonal figure of a health professional.

Groups of parents with children suffering from similar handicaps can be especially helpful to each other. The more experienced parents can inform the newcomers to the group about special services and how to obtain them. The parents can also compare notes on how they have handled specific problems: how to teach a child with cerebral palsy to dress himself, how to show a diabetic child that he can inject his own insulin, what special rules of safety a deaf or blind child needs to learn and how to go about teaching him, and how to deal with the many special problems of daily living that an autistic or retarded child presents. An experienced parent with a handicapped child can sometimes be more knowledgeable about such issues than the professional staff.

Many parent groups also develop cooperative mutual help activities. A parent of a handicapped child often has great difficulty in finding an adequate baby-sitter or car pool. The parents of children with similar handicaps are often very helpful in providing these services for each other and in pitching in when there is a special crisis.

These parent groups are encouraged by hospitals and other centers for the handicapped. Sometimes they form spontaneously as parents become acquainted in a clinic waiting room. Some parent groups stay in existence for many months or several years; others tend to break up after a few months, when the parents feel they no longer need them.

The Effect of the Handicapped Child on Brothers and Sisters

A handicapped child not only creates special stresses and responsibilities for the parents but also can create problems and difficulties for the non-handicapped siblings. They may feel neglected by all the special attention and family resources given to their handicapped brother or sister. They may resent the burdens they may have to bear in assisting in the care of the handicapped child. They may be embarrassed to bring their friends home and have them witness the bizarre appearance or behavior of the handicapped child.

But such negative reactions are not universal. Some children take on a protective role and stop their age-mates from scapegoating their handicapped sibling. Some take on the role of informal teachers and teach their afflicted brother or sister how to cope with at least some of the social demands of the outside world. Some coach a handicapped sibling with imperfect muscular control so that he can participate in group athletics on at least a modest level. On a more subtle but very important level, such active and age-appropriate involvement in the care of a handicapped brother or sister may give the nonhandicapped child a sense of importance in the family's life and increase his confidence in his ability to master unusual demands and stresses, especially those connected with illness and handicap.

In other words, there is no simple formula by which the effect of a handicapped child on his brothers and sisters can be calculated. A recent thorough review of this issue by Denis Drotar, of Case Western Reserve University in Cleveland, and Peggy Crawford, of the Cleveland University Hospital, has emphasized this fact (1985). A number of studies quoted by these authors indicate that the effect of a child's chronic illness on the psychological adjustment of siblings is selective and varies with age, sex, and type of illness. The preexisting stability of the family and the effect of the handicapped child on the parents are also important factors in the nonhandicapped siblings' reactions. Parents can be reassured that a chronic illness in one child does not necessarily increase the psychologic risk for the siblings. They can be open and honest with their nonhandicapped children about the special care that is necessary for their handicapped sibling and give them some appropriate positive role in this special family responsibility. At the same time, the nonhandicapped siblings should be encouraged to lead their own lives as normally as possible under the circumstances.

Occasionally, the problems posed for the family by a severely handicapped child may be so severe that it may be very difficult for the healthy sibling to live a normal life. We remember poignantly the anguished dilemma of Marian, whose brother, Allen, seven years younger, suffered from severe autism. This very serious illness of childhood involves a distortion of development in a host of psychological characteristics and is therefore now designated as a "pervasive developmental disorder." Such a child cannot make a social contact that has any emotional meaning. He learns by rote memory but cannot use his knowledge in any social context, such as in a give-and-take communication with another person. He is prone to develop rituals and obsessive ideas and can have explosive outbursts of rage.

One of us (S.C.) saw Allen first when he was about four years old and the diagnosis was already evident. With cases of autism of this severity, the outlook is very dismal, and institutional care is usually recommended. But Allen's mother was adamant that he would remain at home, and I could not challenge her statement that institutions for such children were uniformly dreadful places. The mother devoted her life to Allen's care, and gradually Marian had to participate as well. By the time she was an adolescent, Marian's own social life began to shrink because of the incessant care and vigilance required for Allen's supervision and training. The father was only peripherally involved because of his outside work responsibilities. Marian became interested in a specific career that took her away from home, but she had to give it up because of repeated urgent calls to come back home because of a new crisis with her brother. Allen, who is now in his late twenties, has been helped by the medications that have become available and is being placed in a small home for autistic adults. If this move succeeds, Marian, now in her thirties, may be able to start a life of her own. But doing so will not be easy, given the many years she sacrificed to her brother's life. Should she have done differently? It is easy to say she should have insisted on pursuing her own social life as an adolescent and her career as a young adult. But when this advice was given her by various people, she would pull back with a frightened look and ask, "But what will happen to my mother and Allen without me?" Fortunately such tragic dilemmas are rare, but when they occur there is no simple answer.

Control and Competence

Two kinds of experiences that are central to the child's development of a healthy and realistic self-esteem and self-confidence are those in which he feels in control over the events in his life and those in which he feels competent in the mastery of the successive challenges of life. The handicapped child usually faces special difficulties in achieving these experiences. Whether his handicap is deafness, blindness, subnormal intelligence, a difficulty with muscular strength and dexterity, or another abnormality in an important function of the body or mind, it is bound to interfere with his easy development of a sense of competence. Surgical procedures or other corrective measures may further threaten his sense of control over his life.

Many such children, faced with difficult and interminable struggles that are not part of the lives of their more fortunate age-mates, may also torment themselves with the question, "Why me, what did I do to deserve this?" Such a question easily leads to guilt feelings ("It must be my fault"), bitterness ("Life has given me a raw deal"), frustrating envy ("I'm as good as they are, and look what an easy time they have compared to me"), or a combination of these demoralizing reactions. Parents, other family members, friends of the family, and professionals should be aware that the handicapped child may be nursing such feelings, which can only compound his difficulties in achieving a sense of self-worth and competence. Encouragement and guidance are essential antidotes, but they have to be applied, not as clichés, but appropriately and specifically—at times of real achievement or at moments of frustration or despair over failure at a difficult task.

Programming step-by-step sequences of increasing difficulty in meeting the demands of a task—whether social, academic, or athletic—is an especially important way in which the child can experience achievement and competence. And open recognition of such expanding competence by the family and friends of the family can give the handicapped child an optimistic view of his own potential and future possibilities in life.

The parents of a child who strikes up a friendship with a handicapped child can also be very helpful. They can encourage the friendship and emphasize to their own child that a child can have a handicap in one area and be entirely normal in all other ways. They can suggest to their youngster that his handicapped friend would be a welcome visitor to their home. On such visits, the parents should treat the handicapped child in a matter-of-fact way and at the same time be alert to avoiding situations that would make for embarrassment or accidents. For example, if the child is blind, the parents and their own child can describe the layout of their rooms and furniture and any potential hazards. If he is deaf, they can find out whether or not he can lip-read and structure their communication with him accordingly.

The Special Stresses of Adolescence

In the previous chapter, we demonstrated that the great majority of boys and girls go through adolescence without significant emotional or behavioral problems. The same benign prognosis for adolescence, however, cannot be given for many handicapped youngsters, if not the majority. Normal adolescence does bring many changes in life style and activities, which most nonhandicapped youngsters can achieve easily and smoothly. Relationships with age-mates shift from the involvement with one or two friends at a time, which is characteristic of the earlier childhood years, to group activities. Boy-girl contacts begin to blossom and take on sexual overtones. The urge for independence creates fashions in dress, hairstyles, and special idiomatic expressions through which the adolescent proclaims that he is no longer a child but is beginning to shape his life on his own. The physical development starting in puberty raises the standards for skills in sports and games.

All these transitions, as simple as they may be for most normal adolescents, may be difficult, confusing, and sometimes even impossible for the handicapped adolescent. The deaf youngster may not be able to follow the rapid banter, kidding, and special idioms of the friends he made in childhood. The blind adolescent may not know that he now appears conspicuous because his dress and hairstyle are out of conformity with the group's. (Such issues may appear trivial, but they can assume great importance in adolescent groups.) The handicapped youngster may find that a childhood friend is now reluctant to have him tag along when the friend is now trying to be part of a boy-girl group. The deaf or blind adolescent may find that the group is deciding on an expedition for which he is not prepared, such as going to a movie. The handicapped youngster with clumsy muscular movements due to cerebral palsy or some other cause may find that it is now hopeless to try to keep up with his friends in a baseball or basketball game, even when he had formerly been able to participate in sports with them on at least a modest level.

Parents, teachers, and a really close friend can do a great deal to ameliorate these difficult problems the handicapped youngster meets in adolescence, but they cannot eliminate these stresses or anticipate all the unexpected issues the handicapped adolescent will face. These youngsters have already been struggling to master the demands of social and academic life in spite of their handicap. The need to make the new and often complex adaptations of adolescence may just be too heavy an additional task for many of them, even for those who have previously functioned well in a mainstream program in a regular school. Several examples from our research studies can illustrate the special problems of these youngsters when they reach adolescence.

Julie, profoundly deaf as a result of congenital rubella, was an avid reader and writer. She used complex sentences with correct grammar and subtle nuances of meaning. She had a number of hobbies and was extremely persistent in all her undertakings. She was in a regular school, and her academic work was not only up to grade level but superior in several subjects, especially English. Her family situation was peaceful, and the family members helped her as needed with special situations, such as telephone conversations. Julie was part of her nondeaf age-group to a limited extent, although her mother also encouraged her to attend a young adult deaf social group.

As Julie came into adolescence, however, her social relationships with her age-mates with normal hearing became increasingly difficult and stressful. In contrast to her earlier childhood experiences, she found that rapid give-and-take verbal communication was an essential part of a teen-age social group. Lip-reading, at which she was adept, was no longer adequate for this purpose. In addition, her own speech was difficult for other adolescents to understand. She became increasingly isolated socially outside her home and her deaf social group, and some of her classmates even began to mock and tease her. As she put it in a poignant autobiographical vignette about a girl named Andrea, "Often, the other children teased and tormented Andrea for being deaf and talking differently, sometimes with an unusual, squeaky high pitch." Though very distressed, she and her mother were facing the realities directly, as they always had. At our last contact with them, she was learning sign language, and they were considering transferring Julie to a high school for the deaf when she finished junior high school, if her social situation continued to deteriorate.

Billy, another of our profoundly deaf congenital rubella children, had also had an academically successful mainstreaming experience in a regular school. Unlike Julie, however, he first went through an initial unhappy and unsatisfactory school experience. His first school failed to provide a special resource teacher, no individual educational plan was developed, and his classroom teacher resented having a deaf child in her class. Billy, who was intensely negative temperamentally when under stress, began having severe tantrums and oppositional, aggressive behavior, both at school and at home.

The parents then combed the other schools in the community until they found a sympathetic principal ready to make a strong commitment to Billy's special educational needs. The boy transferred to this school, an individualized program was developed for him, and a special resource teacher was provided as needed. The principal even started an after-school club in which both deaf and hearing children could learn to sign, with Billy at its head. In this new school, with all these favorable and even necessary conditions for his education, Billy blossomed. His symptoms disappeared, he became a cooperative member of the class, and he began to learn effectively.

Billy's social adaptation in adolescence has thus far been less frustrating than Julie's, although he has been able to make only one hearing friend. He does occasionally join neighborhood ball games, where his deafness is not a disabling handicap. Fortunately, he has also developed mechanical talents, which have served as a social bridge to his age-mates. He fixes neighborhood children's bikes and various items of school apparatus and is in demand for these activities. It is clear to him and his family, however, that his deafness creates an extremely difficult barrier to becoming fully accepted into a hearing social group. He is planning to attend the National Technical Institute for the Deaf, a first-class institution in Rochester, New York, which has joint classes with hearing students attending the National Technical Institute under the same administration.

Julie and Billy are success stories on the academic value of mainstreaming. But this mainstreaming in no way guarantees a successful passage into the mainstream of adolescent social life.

Our study of the developmental course of mentally retarded children comprised a group of fifty-two middle-class mildly retarded children who had all been living at home in childhood. The families were committed to keeping their children at home if at all possible and to giving them the educational and social experiences they could master while living in the community. In adolescence, however, eleven of these youngsters had been in an institution for at least a period of time, and nine other families were actively seeking appropriate residential placement. Thus, twenty of these fifty-two youngsters had been able to adjust and function at home in childhood but not in adolescence.

An analysis of the differences in this group from the remaining thirty-two who were still capable of a positive adjustment at home and in the community showed that the nonadjusted adolescent group had lower IQ scores, a much higher incidence of behavior problems, a higher percentage with brain damage, and a significantly higher number with the difficult temperament pattern (Chess 1980).

All these factors make for a decreased capacity to adapt to the demands and expectations of the home, the school, and the community. During childhood, with the positive support system provided by the families, the difficulties these children had in coping with their environment were not sufficient to make them unmanageable at home and in the community. With the new demands and stresses of adolescence, however, the situation changed. As the mentally retarded children with difficult behavior became older and stronger, this behavior became less and less acceptable to others. Public scenes became more embarrassing to parents, brothers, and sisters. Previously supportive neighbors at best lost patience and at worst became concerned that the retarded youth might be dangerous to their own children. Appropriate recreational facilities were not easily available or were rejected by the youngster. Traveling sometimes was an insurmountable problem because of poor judgment and easy confusion. Parents often had to make an agonizing choice between residential institutional care for their difficult mentally retarded adolescent or sacrificing the interests of their other children if they kept him at home.

Although adolescence is a period of exceptional stress and difficulty for the handicapped youngster, the outlook should not be considered at all hopeless. We all know of many people with even severe handicaps who make the transition to adult life successfully and productively. We need more research to identify the specific issues in individual youngsters and to develop new approaches that will make the passage through adolescence less stressful for handicapped youngsters. Above all, we need a genuine and continuous national commitment to provide the resources necessary to make adolescence less painful and stressful.

14

The Tyranny of
the IQ Score

AT THE BEGINNING of this century the French minister of public education was troubled by the fact that a number of children were failing to learn successfully in normal classrooms. He commissioned Alfred Binet, director of the psychology laboratory at the Sorbonne, to investigate the problem. The commission had a specific practical goal: to develop a way of identifying these children so that they could be given some form of special education.

Binet himself was a remarkable scientist. He had already been interested in the measurement of intelligence and had conducted painstaking experiments based on the work of the eminent nineteenth-century French physician and anthropologist Paul Broca. Broca, and others of that time, firmly believed that the size of the brain was highly correlated with intelligence: the greater the size of the brain, the higher the intelligence. Higher intelligence was said to be especially correlated with the size of the anterior portion of the skull, the presumed seat of intelligence. Furthermore, it was considered an established fact that the brains of the "superior" white races were definitely greater in size than those of the "inferior" black races.

Binet, who was a scientist of great integrity, found to his distress that

AUTHORS' NOTE: Much of the historical material in this chapter is taken from Stephen Jay Gould's fascinating book *The Mismeasure of Man* (1981). Gould, a Professor of Geology and Biology at Harvard University, has made an outstanding contribution to the expansion and elaboration of the concepts of evolution fathered by Darwin. *The Mismeasure of Man* traces with scholarship and clarity the sad history of the attempts of eminent scientists over the centuries to justify blatant racist and sexist prejudices.

his studies did not confirm Broca's assertions. There did not appear to be any relationship between the size and shape of the skull and a student's level of academic achievement. Binet also reported an experience that all scientists must take to heart. "I feared," he wrote in 1900, "that in making measurements on heads with the intention of finding a difference in volume between an intelligent and a less intelligent head, I would be led to increase, unconsciously and in good faith, the cephalic volume of intelligent heads and to decrease that of unintelligent heads." He recognized that such a danger is greater when the bias is submerged and the scientist believes in his own objectivity, and he described an experiment in which his measurements were distorted by just such a subconscious bias. "The details," he said, "the majority of authors do not publish; one does not want to let them be known" (quoted Gould 1981, pp. 146–48).

Binet and his colleague Theodore Simon devised a series of short tests of graded difficulty related to everyday life. The solutions presumably involved processes of reasoning, and the number and difficulty of the tasks a child could accomplish were postulated to correlate with her age and intelligence—that is, her "mental age." On checking this hypothesis, Binet did indeed find that his measurements of mental ages corresponded with teachers' judgments of children's intelligence.

Binet revised his scale several times before his death in 1911, and a subsequent revision was made in 1916 by Lewis Terman, of Stanford University. This final revised form became the Stanford-Binet Intelligence Test, which soon was in wide use. Terman also introduced the concept of the "intelligence quotient," which was calculated by dividing the mental age by the actual age (up to sixteen years) and then multiplying by 100 to eliminate decimals. This IQ score, as it is commonly called, thus presumably identifies a person's intelligence in relation to her age-mates. An IQ score of 100 is average, a score of 70 is retarded, and a score of 130 is superior. The lower the score is below 100, the greater is the retardation; the higher it is above 100, the greater is the intellectual superiority, so the current wisdom goes.

The Stanford-Binet test was developed primarily for use with children and proved unsatisfactory for testing adults. In 1939, David Wechsler, the chief psychologist of Bellevue Psychiatric Hospital in New York City, developed an intelligence test for adults. Known as the WAIS (Wechsler Adult Intelligence Scale), it continues to be the mostly widely used intelligence test for adults. Wechsler later developed two other tests, one for older children and one for younger ones, which have certain measurement advantages over the Stanford-Binet test. Several tests have been devised for the infancy period, starting with one devised by Arnold Gesell of Yale

University. Not surprisingly the scores on these infancy tests have correlated poorly with intelligence test scores at later ages, for a number of
the aspects of "intelligence" measured by the tests of older children or
adults, such as verbal ability, have only just begun to appear in the infancy
period.

What Do Intelligence Tests Measure?

But what does the IQ score really tell us? Is it an infallible measurement
of the quality we call "intelligence"? And what are the factors that shape
the IQ score? These are complex questions, and the answers are not simple.

Philosophers have argued for ages, and psychologists have struggled in
the past hundred years or so, over the question of what constitutes intelligence. How do we compare the creative intelligence of a Shakespeare or
Picasso with the equally creative but differently directed intelligence of a
Newton or Einstein? How do we compare the insights and judgments of
a great statesman with the administrative skills and business acumen of a
successful corporate executive? If several youngsters achieve the same high
IQ score, and one goes on to become an imaginative artist or scientist,
another becomes a brilliant journalist or editor, a third turns out to be a
stimulating teacher, and a fourth settles into a routine professional or
business job, what are we to conclude about the meaning of their similar
IQ scores? Binet himself understood clearly that a so-called intelligence
test is not a true measure of that complex, elusive and many-sided human
quality we call *intelligence.* He cautioned that his scale, "properly speaking,
does not permit the measure of the intelligence, because intellectual qualities are not superposable, and therefore cannot be measured as linear
surfaces are measured" (Gould 1981, p. 151). In other words, if we measure
one stick of wood that is ten inches long and another that is fifteen inches
long, we can say that the second stick is 50 percent longer than the first.
But if we measure the IQ of one child as 100 and that of a second as 150,
we are not justified as saying that the second child's intelligence is 50
percent higher than the first's.

IQ tests presume to measure intelligence through a series of separate
subtests that rate the subject's knowledge, comprehension of the meaning
of words, abstract thinking (through the identification of similarities and
differences), reasoning (through the ability to put a group of pictures into
a series so that they tell a story), and so on. Each subtest is scored on a

rating system in which the average child's performance is marked 100, and progressively lower or higher scores presumably measure lower or higher intelligence. The final IQ is obtained by averaging the sum of all the subtest scores, multiplying by 100, and dividing by the subject's age.

This system of scoring and evaluation of an IQ test has several weaknesses. A child may perform well on all subtests except one, and this one poor subtest result will pull down her total IQ score. Yet there may be many reasons for her poor performance on this one subtest: inadequate instruction by the psychologist; confusion about the meaning of the test; less experience with the content of that subtest than with that of the other subtests; or a specific developmental lag in the particular area tested by that subtest. For example, one subtest gives a list of "nonsense squiggles"—that is, meaningless symbols—each of which is associated with a specific number or letter. The child is then presented with a set of the symbols in scrambled order and instructed to put the correct number or letter under each one. Failure in this test may indicate a difficulty in perception or in the coordination of perception and writing, or it may simply mean that the child does not understand the instructions. The difference between these two possibilities is vital, and further special testing is required to determine which one is true. Yet many psychologists may fail to test further and instead simply label the child's answer as proof of a perceptual problem.

Another problem arises in evaluating the relationships between the subtest scores. The IQ subscores are divided into verbal and performance groups, and the "full IQ" is obtained by averaging the two. Some verbal subtests ask for similarities, such as between an apple and an orange, or for differences, such as between a cow and a cat. These tests are graded according to the complexity and subtlety of the answers. For example, if a child responds that a cow is bigger than a cat, her response is given a lower score than if she says that the cow has hoofs and the cat has toes. In one performance subtest, the child is shown pictures in which one element is missing, such as a table with three legs or a cat without whiskers, and the child is asked to name the missing part.

A substantial difference in a child's verbal and performance subscores is usually interpreted as evidence of some problem in overall intelligence, abstract thinking, or perceptual abilities. But there are many other possibilities, including the child's differential knowledge or life experiences with one definition or another, or one object or another. These possibilities should be investigated, if necessary by other tests, but many psychologists simply accept the test results at face value. A low IQ test score should also be analyzed. For example, if a child gives an "I don't know" to many items, it may mean that the language in which the test is being administered is not the child's primary language and that she is having difficulty understanding some of the instructions, or that the child, for one psychological reason or another, is resistant to taking the test. In such cases, an "I don't know" answer may reflect a child's inability to comprehend the test or her refusal to cooperate with the examiner; it tells us nothing about that child's intelligence.

The IQ test appears to be a relatively simple procedure, and clinical psychologists easily learn to administer it. But although it presumes to follow an objective, unbiased, and scientific method, many factors extraneous to "intelligence" may affect a child's IQ score.

The Social Implications of IQ Testing

Binet himself feared that teachers and others would use his test to label children permanently and segregate them according to their presumed intelligence. He also worried, with good cause, that teachers would designate unruly or unmotivated children as "stupid" and incapable of learning and would give up on them. The whole purpose of his work was to identify those children who needed special concentrated methods of teaching, and he protested vigorously against those who were "affirming that an individual's intelligence is a fixed quantity, a quantity that cannot be increased. We must protest and react against this brutal pessimism, we must try to demonstrate that it is founded upon nothing" (quoted in Gould 1981, p. 154).

Binet's forebodings were not idle worries. They came to pass as he had warned when the IQ tests were expanded and refined in the United States and England by Terman and others. The IQ score was fixed to the child as part of her nature. Decisions of school placement and even job assignment and promotion were based on IQ scores. Virginia and several other states passed laws authorizing the sterilization of young women whose IQ scores were in the extremely subnormal range. In 1927 the Supreme Court upheld this law, with the chilling statement, "Three generations of imbeciles are enough" (quoted in Gould 1981, p. 335). Yet Carrie Buck, one young woman whose fate was decided by this decision, married and led a decent life without evidence of mental deficiency, only in her later years discovering why she never could bear children. "My husband and me wanted children desperately. We were crazy about them. I never knew what they'd done to me" (p. 336).

What was actually the case with Carrie Buck, and others like her, was a story of three generations of women brought up in poverty, with abysmally inadequate education, whose life experiences in no way prepared them to answer the abstract and alien questions of the IQ test. Yet even as liberal a Supreme Court justice as Oliver Wendell Holmes could condemn them as hereditary mental imbeciles who would transmit their condition to their children unless they were sterilized.

On a larger scale, intelligence tests given to army recruits in World War I were used to support the prejudices that led to the Immigration Restriction Act of 1924, which was to have far-reaching effects. The modified Stanford-Binet tests used with the recruits had produced the dismal finding that the average white American had a mental age of 13.08. The validity of the test itself and the manner in which it was administered were not questioned, yet it was heavily based on educational knowledge and on American life. Three questions are typical of the test: Crisco is a: patent medicine, disinfectant, toothpaste, food product. The number of a Kaffir's legs is: 2, 4, 6, 8. Christy Mathewson is famous as a: writer, artist, baseball player, comedian. How many modestly educated recruits would know what a Kaffir was? And how many foreign-born would recognize Crisco or Christy Mathewson? In the completion items, in which the recruits were asked to draw in the missing part in a picture, missing items included a rivet in a pocket knife, a horn on a phonograph, a net on a tennis court, and a ball in a bowler's hand. How many working-class Americans or immigrants were familiar with such items? Moreover, the tests were given under all sorts of inadequate conditions, such as in barracks where the instructions could not be heard, or the lighting was inadequate for reading the questions. In one survey of a number of camps, the minimum score on the test ranged from 20 to 100 (pp. 199–202).

Nevertheless, these tests were devised by prominent scientists who proclaimed the objectivity and validity of the procedures, and as a result, many eminent academicians bemoaned the future of American democracy with such an unintelligent population. Going even further, C. C. Brigham, a psychologist at Princeton University, analyzed the Army data and concluded that there had been a gradual deterioration in the class of immigrants who had come to this country in each succeeding five-year period since 1902. He did not fail to emphasize that these recent immigrants had come from southern and eastern Europe and that the previous generations of immigration had been of "Nordic stock." There were many contradictions in his own findings. For example, Northern blacks, who had more education, scored higher than Southern blacks. Brigham simply said that Northern blacks had more white blood and that the more intelligent blacks were drawn to the north. The Army tests had rated Jews (primarily recent immigrants) as low in intelligence. But what about the impressive accomplishments of so many Jewish scholars, writers, and scientists? Brigham had a ready answer. We are aware of these outstanding Jews, he said, because it surprises us by contrast to the mass of Jewish people. With this kind of tortuous "reasoning," Brigham was able to stick to his basic thesis.

Brigham's book, published in 1923, had a profound political effect. Congress at the time was under pressure from a number of groups who for one reason or another wished to restrict immigration into this country. And here was an impressive "scientific" report that buttressed their cause and became, as Gould puts it, "the most powerful battering ram for these groups" (p. 231). The 1924 Immigration Act was passed, setting the ethnic composition of the country's population in 1890 as the baseline for deciding immigration quotas from each country. Why was 1890 picked? The reason was clear and openly stated. It was only after 1890 that southern and eastern European immigrants began to flood into the United States, threatening to dilute and degrade the precious American Nordic stock. President Coolidge signed the bill with the proclamation, "America must be kept American" (p. 232).

This immigration act had many unhappy effects. Most tragic of all was that it slowed Jewish immigration to a trickle. It has been calculated that the act kept six million southern and eastern Europeans from immigrating to this country between 1924 and 1939 (Chase 1977). One can presume that several million were Jews who would have escaped the Holocaust and that Brigham's "scientific" racist report played a powerful sinister role in their deaths.

In his later years, Brigham had a profound change of heart and stated that his previous work was hopelessly in error. He acknowledged in 1930 that he had combined two different tests which measured different things, that the tests themselves were internally inconsistent, and most important of all, that the tests really measured familiarity with American language and culture and not innate intelligence. "Comparative studies of various national and racial groups," he wrote, "may not be made with existing tests. . . . One of the most pretentious of these comparative racial studies —the writer's own—was without foundation" (quoted in Gould 1981, p. 233). Brigham's recantation took courage and is rare for a scientist, but it came too late. The damage in the 1924 Immigration Act had already been done.

The Weaknesses of IQ Tests

It may be argued that these shocking errors took place several generations ago and that present standards for research in intelligence tests would prevent their reoccurrence. If only this were true! Time after time we have seen mental health professionals and educators accept a psychologist's report of a child's low IQ score and place the child in a class for slow or retarded children without inquiring into the conditions of the test procedure. The child may have been ill that day; she may have been anxious or resistant to the test or to the examiner for some reason; she may have had an unrecognized visual or hearing loss that interfered with her performance; she may have been a recent immigrant whose knowledge of English was still shaky; the examiner may have had a bias against black or Hispanic children. Rarely do the educational authorities inquire into these possibilities and ask that a second test be done.

More subtle factors can also play their part in influencing the IQ score. In our working-class Puerto Rican families, we tested the IQ of 116 children between the ages of six and sixteen years (Thomas et al. 1971). These were older brothers and sisters of the subjects in the longitudinal study. The families were stable geographically. Ninety percent were two-parent families, and over 95 percent of the fathers were employed, the majority as unskilled workers. To ensure comparability and validity of findings, we used two experienced psychologists who were both female, of Puerto Rican origin, and fluent in Spanish and English. Both were familiar with the Wechsler Intelligence Test for Children, which we used for all subjects. In short, we tried to eliminate all the possible sources of bias that might influence the test results. The major difference was that examiner B had never met any of the children before testing them, while examiner A had known their families for years as a result of her participation in other phases of our longitudinal study. Children were assigned arbitrarily to the two examiners for testing.

The results were startling. All 71 children tested by examiner A were found to have IQ scores that were 10 points higher on the average than the 45 children tested by examiner B. Moreover, only 5 percent of the youngsters tested by examiner A had scores that were borderline or defective, in contrast to 45 percent of those tested by examiner B. To check on a possible unrecognized bias in the assignment of children to the two examiners, we selected nine children tested by examiner A and ten by examiner B, making sure that the IQ scores and age distribution were comparable. These children were then tested by the examiner who had not tested them earlier. The examiners were told that this retesting was a "routine check," and no hint was given to them as to the real reason for this procedure.

The retesting showed the same difference. In every instance, the scores attained by the children tested by examiner A were higher than when they were originally tested by examiner B. In no case had these children tested by examiner A been tested by her originally.

At first glance these findings were puzzling. We had controlled for the various sources of bias in test results reported by other investigators: sex differences between examiner and child, differences in race and cultural background, and the testing experience of the examiner. All the testing had been done in a similar environment, in middle-class high-rise apartments adjacent to the Spanish Harlem area.

We therefore hypothesized that differences in examiner style in test administration might be the crucial cause of our findings. We enlisted the aid of Paulina Fernandez, a highly competent clinical psychologist fluent in both English and Spanish. Dr. Fernandez first analyzed the examiners' description of each child's attitude in the testing session. She found that examiner A used positive terms, such as "friendly," "pleasant," "spontaneous," and "relaxed," in 57 percent of the cases, in contrast to negative terms, such as "shy," "hostile," "aloof," and "stubborn." By contrast, examiner B used positive terms in only 45 percent of cases, a statistically significant difference. With regard to the child's behavior, the story was the same. Examiner A used positive terms, such as "involved in tasks," "expressed interest," and "persisted with difficult tasks," in 97 percent of cases, in contrast to 67 percent with examiner B.

The two examiners were then interviewed concerning the way each conducted the testing session. Both examiners had operated within the rules set by the standardized test, but they differed markedly in the manner in which they made initial contact with the children and sustained their interest. Examiner A spent considerable time with the children before starting the test, chatting with them, encouraging their questions about the test, and showing them around the apartment. She also encouraged the children to try again if their first response was "I don't know." In contrast, examiner B described herself as reserved and quiet. She tended to follow a set and impersonal routine that varied little from child to child, did not encourage spontaneous informal chit-chat, and tended to accept a first "I don't know" as a final answer. Examination of the test protocols themselves also showed that the children tested by examiner A gave significantly longer and more elaborate responses than those tested by examiner B.

It is of interest that we did not find these differences in IQ test scores in the middle-class children of native-born parents in our New York Longitudinal Study. The mean IQ scores obtained by three different examiners were identical, despite the fact that the examiners' testing styles and ways of making contact varied greatly. It is our hypothesis that this difference in our findings lies in the different life experiences of the two sets of children. The middle-class children were brought up with all kinds of educational toys and puzzles, and games with their parents often involved solving riddles and problems. For them, the IQ test was just another such game, and the content, rather than the examiner's style, held their attention. The working-class Puerto Rican parents on the whole did not have such achievement-oriented and task-mastery goals for their children. For these children the IQ test represented a strange and even bewildering set of demands. With such a reaction, the examiner's manner of making contact with them—friendly and encouraging or stiff and informal—might make a significant difference in how they performed.

Our findings are similar to those reported in a study of disadvantaged children by Edward Zigler and Earl Butterfield, of Yale University (1968). These researchers contrasted the IQ scores obtained when "optimizing" rather than "standardized" testing procedures were used. In the optimizing procedure, the order of items presented was altered to ensure some degree of initial success and to maximize the number of successes early in the testing procedure. Gentle encouragement was also used. In the standardized situation the items were given in their standard order, and the examiner tried to be neutral though friendly. The techniques used by Zigler and Butterfield to improve performance appeared to be very similar to those used spontaneously by our examiner A, while their standardized procedure closely approximated the behavior of our examiner B. In their study, as in ours, significantly higher levels of IQ were obtained when the optimizing procedures were used.

We went one step further in our study. We obtained the written achievement scores on standard group tests administered by the school. These school test procedures were even more impersonal than the IQ tests done by our examiner B. It was therefore no surprise to find that these school test scores correlated significantly with those obtained by examiner B, but *not* with examiner A's scores.

We can only guess at how many disadvantaged children are labeled as borderline or defective on the basis of impersonal intelligence tests and are therefore tracked into special classes that deprive them of normal learning possibilities. A number of surveys and our own experiences with individual children in mental health clinics suggest that the number is scandalously high. The cost to the individual children, their families, and the community at large must be enormous.

The implications of our study and that of Zigler and Butterfield are many. A standard method of test administration does not mean that all children will respond the same way. The standard testing procedure may bring out optimal performance in one group of children (or adults) but fail drastically to do so in another group from a different sociocultural background. Before any child is labeled as defective or borderline subnormal and assigned to a special class for such children, therefore, it is imperative that the testing procedure be carefully evaluated and that retesting under more favorable circumstances be done if necessary.

Can IQ Change?

Binet himself, as we saw earlier in this chapter, protested strongly against the idea that intelligence was a fixed quantity that could not be increased. But as the IQ movement was taken over in this country and in England, the thesis that intelligence was unchangeable began to dominate the field of clinical psychology. This concept was linked with the eugenics movement, which saw it as leading to a method of raising the level of American society. As a leader in this movement, Lewis Terman asserted that "in the near future intelligence tests will bring tens of thousands of these high-grade defectives under the surveillance and protection of society. This will ultimately result in curtailing the reproduction of feeble-mindedness and in the elimination of an enormous amount of crime, pauperism, and industrial inefficiency" (quoted in Gould 1981, p. 179). Binet wanted to identify these "high-grade defectives" so that they could be given special education and become useful members of society. Terman wanted to identify them so that they could be placed under "surveillance" and prevented from having children.

One study after another, however, has demonstrated that the IQ of a child is not fixed and immutable. In one British study of 109 subjects from varied social backgrounds, the IQ score of 50 percent of the sample changed by 10 points or more between the ages of three and seventeen, and in 25 percent by 22 points or more. Between the ages of eight and seventeen the point spreads were almost as wide, and from infancy even greater (Hindley & Owen 1978). These findings are similar to those from an earlier California study (Pinneau 1961). In our own longitudinal study, though we have not as yet made a systematic study of this issue, there have been a number of significant changes in IQ scores between three and six years and between six and nine years.

The accumulated evidence that the IQ score, like all other psychological attributes, can be changed by environmental factors became so convincing that even Terman himself recanted his previous views. In *Measuring Intelligence* (Terman & Merrill 1937) he said very little about IQ and heredity. All the potential reasons for IQ differences between groups were now couched in environmental terms. He took note of the finding that the IQ of rural children dropped after school entry, while that of urban children of working-class parents rose, and suggested that the difference in IQ change might be due to the better schooling received by the urban children.

By the late 1930s the ideas that the IQ is fixed and that eugenic measures should be taken to restrict the reproductive activity of "mental defectives" seemed to be dead and buried. But like the proverbial cat, these ideas have many lives, and the thesis has come alive again in recent years in a more sophisticated form.

Is Intelligence Hereditary?
The Cases of Arthur Jensen and Cyril Burt

It is now generally accepted by the psychological profession that intelligence is the product of both biological-hereditary and environmental factors. It is evident that as a group children of highly educated families have higher IQ scores than children from poorly educated families. This difference was clearly evident in our middle-class New York Longitudinal Study children as compared with our working-class Puerto Rican children. (With all our caveats regarding the misinterpretation and misuse of the IQ score, it still remains in many types of studies our best measure in comparisons of intellectual ability, as long as we keep its limitations in mind.) But how much is environmental and how much is genetic (hereditary) is difficult to know. That environment was important was evident from the studies mentioned above and from the many reports of children whose IQ scores rose dramatically after adoption into families where they were given richer educational opportunities. But estimating the genetic factor was more difficult. Brothers and sisters share 50 percent of their genes; the question is *which* 50 percent. And even children who grow up in the same family may be exposed to different environmental influences—parental attitudes, peer relationships, school and other life experiences. Such differences in environmental influences further compound the difficulty of determining the genetic factor in the intellectual level of brothers and sisters. Even the great similarity between monozygotic twins—those conceived from the same egg and sperm cell, who share 100 of their genes—cannot be assumed to be entirely genetic. At least in some cases, it may be that their close physical resemblance and their identical ages lead them to be exposed to similar environmental experiences.

But most psychologists and educators were able to live with this ambiguity of genetic versus environmental influences and accept the necessity to give children the best possible education, whatever their level of intelligence or its causes. The general consensus was expressed by a leading psychologist, Florence Goodenough, who herself had sought to devise a culture-free test in the Goodenough-Draw-a-Person Test:

> The search for a culture-free test, whether of intelligence, artistic ability, personal-social characteristics, or any other measurable trait is illusory, and . . . the naive assumption that the mere freedom from verbal requirements [that is, test items that do not require verbal ability] renders a test equally suitable for all groups is no longer tenable. (Goodenough & Harris 1950)

Then, in 1969, Arthur Jensen, a psychologist at Stanford University, startled educators and mental health professionals with an article in which he propounded several assertions for which he claimed scientific evidence: (1) Intelligence was primarily a hereditary genetic trait, accounting for perhaps 80 percent of an individual's intelligence. (2) Blacks were genetically inferior to whites in intelligence. (3) There are two types of learning, Level I, which is associative or rote learning, and Level II, which is conceptual. Blacks learn largely on Level I, and whites on Level II. Education for blacks should therefore concentrate on rote learning and not conceptual learning. (4) With this genetic inferiority in intelligence, compensatory educational programs, such as Head Start, are bound to fail.

The popular media, with few exceptions, accepted uncritically Jensen's conclusions with all their racist implications. Among social scientists the reaction was mainly, though not entirely, one of shock and condemnation. Criticisms came in a flood and concentrated on the many defects in Jensen's data and the inadequate scientific basis for his conclusions. Martin Deutsch, of New York University, a recognized pioneer in the study of the psychological and educational issues of disadvantaged children, prepared a detailed critique of Jensen's article after consultation with a number of psychologists and social scientists (1969). Regarding Jensen's article, Deutsch comments,

I found many erroneous statements, misinterpretations, and misunderstandings of the nature of intelligence, intelligence tests, genetic determination of traits, education in general, and compensatory education in particular. . . . All the errors are in the same direction: maximizing differences between blacks and whites and maximizing the possibility that such differences are attributable to hereditary factors. (p. 524)

Deutsch further points out that Jensen's condemnation of compensatory education is based primarily on the studies of summer Head Start programs, which were brief, often taught by inexperienced teachers, and not followed up with experiences in the regular school session. He cites by contrast a number of long-term compensatory programs for disadvantaged children, staffed by skillful teachers, in which the outcome was uniformly positive in raising the children's academic levels.

A basic error in Jensen's thinking is worth emphasizing. Let us assume that there is a large genetic component to intelligence *within* groups—that is to say, among blacks, among whites, among Chinese, and so on. Such a finding, even if proved valid, would have no significance as to whether differences *between* groups (whites and blacks, or blacks and Chinese, for example) are or are not genetically determined. In the same way, it might be true that the heights of individual American white adults and Japanese adults are each largely influenced by genetic factors. But that fact would not prove that the differences in height between Americans and Japanese as a group are genetic in origin. They may be due to differences in nutrition or other environmental factors.

As long as American black children start off at an environmental disadvantage, there is no way that we can say that genetic factors determine their lower performance compared with whites, or even with other minority groups, on IQ tests. There is even a question of what we mean by "race." The term *race* is a loose, popular one that has very little support genetically. Different specific nationalities may be similar in their genetic composition, but American blacks, because of their differing ancestries and their history of intermarriages, can be presumed to have different genes.

As the years have passed, the critical judgment of Deutsch and others on Jensen's work has crystallized into a firm consensus among most leading social scientists. A special blow to Jensen was the discovery that one of his main sources of "scientific evidence," Cyril Burt, had been guilty of pernicious and prolonged scientific fraud.

Cyril Burt was undoubtedly the most eminent British psychologist of the first half of this century and deeply respected by fellow psychologists throughout the world. He held many professional positions and was justifiably knighted for his contributions to psychological theory and their educational applications. A number of his studies have stood the test of time.

In addition to his other work, Burt published a number of papers reporting extensive studies of twins and their relatives which "proved" that intelligence was genetically determined. Jensen, in his 1969 article, quite accurately referred to Burt's work as "the most satisfactory attempt" to show the genetic basis of the IQ score. But gradually suspicion regarding Burt's data began to grow from a number of different sources. The first serious doubts came from Princeton psychologist Leon Kamin (1974), who identified a number of numerical impossibilities in Burt's published articles. In three sequential papers published between 1955 and 1966, Burt reported increases in the sizes of his sample of separated identical twins, but in each report the IQ correlations of the twin pairs were identical— .771. Such a duplication of exact correlations to the third decimal place was unheard of in psychological research. Then the medical correspondent of the London *Times* tried to locate two of Burt's research associates, the Misses Conway and Howard, who had published papers supporting his views in a journal edited by Burt. They could not be located, nobody had heard of them, and the newspaper correspondent suggested that the two women had been invented by Burt. The journalist accused Burt of perpetrating a major fraud, a charge which was then supported by two of his former students, Alan and Ann Clarke, now themselves eminent and respected psychologists.

Those psychologists who supported Burt's views, such as Arthur Jensen, tried to rally to his defense and accused his critics of "character assassination" and "McCarthyism." But this defense was short-lived. When Burt died, in the early 1970s, his sister commissioned one of his admirers, Leslie Hearnshaw, to write a biography of her brother. All of Burt's private papers and diaries were made available to Hearnshaw. As he went through these papers and studied them carefully, Hearnshaw found one evidence after another of dishonesty, evasion, and contradiction. In the biography, published in 1979, Hearnshaw was forced to conclude that the charges made by Burt's critics were essentially valid. Burt had fabricated and falsified data, and all his findings on the genetic basis of the IQ had to be discarded. And these were the conclusions of an honest scholar who had started out as an admirer of Burt. (The full story of Burt's fraud is related in Lewontin, Rose, & Kamin 1984.)

We can only speculate why a man of Burt's distinction and reputation would engage in such shocking fraudulent behavior. But there is also a larger question. Why were his data, which appeared suspect and contradictory, published and accepted without question by his colleagues? It did not require Hearnshaw's study of Burt's private papers to detect the inadequacies and contradictions in Burt's reports, yet his writings went unchallenged and were quoted with reverence by many in the scientific community for over ten years. The hard lesson to be drawn is that even scientists can be overly impressed by the weight of an authoritative figure and can also lose their objectivity when evaluating a study that confirms or challenges their own personal biases.

The Value of the IQ Test

After this distressing account of how the IQ score has been misused, so often with serious consequences, it might seem as though we would be better off to discard the test entirely. Some groups have been advocating such a solution.

But the IQ test has value, if we recognize its limitations. Given properly by a sensitive and trained psychologist, the subtest scores and the full IQ score can tell us a great deal about certain aspects of the intellectual functioning of a middle-class white child. Stephen Gould himself feels that his son's IQ test, with the proper analysis of the subtest scores, was helpful in the proper diagnosis of the boy's learning disability (1981). In many such cases, as well as with various other psychological or psychiatric problems, the IQ test may be very useful.

A child's IQ score may also be predictive of her later academic achievement. This is not surprising, inasmuch as many of the items in the test are very similar to the curriculum items of most schools. In some cases the IQ test may be helpful with a student who is resistant to school, in identifying whether or not the problem is one of intellectual capacity. The subscore test scores of an IQ test may also be helpful in identifying a particular area of intellectual functioning where the youngster is weak, so that remedial measures can be focused on that specific area.

But the IQ test is a fallible instrument in many cases. A dramatic illustration occurred with one of the boys in our longitudinal study. He was tested at three and six years of age, as part of our routine procedures. The tests were given by our most experienced and competent staff psychologist, who detected nothing unusual in the boy's behavior during these tests. His IQ score at three years was 108, and at six years was 111, practically identical scores. The conventional wisdom is that scores at this level are too low for a student to perform even modestly at the college level. Yet this youngster went through one of the most demanding and prestigious colleges in the country, was graduated with honors, and then went through a leading medical school successfully. We can only speculate why his early school-age IQ score so drastically failed to predict his later intellectual abilities. Perhaps there was an unusually slow maturation of the brain capacities that are measured, at least to some extent, by the IQ scores. (We do not have any later IQ scores on this boy after the test at age six.) Perhaps he was confused in some way by the test requirements themselves, although no such difficulty with the actual test-taking was detected at the time. Whatever the reason for his low IQ score in relation to his later brilliant academic achievement, the moral of this case is that any hard and fast prediction from an early IQ test score rests on a shaky foundation.

It is clear from the discussion in this chapter that decisions based on IQ scores should be made cautiously, if at all, with minority children, especially those from disadvantaged backgrounds or for whom English is not their primary language. Even for middle-class native-born children, the IQ score is only one of many predictors of future success or failure in life. Socioeconomic status, motivation, special talents and interests, temperament, and sometimes even pure luck, all play their part.

An analogy can be drawn between a low IQ score and the childhood disease phenylketonuria (PKU). In this illness, the lack of a certain enzyme prevents the young child from digesting completely the many foods that contain phenylalanine. Instead, a toxic substance is formed that is likely to cause mental deficiency. There is no doubt that this condition is hereditary. But if the child is given a special diet low in phenylalanine, she can develop normally. The environment (food intake) determines the effect of the hereditary deficiency.

We must treat a low IQ score as we do PKU. In the tradition of Alfred Binet, we should not label a child with a low IQ score as inferior for life. Rather, as Binet did, we should look for the special environmental changes that could ameliorate the unfavorable consequences of such an IQ score.

Alternatives to the IQ Test

The limitations of the IQ test have led a number of investigators to search for alternative measures and concepts of cognitive ability. In the 1930s the Russian psychologist Lev Vygotsky criticized the standard IQ test procedures because they gave a child credit for a correct answer only if she achieved it on her own; the child gets no credit for a correct answer with the help of the psychologist. "Even the profoundist thinkers . . . never entertained the notion that what children can do with the assistance of others might be in some sense even more indicative of their mental development than what they can do alone" (1978, p. 86). He then went on to say that two children who show the same standard test level may show different levels of "potential development as determined through problem-solving under adult guidance or in collaboration with more competent peers" (p. 87). Vygotsky called this difference between what the child can do alone and what she can do with help "the zone of proximal development" and considered it a very useful guide not only to what the child has already achieved intellectually but also to "what is in the course of maturing" (p. 87). He postulated that the measurement of the zone of proximal development might have profound significance in the education of both normal and deviant children and in the analysis of the relationship between learning and development.

Vygotsky's intriguing concept has never been put to any full-scale testing, although a few investigators have used modified forms of his formulation in research, such as our own study of children with congenital rubella. Many teachers have also used this approach empirically in their day-to-day work with their students. A real test of Vygotsky's concept would be important, because if he is correct, the measurement of both the IQ score and the "zone of proximal development" could greatly enhance our ability to evaluate a child's cognitive capacities.

In 1973, Harvard psychologist David McClelland wrote a searching critique of the validity of IQ tests and similar tests of intellectual ability. His reasoning is close to Gould's, quoted earlier in this chapter. McClelland asks,

> Does this mean that intelligence tests are invalid? As so often when you examine a question carefully in psychology, the answer depends on what you mean. Certainly they are valid for predicting who will get ahead in a number of prestige jobs where credentials are important. So is white skin; it too is a valid predictor of job success in prestige jobs. But no one would argue that white skin *per se* is an ability factor. Lots of the celebrated correlations between so-called intelligence test scores and success can lay no greater claim to representing an ability factor. (p. 6)

McClelland's thesis is that instead of emphasizing IQ tests, which presumably measure "general intelligence," we should develop and emphasize tests that measure competence. "If you want to know how well a person can drive a car, sample his ability by giving him a driver's test. Do not give him a paper-and-pencil test for following directions, a general intelligence test, etc. . . . If you want to test who will be a good policeman, go find out what a policeman does" (p. 7). McClelland also suggests other tests of competence, such as assessing communication skills and patience. He cites several specific approaches to testing competence instead of IQ, but he is pessimistic about the negative responses he has met to his ideas. Again, McClelland's concept deserves a full-scale test of its usefulness as compared with the standard reliance on an IQ score.

Recently Howard Gardner has proposed that we try to forget "the concept of intelligence as a single property of the human mind; or of that instrument called the intelligence test, which purports to measure intelligence once and for all" (1985, p. ix). Instead Gardner asks us to consider all the different roles that have been prized by cultures over the ages and to realize "the possibility that many—if not most—of these competencies do not lend themselves to measurement by standard verbal methods" (p. x). As an alternative approach, Gardner proposes seven types of human competencies, such as musical intelligence, linguistic intelligence, and spatial intelligence, each of which fulfills his eight criteria for an intelligence. His concepts are detailed in chapter 8. This approach represents another promising alternative to standard IQ testing, not only in theory but also in its application to educational methods.

Finally, there is the new exciting work on metacognition, also described in chapter 8. Workers in this field are not content with the issue of what a child actually knows (cognition), as is the IQ test. Rather, they are exploring the equally if not more important question of how a child knows she knows something and how she goes about planning to acquire additional knowledge.

These new approaches to the study of a child's intelligence open up all kinds of new possibilities for understanding how a child thinks, for measuring her potential for additional learning, and for using this knowledge to develop new approaches to education. The standard IQ test will probably continue to be used with a greater awareness of its limitations. But one can predict that the new methods will make the IQ score only one of a number of methods used to assess a child's intelligence and to plan her educational curriculum.

15

The Parent as Teacher and Friend

I N chapter 3 we discussed "The Many Ways of Parenthood." Some parents are permissive, others are strict; some are basically secure and self-confident, while others may be insecure and unsure of themselves; some may feel intimidated or victimized by a child who is difficult to manage, while others may be able to be more objective; some are openly expressive of their feelings, others are reserved and self-contained. And some parents may have psychiatric problems of their own.

As we saw, these different parental characteristics and styles can affect the child's functioning and may promote goodness or poorness of fit, depending on the child's attributes. But out of all these styles, is there any one special characteristic of the primary caregiver, be it the mother or a mother-substitute, that is of basic, decisive importance if the child is to thrive psychologically? Is there some emotional nutrient that the young child must have, just as he needs essential nourishing foods?

Maternal Love and Tender Loving Care

At one time, it was supposed that there was, indeed, a basic psychological ingredient that all children needed from birth onward. Without it, they could not flourish. This was maternal love, or tender loving care—TLC, as it came to be called. Occasionally the father was also called upon to provide TLC. This prescription gained increasing prominence over a number of decades and reached its height in the 1950s and the 1960s. It is still the main stock in trade of many professionals dealing with young mothers, who consider it not only a basic need but panacea.

There is no doubt, of course, that the mother's love for her child is a powerful positive influence on the child's development. The innumerable paintings of the Madonna and Child in many different cultures and historical periods attest to this universal recognition of the importance of maternal love. But this importance does not make it a universal cure for the ills of children. In the 1950s and 1960s it was handed out by mental health practitioners as a routine prescription for a child's behavior disorder, even when there was no evidence that the child was deficient in TLC. If the mother protested that she did indeed love her child dearly, all too often her very vehemence was taken as "proof" that she must be covering over some "deep unconscious hostility." All too often, such mothers ended up on a psychoanalyst's couch in the search for this "unconscious hostility." And if the mother believed in the prescription and embraced the idea that if she gave her child this TLC all would be well, she was immediately faced with a gigantic problem. How could she generate this magical TLC? She couldn't go to the drugstore for it, as if it were a bottle of aspirin. And if she overdid the routines of hugging and kissing her youngster and repeating "I love you," at least some children might feel at times that they were being pestered and taken away from what they were busy doing.

Many times over the years we have seen confused and anxious parents who have been given this prescription of TLC by a professional or a friend and have tried to be more "loving," only to find that their child's problem was no better. Sometimes it is a case of improper management of a temperamentally difficult child, when the parents need specific advice and guidance on how to handle that kind of youngster. Sometimes the child is suffering from an undiagnosed learning disability, with anxiety symptoms over his school performance, and needs remedial educational instruction. The child may have a motor clumsiness that makes him the scapegoat of his play group and requires the right kind of practice and training to overcome. Or there may be a serious psychiatric disorder that requires special treatment. In all such cases TLC will be little more than a Band-Aid prescription, and even a Band-Aid applied to the wrong spot.

The Origins of the TLC Prescription

How did this one-sided emphasis on maternal tender loving care originate? First there was Freud's description of the child's relationship to the
mother as "unique, without parallel, established unalterably for a whole
lifetime as the first and strongest love-object and as the prototype of all
later love relations—for both sexes" (1940, p. 188). Then during the 1930s
and 1940s a number of psychiatrists, psychologists, and pediatricians
began to report evidence that a long stay in an impersonal institution could
lead to permanent damage to infants' development of intellect and personality. Especially noteworthy was the series of studies done by William
Goldfarb, then a psychologist at the Hebrew Home for Infants in New
York City (1943; 1947). Goldfarb systematically evaluated the mental development of a group of young children brought up until the age of two
in an institution and then placed in foster homes. He compared these
findings with the functioning of another group who had gone straight from
their mothers to foster homes in which they had remained. There were no
significant differences in the foster homes or in the mothers' occupational,
educational, and mental status in the two samples of children. The only
significant differences appeared to be the result of their differing experiences in infancy.

Goldfarb found striking differences in the two groups of children. The
institutionalized children were aggressive, distractible, and impulsive. Social activities with other people were limited, and relationships were easily
broken. The children's intellectual levels, as determined by test procedures, were significantly lower than those of the group who had gone
directly to foster homes. Furthermore, Goldfarb emphasized, these differences were not transitory but persisted into later childhood and adolescence.

Following these reports came the most influential study of all. In 1951,
British psychiatrist John Bowlby, at the request of the World Health
Organization, wrote his now-famous monograph *Maternal Care and Mental
Health,* in which he reviewed the various studies that had been reported
and added a number of his own observations. His conclusion was precise
and emphatic: "Mother love in infancy and childhood is as important for
mental health as are vitamins and proteins for physical health" (p. 158).
Later Bowlby extended his thesis to assert that the loss of a mother figure
in early life is capable of causing later psychiatric disorders (1969, p. xiii).

Bowlby's 1951 report received immediate and widespread recognition.
Together with Goldfarb's studies, it led to a change in public policy.
Whenever possible, the traditional orphan asylum was closed, and infants

who required residential placement were placed into foster home care as quickly as possible. According to Michael Rutter, the concept of maternal deprivation "has been held to be the cause of conditions as diverse as mental subnormality, delinquency, depression, dwarfism, acute distress and affectionless psychopathology" (1981a, p. 15).

Current Views of Maternal Deprivation and Tender Loving Care

Bowlby's findings stimulated a number of studies and professional reports, some supporting his thesis, but others challenging the data on which he based his conclusions. Questions arose more and more insistently. Bowlby's data came primarily from young children who were grossly deprived of consistent, affectionate contact throughout their early years. Granted that such deprivation had most undesirable effects, could these findings be applied to children brought up in stable homes with parents who cared for them? Was it "maternal deprivation" if an infant had several primary caregivers, and not an exclusive caregiving relationship to the mother? Was there a unique, even mystical quality to "mother love" that the infant could not obtain from the father, other family members, parents who cared for them, but perhaps not full-time, or an affectionate baby nurse? And if the baby did suffer real deprivation in infancy, was this bound to have permanent psychological effects?

The many studies conducted in the past thirty years have provided answers to these most important questions. The relevant reports, numbering almost a thousand, have been systematically analyzed by Michael Rutter. Rutter, who is perhaps the most distinguished child psychiatrist in the world today, has conducted a number of important research studies of his own. He also has the extraordinary ability to assemble the world-wide reports on a topic of broad interest in child psychiatry and child development—psychosexual development, stress and coping, prevention of behavior disorders, delinquency, brain damage in children, and autism, to name only a few—and to subject the findings to an incisive critical review. This he has done with the subject of maternal deprivation, and his authoritative monograph *Maternal Deprivation Reassessed* (1981a) is already a classic overview of our present state of knowledge on this subject. In this monograph, Rutter also points up the directions for further research.

On the basis of the analysis of this vast professional literature that has accumulated since the publication of Bowlby's monograph, Rutter first points out that the evidence of the importance of deprivation and disadvantage on children's psychological development has continued to mount, confirming Bowlby's original arguments. We would all join in this conclusion, and Bowlby's work certainly played an important part in demonstrating that children need a healthy psychological environment as well as a healthy physical one in order to flourish.

There are, however, many dramatic testimonials to the fact that children are not necessarily permanently damaged by even the most appalling deprivation. Rutter cites several cases of this kind, including the carefully documented report of a pair of Czech twin boys who were severely abused as infants and young children. The boys' mother had died after childbirth, and they were brought up by an indifferent stepmother and a harsh father who was away from home most of the time as a railroad worker. The boys grew up in almost total isolation. They lived in a small, unheated closet, were often locked in the cellar for long periods, and were never allowed out of the house or even into the other rooms of the house. They slept on the floors and were often cruelly punished. When they were seven years old, they were finally discovered by the public authorities, removed from the home, placed in a children's institution, and finally settled with a good foster mother. Continuous care was then given them by the foster mother, their teachers, a pediatrician, a psychologist, and a speech therapist. Their IQs rose gradually from 82 and 72 at age eight until they reached a normal average level of 100 and 101 at age fourteen. They have attended community schools, their speech is adequate, and they have made friends. They love reading, and they can ride bicycles, swim, ski, and play the piano well (Koluchova 1976).

Equally dramatic is the case of Genie, an American girl who was not removed from an appallingly deprived atmosphere until she was thirteen. When discovered, she was incontinent, without language, and able to walk only with difficulty. Four years later Genie still had many problems, but she had already learned to talk in phrases, and her basic mental age had risen from less than five years to eleven years (Curtiss 1977).

From these cases and similar if less dramatic studies, Rutter emphasizes that "it is clear that even the damage due to very severe early deprivation is to a considerable extent reversible later in childhood if the environmental change is sufficiently great and if the later experiences are sufficiently good" (p. 181). Again, this is a testimonial to the flexibility and plasticity of the human brain.

What about the disturbances that Goldfarb and Bowlby reported in the social and intellectual development of children raised in impersonal institutions? An important British study has been done by an expert team led by psychologist Barbara Tizard, of the University of London (1974). The group studied a number of residential nurseries run by three voluntary societies. These nurseries provided a rich cognitive environment, with a high staff-child ratio and generous provision of toys, books, and outings.

There were multiple caregivers and constant staff changes, however, and close staff-child relationships were disapproved. Stimulating as the environment was, therefore, the children lacked a close or continuous relationship with a single mother figure. Of the sixty-five children brought up in these institutions since infancy, twenty-six were still living there at four years of age. Twenty-four had been adopted, and fifteen had been restored to their natural mothers at age three. Various assessment procedures were used, including testing response to strangers, IQ testing, and assessment of breadth of experience. No evidence of cognitive retardation, verbal or otherwise, was found in the four-year-old children. The children restored to their mothers a year previously had slightly lower test scores. The adopted children, however, were intellectually more advanced, friendlier, and more talkative than the institutional children. The authors speculate that this same improvement could occur in the institutional children if the institution provided the personal closeness that the adopted homes did. A later follow-up study showed that even children adopted after the age of four years usually developed deep relationships with their adoptive parents, although they did tend to show social and attention problems in school.

These findings from children brought up in good institutions but with "maternal deprivation" indicate that while such deprivation may lead to less than optimal development, it does not have the grim implications suggested by Freud, Bowlby, and others. The issue may not be the institution as such, but a good one versus a bad one.

Is Mother Love Unique?

The emphasis on mother love and tender loving care in infancy implies that mother love has a unique importance for the infant's mental health, just as vitamins and proteins have for physical health. In other words, does the infant's attachment to the mother show some unique quality? Rutter also investigated this question and answered it with a resounding "no."

An infant's attachment to another person may be shown in various ways: by protest or distress if the attached person leaves the child, by a greater tendency to explore in a strange situation when the attached person is present, and by following or seeking closeness with the attached person. Each of these qualities has been shown by a large number of investigators to be present in attachment to fathers, to sibs, to peers, to adult caregivers in a nursery, and even to inanimate objects, such as a favorite toy or blanket (Rutter 1981a). The attachment to the mother may be stronger in *quantity*, but it is not different in *quality*.

A recent careful review has confirmed Rutter's conclusions. Dale Hay, of the State University of New York at Stony Brook, has made a thorough analysis of the research literature in the fields of parent-infant attachment and early age-mate relations (1985). Hay points out that the research trends in these two fields have in the main gone in separate directions. Studies of attachment have concentrated on individual differences in how infants make their attachments to parents, the different forms this attachment takes in different children, and the consequences of this type of attachment for the infant's development. Studies of early age-mate social relations, by contrast, have focused more on general group trends rather than on individual differences.

Hay makes a comprehensive comparison of these two bodies of research and demonstrates that the development of young children's attachment to their parents parallels the steps they take in relating to their age-mates. The research data in both areas shows that with both parents and age-mates infants first recognize prospective social partners, then communicate with them, then engage in patterns of interaction with them, learn from these experiences, and subsequently interact in different ways with them. She ends her comprehensive analysis by pointing up how much we still have to learn about the development of the child's early relationships. But even with our incomplete knowledge, she is convinced that the attachment relationship to the parent is not without parallel in social development. She thus considers it imperative to integrate the study of attachment to the parents into more general theories of social life.

These clear-cut findings that mother love does not have a unique mystical quality should come as an enormous relief to the host of mothers who are not able to assume primary continuous caregiving responsibilities for their babies. Mothers who return to work outside the home or who have other demanding responsibilities can be reassured that as long as they maintain an active relationship with their babies, and as long as the substitute caregiver is competent and affectionate, their babies will thrive. Nothing unique is being lost.

The Significance of Attachment Research

Attachment of the infant to the mother or other primary caregiver may not be a unique process, but it certainly does occur. We can conceptualize attachment as a developmental process, in which the specific manifestations are shaped by the infant's maturational level and life experiences. In the early weeks of life, the baby who will not stop crying when held by another person often quiets when held by the mother. By two or three months the infant may be smiling more often and more actively at his mother than at other people. By the second half of the first year, the expressions of attachment become more evident and complex, as an evidence of the child's advancing level of cognition and feeling. A child of this age may cling or crawl to his mother if confronted with a stranger who tries to pick him up, and he may turn first to his mother when unable to master the use of a new toy. In this same age period, the infant may begin to show what we call *stranger wariness*. If approached quickly by a stranger, a nine- to twelve-month-old infant may become silent, stop playing, shrink back, and even begin to cry, when he has not manifested this reaction in earlier months. Jerome Kagan interprets this stranger wariness as a new stage of cognitive development, in which the child is now able to compare the stranger's face with his mental representations of the familiar faces in his memory, so that a great discrepancy will create uncertainty and uneasiness in the infant (1984, p. 44).

But this stranger wariness is only a relative phenomenon, elicited in the first moments of contact with a stranger. Inge Bretherton, of the University of Colorado, has shown that after even a few minutes, one-year-old infants begin to show a positive response to strangers and become willing to engage in play with them (1978).

Alan Sroufe, of the University of Minnesota, has also reported that infants may show strong positive reactions to strangers as well as wariness and that both may occur in the same exposure (1977). Some developmental psychologists question the usefulness of the concept of stranger wariness because of its inconsistency and instability (Rheingold & Eckerman 1973). In any case, stranger wariness, when it occurs, disappears gradually in the second year of life and does not appear to play a significant role in the child's development.

We have discussed this phenomenon of stranger wariness because it has been incorporated into a widely used test of the character of an infant's attachment to his mother. This test, devised by psychologist Mary Ainsworth, of the University of Virginia, and known as the Ainsworth Strange Situation, is usually given to infants between eight and eighteen months of age. The child is taken into a strange room with his mother, who then leaves him, the first time alone and the second time with a stranger, each time returning a few minutes later. Those children who show mild distress at the mother's leaving, approach the mother on her return, and are quickly soothed are characterized as having a secure attachment to the mother. Insecure attachment is considered to take one of two forms, personified by infants who do not show distress at the mother's leaving and actively turn away at reunion, or those who are difficult for the mother to console on her return (Ainsworth et al. 1978). Ainsworth also reported that the mother's sensitivity to her infant's signals during feeding, play, and bodily contact during the first three months of life correlated significantly with whether the child showed "secure" or "insecure" attachment in the Strange Situation at one year of age.

Because of the ease with which it can be administered and its claims to measure the nature of the infant's attachment to his mother, the Ainsworth test has spawned a great many studies and reports based upon its use. Its claims have been extended, so that it now is considered an index of the mother's adequacy as a caregiver in the infant's early months as well as a measure of an important aspect of the child's emotional state almost a year later.

The Ainsworth test has its enthusiastic supporters and its skeptics. Prominent among its advocates are Alan Sroufe and others who claim that the infant's rating on the test correlates significantly with his later psychological development. Sroufe and his co-workers have reported correlations of the test ratings with quality of play, problem-solving, and social competence with peers in the two- and three-year age periods. They consider that a secure attachment, in the Ainsworth sense, "is an important aspect of infant emotional development, the secure base serving as a context within which the infant develops its first reciprocal relationship with another individual, its rudimentary sense of self, and its first sense of the emotional availability and sensitivity of others" (Matas, Arend, & Sroufe 1978, p. 1554).

The skeptics include ourselves. We, and others, have a number of reasons for doubting the meaning of the Ainsworth test and the significance ascribed to the infant's attachment to the mother. First there is the question of what the Ainsworth test actually measures. Does it measure attachment, as claimed? Rutter has properly cautioned against drawing conclusions from "curious procedures involving mother, caregivers and strangers not only going in and out of rooms every minute for reasons quite obscure to the child, but also not initiating interactions in the way they might usually do" (1981a, p. 160). The Ainsworth test, given these strange and bewildering qualities for the child, might be rating any number of the child's characteristics. One possibility is that it might, at least in part, reflect a child's temperamental attributes of reaction to a strange situation and quickness of adaptation to the new. The correlation between the Ainsworth test rating and the later measures of the child's social competence and approach to play and problem-solving may reflect a consistency in temperament between these two age periods. From Sroufe's report, it is not possible to resolve this question, inasmuch as no independent measures of temperament were done. Jerome Kagan (1984, p. 58) has raised this issue, emphasizing that differences in the proneness to distress in uncertain situations confound the assessment of attachment in the Ainsworth test. Some support for this view also comes from a joint American-Japanese study done with Japanese babies. These investigators found that irritability in very young infants (which probably corresponds to our categories of negative mood and adaptability) did influence the child's later behavior in the Ainsworth test (Miyake, Chen, & Campos 1985).

Studies in other cultures, such as in North Germany and Japan and on Israeli kibbutzim, have found different percentages of "secure" ratings and the two types of "insecure" ratings from the groups in Ainsworth's study. These findings suggest that cultural factors, which may or may not include maternal competency in the child's early months, as claimed by Ainsworth, may influence the child's test rating (Bretherton & Waters 1985). The Japanese study, for example, points out that separation from the mother even for brief periods is a very unusual occurrence for Japanese infants and that this factor may influence the child's reaction to the mother's leaving the room during the Ainsworth test, whatever the degree of attachment security.

Michael Lamb and his associates have made an exhaustive analysis of the voluminous body of research reports that have used the Ainsworth test (1984). They conclude that there is little reliable evidence concerning the specific dimensions of parental behavior that affect behavior with a stranger. Also stability over time in security of attachment is high only when there is stability in the lives and behavior of family and caregivers (p. 127).

We have reviewed the Ainsworth Strange Situation test in such detail for several reasons. It is a widely used test, and it is assumed by all too many developmental psychologists to be a valid test of the older infant's emotional attachment to his mother. This conclusion has by no means been demonstrated. Moreover, the test findings are assumed to reflect the mother's adequacy as a caregiver in the infant's early months and to predict the level of the child's social and problem-solving competence a year or two later. Here again, it seems to us, we have a new and more sophisticated version of the "blame the mother" ideology, in which the mother's attitudes and handling of the infant determine the child's psychological fate.

Finally, the use of the Ainsworth test reflects a general problem in developmental psychology and psychiatry. Many research workers keep looking for a pot of gold at the end of the rainbow—some simple, quick test, with easily measurable ratings, that can identify the child's present psychological state and his future development. A number of leading psychologists are disturbed at this trend, which ignores the complexities of the child's mental characteristics even as a newborn, the variability of environmental influence from one family to another, and the many different outcomes that occur in the interaction between different children and different environments. Urie Bronfenbrenner, of Cornell University, has complained that "much of American developmental psychology is the science of the behavior of children in strange situations with strange adults" (1974, p. 3). Robert McCall, of the Boys Town Center for the Study of Youth Development, has warned that "the experimental method now dictates rather than serves the research questions we value, fund, and pursue; as a result the process of development as it naturally transpires in children growing up in actual life circumstances has been largely ignored. . . . What use is our knowledge if it is not relevant to real children growing up in real families and in real neighborhoods?" (1977, p. 334). And Judy Dunn and Carol Kendrick, of Cambridge University, have spelled out the issue clearly: "It is obvious that to assess a relationship as complicated and as rich as that of mother and child solely in terms of the conventional measures of attachment, such as those derived from separating the child from the mother in laboratory experiments (as in the 'strange situation' of Ainsworth), would be deeply misleading" (1982, p. 86).

We have been concerned that our own findings on temperament might be misused as the basis for quick, artificial laboratory tests that would claim to identify the child's temperament and his future personality development. We voiced this apprehension as long ago as 1968:

> As in the case when any significant influencing variable is identified, there is an understandable temptation to make temperament the heart and body of a general theory. To do so would be to repeat a frequent approach in psychiatry which, over the years, has been beset by general theories of behavior based upon fragments rather than the totality of influencing mechanisms. A one-sided emphasis on temperament would merely repeat and perpetuate such a tendency and would be antithetical to our viewpoint, which insists that we recognize temperament as only one attribute of the organism. (Thomas, Chess, & Birch 1968, p. 182)

The same is true for the infant's attachment to his mother. It is only one attribute, although an important one, and should not be made the heart and body of a general theory of development.

How Important Is Tender Loving Care?

What we and others have said does not negate the value of tender loving care for the young infant. We can certainly presume that a baby reared in such an affectionate atmosphere is likely to find his explorations and experimentations with the world around him meeting with approval and encouragement. His maturational achievements—standing, walking, talking, and self-feeding—will be greeted with pleasure and applause. All this, we believe, helps to build the foundation for the development of a positive sense of self and a high degree of self-confidence as he grows older. The infant is also more likely to take corrective criticisms, scoldings, and denials as positive learning experiences if they are given by caregivers who are fond of him. The fact that some infants deprived of such an affectionate, loving relationship to their caregivers still flourish in spite of this lack does not make tender loving care an unimportant ingredient in a baby's development.

But tender loving care is not some mysterious quality that is created only by special routines or rituals on the parents' part. Nor is it a hidden quality tucked away in the depths of the unconscious, waiting to be called out by the baby's birth. Unless the parents have special psychiatric problems, love for the baby is a natural spontaneous development. Those who care for an infant even on a temporary basis easily find themselves becoming attached to the child. In the very actions of nurturing, in the infant's responses to his care and the caregivers' responses to the baby, caregivers become tender and loving without needing to remind themselves to be so.

Yet Americans have a habit of saying, "If so much of this ingredient is good, more must be better." An increase in TLC is like an increase in vitamin intake. If a child has enough vitamin C or D in his diet, doubling or tripling the amount will not bring more benefits; the excess will simply be excreted. Harm has rarely been done by extra vitamins, but neither have they been helpful. The same goes for tender loving care. Under ordinary circumstances, enough TLC is there. A baby likes to be held and cuddled, but if held too long he may struggle to get free. This does not mean that he is rejecting the parent's love; he simply now wants to do something else.

Moreover, parents have different styles of giving and expressing love. Some do it with active physical contact—hugs and kisses. Some do it by spending time with their child, playing or talking or reading at his level. One mother was bored to tears by the standard nursery books. She found that reading a geography book, with explanations, satisfied her own interests and fascinated her daughter as much as the make-believe places and events of the nursery books. This mother gave her daughter love and attention in her own special way, a way that gave pleasure to both of them.

Even the most loving parent can find a child annoying and irritating at times, and a normally loving child may in a moment of frustration blurt out, "I hate you!" Such episodes occur between some adults deeply in love with each other; why not also between parent and child? There are parents who become terrified with guilt if they feel angry at their child. They worry that they may be nursing some ominous buried hatred, when in fact the annoyance is trivial and transient. Such parents may try to appease their guilt feelings and express their TLC by giving into the child's every demand. This is not love but rather abdication of the parent's responsibility to teach the child when and why prohibitions must take precedence over immediate gratification. Such lessons can be given lovingly and with concern for the child's welfare.

Of course, there are parents who do not love their children. There are those who physically or sexually abuse their helpless children. There are those who are embroiled in bitter quarrels with each other, each trying to make an "ally" of the child, without concern for his welfare. There are those whose goals and ambitions in the outside world are so all-consuming that their children's welfare became of little or no concern to them. And there are those who are suffering from some serious psychiatric disorder that blocks their deep wishes to be close to their children. Sometimes such parents can be helped sufficiently to turn their abuse or indifference into affectionate attention, but sometimes no help is possible and a substitute for mother love has to be found.

We well remember the ten-year-old child whose grandmother brought her to our clinic at Bellevue Hospital with symptoms of severe anxiety. The poor child's mother, a single parent, suffered from severe schizophrenia, with symptoms that waxed and waned. When the mother's symptoms increased, she imagined that her daughter had a devil inside her and came after the child with a knife, to stab and kill this devil. The terrified child would have to run for her life to her grandmother, a warm, supporting figure. After every such episode, the mother was hospitalized, improved with treatment, and was released. But then she would stop taking her medication, and the life-threatening behavior to her daughter would start again. Once we had the facts, we tried to arrange transfer of the girl's legal custody to her grandmother. To our amazement, the lawyer in charge of the responsible legal agency refused to go along with this recommendation. His self-righteous position was, "We always take the mother's side. Mother love comes first." The facts were so clear, and the danger to the girl so evident, that in this case we were able to override the lawyer's opposition and place the child with her grandmother. With this change of environment, her symptoms gradually disappeared.

An extreme case, yes. But this pat formulation that mother love transcends all other considerations, and that a mother's love will heal all wounds, still comes up all the time. It is the same viewpoint that insists, "If your child has problems, he needs more tender loving care from his mother."

Parents as Teachers

The concern with the emotional attachment between parent and child, as important as it is, has tended to overshadow another equally important aspect of the parent's influence on the child. Parents are not only the supportive, nurturing caregivers who take care of the child's essential needs and soothe, comfort, and reassure him when distress or problems arise. Parents are also the child's first and most important teachers. As we have noted, the infant comes into the world ready to begin to learn what the world is all about. And the parents are there to act as his primary teachers, just as they are his primary caregivers. And most parents are eager to teach their children.

The process of teaching is not necessarily a conscious effort. The parent need not worry about presenting the baby with visual stimuli that are too complex or missing magic moments by failing to offer new stimuli for which the infant has just become ready. The baby sees and hears what he can, maintains his attention selectively on those sights and sounds that he can absorb, and when he has had enough turns his attention away or falls asleep. Since the world is full of interesting shapes, colors, and sounds, no one need take a course in infant development to do the right thing. The parent can just go ahead doing everyday things with everyday objects and talking at will. As the days and weeks go by, the baby receives all kinds of visual and auditory stimulation, as well as other stimuli like touch, taste, and temperature. Gradually he associates specific sights with specific people and sequences of events. His parents and others who nurture him become associated with what they do and how they do it—not all at once, but little by little.

As this process goes on, the baby is learning. The fifteen-month-old who has learned the word "door" keeps pointing to every door in the house, asking "door?" His parents nod with approval and repeat "door" after him. When he makes a mistake, pointing to a window and asking "door?" they correct him gently. He goes on for many minutes with this routine and comes back to it several times a day. The parents, entranced at first by his new accomplishment and his evident delight in it, may begin to get bored and wish he would stop. Perhaps, then, one reminds the other of the time they were taking tennis lessons. Didn't they stand hour after hour, day after day, swinging at the ball to perfect their game? And didn't the instructor comment each time, "Good shot," "Just right," or "You didn't get your racket back"? Their child is now practicing words and categories in the same way they had practiced all kinds of new skills and tasks in their lives.

Parents are teaching their young children all the time. Most would be surprised if they were told this, just as Moliere's character was amazed to learn he had been speaking prose all his life. For example, at the dinner table with her two-year-old son, the mother pretends to eat her glasses. The child is convulsed with laughter, takes the glasses and hands them to his father, who also pretends to eat them, to the baby's continued amusement. The youngster hands over his napkin for similar pretend eating. He then says "nose," and his father solemnly pretends to take the baby's nose and eat it, while the baby roars with laughter. The child continues to cue his father—"eyes," "mouth," "teeth"—and each in turn is made into a pretend meal. This happy game takes a few minutes, and then the business of finishing the meal is resumed. But it has been more than a brief game for the child. He has practiced dividing objects into those that are foods and those that are not foods. He has also practiced naming a number of objects.

The child's teachers are first and foremost his parents, then other caregivers who fill in as needed, older brothers and sisters, visiting members of the family, and friends. Jerome Bruner and his associates point up the special nature of teaching as a human activity:

> Whether [the child] is learning the procedures that constitute the skills of attending, communicating, manipulating objects, locomoting, or indeed, a more effective problem-solving procedure itself, there are usually others in attendance who help him on his way. Tutorial interactions are, in short, a crucial feature of infancy and childhood. Our species, moreover, appears to be the only one in which any intentional tutoring goes on. . . . What distinguishes man as a species is not only his capacity for learning, but for teaching as well. (Wood, Bruner, & Ross 1976)

Should Parents Do Formal Teaching?

Sandra Scarr, of the University of Virginia, in her excellent book *Mother Care/Other Care* (1984), warns parents against assuming responsibility for formal teaching of a child, saying, "Informal instruction is always appropriate between a parent and an eager child. Formal instruction that ignores the child's motivation is not" (p. 197). She is concerned that parents who become formal teachers will lose the intensity of affect, spontaneity, and partiality to their children that should characterize their relationships with them. Concerning formal instruction to produce a "superchild," Scarr makes the telling point that "with preschoolers, intense instruction in reading skills may accelerate the acquisition of reading by a few years, but at ten the accelerated child will not read more fluently or with more comprehension than a similarly bright child who learned to read at six or seven" (p. 197).

Scarr emphasizes how much the child learns informally from his parents in the spontaneous everyday events that need adult interpretation. We agree completely with this emphasis. We do not see that formal instruction by a parent is *always* undesirable, however. Under certain circumstances it may be very useful and may even enhance the overall positive attachment of the child to the parent. We can illustrate this proposition by an incident from our personal lives.

One of our sons had difficulty with arithmetic in his early school years. In the third grade his teacher informed us that he was falling behind the class in this subject and often did not complete his arithmetic homework. One of us (A.T.) stepped in and informed our son that he needed special drilling in arithmetic. Every Saturday morning I would assign him a number of problems that should take him about an hour to complete. Until he completed this assignment and I had checked it for correctness, he could not leave the house to play with his friends. He protested loudly at this edict, but he knew he had no alternative. During the first few sessions, he hurried through the assignment so that he could get outdoors quickly, but he made many errors, which were pointed out to him. He had to repeat the calculations until he got the right answers, and he quickly learned that hurrying through the assignment would only delay his playtime. The Saturday morning arithmetic drills then became serious sessions to which he gave his full attention. He learned quickly, and within a few months he was up to grade level. We then stopped the Saturday morning sessions, and he continued to maintain a good level in arithmetic in school on his own.

Some months later, in late June, one of us (S.C.) was sitting on the porch and overheard our son chatting just beyond the porch with one of his friends. The friend was unhappy; he was being left back in school because of his poor grades, especially in arithmetic. Our son asked, "Didn't your father help you?" and was told, "No. He said it was up to the school to teach me." Our son exclaimed, "What kind of a father do you have? You should get yourself adopted into another family where your father would care about your school work."

This story makes an important point. Our son was not motivated to learn arithmetic, and the formal instruction was forced upon him by his father. But his success in mastering arithmetic was important to him, and he recognized his father's role in this achievement. The formal instruction therefore did not interfere with his relationship with his father but rather enhanced it.

In another example, one of us (S.C.) had a developmental delay in the ability to learn to read. By the end of the second grade, I had fallen behind the rest of the class and was very unhappy at this situation. My mother, a schoolteacher herself, then took a hand in dealing with my difficulty. Every day throughout the summer, over my protest, she drilled me in reading. By the fall I was up to grade level and even became an avid reader.

Whenever I recall the active instruction my mother gave me, I feel a special glow of affection for her. It was formal, it was not spontaneous, but I know she did it because she was concerned for me and my welfare.

In our opinion there can be many instances of this kind when a parent's intervention in formal teaching is desirable, if the need for it is clear and if it is confined to a specific objective. Parents, like other people, can play many roles in life, even contradictory ones at times. If there are valid reasons for one role, it does not have to take over a relationship completely or harm the other roles the parent plays in the child's life.

Parents as Role Models

Parents become models for their young children for all kinds of activities. The three-year-old boy imitates his father's shaving with his own toy brush. So does his sister. Both imitate their mother's shaving her legs. Later each will learn sex role differentiation—at least regarding shaving. Both imitate their parents' brushing their hair, brushing their teeth, throwing a ball. Both want to help clear the table and put the garbage into the garbage can. When we watch them going through these routines, there is no doubt that they have been watching their parents closely and are highly motivated to imitate them.

Parents continue to provide role models as their children grow older, modeling grown-up behavior, marital relationships, moral and ethical standards, and work roles. Jerome Kagan emphasizes the significance of this role modeling by the parents. In his view,

The major consequence of an undiluted and exceptionally close parent-child bond is to make the child receptive to adapting the values of the family. If those values happen to be consonant with those of the society, all is well. If not, a close mother-infant bond may not be an advantage. The mother who establishes a deep mutual attachment between herself and her infant daughter but who promotes the traditional female values of passivity, inhibition of intellectual curiosity, and anxiety over competence may be preparing her daughter for serious conflict in young adulthood. In this hypothetical case it is not clear that the infant's close bond to the mother is beneficial. (1979, p. 28)

Other similar possibilities come to mind: A close parent-child bond might promote values of sexism, racism, or ruthless competitiveness.

Parents are also prime influences in shaping the child's self-image, self-confidence, and sense of assurance that he can deal with the challenges and opportunities he will meet as he grows up. With regard to these more complicated psychological and social issues, we know much less about how the parent influences the child. Why does one young man, brought up in a harmonious family, embrace the moral and ethical values of his parents, copy their life style, remain close friends with them, and choose a career similar to his mother's or father's, while another young man, also reared in a relaxed family with parents who loved him and each other, ends up by rebelling against their standards and way of life and making his own way in the world at an emotional and geographic distance?

In truth, we have very little hard research data to answer these questions. We can say that harmonious parents who love their child, who are good teachers for him but do not try to force their own beliefs and standards on him, and who are not themselves subject to severe economic problems are most likely to give their child a good start in life. We have seen this clearly in our longitudinal studies. But the specific outcome is another matter. So many other facts enter to influence the youngster's development—what he learns from friends, teachers, and other adults, what he absorbs from television, the influence of a social trend such as the student rebellion during the Vietnam war, the impact of prejudice and bias —all these, and many more, may play a part in the emerging adult personality and life style.

The Child as Apprentice

Kenneth Kaye, of Northwestern University, an important contributor to our knowledge of child development—a serious professional baby-watcher, as we like to call such people—has put forward an intriguing theory about one way in which parents teach children. His concept does not arise from armchair philosophizing but from a long series of painstaking experiments and observations of parents with their children. He likens the structure by which a child learns from his parent to the relationship between a master craftsman and his apprentice. The master provides protected opportunities to practice selective subtasks, monitors the growth of the apprentice's skills, and gradually presents more difficult tasks. We can see this basic parental role in many domains, at all ages. Kaye recalls, "When my father taught me to swim, he backed away as I paddled toward him. I remember crying that it was unfair—but twenty-five years later I did the same thing to my son. . . . In each case the main thing we do is pose them manageable subtasks, one step at a time, and gradually pull that support away from them as their competence grows" (1982, pp. 55–57).

In this apprenticeship system, Kaye argues, parents treat their infants as more intelligent and more mature than they really are. "It is precisely because parents play out this fiction that it eventually comes to be true, that the infant does become a person and an intelligent partner in intersubjective communication" (p. 55). Kaye suggests that parents are usually unaware, at least with young children, that they are taking this master craftsman role but that it works effectively all the same.

Like all methods, however, the apprentice system may not work perfectly all the time. It may even boomerang. A mother may set out to teach her daughter a new skill that is well beyond her capacity, become impatient at her youngster's slow progress, and give up in disgust, telling the girl, "You're just too stupid to learn." After a few such episodes, the daughter will begin to believe she really is stupid. Or a father may set a high goal for his son's academic achievement, perhaps to be at the top of his class. The boy may become a reasonably good student but not live up to his father's expectations. Again, the boy may be labeled "stupid" and finally come to believe it. On the other hand, parents may be shocked, and even feel betrayed, when they discover that their older children are turning to other teachers instead of relying on Daddy and Mother. The apprentice may finally believe he has outgrown his craftsman, and he may be right.

Some traditional chestnuts of advice still retain their usefulness: Let your child learn at his own pace. Don't set unrealistic standards for him. Don't expect that you will be his prime teacher forever, even if you were his first and most important one.

Language Acquisition

As in so many other areas of social learning, the child's first language teachers are the parents and other caregivers. Older brothers and sisters and visitors also play a part.

Everyone talks to the infant as they change his diaper, wipe his nose, help him reach a toy, applaud his new ability to turn over, to walk, to climb. Generally these teachers are ahead of the child in the language they use. They assume he has thoughts and put them into words: "Yes, you want to burp now"; "It's time to put teddy to bed"; "Yes, you have a telephone just like Daddy's"; "You want your bath now." The baby's single words or approximations of words are repeated back to him. When he says "po," the parents translate it as "pillow" for a visiting aunt, who picks up a cushion. The child collects cushions and pillows one by one and brings each to the aunt, watching for recognition that her action has been correct and for praise in her part of the game. If the adult does not understand this "baby talk" word, Jennifer pulls her to a cushion and instructs her as to its proper designation. The teacher becomes the pupil, and the pupil becomes the teacher.

Some parents worry about whether it is better for the baby if they use baby talk or adult language. Actually, there is no evidence that the choice makes any significant difference. If the parent uses baby talk, the child will learn the correct language usage from contact with his age-mates and other people. Or if the parents use adult language, the child will eventually correct his baby talk. "Pisgetti" will become spaghetti; "po" will become pillow. Many parents actually use combinations of baby talk and adult language, as they see fit, and this also works out well in the end.

But learning a language is no simple matter. Language requires the ability to put sounds together to form words, to put words together to form sentences, and to interpret the meanings of words and sentences. The child also has to learn how to participate in the give and take of a conversation, which requires a knowledge of how to alternate vocal expressions with another person. Yet almost all normal children master these complicated rules by five years of age, in addition to learning and retaining a vocabulary of many hundreds of words. Many young children learn two languages, and some even three. Learning a language also requires a substantial level of social competence, for language acquisition always takes place in a social context. A socially isolated child who hears no language learns no language (Bruner 1978).

Language development in the human being is unique in its scope and quality. We take it for granted, yet "no animal society has ever developed a language with the diversity and complexity of human language or one that makes possible the transmission and understanding of an infinite variety of messages. Every human society, however primitive or isolated, has a language" (Mussen, Conger, & Kagan 1979, p. 197).

The truly incredible ability of all normal children to master the many complex and interlocking rules of language use and to acquire an extensive vocabulary—and to do this within the space of five years or less—strongly suggests the existence of a built-in mechanism in the brain that makes this possible. This hypothesis is supported by the condition known as developmental aphasia—difficulty in either comprehending language or speaking it, or both—which can afflict children of good intelligence. No emotional factors account for this developmental disability, which must have a biological basis.

To explain the highly creative and extraordinarily rapid mastery of language by the young, Noam Chomsky, of the Massachusetts Institute of Technology, has postulated an innate brain mechanism for the processing of language (1957). Chomsky's work in defining the complexities and depths of language structure have provided a major stimulus to the rapid development of language studies in the past thirty years. A number of Chomsky's specific ideas have been challenged, but he remains a pioneer in this field of research.

The ongoing research in language acquisition and use promises to bear practical fruit, but this has not yet occurred. For example, no way has been found to speed up and expand the process of learning a language. Parents and others may correct a preschooler's grammar and drill him in the alphabet and in recognizing and voicing simple words. This instruction may make a little easier the child's task of learning to use language effectively, whether in speaking or in reading and writing. But there is no evidence that it will make him more expert in the use of language as he grows older (Moskowitz 1978). Unfortunately, the converse is not true. That is, children brought up in a culturally impoverished environment and attending an inadequate school may end up with a level of spoken and written language use that is tragically below their potential capacities.

For both parent and child, the child's acquisition of language is a landmark event. Communication between them expands enormously, the child is able to express his thoughts and ideas much more clearly, and the parent's role as an informal teacher is enhanced. The child's mastery of language also provides a vital stimulus to the growth of self-esteem and self-confidence. The child can feel that he is now a big boy and can talk just as his parents and brothers and sisters do. They now will listen to him, and he can now have all kinds of conversations with them. His parents' delight in his progressive mastery of language reaffirms his own sense that he has achieved something very important.

Stuttering

It is not unusual for a child who is beginning to acquire language to experience a period of stuttering. It may even happen after the child seemingly has acquired good basic mastery of language. Stuttering usually occurs at the first syllable of a word, and most often with the first word of a sentence. For some children it is the consonants that give trouble, and for others the vowels alone are repeated. Typically, once the problem word has been said, the words that follow give no trouble—until there is a pause, and a new idea comes to the fore.

For other children, stuttering appears after a long period of smooth speech, at age three, four, or five. Some children give up trying to voice a particular sentence and start over again. But most persist, using their own devices to get started, such as shouting the beginning of the word or repeating the sound until, without warning, the words begin to move smoothly. As a general rule, the child stutters less or not at all when singing or reciting poetry.

Stuttering in the normal young child appears to be the result of his thoughts racing ahead of his ability to voice the words easily and quickly. Once his speech development catches up with his thoughts, the stuttering disappears.

It is natural that many parents become worried if their two-year-old or four-year-old begins to stutter. The child may also become frustrated or socially embarrassed and self-conscious. Parents can be reassured that in the vast majority of cases stuttering is only a temporary problem and will disappear by itself. They and other caregivers can be helpful by saying nothing, or by saying quietly and without emphasis that it doesn't matter, or that the child may talk slower whenever he wishes. Usually, after a few weeks or sometimes months, the stuttering ceases gradually. It tends to be most prominent when the child is tired or under stress. Most often, there is no clear relationship between the appearance of the stuttering and other factors in the child's life.

In a very few children, stuttering remains a permanent problem. There is no way of knowing, when stuttering first appears, whether this will be the case. It is best at first to function with the child as if the problem will be temporary. If the stuttering persists, a trained speech pathologist should be consulted.

Children's Fantasies

One important way in which children strive to understand the world around them and to master its expectations is through the use of fantasy. The fantasies in children's play and stories reflect cultural realities. Fifty years ago, it would have been unusual and in some cases abnormal for a child to express elaborate fantasies about space travel, but today it would be as normal as playing house or playing doctor. Parents should certainly not discourage such fantasies or try to point out their illogical or unreal elements. The fantasies represent a normal aspect of development, and the child himself is well able to distinguish fantasy from reality.

Children with fears of one kind or another will frequently express them by fantasies. A child may report that a monster tried to get into his room during the night and kidnap him, or that devils live in a certain house, and he has to avoid going past that house. Parents should take such fantasies seriously; they are the child's way of communicating that he is afraid of something or somebody. Professional help is often necessary in such cases to identify and remedy the real cause of the child's anxiety.

A special issue comes up when a school-age child reports sexual abuse by an adult. Is this fact or is it fantasy? In a recent review of this question, Allan DeJong, of Jefferson Medical College, concludes that "sexual abuse experts generally agree that children do not fantasize or fabricate sexual encounters" (1985). Normal sexual behavior in children can be very varied, from masturbation and "playing house" to flirtation with adults of the opposite sex, especially their parents. They may also have many different kinds of fantasies, such as running away with a "boy friend" or "girl friend" or a parent. DeJong points out from his review of various studies, however, that "these sexual fantasies do not include sexual acts. Children do not graphically describe sexual acts unless they have actually witnessed or participated in them"(1985). Yet when this question is brought up in a court of law, a child's testimony is all too often challenged as a fantasy, and proving that it is real may be difficult.

Sex and Sex Education

Many parents are concerned if, when, and how they should introduce the subject of sex education to their teenaged children. This is especially true when the youngsters do not bring up the subject themselves.

The first sexual issue that parents generally encounter is masturbation. In an NYLS study, the parents as a group were permissive, commenting that since they knew masturbation to be "harmless and normal" they did not interfere with it. The staff interviewers sometimes had the impression that the parents were not fully at ease with this attitude, however, and that they might have intervened if it were not for the weight of authority.

It is, of course, true that a child's masturbation is harmless. It becomes a matter of concern only in the rare cases when it is a compulsive activity, repeated frequently each day. Professional consultation then becomes necessary. If an infant boy pulls at his penis while being diapered or bathed, it does not mean that he will become a "pervert" if it is allowed or that he will be psychologically harmed if his hand is pulled away. His behavior should be treated in the same casual way as if he were pulling at his ear, his foot, or any other part of the body. It should be ignored until it interferes with the dressing, when the hand should be removed quietly. If the child fusses, no matter.

When children are older, the parents need to be prepared with appropriately simple and matter-of-fact responses to questions like "Where do babies come from?"

As we noted in chapter 12, few adolescents are interested in discussing with their parents such issues as premarital intercourse, birth control, abortion, and venereal disease. This is true even where there has been free and easy communication between parent and youngsters over the years and where the adolescents know that their parents will take a liberal view of their sexual interests and activities. In such cases, parents can simply indicate that they are available for discussions about sex. If the adolescent youngster does not take them up on this offer, the parents should drop the issue, and certainly should not try to force a discussion.

Parents as Friends

Parents play many roles in their growing child's life. They are his caregivers, nurturing and protecting him. They are his models and teachers. They introduce him to the rules, standards, and expectations of the family and the outside world. They help him to organize what he learns from them and from others and to reconcile differences and apparent contradictions.

Parents also learn from their children, often without realizing it. We think of one good friend, Bobby, whom we have known since he was a child. In his adolescent years, Bobby became immersed in literary and philosophical studies and began to take on some pedantic qualities. We and his other friends put up with his occasional stuffy comments on an abstract intellectual topic because his basically attractive and engaging personality did not change. When Bobby married and became a parent, a new world seemed to open up to him. He discovered that simple, affectionate play with his young children could be fun, and he displayed a previously unsuspected talent for inventing imaginative games. His sense of humor—always present, but in the past always in the background—flourished, and his stuffiness and pedantry disappeared. Perhaps he might have learned to relax and become playful anyway, but to those of us who knew him well it was clear that his children had taught him some profoundly important lessons for his own development as a human being.

When these mutually helpful and stimulating activities are carried out between parent and child in a friendly atmosphere, the basis for an enduring friendship is formed. Such a friendship is a cherished aim and hope of most parents as they relate to their children day by day, month by month, and year by year.

Friendship between parent and child is indeed one of the treasures of life. Its development is, of course, a dynamic process, and its character necessarily changes as the child moves on from one age period to the next. A parent can be friends with a young infant, a three-year-old, an adolescent, and an adult son or daughter, but each phase of the friendship will bear the marks of the age, capabilities, and experiences of the child. The changes in parent-child friendships will also reflect changes in the parents themselves—crises, life-cycle changes, and job changes, to name only a few.

Some parents, unfortunately, lack the flexibility necessary to perpetuate, let alone expand, the initial friendships as their children grow older. One father was devoted to his two young daughters, attentive to their needs and solicitous for their welfare at all times. In return, to quote their neighbors, "the girls adored him." As the girls grew older and their needs changed, however, the father was unable to modify his attitudes. His solicitude for their safety, a legitimate concern when the girls were toddlers, became an increasingly restrictive prohibition as they grew older. Any activity that might pose any risk—bicycling, traveling by bus around the city, or learning to ice-skate, for example—was sure to be labeled as dangerous. By the time the girls were adolescents, they had learned various strategies for keeping their father in ignorance of how they spent their time. A close parent-child friendship had in this way been transformed into an estrangement.

Occasionally one can see a different and happier sequence. A parent may find the chores of caring for an infant messy and tiresome and may resent the time they take from more "interesting" activities. These feelings may be so strong that the parent misses all the pleasurable give-and-take play that can so easily become a part of the routines of dressing, feeding, and bathing a baby. But as the child grows older, begins to talk instead of just babbling, and becomes increasingly more organized and ingenious in his play, it may dawn on the parent that here is a truly human being who gives of himself freely and responds to the parent's affection with quick and evident delight. The lost early years can then be made up, and parent and child begin to be friends.

A generation ago it was fashionable in some communities for presumably enlightened parents to have their children call them by their first names, in place of "Mommy" and "Daddy." In this way, the parents figured, friendship would be furthered. Friendship between parent and child does not grow out of such artificial devices, however, but rather through the actual life of parent and child with each other, from infancy onward. Whether a child calls his parent by first name or not probably makes very little difference in the long run. This is one of the many questions on which we have little evidence, one way or the other. Our guess is that it may be harmful if, by giving the parent the illusion of friendship, it conceals the need for the daily give-and-take out of which true friendship grows. It may also be an unnecessary source of resentment to the child, who can't understand why he shouldn't call his parents "Mommy" and "Daddy," as all his friends do.

Some parents are afraid that if they frustrate their child, he will "hate" them, and friendship will fly out of the window. But in real life, concern for one another's safety and long-term welfare is a hallmark of true friendship. Little by little, the growing child learns that when his father or mother stops him from doing something dangerous or something that will alienate his friends, it is a sign of true friendship.

Some parents try to force their friendship with their children as though it were a hothouse flower that would blossom with special vigor, given the right amount of warmth, water, and fertilizer. They try to be "buddies" with their children by seeking to exchange intimacies with them and showing an active involvement in their activities. This may work in some cases, if parent and child do have similar interests and do communicate easily with each other. But some youngsters prefer to have their own separate activities and special friends and may be temperamentally reticent about expressing feelings and confidences. If the parents respect such a child's individual style, they can still be good friends. But if they feel left out and try to force their way into a closer involvement with the child's activities, their efforts are likely to boomerang. The youngster will resent the intrusion, the parent will be hurt and angry, and there goes the friendship.

Even when parent and child have been close, a change comes with adolescence. The teenager suddenly confides in his friends instead of in his parents. Family outings now take second or third place to his other activities. Some parents can accept this change reasonably, if a little sadly—their child is growing up, and something has been lost for them, though not for him. But they know they have not lost his friendship. Other parents, however, have heard the ominous term "generation gap" and see their teenaged daughter or son slipping away from them forever.

As we saw in chapter 12, this so-called generation gap between parents and their adolescent sons and daughters does not merit the emphasis and concern expressed by so many mental health professionals and lay commentators. The friendship between parent and child need not disappear in adolescence, but its nature has to change. The adolescent should not be subject to the same parental rules and monitoring as he was earlier in life. On his side, the adolescent's striving for independence should not blind him to the fact that his parents still have all kinds of economic, medical, and moral responsibilities for him. The adolescent's freedom is only relative; it cannot be absolute with regard to his parents. A flexible give and take between parent and adolescent, with respect for each other's legitimate needs and responsibilities, is the best guarantee that their friendship will continue.

As to adult life, there is no simple predictive rule. Some adults remain active friends with their parents, seeing them frequently, confiding in them, seeking their advice, and engaging in social or athletic activities with them. Others become distant from their parents or maintain what might be called a casual friendship. The type of relationship that will ultimately develop is difficult to predict during the child's younger years. Many factors enter into the parents' and the child's lives as he grows to maturity —similarities or difference in interests, geographical closeness or separation, divorce, illness, and so on—and all may affect the way the friendship is sustained or changed.

Occasionally a parent and a grown son or daughter become overly attached to one another. This may interfere with the young person's development of his or her own life as an independent adult. It may even lead to disputes that jeopardize a marriage if, for example, a parent becomes excessively intrusive and the son or daughter sides unfairly with the parent instead of supporting his or her own spouse in an argument.

Not all parents can make friends with their children. An authoritarian parent who insists on supervising all a child's activities will likely find that the youngster leaves home and cuts his ties as soon as he can. A parent who becomes jealous of a child's special talents and tries to compete with or undercut him will also lose—or never gain—the youngster's friendship. A parent who is absorbed in activities outside the home and has no time to spend with a child cannot make friends with him.

But just as there are many differences in children and many ways of parenthood, there are many ways of friendship between parent and child. The character and intensity of the friendship may change with time, as the child becomes an adolescent and then an adult. But it can always remain a friendship, whether the parent and the adult child see eye-to-eye on most issues or have friendly disagreements.

16

Brothers and Sisters Can Be Friends

T HUS FAR in the book our focus has been on the parents as the key family members involved in the development of the infant and child. As central as they are, parents are not the whole story. In many families, brothers and sisters are an important part of the constellation.

The Birth of the Second Child and Sibling Rivalry

For the firstborn child, the arrival of a new baby in the family constitutes a sudden, dramatic change in her life. No longer does she have the exclusive attention of parents, relatives, and visitors. No longer are her desires immediately attended to by her mother or other caregivers, who now may be busy taking care of the new baby.

The firstborn shows her distress at these developments with all kinds of disturbances in behavior, which are easy to observe. Yet early psychiatric theory paid little attention to this transformation in a child's life. The first systematic report on sibling rivalry and its psychological importance came in a monograph in 1937 by child psychiatrist and psychoanalyst David Levy. (*Sibling* is the term used to categorize brothers and sisters. Originally, *sibling* applied only to young children, just as duckling means "little duck," and the term *sib* was used for older brothers and sisters. In recent years, however, *sibling* has come into common usage for older as well as younger children.)

Levy's report was based on the study of children seen in his clinical practice, especially on observations of their reactions in doll play. He believed that the degree of the firstborn's disturbance at the arrival of a rival was directly related to the closeness of her relationship with her mother. The closer the relationship, the greater the firstborn's distress, according to his observations. Levy's report was influential in turning the attention of mental health professionals to the importance of sibling rivalry. A number of reports have confirmed the frequency of its occurrence, and some have also emphasized Levy's association of its degree with the child's dependency on the mother (Dunn & Kendrick 1982). In a swing of the pendulum, sibling rivalry has now gone from being largely ignored to being overdiagnosed by some mental health advisers. In our own practice we have seen a number of instances in which a behavior problem thought to be due to poorly handled sibling rivalry proved to stem from an entirely different cause. Yet sibling rivalry does exist, and child care manuals now give detailed advice to parents on how to handle their firstborn's jealousy, clinging, fussing, regression to baby-like behavior, and other evidences of sibling rivalry. As might have been expected, much of the advice given by different experts is contradictory.

Until recently, there has been very little systematic research on this issue of sibling rivalry. We know that while the arrival of a second child frequently arouses intense emotional reactions in the firstborn, the second child, who has never been "King of the Walk," does not experience the same kind of distress on the arrival of a third child, though he may show some adverse behavioral change at no longer having the privileges of the baby of the family. It was also known that if the firstborn is an older school-age child, she will experience much less intense sibling rivalry than of the two- or three-year-old firstborn.

But many questions remained unanswered: How does the quality of the firstborn's relationship to the parents before the birth of the second child affect her response to that event? How does the firstborn's relationship with the parents change after the birth of the second child? Are there individual differences in the way firstborns react to the arrival of a sibling? If there are such variations, what factors are responsible for them? What is the nature of the relationship established by firstborns with their siblings? How does this relationship persist over time, and why? All these issues are pertinent to our understanding of the child's psychological development. They are also important for parents, for the answers to these questions can lay the basis for effective guidance on handling the problems that may be created by sibling rivalry.

To probe a number of these questions, psychologist Judy Dunn and her associates undertook a painstaking systematic study that has provided us with a solid body of information on sibling relationships. Dunn's research project and her findings are spelled out in *Siblings* (1982), written with her principal collaborator, Carol Kendrick.

As in any such research study, it must be remembered that the data were obtained from a group of families with a specific sociocultural and national background. Generalization of the findings to other social or national groups must be done cautiously, and some aspects of the study should be repeated elsewhere. But Dunn & Kendrick have blazed a trail for others to follow, by spelling out their methods carefully and in detail. A number of their findings dovetail with related child development studies in other research centers, which provide evidence that their conclusions can be applied to other social groups and cultures.

Dunn and Kendrick's study group comprised forty firstborn children living with their parents in Cambridge, England, or in nearby villages. Sex distribution was equal. The great majority of the families were working class and had no contact with the university. The mothers did not work outside the home, and their housing situation was relatively good. The families were stable, play space was adequate, and most of the children had a network of relatives living in the area. At the beginning of the study, the children ranged in age from eighteen to forty-three months, and the mothers were within a few weeks of the birth of their second child.

Methods of data collection included both lengthy interviews of the mothers about their children's behavior and extensive observation of the children at home. The authors comment about the great advantage of observing children in their own home settings rather than in artificial laboratory settings, a judgment with which we strongly agree. The families were visited four times: during the last month of the mother's pregnancy, during the first month after the birth of the new baby, when the baby was eight months old, and when the baby was fourteen months old. The authors used a variety of descriptive units to rate the mothers' and children's behavior. These included positive items, such as affectionate tactile contact—mother helps or shows, or child gives baby a toy—and negative items—mother prohibits, child fusses, or child wonders. In addition to these specific items, lengthier interactions were also included, such as sequences of joint play. Other categories of special interest, such as imitation of actions or sounds, or mutual looking, were also rated. Ratings of the firstborn's temperament prior to the birth of the sibling were also made, using a modified scheme of our own basic categories of temperament. A follow-up by one of the authors' colleagues was also done when the firstborns reached six years of age, though only nineteen of the forty children had reached this age by the time *Siblings* was written.

The authors found a close agreement between the mothers' reports and the observations made by the staff members in the home. This finding corresponds to our experience in our own study, that with a proper approach to the mother and an emphasis on obtaining descriptions of a child's behavior, rather than what the parents think it means, accurate information can be obtained from the vast majority of mothers and fathers.

The data of Dunn and Kendrick's study included both qualitative narrative descriptions of individual children and quantitative ratings, permitting the study of specific children as well as a statistical study of the group as a whole. We have also found this combination of qualitative and statistical methods of analysis to be most effective in identifying and evaluating the significant findings of a behavioral study.

Dunn and Kendrick found that almost all the firstborn children showed distress at the arrival of the new baby. The most common expression of disturbance (in 93 percent) was an increase in disobedient and demanding behavior, especially with the mother. More than half the children showed an increase in clinging and tearfulness, and a minority experienced increased sleeping and feeding problems. Two of the twenty-six children who had been toilet trained began to lose this control, and several showed signs of withdrawal tendencies. There were signs of regression in twenty-eight. For fifteen these were mild—occasional baby talk, demands to be carried, or requests to be fed. Many mothers observed reactions of jealousy when the father or a grandparent showed pleasure or interest in the new baby. This jealousy was expressed either by "looking unhappy" or by direct comments, such as "Daddy is not Ronnie's daddy." Direct aggression toward the baby, such as hitting or poking, was not common. A larger number, approximately half the firstborns, did on occasion irritate the baby by what appeared to be deliberate actions—shaking the crib or taking away his bottle, for example.

A number of the children showed more than one of these expressions of distress and jealousy. The severity of the disturbances varied greatly, as did their duration. The authors investigated the reasons for these differences by means of the statistical technique called multiple regression analysis. (With this procedure, one can determine whether two factors that appear to be linked are actually causally related or being influenced by a third factor.)

A highly significant correlation was found with the firstborn's temperamental characteristics. The influence of temperamental factors was most evident in the firstborn's relationship with the mother but did not appear to be significantly involved in the child's relationship with the father or younger sibling. Those children rated before the baby's birth as having negative mood, high intensity of reactions, and a tendency to withdrawal responses to the new were more likely to show disturbed reactions to the new baby. The nonadaptable children (the term used by Dunn and Kendrick is "unmalleable") were also more likely to have feeding problems and to demand more attention. Children who were already anxious and fearful before the baby's birth were likely to become more so after the sibling's birth. It is of interest that these temperamental factors correspond closely to our own categorization of the temperamentally difficult child. We and others have found that children with this temperamental pattern are more vulnerable to demands for change and new adaptations. It is therefore not surprising that temperamentally difficult firstborn children find the radical change in their life produced by the arrival of a new sibling to be more stressful and disturbing than do other youngsters.

Besides these temperamental differences, Dunn and Kendrick reported that the firstborn boys were more likely to be more withdrawn after the baby's birth than were the girls. The same withdrawal was also more frequent, in both boys and girls, if the mother felt especially tired or depressed after the baby's birth. When the child had a close relationship with the father, the extent of the child's disturbance was significantly diminished. Finally, in the families where the mother had a particularly close and harmonious relationship with a firstborn daughter there was a greater tendency for the sibling relationship to be especially difficult.

The finding of sibling rivalry, emphasized so much by mental health professionals, is only one part of the story, however. Equally important in the Cambridge study were the many evidences of positive responses of enjoyment that the firstborns had to their baby brothers and sisters. Almost all were eager to help in the care of the baby and to cuddle her, and over half tried to entertain her with toys, books, or play. The majority of the mothers also reported increased independence in the older child, such as increased insistence on self-feeding or dressing or going to the toilet alone.

But a number of the children who were conspicuously affectionate and warm toward the baby also showed evidence of disturbance and jealousy. Some of those with increased independence in some areas regressed in others. The authors emphasize this complex and contradictory pattern of sibling reaction: "It appears from these findings that a simple notion of 'degree of disturbance' is inappropriate to describe the children's reaction to the arrival of the baby" (p. 34). This finding provides additional evidence of the great individuality and differences in behavior of normal children (and their parents) in all areas of life. Any attempt to find a simple formula that can be applied in the same way to all children is indeed a futile search.

Some theorists, especially in the psychoanalytic movement, place great emphasis on the symbolic importance of the mother's breast in the child's psychological development. They suggest that the older child may be especially disturbed if the mother breast-feeds the baby. Dunn and Kendrick found no evidence to support this idea and state flatly that "mothers who are expecting a second child need not feel that a decision to breast-feed the second will subject their first child to additional stress" (p. 51).

The authors point to the contradictory advice given to parents about the value of preparing the first child ahead of time for the birth of the second. Some experts consider such preparation very valuable, others doubt its usefulness. Dunn and Kendrick do not have systematic data on this issue. They did find that there was no significant difference in the firstborn's reactions whether the baby was born at home or in the hospital. In other words, separation from the mother did not constitute a noticeable additional stress. It is true that the mother's hospitalization lasted only two days on the average, and the father and grandparents or other relatives were available during the mother's absence. The study also found no appreciable effect on the firstborn of the different ways in which she first met the baby. As the authors comment wisely, "Even as adults we may be *rationally* prepared for a change in our relationships, yet devastated by the experience of that change" (p. 49).

Sibling Relationships

The Cambridge study also provides much valuable information on the patterns of the relationship of young siblings with each other. The study found a wide range of differences between the sibling pairs in the relative proportion of friendly versus unfriendly behavior of the firstborns toward their younger siblings. By contrast, there was greater uniformity in the reactions of the younger to the older siblings. The younger child was likely to approach her older brother or sister in a friendly way and respond with pleasure to positive overtures from the older sibling. These observations are consistent with the findings of other investigators. In our own studies, parents consistently reported on the special ability of the older sibling to entertain, amuse, and divert her baby brother or sister.

Empathy

Dunn and Kendrick were impressed by the richness and variety "of communication and social understanding between the children that current approaches to the study of early communication hardly begin to consider" (p. 133). This was true for both verbal and nonverbal interchanges between the children and suggests a fruitful field for further research in early social development. This level of social communication and relationship between young siblings is also of special interest in relation to the human personality characteristic we call *empathy,* and the Cambridge study provides new and fascinating information in this area.

Empathy can be defined as one person's sharing of another's feelings and thoughts. Empathy does not necessarily mean having the same feelings and ideas as the other person, but understanding and sympathizing with them and perhaps even trying to do something to correct the distress that the other person may be experiencing. Empathy has both cognitive and emotional components. It requires both the capacity to understand what the other person is feeling and why and the ability to experience the emotional quality appropriate to this understanding. It goes without saying that empathy represents a complex and important attribute of human social functioning. In Piaget's system of cognitive development, children below the age of seven are not considered to be capable of empathy. In his scheme, the child's thinking is egocentric; she cannot consider points of view different from her own (1954). Dunn and Kendrick, however, found definite evidence of empathy in the firstborn child in their home observations done when the baby was eight months old and again when she was fourteen months old. The investigators set up strict criteria for their ratings of empathy. For example, giving the younger one a toy to play with indicated an interest in the baby's welfare but was not considered definitive evidence of empathy. But if the younger child was frustrated or distressed or had hurt herself, and the older child gave her the toy unsolicited, this was clear evidence of empathy. In this case, the older child's behavior showed that she understood the feelings of her younger sibling, sympathized with them, and wanted to do something to make the baby feel better. Such incidents that could be definitely rated as empathy were noted in 65 percent of the firstborns in the home observations when their ages ranged from 28 to 57 months and their siblings were fourteen months old.

The data of this Cambridge study could not identify what factor or factors were responsible for the development of empathy in these young children. As Dunn and Kendrick point out, the systematic study of this issue would be a most desirable research project. Being able to stimulate the development of this quality of empathy in children systematically would have enormous social implications for parents and others. Empathy creates positive human bonds between individuals and counteracts the forces in society that tend to alienate people from each other. One suggestive finding of the Cambridge study is that the way the mothers talked to the firstborn about the baby had a significant effect on the relationship that developed between the children. The study identified a group of mothers who talked about the new baby from the beginning as a *person*, a real human being with needs, likes, and dislikes. They discussed the care of the baby with the firstborn as if they were working together for the baby's welfare. These mothers gave genuine encouragement to the older child's attempts to help with the baby's care. They also called the older child's attention to the baby's positive interest in her behavior. Dunn and Kendrick found that in these families, friendly interaction between the children became much more frequent than in families where the mother did not express such attitudes.

The mother who responds to her newborn baby as already a person is intuitively making the same judgment that has crystallized from the recent research challenging the mystique of the newborn as something other than normal and human—a bundle of instincts, autistic, narcissistic, unhatched psychologically, and so on. This finding of the Cambridge study indicates that these other research findings have practical as well as theoretical importance. It is well within a mother's ability to consider her newborn baby as already a person and to communicate this approach to her older child or children. According to the findings of the Cambridge study, this specific concrete action may well have a positive effect on the kind of relationship that develops between her children. It is plausible to speculate that it will also stimulate the capacity for empathy in the children.

The Bond Between Siblings

The Cambridge study has provided us with a vivid picture of the complexities, individual differences, and contradictory attitudes of an older and younger sibling to each other that crystallize in the weeks and months after the birth of the younger child. The partial follow-up of their sample when the firstborns were six years of age highlighted again the tremendous variation in patterns of relationship of the different sibling pairs. Some engaged actively in play with each other; some had frequent fights, and some had less intense hostile interchanges with each other. There was strong continuity with the earlier findings in the proportion of friendly versus antagonistic interactions between the siblings. These findings are of interest, but they have to be considered as preliminary and tentative.

Other studies of sibling relationships in the older childhood years and in adult life have in the main been fragmentary, unsystematic, and impressionistic. Psychiatrists and clinical psychologists have tended to concentrate on the issue of sibling rivalry. Some family therapists have made much of the concept that one child is made the family scapegoat. Actually, it has been the novelists and dramatists such as Shakespeare and Dostoevsky who have provided us with insights into the subtleties, complexities and importance of relationships between brothers and sisters. There has been one major attempt to explore the nature of the bond between siblings throughout life, a study by two clinical psychologists, Stephen Bank and Michael Kahn, reported in *The Sibling Bond* (1982). Their information came from their case material from patients in psychotherapy, from patients of colleagues, and from interviews with a number of persons who were not patients. *The Sibling Bond* emphasizes the richness and variety of sibling relationships at all ages and the importance of this relationship in people's lives. The authors point up the positive features of many sibling bonds and address a much-needed plea to psychotherapists to pay attention to that factor in the treatment of their patients. Unfortunately, their analysis of their data appears to have been impressionistic, in contrast to the rigorous research methodology of Dunn and Kendrick's Cambridge study.

In our New York Longitudinal Study we too have been struck by the great variety of relationships between brothers and sisters. In the early adult follow-ups, many of the subjects have said, "When we were kids, I used to fight all the time with my brother (or sister), but now that we have grown up, we have become good friends." Others, however, have reported antagonistic, distant, or only casual friendly relationships with their siblings. We have not yet analyzed these data to determine what factors may have been responsible for the different types of evolution of the sibling bond from childhood to adult life.

Children of Divorce

The sibling bond can assume special importance for children whose parents are divorced. Judith Wallerstein, director of the Center for the Family in Transition in Corte Madera, California, and one of the leading researchers of the impact of divorce on children, makes this point emphatically. In a recent paper on the children of divorce, she reports, "We were impressed with the solidarity between siblings in a subgroup of these families—with the love, intimacy, and loyalty among brothers and sisters and the candor and pride with which this was acknowledged" (1985, p. 552). She cites several instances, each with a similar theme: "Divorce forced my brother and me to grow up and to be close to each other"; "My relationship with my sister has been the saving of our emotional and physical selves"; "I rely a lot on my brother. We're intimate in our discussions" (p. 552). The close sibling bonds between these children served to maintain positive concepts of the possibility of faithfulness, enduring love, and emotional intimacy with another person.

Unfortunately, a positive sibling bond did not develop in all the divorced families in the study. In some cases, antagonism was rather the outcome. One young adult put it that "I had to take care of my brothers and sisters and got blamed for everything" (p. 552). (Of course, this can also happen in intact families.)

It behooves parents planning divorce to take these findings seriously. Whatever their feelings toward each other may be, they will have a continuing responsibility toward their children. Divorce is a disturbing and even disruptive event for the children. If a strong sibling bond can be an important factor in minimizing the harmful effect of their parents' divorce, then it is clearly the responsibility of the parents to work together to cement this sibling bond before, during, and after the divorce. The specific methods used will vary from family to family. In general they involve working out ways to encourage the children to pursue similar interests and activities together, to respect each other's differing interests, and to neutralize potential or actual sources of friction.

The Implications of Sibling Research

There are a number of important lessons both for parents and for mental health professionals in the findings of Dunn and Kendrick's Cambridge study. The study found that the adaptations required of the firstborn with the birth of the new baby almost universally create stress, which is evident in the older child's distress and disturbed behavior.

But stress, as we have emphasized in earlier chapters, can have either healthy or unhealthy consequences for the child's development. The outcome depends on the capacity of the child to master the stress and on the attitudes and behavior of the parents and others, which either reinforce or hinder the child's efforts at coping.

The study also found positive change in most of the firstborns, such as growth of independent functioning, eagerness to help with the care of the baby, and the development of empathy. These indications of healthy change are ignored by most writers, who tend to focus only on the sibling rivalry issue. Dunn and Kendrick, however, highlight this positive change, as we would. They ask, "Is it possible or likely that the emotional upheaval for the elder child contributes in an important way to the developmental advances that follow the birth of the sibling?" (p. 211). More research data is needed for a definitive answer to this question, but the evidence from the Cambridge study, our own longitudinal study, and the case records reported by Bank and Kahn make us confident that the answer will be a resounding *yes.*

Books on child care usually emphasize the responsibility of the parents in determining whether or not sibling rivalry becomes severe. But the Cambridge study has shown clearly that the relationship between parent and child is only one of the important factors determining the severity of the firstborn's jealousy and disturbance: "The sex constellation of the sibling pair and the temperament of the first child were both of major importance; it would be quite unjustified, indeed invidious, to suggest that the expression of jealousy and disturbance depended predominantly on the parents" (p. 219). Furthermore, Dunn and Kendrick found that where the mother's relationship with her daughter was particularly sensitive and harmonious, the sibling relationship was especially difficult. They ask pointedly whether "the mother should be blamed in this case—blamed for *what* precisely? Surely not for the sensitivity of her relationship with her daughter?" (p. 219).

To emphasize that the parents are not all-decisive in determining the course of their children's relationship with each other does not mean that they have no influence. Quite the contrary. The Cambridge study gives definite evidence of the importance of the parents' attitudes and behavior for the early years. Our own longitudinal study, the observations of Bank and Kahn, and a number of other reports confirm this finding and extend it into the later years of childhood as well. There is much that parents can do to minimize the severity of sibling rivalry and encourage the growth of healthy, affectionate relationships between their children.

Practical Advice for Parents

From their Cambridge study findings, Dunn and Kendrick offer a number of practical suggestions to parents for the first weeks and months after the birth of the second child. They recommend that parents minimize changes in the firstborn's life, and especially that they try to avoid any drastic decrease in the level of play and attention the first child had been receiving. For the early weeks the mother should have as much help and support as possible from the father, other relatives, and friends. If the firstborn's disturbance appears unusually severe, the question of whether it is due to difficult temperament should be given special consideration. If this is the case, then the approach that is best for such a child in other situations will apply here as well (see chapter 5). The older child is likely to be most upset when the mother or other primary caregiver is actively caring for the new baby. Planning ahead for ways to distract the older child's attention at such times are useful, such as engaging her in play with the father or another relative, bringing out a favorite food treat, or telling the older child a story while feeding or bathing the baby. Involving the firstborn in the care of the baby and talking to her about the baby as a person have particular value.

We agree emphatically with these recommendations. A number of them are as appropriate for the later months and years as they are for the first months. Parents and visitors should pay attention to the older child as well as the younger. If a gift is brought for one child, there should also be a gift for the other child. The parents should not attempt to duplicate everything for the children, however. If one child needs a new pair of shoes, for example, and the other child or children do not, the approach should be, "When you need new shoes you will get them. But you don't need them now."

We can add additional suggestions for the later childhood years. They are presented as our views, based on the impressions gained from our experience as parents, researchers, and therapists. They appear reasonable to us, but hard research evidence to back them up is not available.

Parents should treat children equally, but that does not mean identically. Helping with household chores and good table manners can be demanded of all the children, but the level of demand should vary with the age and developmental stage of each child. This differentiation should be spelled out clearly to the children. The same issue of equal but not identical treatment will apply to a number of other issues: special treats or trips, amount of allowance, type of clothing or athletic equipment, and various privileges. Some younger children are delighted to wear clothing handed down from their older brothers and sisters; others feel deprived if new clothing is not bought for them. In the latter case, parents should use their judgment. If they decide that a hand-me-down item of expensive clothing is just right for the younger child and buying a new one would be a strain on the family finances, they can stand firm on this judgment. Often the younger child can be satisfied with a simultaneous purchase of some other garment she also needs. In any case, a child's protest over "unfair" treatment will not cause any real harm if the issue is clearly, quietly, and patiently explained. Otherwise, appeasement of the child only invites similar blackmail on future occasions.

Parents should remember that problems of sibling rivalry come up at all ages. The younger child may want the same bedtime, the same freedom to cross the street and travel, or the same allowance as her older brother or sister. Parents should be clear that differential treatment does not mean inequality or favoritism. If they are consistent in their rule that "when you are Danny's age, you will get the same privileges as he has now," the younger child's distress will subside.

A great deal of commotion between siblings is aimed for the parents' attention. Children who have been playing peacefully with or alongside each other will often start a quarrel as they hear one or both parents enter the house. On the other hand, parents should not automatically shrug off such commotions as "sibling rivalry." There may be a justified complaint or problem, and the parents should check out the content of the quarrel before making a judgment.

Parents are best advised to tell their children, once they are of school age, to settle their own quarrels among themselves unless a really important issue is involved. Intervening in minor quarrels may simply encourage the children to escalate their protests to win over the parents.

There are times when a younger child gets upset because she cannot duplicate her older sibling's level of accomplishment, whether in block building, athletic skill, or piano playing. This fact of life cannot be changed. But encouragement of the youngster's efforts and praise of her increasing abilities as she grows older should be helpful in teaching the important lesson that an initial failure is not fatal.

Parents can also be alert to the evidence of shared interests and encourage their development by increasing the children's opportunities for such mutually satisfying activities. Above all, parents can do a great deal to create a family atmosphere in which each child's accomplishments are held up as a source of pleasure and satisfaction for the whole family.

Finally, parents should be clear that there is no simple rule that can be applied like a blueprint to all situations and that will guarantee the elimination of sibling rivalry. Like all issues in the child's psychological development, the relationship between siblings over the years is shaped by multiple factors. Some of these influences are predictable and partially within the parents' control. Many more are unpredictable and beyond the parents' control. Individual differences in psychological development are a central fact that we recognize more and more. Nowhere is this more evident, perhaps, than in the kinds of relationships brothers and sisters develop as they live and interact with each other and the rest of the family through childhood and adolescence and into adult life.

17

Other Family Issues

IN chapter 15, we considered a number of ways in which parents relate to their children. With some of these issues, such as the parent's roles as friend and teacher, the discussion involved both parents as a unit. With other questions, such as whether mother love is unique, the effects of maternal deprivation, and the nature of the young child's attachment to the mother, the focus was on the mother, reflecting the major trend in developmental research, which has largely been concerned with the mother's functioning and influence on the child.

In recent years, however, a number of researchers have begun to examine the role of the father in the development of the infant and older child. This interest has paralleled a significant increase in the past two or three decades in the level of responsibility that many fathers take for their children's care. Fathers have become active caregivers, instead of leaving this function entirely to their wives. Professional interest is also just beginning to turn to an examination of the influence of grandparents in their grandchildren's lives.

This chapter will consider the roles of the father and the grandparents as well as a number of other topics involving the structure of the family: the single parent; separation, divorce, and remarriage; joint custody of the child after divorce; and adoption. Most of these areas are interrelated, and our prime concern will be the effect of each of these factors on the child's functioning and development.

The Role of the Father

The traditional views of the father's role with his child have been summarized in a review article by Ross Parke, of the University of Illinois (1979). As Parke points out, until recent decades in Western industrialized society sex roles had been clearly prescribed. Child care was assigned almost exclusively to the mothers, and as recently as a generation ago it was even considered inappropriate for fathers to take a nurturing role toward their infants. Most other cultures, though not all, took a similar view of sex-role stereotyping. Parke quotes anthropologist Margaret Mead's comment that "fathers are a biological necessity, but a social accident." Fathers were said to influence their children's development, but only in older childhood (Biller 1971).

This traditional sex-role stereotyping was justified in the past, and not too distant past, by citing evidence from other animal species that presumably showed that the males took very little part in the care of their infants. But recent, more careful research has changed this finding drastically. A thorough review of research with monkeys and other nonhuman primates some ten years ago concluded that "adult males form attachments with infants and infants form attachments to adult males" (Redican 1976). Animal researchers had also reported that the female hormones associated with pregnancy and delivery "primed" her to engage in caregiving activity. Aside from the fact that generalizing from animal research on rats to humans is of dubious validity, recent studies have given quite a different picture of hormones and animal behavior. A comprehensive survey in 1974 concluded that "the hormones associated with pregnancy, childbirth, and lactation are not necessary for the appearance of parental behavior" (Maccoby & Jacklin 1974).

In the early 1950s Henry Harlow, of the University of Wisconsin, carried out a series of dramatic experiments with infant monkeys isolated from their mothers after birth (1958) that startled child development students. He devised two types of inanimate "surrogate mothers." These were frames with a bottle and nipple arrangement in an appropriate spot, so that the infant monkey could suck and obtain adequate nourishment. One surrogate mother was a wire frame, the other was a terry-cloth-covered frame. The infant monkeys who used the terry cloth frame fared much better than those who used the wire frame. The former fed more vigorously, thrived physically, and clung to the frame when they were frightened in some way. The monkeys who used the wire frame did significantly less well and did not turn to the frame for comfort when frightened. Harlow commented, "We were not surprised to discover that contact comfort was an important basic affectional or love variable, but we did not expect it to overshadow so completely the variable of nursing" (p. 677). Then, speculating beyond his data (although speculating from monkeys to humans is much less risky than speculating from rats), he concluded that "the American male is physically endowed with all the really essential equipment to compete with the American female on equal terms in one essential activity: the rearing of infants" (p. 685).

The human studies in the 1930s to the 1950s, especially by Goldfarb and Bowlby, appeared to demonstrate the serious consequences of "maternal deprivation" and the "unique" quality of mother love. But as we saw in chapter 15, critical analyses of their findings and an impressive series of studies by other investigators have dispelled these notions. In particular, Michael Rutter's exhaustive and analytic review of the research literature, reported in *Maternal Deprivation Reassessed* (1981), led him to conclude that Bowlby's concept of a decisive and unique mother-child relationship was not supported by the accumulated research evidence. Also influential was a study by two British psychologists, Schaffer and Emerson (1964), who found that of a group of eighteen-month-old children, the principal attachment of the infant was to the mother in only half the subjects; in nearly a third of the cases the main attachment was to the father. A majority of the children showed multiple attachments of varying intensity to other persons in their lives.

These findings have fostered a whole series of studies of the child's relationship with his father. To further complicate this family system, the father's and mother's influence on the child may also be indirectly influenced by their relationships with other members of the family, such as brothers and sisters. For example, a father may admire his own brother's manner of handling children and try to emulate this whether it fits or not.

The role of the father is also greatly influenced by whether he holds to the traditional male image of the routines of child care as "feminine." One typical study found that those fathers with this concept spent much less time in day-to-day child care and even in play and helping with school work than did other fathers without such a *machismo* orientation (Russell 1978).

The recent massive influx of mothers of young children into the work force has also served to blur the traditional sex role differentiation, in which the father worked outside the home and the mother worked exclusively in the home caring for the home and the children. Fathers have been stimulated or impelled to the understanding that the care of their children

is their concern as well as their wives.' In many communities, especially
among middle-class families, we now find many fathers attending prenatal
classes with their wives, staying with their wives throughout the delivery
of the baby, and arranging vacation time to be home in the first weeks of
the infant's life.

Research on the Father's Role

With all the complexities of the family system and the father's part in
it, research studies of the father's role as a parent are not simple. Much has
been learned, but many questions still remain unanswered. Perhaps the
most knowledgeable and thoroughly committed investigator of the father's role is Michael Lamb, co-director of the Fatherhood Project at the
University of Utah. For testimony he presented on November 10, 1983 to
the Select Committee on Children, Youth and Families of the U.S. House
of Representatives, he prepared a summary of the findings in the key issues
of the role of the father in child development. A condensed version of his
authoritative testimony will serve to summarize the present stage of our
knowledge of this subject.*

1. *How much do fathers really do with their children?*
    Fathers in two-parent families spend on the average about a third as much
    time as mothers do actually interacting with their children, and about half
    as much time as mothers do being available to their children. Fathers are
    relatively more involved when mothers are employed and when the children
    are older. The degree of paternal interaction, accessibility, and probably
    responsibility have significantly increased in the past fifteen years.
2. *How well do fathers perform as parents?*
    Fathers *can* be quite as sensitive or competent as mothers in relation to young
    infants, although they tend to yield responsibility to their wives. "With the
    exception of pregnancy, parturition, and lactation, there is no reason to
    believe that men are inherently less capable of child care than women,
    although these potential skills often remain undeveloped or under devel-
    oped" (p. 3).
3. *Do mothers and fathers behave differently with their children?*
    Mothers tend to be identified with caregiving, nurturance, and the day-to-
    day business of childrearing, whereas fathers become associated with play-
    ful social and physical interaction. We do not know whether these differ-
    ences between maternal and paternal behavioral styles have any formative
    significance.
4. *What effects do fathers have on their children's development?*
    There is persuasive evidence that when fathers have close, positive relation-
    ships with their children, children tend to evidence higher achievement

---

*A bibliography of studies of the father's role is provided in Lamb's 1982 article "Paternal
Influences on Early Socio-economic Development," *Journal of Child Psychology and Psychiatry,*
23:185–90.

motivation and cognitive competence, better social skills, and better psychological adjustment. These influences are similar to the significant aspects of mother-child relations, and the parent's gender seems relatively unimportant. Effects on moral development have not been well established.

5. *To what can these effects be attributed?*
   Fathers serve as models for their children to emulate, help shape their behavior by selective rewards and punishment, and along with their wives provide models of heterosexual interactions and relationships. In each of these modes of influence, the emotional quality of each relationship and of the family as a whole is very important. We cannot differentially rate the importance of each of these influences, but because they tend to go together, it is not really fruitful to assess their relative importance.

6. *What effects does father absence have on children?*
   Most studies of this question have been unsatisfactory because of inadequate research methods. It does appear that boys whose fathers are absent (usually due to divorce) tend to show problems in achievement motivation, school performance, psychological adjustment, and heterosexual relationships. The effects on girls have been less thoroughly studied, but they appear to be less severe than the effects on boys. The effects of the father's absence on psychological functioning are not necessarily enduring, however.

7. *To what should the effects of father absence be attributed?*
   Many factors appear important, beyond the absence of a male role model. They include the absence of a second parent to back up the mother, financial stress on the mother, the mother's social and emotional isolation and stress, change in the mother's role (such as having to go to work if she had previously stayed at home), the amount of predivorce parental conflict, the character of the relationship with both parents after the divorce, and the child's age and sibling status. Because so many factors may be operating, no single intervention strategy is possible in all cases.

8. *What effects does increased parental involvement have?*
   The effects are positive when fathers share equally in child care. These effects are probably due to many factors—the close involvement of two parents, cooperation between the parents, less marital conflict, and common sets of values. Not all these factors are always present with greater parental involvement, but they are more likely to be present.

Lamb concludes by emphasizing that paternal effects can only be considered within the entire context of the special family circumstances. He concludes that "unfortunately, there is no 'magic bullet' where childcaring is concerned," a formulation that is a basic theme of this book.

Data from the NYLS

Our own information from the New York Longitudinal Study conforms in general to Lamb's summary of the research literature. Of course, our study started thirty years ago, but the trends described by Lamb were evident in many of the families even then.

Our most striking finding was the tremendous variability in the father-child relationship in these middle-class families. In some families the father was equally involved in the daily child-care routines—feeding, bathing, dressing, diaper-changing, answering the child's night calls or cries—from the time the baby came home from the hospital. These fathers usually continued this active involvement with age-appropriate activities as the child grew older. Many other fathers played an active but more limited role. Typically, this group left most, though not all, of the daily chores to their wives and involved themselves with their children in specific activities, such as roughhouse play, discipline, and reading to the children. A small number of fathers maintained a distance and even aloofness from any specific responsibilities for or regular interplay with their children.

Many factors played a part in shaping the nature of the father's involvement with their children, as well as the amount of time spent with them. If both parents worked full-time, then the issue that both should share household chores and child care became a clear one. That did not mean a mechanical fifty-fifty division of daily chores, however. More often, one parent took major responsibility for certain areas and the other for other areas. For example, the mother might look after the children's clothing needs and the father would take the night calls.

These divisions of labor took shape gradually but differently in those families in which the father assumed equal responsibility and, yes, equal tenderness in the care of their children from infancy onward. Differences in the parents' interests, energy level, temperament, time schedules—all these factors meshed to form different types of equality in paternal and maternal relationships with their children, from which the children could only benefit. Mutual support of the parents was evident and important in a number of cases. In one family with an extremely temperamentally difficult infant son, the mother reacted with anxiety and strong guilt feelings, blaming herself for the child's loud crying spells and slow adjustment to everything new. The father, of a quiet, patient temperament himself, understood his infant's behavior with great sensitivity and clarity. He proved a tower of strength to his wife, constantly reassuring her and taking over one difficult chore after another as necessary. It is of interest that now his son and his son's younger brother, as young adults, both have great affection and respect for their father, which they remember as a continuous feeling from their early childhood onward. They also have deep affection for their mother, but they are clear that it was their father who played the dominant positive role in their family. In other families, it was the mother who felt secure and self-confident as the child's caregiver and who helped the father overcome his initial self-doubts in assuming responsibility for this tiny, fragile infant who had entered his life.

A father's active role was not always so benign. In some cases fathers who were involved with their child's care labeled as weaknesses characteristics that in reality were normal temperamental characteristics, such as high intensity, high activity, slow adaptability, or extreme distractibility. In such cases, the father's active involvement in child care was far from a blessing, when he demanded that his child change these undesirable traits and change them quickly. This kind of poorness of fit commonly produced excessive stress on the child, resulting in behavior problems.

When the father worked full-time and the mother worked only part-time or not at all outside the home, the mother most often assumed the major responsibility for the child's daily care, as might be expected. Even so, some fathers in this situation were eager not just to help but to assume more than their share of caregiving activities when they were at home. At the other extreme, a few fathers used their work commitments as an excuse to detach themselves from most if not all domestic responsibilities. If the mothers accepted this situation, the household might appear to function smoothly on the surface, but the father was sometimes disconcerted to find later on that a relationship he had looked forward to having with his older son or daughter just did not exist. It had never been built.

There were several different reasons why fathers were emotionally distant from their children. In a few cases, these were men who were psychologically unable to make a close emotional tie to any human being. There were also several men who could not sustain a personal relationship with another adult, whom they automatically saw as a threatening, competitive figure, but could do so with a young child. These fathers built positive emotional ties with their young children, but as the youngsters grew into adolescence and adult life, the fathers were unable to maintain the tie, and the relationship grew progressively more distant. Other fathers showed just the opposite tendency. They were either bewildered or annoyed with the child-care necessities of their young children, but as their youngsters matured and began to develop interests and abilities they found attractive, the fathers began to appreciate their children as interesting human beings. A closeness could then develop, unless by that time the child had been so alienated by his father's previous aloofness or irritability that nothing more than a superficial friendship could develop.

In some families in our longitudinal study, a domineering, controlling mother has insisted on an exclusive authoritative, even authoritarian, role with the children. The fathers with passive personalities have responded by withdrawing from the domestic scene. By contrast, if the fathers were assertive, open conflict with their spouses was common. In these cases the father's relationship with the children may have been preserved, but such open parental conflict in the child's early years correlated significantly, in a negative direction, with the youngster's overall level of functioning and adjustment in early adult life (Chess et al. 1983).

There were other families in which the father assumed the dominant authoritative role at home and unilaterally set the rules and demands for the children's upbringing. In such cases, mothers who were passive tended to be submissive to the father's standards, even if they disagreed. When they did disagree, these passive mothers usually vacillated and even became confused in their handling of the children. If the mothers were firm and assertive in a reasonable, flexible way, the fathers sometimes retreated, and excessive stress in the home was avoided. If not, or if the mothers rigidly demanded their own way, the stage was again set for the open conflict that we found to be harmful to the children even into adult life.

Implications for Parents

A basic lesson to be drawn from the research findings of recent years is that from the beginning the father can and should play an equal role with the mother in child care and in the parent-child relationship. The mother's role is deeply important, but not unique.

But this equality of partnership between father and mother in the care of their children will vary tremendously from family to family. Equality does not mean sharing all tasks equally. One parent may find changing a soiled diaper distasteful, and the other may not mind this chore. In such a case, there is no reason why the parent who doesn't mind shouldn't take over this task. Other ways of equalizing the child-care burdens are possible. The same parent who takes on the diaper-changing may find it burdensome to handle a highly active young child in the bathtub. The spouse may enjoy this tumultuous water play and take on this responsibility. Equality in the child-care partnership is best achieved in these kinds of give-and-take arrangements, and not by adding up minutes and hours spent with the child to achieve some kind of mechanical bookkeeping balance.

Open parental conflict over child care is a potentially harmful source of stress to a child. Parents can privately agree to disagree when they have different views and can work out some common approach. If the child occasionally says "Daddy, you want me to do this, but Mommy tells me the opposite," it is usually sufficient to reply quietly that parents, like other people, don't always agree, and the youngster can do it the one way with Daddy and the other way with Mommy. If there has to be a choice, this can be decided in a relaxed discussion with the child present.

The Role of Grandparents

Very little attention has been paid in the research and other professional writings on the influence of grandparents on the lives of their grandchildren. Even the more popular volumes on child care, with a few exceptions (such as Kornhaber & Woodward 1981), have been silent on this subject.

It is true that systematic research on the role of grandparents with their grandchildren presents a number of special problems. In these days of divorce and remarriage, there may be as many as eight grandparents in a family, each with a separate set of psychological characteristics. One or more grandparents may live nearby or with the family and be actively involved with the children. Others may live at a distance, and the relationships with the children may be only occasional and brief. A grandparent's interchange with a grandchild may also be affected by complexities of the relationships with his or her own child, the parent of the grandchild, as well as with the son- or daughter-in-law. Conflicts between the grandparent and parent over child-rearing practices can reflect both ongoing personal struggles and changes in prevalent opinions over the course of a generation.

Yet grandparents can be important influences in the lives of their grandchildren. This fact was clear in the recollections of some of the subjects of our longitudinal study. More specific information comes from the thorough and comprehensive study of effect of divorce on children done by Judith Wallerstein and her collaborators at the University of California, Berkeley (1983). They found that only 25 percent of the children were helped by grandparents or other members of the extended family when their parents separated. They comment that "although grandparents often are unavailable, there is evidence that a significant number of grandparents are hesitant about intruding at the time of crisis and, if called upon, would happily make themselves available as a resource for their grandchildren" (p. 246). Grandparents and members of the extended family can be especially helpful in visiting regularly, providing special treats, babysitting, and offering other forms of support.

Wallerstein's finding of the lack of involvement of grandparents with their grandchildren in a time of crisis is extended further by psychiatrist Arthur Kornhaber. He laments, quite correctly, the overall trend in our society in which "grandparents are no longer 'part of the family.' In too many cases, unfortunately, this is literally true" (1981, p. xx). He feels that the social encouragement to older people to continue to live their own lives and pursue their own interests has contributed to the emergence of older Americans "who no longer conform to negative stereotypes of 'old Granny and old Granpa.' . . . The brutal fact is that more and more grandparents are choosing to ignore their grandchildren. In turn, grandchildren are ignoring them" (p. xxii). His book is a plea for the reaffirmation of the "vital connection" between grandparent and grandchild, which could mean so much to both.

We may be biased on this issue, with six grandchildren of our own. But to us, the research evidence, as fragmentary as it is, suggests strongly that grandparents can play an important role in their grandchildren's lives. Wallerstein emphasizes their value in times of crisis, such as separation and divorce of the parents. But it seems to us that grandparents and grandchildren who are fortunate enough to establish close ties have a great deal to give to each other in the ordinary course of everyday life. For the grandparents, the growing and maturing child who is linked to them genetically and emotionally reaffirms the continuity of life into the future. For the child, the grandparents provide a sense of continuity with the past and with their cultural heritage. And it is the grandparent who has this kind of tie with his or her grandchildren who can be most effective as a supportive figure if and when a family crisis develops.

As in all human relationships there is no single blueprint for establishing a close tie between grandparent and grandchild. Certainly it is easier if they live close to each other. But even if they are separated geographically, there are many ways of keeping in touch, such as visits back and forth, frequent letters and telephone calls, and birthday remembrances.

Parents sometimes worry that the grandparents will "spoil" their child with their loving time and attention and frequent gifts. We can only offer our opinion that this is almost always an overexaggerated concern. Children are very good at differentiating their relationships with different members of the family. They may know that Grandma is lenient and permissive and will press limits with her that they will not try with their parents. Each relationship is different, and the one between child and grandparent should not be a carbon copy of the one between child and parent.

The Single Parent

Single parents make up a very heterogeneous group. There are the mature divorcée, the widow or widower, and the teenager hardly out of her own childhood and deserted by her lover. There is the woman who has had several unsatisfactory marriages or love affairs and decides that she will never find the right man but deeply wants to be a mother, so she has a casual affair in order to become pregnant. There is also the homosexual woman who has no desire to live with a man but wishes to be a mother and has a brief heterosexual relationship to achieve this purpose. A report by the National Center on Health Statistics on babies born out of wedlock in 1983 showed an increase in the number born to women aged thirty-five to thirty-nine, as compared with previous years (*New York Times,* 29 September 1985). This may indicate that more single women are deliberately becoming pregnant before it is too late for them to become mothers.

Certainly, there is no generalization that will fit all these diverse types of single parents. Most are women, but there are also single fathers, whose wives have died or been institutionalized or who have custody of the child or children. One can say that a single parent requires a special support system, such as an additional caregiver or adequate day-care facility, to cope with the demands resulting from sole responsibility for the care of the child. But there is no substantial evidence in the research literature that a child necessarily suffers psychological harm because he lacks a "father figure" or a "mother figure" to provide a model for future adult relationships. There are almost always one or more substitutes available to the child—an older brother or sister, uncles, aunts, and grandparents. Sometimes even the parent of a close friend serves this function. What matters are the circumstances and stresses created by single parenthood. And these are vastly different for a mature educated woman with an ample income than for a barely literate fifteen-year-old girl living on welfare in a crowded slum tenement where there is hardly room for her, let alone her new baby.

If the child has no contact with the other parent, it is predictable that he will want to know why he has no daddy or mommy, as his friends do. Where the other parent has died, the child should be given a direct, truthful answer, no matter how painful. Often the child will ask the same question at succeeding age periods. This does not mean that he has forgotten the answer, but rather that at a new stage of intellectual development he wants and needs to have a more detailed explanation.

It is reassuring that studies have consistently shown that the death of a parent need not in itself have long-term harmful psychological effects on the child. Rutter, in summarizing a number of reports, concludes that despite the major readjustment that may be entailed, most children develop normally (1966). Another British study by Michele Van Erdewegh and associates confirms this conclusion (Van Erdewegh, Clayton, & Van Erdewegh 1985). And our own longitudinal study found that the earlier death of a parent did not significantly affect the overall level of adjustment of the subjects in early adult life.

There may, of course, be individual instances in which the death of a parent is not followed by long-term readjustment. One of our study subjects was temperamentally quick and intense in her reactions, which gave her a tendency to impulsivity in behavior. The result was some behavior problems in her early school years, but the parents, working together to set firm and consistent rules for her, with our advice, succeeded in eliminating these problems. When she became a young adolescent, with new and more complex social and academic demands, her impulsiveness again threatened to give her difficulties. Unfortunately, her father, a forceful and respected figure in the family, died suddenly at that time. The mother was overwhelmed by her bereavement, her necessity to take a full-time job, and her sole responsibility for her four children. Without the father, she was unable to control her daughter's impulsiveness, which led to increasingly serious antisocial behavior and school truancy.

Where the single mother has made the deliberate choice of motherhood without marriage, or where she has had an accidental pregnancy with scruples against abortion and has not married the father, it is our judgment that she should also give her child a direct and honest answer. It may confuse or anger the child, but if the mother speaks with dignity and without apologies for her principled decision, she can expect that the child will understand her position, even if he wishes it could have been otherwise.

It is quite another matter, however, for the child to reveal his paternity in the outside world. We have come a long way in recent years in our tolerance of unconventional sexual situations. A child whose parents are not married, however, still faces the real danger of being scapegoated by age-mates and neighbors as illegitimate. In our opinion the mother is well advised to tell her child to keep the facts a secret between themselves and other close family members. For the outside world, a white lie such as "my father died before I was born" will give him needed protection. The mother should emphasize that such a cover-up is necessary not because they have anything to be ashamed of but because so many other people still make unreasonable and unfair judgments.

If the child insists on meeting his father and even having a relationship with him, and this is agreeable to the father, the mother should not stand in the way. If the father rejects the child, it will be clear that mother is not to blame. To make this an issue of contention with her son or daughter can only boomerang and make the youngster wonder whether the mother has something sinister to hide.

Separation, Divorce, and Remarriage

Permanent separation of the parents, whether or not accompanied by legal divorce, creates serious stress for the children. Even if the children have been aware of frequent and fierce conflicts between their parents, with the threat of divorce always in the air, the actual separation comes as a shock. Many children cannot help asking themselves "Was it somehow my fault?" or wondering "If my parents can stop loving each other, maybe they can stop loving me." There are often major readjustments in life style for both parents and children, some of which may be stressful.

Evaluation of the long-term effects of parental separation and divorce on children is quite complex. Many factors have to be considered: the financial consequences, the behavior of the parents with each other and the children, the age and sex of the child, the nature of the child's relationship to each parent before the separation, the support given by the extended family, and the nature of the custody arrangements. Unpredictable intervening events, such as the emergence of a special talent that brings the child closer to one parent, may also play a part. And remarriage of one or both parents, a frequent occurrence after divorce, brings a series of new issues: relationships with a stepparent, and with stepbrothers and sisters, and perhaps the birth of younger half-siblings.

Fortunately, we now have a wealth of significant information on the effects of divorce and remarriage, primarily from two thorough and methodologically sophisticated longitudinal studies. Judith Wallerstein's study comprised sixty divorcing families, primarily but not entirely white and middle-class, with 131 children aged three to eighteen at the time of separation. One child was chosen from each family. Follow-up studies were done after five years and again after ten years, when fifty-one families with ninety-eight children were located and reevaluated (1983; 1985). The other study, by Mavis Hetherington and her co-workers at the University of Virginia, started with 144 white middle-class children and their parents (Hetherington, Cox, & Cox 1985). Half the children were from divorced, mother-custody families, and the other half, used as a control group, were from nondivorced families. The families were first studied at two months, one year, and two years after the divorces of the first group. A new follow-up has now been done six years after the divorce, in which 124 of the original 144 families were available for reevaluation.

Both the Wallerstein and the Hetherington studies used a number of data-gathering procedures, and the information was analyzed statistically and by the evaluation of individual families. Only the highlights of their extensive findings and conclusions can be presented here.

Wallerstein points out that the initial responses of a child to divorce are more observable, "whereas the long-lasting effect on development is complex and impossible to predict . . . the child's age and developmental stage appear to be the most important factors governing the initial response" (1983, p. 247). According to her observations, preschool children are most likely to show regression, such as in toilet training and clinging to the parents. Children aged five to eight are likely to show open grieving, including sighing and sobbing. Children nine to twelve years old are frightened by the divorce and often worry about entering adolescence without the support of an intact family. They are also likely to be intensely angry at one or both parents for divorcing. Adolescents may worry about their own future marriages and the possibility that they too may experience sexual and marital failure.

Wallerstein is optimistic regarding the beneficial effects of most remarriages. "There is encouraging evidence from social agencies, parent self-help groups, life education courses, adult education courses, and some preliminary research that adults enter the second marriage more realistically. . . . Overall, remarriage appears to enhance the lives of many children, particularly those who have not yet reached adolescence" (1983, pp. 252–54). As Wallerstein emphasizes, however, such a benign outcome of remarriage is not automatic. If the stepfather enters too abruptly and authoritatively into the paternal role, he may generate anxiety in the children and alienate them. Problems may also arise in the remarried family if the stepparent fails to recognize that the development of a positive relationship with the stepchildren requires time, attention, and patience. Instant love, respect, and obedience are unrealistic expectations.

Hetherington's study in general confirms Wallerstein's findings on the disturbing effects of divorce on children. One difference is that Hetherington found that divorce had more adverse effects for boys, but that remarriage was more disruptive for girls. Both findings appeared to stem from the benefit that children receive from having an involved same-sex parent or parent surrogate in the home. For the boys in these mother-custody families, a stepfather might fill that need. In contrast, stepfathers may disrupt the close relationships formed by divorced mothers and their daughters (1985). Like Wallerstein, Hetherington emphasizes that the most successful stepfathers are those who first cement a positive relationship with the child before taking over an active role in the family's discipline and decision-making.

Our New York Longitudinal Study has not included an in-depth study of the effects of divorce and remarriage, but our data have been sufficient for an analysis of the overall effect in early adult life of parental separation or divorce in the subject's earlier life. The analysis included a rating of parental conflict obtained from both parents simultaneously but separately when the children were three years old. Correlations calculated for separation or divorce appeared to show a definite negative effect on the level of early adult adjustment. A similar finding was found with parental conflict and adult adjustment. Parental conflict and subsequent separation or divorce were also significantly correlated. But when the effect of parental conflict on early adult adjustment was separated out by multiple regression analysis, there was no significant residual effect for separation or divorce. In other words, parental conflict in the child's early life appeared to be of greater long-term harmful significance for the child than actual separation or divorce. This finding is in accord with a report by Michael Rutter emphasizing the deleterious effect on the child of parental discord as contrasted with actual separation or divorce (1981b).

Joint Custody

Until recently, custody of a child after parental divorce was usually granted to the mother, unless there were special circumstances that made this decision undesirable. This decision has the unfortunate effect of separating the child from the father, even if frequent visiting is possible, and also leads to many disputes over the rights of the father. In recent years joint custody, in which both parents share the time and care of the child after the divorce, has been advocated as a solution to the battle over child custody. In this arrangement, the child in effect has two homes, one with the father and one with the mother, alternating between them. The parents share the responsibility and authority for their child's care, or the child lives with one parent but there is joint responsibility. Provisions for such joint custody arrangements have now been enacted in thirty-two states.

The joint custody movement has sprung from several sources. Several courts found that the presumption that mothers should have custody violated fathers' constitutional rights of equal protection (Derdeyn & Scott 1984). The increasing number of mothers working outside the home, even mothers with young children, has weakened the presumption that the mother is always best able to give continuous care to the child. Finally, joint custody has relieved judges of the responsibility for making the difficult choice of which parent is best suited to raise the children. As one judge has put it, "Joint custody is an appealing concept. It permits the court to escape an agonizing choice, to keep from wounding the self-esteem of either parent, and to avoid the appearance of discrimination between the sexes" (quoted in Derdeyn & Scott 1984, p. 204).

Experience with joint custody is as yet too brief to allow for definitive conclusions. Two recent articles, by Andre Derdeyn and Elizabeth Scott, of the University of Virginia (1984), and by Susan Steinman and her associates in the San Francisco Joint Custody Project (1985), have reported preliminary impressions, both favorable and critical.

Derdeyn and Scott weigh the possible advantages and potential problems of joint custody. On the positive side, it may avoid the emotional and financial costs of court battles over custody. It holds out the promise that the child will lose neither parent but will be able to maintain close relationships with both parents. Mothers may also benefit as the burden of single parenthood is lifted.

These features of joint custody have stimulated many judges to order joint custody when only one parent is in favor of it, and even when neither has requested it. In such cases there is the danger that the divorcing parents will miss the opportunity to resolve their conflicts in court and that these conflicts will be perpetuated by the joint custody decision. Two very angry parents may even be pressured to agree to joint custody, which may then not be in the child's best interests. On the other hand, joint custody may impel the father to have more frequent contact with his children, a consequence that a number of studies have found beneficial to the children (Derdeyn & Scott 1984).

Derdeyn and Scott emphasize, however, that there is as yet little empirical research on joint custody that can give us answers to questions about its positive and negative effects. They conclude,

Joint custody may provide the optimum solution for many children. However, the enthusiasm for joint custody seems to be related primarily to our desire to mitigate the pain and loss caused by divorce for both children and parents, and to have a rule for making these difficult decisions. There is a marked disparity be-

tween the power of the joint custody movement and the sufficiency of evidence
that joint custody can accomplish what we expect of it. (p. 207)

Steinman and her co-workers report a follow-up of a study of fifty-one
joint-custody families, done one year after this arrangement had been
implemented. The psychological characteristics of the parents were evaluated in detail, in an attempt to differentiate the families for whom joint
custody is likely to be beneficial from those families for whom it may be
stressful. The findings indicate that "the parents represent a wide spectrum
with respect to reaching a joint custody agreement, and sustaining the
arrangement, and the degree of conflict and stress they experience in joint
parenting" (p. 554). Those families that were most successful in imple-
menting a joint custody arrangement were characterized by (1) respect and
encouragement of the bond between the child and the former spouse; (2)
some degree of objectivity of the parents with regard to the children, no
matter what their other conflicts may be; (3) empathy with the point of
view of the child and other parent; (4) the ability to shift role expectations
from those of mate to those of coparent; (5) the ability to establish new
role boundaries; and (6) high self-esteem and flexibility in the parents.

It may be asked how many parents can live up to such high standards,
especially when they have been engaged in the severe conflicts leading to
a divorce. But we have seen a number of parents with enough of these
characteristics, especially the ability to separate the needs of the children
from their own conflicts, that we were confident they could successfully
share custody.

Steinman and her co-workers also list the characteristics that seem to
predict a negative outcome for joint custody. Not surprisingly, they emphasize continuing intense hostility and conflict between the parents that
cannot be diverted from the child and the fixed belief that the spouse is
a bad parent and should be punished. A history of substance abuse or of
physical abuse between the parents was also predictive of a negative
outcome. The authors recommend professional help for those parents who
are struggling to make joint custody a success. This should prove useful
in at least some cases.

Parents who have decided on permanent separation and divorce have a
deep responsibility to minimize both the short-term and the long-term
harmful effects on their children. And there is a great deal that they can
do, as the carefully documented research in this area attests. Our suggestions are an amalgam of those proposed by Wallerstein and Hetherington
and those that derive from our own research and clinical experiences.

First of all, be honest with the children. Postponing the truth with subterfuges such as "Your father can't live at home all the time because he has a new job" can only magnify the damage. As Wallerstein puts it, "Children who are told of the divorce before the parent's departure from the household and who are also assured that they will continue to see the departing parent are significantly calmer than those who must confront the divorce without any preparation" (1983, p. 246).

Next, assure the children emphatically and repeatedly that they are in no way responsible for the separation. Emphasize that the fact that the parents have stopped loving each other does not in any way mean that they love their children any less or that they will love them less in the future. The absent parent should keep all commitments for visitation time religiously, giving them first priority over all but extraordinary unexpected events. On the other hand, the absent parent should be ready to give up any one scheduled visit at the child's request if the visit will interfere with some important event the child wishes to attend.

Issues of parental conflict should be hidden or at least muted in front of the children. It is especially dangerous for one parent to try to draw the children into an antagonistic position toward the other parent. When this happens the children can be torn by serious and highly destructive divisions of loyalty. In cases where we have been unable to stop one parent from engaging in this tactic, we have always urged the other parent not to be drawn into trying to defend his or her position or to counterattack. It is always possible to say to the children, for example, "Your mother believes this or that about me. I'm sorry she feels that way, but that's between her and you. You and I have our own relationship, and it is apart and separate from what your mother thinks." That way, the children will know that they have at least one parent who will not press them into a position of divided loyalty.

We remember one case in which the father divorced his wife to marry another woman when his two children were very young. He was faithful in his alimony payments but otherwise ignored his children completely. When his children became adolescents, however, they blossomed into attractive and intelligent youngsters. Now that they were no burden, the father suddenly intruded himself into their lives, courting them with all kinds of special treats. Inasmuch as he was highly successful in a glamorous field of work, he was able to do this on a grand scale, and the children delighted in visiting him. The mother became both angry and threatened. She had borne all the burden of the children's care when they were young, and now that they were grown and a pleasure to have around, her former husband was threatening to seduce them away from her. We cautioned her strongly not to interfere and to pretend, if necessary, that she was glad her children were having all these new exciting experiences. She followed our advice, although she often had to bite her tongue. Eventually the glamour wore off, and the father became rather bored with these expeditions. The children sensed the waning of his interest in them, and their relationship with their mother remained close and affectionate.

Finally, play it by ear. If the child has a disturbed reaction, treat it supportively and patiently. Do not force discussion of the divorce on the child. Let him bring it up in his own time and own way.

In the case of remarriage, as Wallerstein points out, the readjustment requires slow, careful work to make the new family arrangement functional. In no way should the stepparent intrude on or try to compete with the child's relationship with the absent parent. If it is the absent parent who remarries, the same approach applies; every care should be taken to ensure that the parent's remarriage will not alter the relationship with the child.

We have been impressed in the early adult interviews in our longitudinal study with how well most of the subjects with divorced parents have been able to resolve this issue positively. Some have done it with genuine help from one or both parents. Sometimes a stepparent has helped, and sometimes the youngster has managed the task on his own. Where the issue of the parents' divorce was still a source of bitter distress, there were usually other unfavorable factors that were preventing the mastery of other problems as well as this one.

Adoption

Adoption is widely accepted in our society. Does it, however, create special problems for the child and the adoptive parents? And, if so, how should they be handled? A comprehensive survey of the research findings has been made by Burton Sokoloff, of the Department of Pediatrics at the University of California at Los Angeles (1983). Our discussion here is based on his review, supplemented by our own experience with adoptive parents who have consulted us over the years.

First, and most important, the majority of adopted children make a healthy adjustment to the family on a par with their nonadopted agemates. They adjust well even if the adoptive parents have other children who have been born to them. This favorable outcome requires the adoptive parents to be truthful with the child and to make it clear by their attitudes and behavior that they regard the child as much their own as if they were the biological parents. Studies also show that adopted children have fewer educational and psychiatric problems than children who remain with their single biological parents. This finding is not surprising, inasmuch as the adoptive parents can usually provide a more stable and advantaged environment for the child than the single biological mother can.

Several reports have indicated that adopted children constitute a disproportionately large percentage of cases at mental health facilities, greater than their percentage of the total population of children in the community. However, these studies have not shown whether adopted children actually have more problems than other children do or whether adoptive parents utilize these facilities more than other parents. The latter possibility may very well be true. Many adoptive parents worry that the child may have some unknown genetic defect or may be secretly disturbed at being rejected by his biological mother. They may interpret even a minor deviation in the child's behavior as a sign of serious psychological disturbance and rush to get professional help. Even general population surveys rather than mental health clinic statistics have not settled the question of whether adopted children have more problems. One done in Sweden showed a higher rate of disturbance among adopted children, but a similar study in England found no significant difference between adopted and nonadopted children.

An adopted child should know the fact of his adoption from the beginning. Perhaps the word will have little or no meaning when it is first used —this is so for all complex words. As the child moves to successive developmental stages, he will ask questions in accordance with his growing conceptual abilities. The parents should welcome such questions and answer them truthfully. If they try to hide the fact that the child is adopted, the child may learn it in a painful and damaging way. Many of the problems of adopted children, as we have seen them, arise from such evasions by the parents and a distressing and at times even malicious revelation from other sources. Such unexpected news may make the child wonder whether there was something shameful about his origin, leaving him frightened, confused, and even ashamed of himself as a person. This is one situation where honesty is truly the best policy.

In recent years, a number of countries and some states in this country have made it legally possible for mature adopted children to identify, locate, and even meet their biological parents. The justification for doing so is that it will give the adopted person a greater sense of identity, overcome hidden feelings of rejection, and eliminate unrealistic fantasies that may have developed over the years regarding the biological parents.

It also reassures the biological parent or parents that the child has been well brought up. Sokoloff reports that the results of such meetings between adopted young adults and their biological parents have often been favorable.

We are uneasy about the hazards involved in such a meeting, however. One adopted youngster in our longitudinal study was able to locate her biological mother and was shocked to find her living a sordid alcoholic life, in no way interested in her biological offspring. Rather than alleviating any feelings of rejection, the experience inflicted a new and disturbing rejection.

In some cases, the biological mother may have built a new life for herself, with marriage and a family, in which she has concealed the existence of the previous child. The exposure of her secret by the sudden appearance of this son or daughter may do great harm to her new life. We would suggest that a meeting between adopted child and biological parents not be encouraged until adequate information is available indicating that such a meeting will not be harmful to either the child or the parent.

Sokoloff recommends that at the time of adoption the adoptive parents obtain as much medical and background information on the biological parents as they can. They will then be in a position to answer questions the child may raise as he grows older. This is especially important as the child matures and may begin to worry that he carries some genetic defect that he may transmit to his own children.

It is important for an adoptive parent to distinguish between genuine questioning by the adopted child as to his own worth if his mother "gave him away" and a ploy to gain special advantage. It is essential to make clear to the child that his biological mother was unable to give him a secure home, and because she loved him, she did her best to arrange for him to be adopted by parents who would love him and bring him up. The news that he did not grow in his adoptive mother's belly should not in itself be cause for estrangement of child from parents. The attachments and mutual bonds between adopted children and adoptive parents will be the product of the myriad features of their interaction over the years, just as with other children.

An adopted child may try to use the fact of adoption for some immediate advantage. One adopted boy had fallen behind in his algebra and his mother had begun tutoring him in daily twenty-minute sessions, which were to continue until he really understood the work. One Saturday morning, with a baseball game lined up, the boy said, "My other mother wouldn't make me stay in." The mother merely replied, "Maybe so, but we can talk about that after we finish today's lesson." The teaching session began with no further fuss, and when it came to an end the boy started to run out to his friends. The mother, with a slight touch of tit-for-tat, said, "Wait a minute. Didn't you want to talk about your 'other' mother?" To which the son replied good-humoredly, "Oh, Mom, you knew I was only trying to get out of doing my algebra!" and off he went, to the satisfaction of both.

The major points to stress with an adopted child, then, are: (1) You are our child, emotionally and legally; (2) Your biological mother could not care for you and out of love provided you with parents who wanted you and could give you good care; (3) It would be nice to agree on everything, but as with all parents and children there will be times when we differ, and when we do, it has nothing to do with your being adopted; and 4) We are your real parents, and as all parents do we will make decisions as the need arises—for safety, for provision of opportunities to develop, for adaptation into the rules and values of the family.

18

Working Mothers and Their Children

"He has monopolized nearly all the profitable employments, and from those she is permitted to follow, she receives but a scanty renumeration. He closes against her all avenues to wealth and distinction which he considers most honorable to himself. As a teacher of theology, medicine, or law, she is not known."

—*Declaration of Sentiments,* First American meeting for women's rights, Seneca Falls, New York, July 1848

ABOUT twenty-five years ago we knew a young woman doctor who was scheduled to begin her psychiatric residency training in a leading hospital in her field. When the director of the psychiatric service learned that she was pregnant and would have her baby shortly before she began her residency, he pressured her to postpone her hospital work and stay home with her baby. Another young woman, a psychologist, was delighted at finding what seemed the perfect job for her. She had a three-year-old son who had just started nursery school, and her work hours would match his school schedule. However, her husband, a psychiatrist, insisted that she turn down the job and stay at home. According to him, the "facts" were that if she had an outside interest, she would not be able to give their son the full emotional attention that a young child needed from his mother, and the boy would be "emotionally damaged."

Traditional Views of Maternal Employment

The views represented in these incidents were not the extreme opinions of a small minority of professionals of the time. Rather, they were typical of the judgments of a large and influential segment of mental health professionals, who believed firmly that the mother's place was in the home. Even Abram Kardiner, a prominent psychoanalyst at Columbia University, and one of the few analysts of the time who emphasized the importance of social and cultural factors in psychological development, wrote: "My own experience with working mothers indicates once again that the predominant emotion they feel is guilt. I have no choice but to believe this guilt is the price exacted for maternal neglect in the interest of self-enhancement" (1954, p. 223). Having offered this grim judgment, he then offered a solution: "Marry young, have your children between eighteen and twenty-four, spend the next fourteen years giving them effective care, and then enter on a career" (p. 225). How a woman who even in her twenties might have a hard time overcoming sex discrimination and starting a career could carry out this totally unrealistic prescription, Kardiner did not bother to say.

Even Spock and Brazelton were caught up in this dim view of the mother's working unless it was absolutely necessary. Spock included his discussion of working mothers under "special problems" until his 1976 revision and declared that their children were in danger of growing up maladjusted. Before 1976, he was emphatic in stating that unless the mother had to work, it made no sense for her to do so and "pay other people to do a poorer job of bringing up her children" (1967, p. 570). In the late 1960s Brazelton was arguing, with no ifs or buts, that "two mothers are not as good as one in the first crucial years. It is better for an infant to have one figure to relate to, to understand, to absorb as he sorts out his own reactions to the world" (1969, p. 164).

What accounted for this unrelieved picture of the harm done to children if their mothers worked outside the home? The reasons are discussed in chapter 15 and will be summarized briefly here. First, there was Freud's dictum that the child's relationship to the mother was unique and unparalleled, a prototype for all subsequent relationships. There was also William

Goldfarb's study (1943; 1947) of the harmful effects on infants raised in institutions. Most influential of all was John Bowlby's monograph *Maternal Care and Mental Health* (1951), in which he concluded that mother love in infancy and childhood was indispensable for mental health. His report received wide circulation and publicity and led most psychiatrists and other mental health professionals to conclude that the mother was a unique, all-important nurturing caregiver for the infant and that she could not be adequately replaced by anyone else.

Leon Eisenberg, chair of the Department of Social Medicine at Harvard Medical School, has also pointed out that social scientists, like other people, are inevitably influenced by the sociocultural forces of their time.

> The Zeitgeist shapes the way problems are formulated, data are collected, and findings are interpreted. . . . During World War II, when the war effort demanded woman power in industry, government subsidized day care. . . . The public was reassured to learn that systematic research revealed no deleterious effects. With the war over, it was essential to find jobs for men and to ease women out of the labor market; not only did child development become less interesting to policy makers, but the old myths about child rearing in the home flowered once again, in total disregard of the evidence. (1981, p. 708)

Finally, Jerome Kagan has speculated,

> Every society needs some transcendental theme to which citizens can be loyal. In the past, God, the beauty and utility of knowledge, and the sanctity of faithful romantic love were amongst the most sacred themes in our society. Unfortunately, the facts of modern life have made it difficult for many Americans to remain loyal to these ideas. The sacredness of the parent-infant bond may be one of the last unsullied beliefs. (1984, pp. 56–57)

The Changing Work Force

In spite of the strictures and dire predictions of so many of the experts, the past thirty years have witnessed an enormous increase in the number and percentage of working mothers. This is indeed one of the most dramatic social changes to occur in so short a time.

A comment on the term "working mother" is in order. The use of this term is almost always restricted to women working outside the home. But the mother who stays at home and takes care of her children is also a working mother, and a hard-working one to boot. She works long hours at responsibilities that require planning, organization of time, and a considerable demand on her physical energies. The rub is that she is not paid for this work, and in a society where money is a prime criterion of value, this means that she is not really "working." With this caveat in mind, we will use the term "working mother" as a convenient shorthand for the mother working outside the home, as the term is almost universally used in popular and professional discussions. For the mother working full-time taking care of her child and home, the term "domestic mother" will be used.

In 1950 only 11.9 percent of mothers with children under six years of age and 28.3 percent of mothers with children aged six to seventeen worked outside the home. In 1980, the comparable figures were 43.2 and 59.1 percent (Gerson 1985). In 1982 the Census Bureau reported that 41 percent of women with children under one year of age and 38 percent of women with children under three were employed outside the home. A year later, the statistics were 45 percent and 44 percent respectively (Young & Zigler 1986, p. 43). And in 1985, a U.S. Labor Department study found that 49.4 percent of women with children under a year old, and more than half of all women with children under six, worked outside the home (*New York Times*, 16 March 1986). Many mothers, even those with small children, have entered the job market, entering fields that were previously closed to them, such as the clergy, police, and firefighting, and swelling their numbers in fields where previously they had had only token representation. All the evidence is that they function on the job as effectively and efficiently as men do.

Furthermore, an impressive body of substantial research has accumulated during these years that comes to the same conclusion: Maternal employment outside the home in itself poses *no* hazard either to the welfare and healthy psychological development of her children or to her own well-being. The research reports can be roughly divided into two groups: empirical studies comparing groups of working mothers with groups of domestic mothers, with regard to the functioning and adjustment of the mothers and their children, and studies to test the hypothesis that the mother-infant relationship is unique, so that the child necessarily suffers if the mother works outside the home.

Research Findings on the Effects of Maternal Employment

As early as 1959, Alberta Siegel, of Stanford University, and her co-workers studied a group of kindergarten children and found no significant differences in the adjustment and functioning of the children of working mothers as compared with children of domestic mothers. A review of the existing studies conducted the following year by Lois Stolz, of Stanford University, came to a similar conclusion: "It looks as if the fact of the mother being employed or staying at home is not such an important factor in determining the behavior of the child as we have been led to think" (1960, p. 779).

In recent years the research literature on this subject has expanded dramatically. Siegel reviewed these reports in 1984 and found the conclusions about the same as those of the earlier studies. "Some studies show that children of working mothers, especially daughters, are more favorably disposed than others to outside employment for women and to educational achievement. . . . But in most ways the children of working mothers are not importantly different from their peers" (p. 486).

The National Academy of Science sponsored a special study by an eminent panel of social scientists, who reviewed all the studies of working mothers and concluded, in a 1982 report, that there were no consistent effects of mothers' employment on any aspect of child development (Kamerman & Hayes 1982). Sandra Scarr, another distinguished social scientist, also reviewed the research literature and commented, "All we know is that the school achievement, IQ test scores, and emotional and social development of working mothers' children are every bit as good as that of children whose mothers do not work" (1984, p. 25). But that is quite a lot to know!

By now, therefore, the volume and quality of research studies have made it abundantly clear that a mother's working outside the home is not harmful to her children. But several "ifs" have to be added. This finding is true only if the substitute child care, whether in the mother's own home or in some child care arrangement, is of high quality. (We will consider what makes for high quality child care later in this chapter.) This finding is also true only if the working mother's job does not drain her energy and time to the extent that she does not have the vitality and time to develop and maintain an active, affectionate give-and-take relationship with her children.

The fact that so many mothers of preschool-aged children work outside the home is of special concern to pediatricians. They are the ones who are often asked for reassurance and advice by anxious working mothers. The American Academy of Pediatrics therefore set up a special blue-ribbon committee of distinguished pediatricians to review all the evidence and formulate appropriate answers (1984). Their findings are clear and succinctly stated. To the basic question "Is my working harmful to my child?" their answer is that this "depends upon (a) the provision of a safe, caring environment for the child; and (b) the mother's satisfaction in her outside work, the support and help of her family, and her vitality at the end of the day to nurture her children" (p. 874). They provide specific guidelines for evaluating a substitute caregiving situation.

Another question often asked concerns the right time to return to work after the birth of the baby. The committee gives no pat answer but points out that it should depend on the health of the mother and the child, practical need, the relationships developing between mother and child, family equilibrium, the availability of adequate child care. The committee reaffirms that if the infant receives satisfactory substitute care, she will be as much attached to her mother as an infant whose care is given exclusively by the mother, an issue that worries many mothers. The committee further notes that "women who feel fulfilled because of their work away from home may be better mothers than if they stayed home and were continually dissatisfied and frustrated" (p. 875).

The data of our longitudinal study have been sufficient for us to confirm the emphatic point made by the Academy of Pediatrics committee, as well as by other investigators (Hoffman 1963), that the quality of a mother's nurturant role with her baby will be strongly influenced by her feelings of satisfaction or frustration as either a working mother or a domestic mother. The analysis and report of the findings from our study were done by Jacqueline Lerner and Nancy Galambos (1985). The data included the mother's work history outside the home and a rating of maternal role satisfaction, whether as an employed mother or as a domestic mother. The rating was obtained from the special interviews with the mothers and fathers separately, conducted when the child was three years old. The staff members responsible for these interviews were trained mental health professionals who had no other contacts with the parents or children of the study. In addition to exploring child care attitudes and practices, parental and spousal roles, and the effects of the child on the parents and the family, the interview with the mother went into her employment situation, feelings about working, the father's support of her working, and other supports in the home that helped her to fulfill her role obligations, such as the availability and quality of child care and household help. The interviews were audiotaped, and a rating scheme for maternal role satisfaction obtained from these tapes.

From these same interviews, a statistical analysis of eight parental characteristics had already been done some years previously, and three were selected as measures of parent-child interaction because they most clearly resembled categories used in other studies of maternal role satisfaction. These three were: (1) rejection—the mother's tolerance for or disapproval of the child; (2) limit setting—the degree of restrictiveness and strictness of discipline when dealing with the child; and (3) the degree of consistency or inconsistency with which the child was disciplined.

Finally, the data included a rating of the child's temperament along the dimension of easy versus difficult temperament. While the evidence strongly suggests that the child's temperamental characteristics are not created by the parents, it is also a reasonable hypothesis that the parents' interaction with a temperamentally difficult child can either exacerbate or attenuate the difficult behavior and management of such a child. The temperamental ratings at age two and age four were included in the analysis. The earlier measure (age two) was included in order to measure the effect that this early behavioral pattern of the child might have on the mother's role satisfaction a year later, as rated from the special parental interviews when the child was three.

Rather than analyzing these ratings by simple statistical methods, which would only establish correlations between any two sets of ratings (child temperament at age two and mother's role satisfaction, or difficult temperament at age two and age four, for example), Lerner and Galambos used the more sophisticated and powerful statistical model of path analysis. By this means they were able to trace the sequential relationships from early child temperament to maternal role satisfaction to mother-child interaction to later difficult behavior by the child at age four.

The path analysis showed that maternal role satisfaction was significantly related to maternal rejection, and maternal rejection was significantly related to later difficult behavior in the child. The two-year-old difficult temperament was not the causal factor: It was not significantly related to maternal role satisfaction or mother-child interaction. When the working and domestic mother groups were tested separately, the same trends emerged. The authors conclude that the results support the notion that the mother-child relationship has a stronger influence on the child's development than maternal status per se. Mothers who were highly satisfied with their roles, whether or not they were working outside the home, displayed higher levels of warmth and acceptance than did dissatisfied mothers.

The authors caution that the study was done on a homogeneous sociocultural group and that the data were collected some twenty-five years ago, when the attitudes toward employed women were quite different from those widely held today. With these cautions in mind, this study is a valuable one for two reasons. It studies the issue of working mothers in relation to young children, whereas most studies have been done on older children (Siegel 1984), and it utilizes longitudinal data, which minimize the distortions of memory that occur when mothers or others are asked about earlier life events, experiences, and attitudes.

Research Findings on the Effects of Multiple Caregiving

The working mother of a young child must provide substitute caregivers for her child while she is at work. Is something unique lost from the mother-child attachment if there are other caregivers, as Bowlby and others asserted in the past? This question still troubles many working mothers today.

There are many other societies in which the infant routinely has more than one primary caregiver. A conspicuous example is the Israeli kibbutz system, in which children are reared in communal units from birth onward, with multiple mothers—their own working mothers and the kibbutz caregivers. Experts from the United States and England visited these kibbutzim, convinced ahead of time that they would find this communal arrangement having serious harmful effects on the children. As Sandra Scarr put it, "They were puzzled about the lack of evidence for what should have been disastrous outcomes for the children of the kibbutz" (1984, p. 217). (On one of our visits to Israel, various Israeli psychiatrists and psychologists regaled us with amusing anecdotes concerning the confused hustle and bustle of these American and British experts who kept looking for evidence that just did not exist.) In spite of these attempts to find evidence of disturbance in these children, the bulk of the extensive research studies have come to the opposite conclusion. Scarr has reviewed the studies, which used a number of different scales and observations to rate the psychological development of the kibbutz youngsters into adult life. These ratings were then compared with similar ones made on children raised in agricultural villages by traditional families with a single mothering caregiver. The conclusion was clear: "Kibbutz youngsters grow up to be fine adults, just as well adjusted and smart as Israeli children reared by traditional families" (p. 218).

Michael Rutter's authoritative monograph *Maternal Deprivation Reassessed* (1981a), which we reviewed in chapter 15, provides further reassurance.

He concluded, "Bowlby's argument is that the child's relationship with mother differs from other relationships specifically with respect to its *attachment* qualities, and the evidence indicates that this is not so" (p. 142).

Anthropologist Margaret Mead has even suggested that children reared in cultures in which caregiving is shared by a number of mother figures instead of being given by a single mother are better able to tolerate separation (1962). She also speculates that such children may even develop more subtle and more complex personality characteristics, as a consequence of having more varied identification figures than do children with a single mother figure. This is an intriguing hypothesis that could perhaps even be tested in this country with children growing up in alternative family arrangements.

Changing Attitudes Toward Maternal Employment

We now have a veritable mountain of evidence on maternal employment outside the home. If any subject has been thoroughly researched within the past twenty-five years by child psychologists, psychiatrists, and pediatricians, this one has. The data are abundant, and the conclusion is clearcut: The children of mothers working outside the home are not harmed if a satisfactory caregiver or caregivers are provided. Of course, the issue for the child will be different if the substitute caregiver is inadequate. But the child will also not prosper with a mother who stays at home if she is an inadequate caregiver. Child abuse can occur in a bad child care center; it can also occur, perhaps much more frequently, with disturbed parents at home. The research evidence also strongly suggests that it is not the mother's employment or nonemployment outside the home that is significant for the child and herself, but rather her role satisfaction or dissatisfaction.

How much have these solid research findings affected the advice given by experts? How much have the attitudes of young parents and the thrust of the popular media been affected? As we would expect, the responsible and thoughtful experts have taken the evidence seriously. In contrast to his earlier editions, for example, Spock's 1976 revision of his *Baby and Child Care* takes a positive attitude toward working mothers and emphasizes the father's role as a parent. Acknowledging his earlier prejudices (a rare event among experts), Spock states that "both parents have an equal right to a career if they want one . . . and an equal obligation to share in the care of their child. . . . If the mother has resolved her guilt and doubts, her children will not only accept but be proud of her working" (p. 37). Brazelton was a member of the Academy of Pediatrics committee whose positive approach to the working mother was cited earlier in this chapter. In his latest book, *Working and Caring* (1985), Brazelton with his usual wisdom and clarity gives specific advice to help and reassure working mothers. We have only one objection. Though he points out that "we need to know more than we do about ages at which babies can be left" and that "in long-term follow-up studies of babies who have been in day care situations in infancy, many researchers find that there is no recognizable difference in later intellectual or emotional development" (p. 24), Brazelton then strongly recommends that the mother stay at home for the first four months; otherwise "new parents will never feel competent or truly 'attached' to their baby" (p. 60).

As Brazelton himself indicates, there is no solid research evidence to support such an emphatic judgment, and we feel that this generalization is not justified. It is our impression that many mothers feel competent and fully attached to their babies even if they go back to work when the baby is younger than four months. Other mothers may not feel competent even if they stay home for many months before returning to work. The desirable time for returning to work can also be influenced by the child's temperament. If the baby is temperamentally easy, develops regular sleep and feeding schedules quickly, begins to sleep through the night by two months, and takes cheerfully to a new caregiver, then the mother can return to work when the baby is still a very young infant. If the infant is temperamentally difficult, feeds and sleeps irregularly, awakens crying several times at night, and will have nothing to do with a strange caregiver, no matter how expert, then the issue will be different. The mother is likely to be too drained physically if she combines this difficult caregiving with a return to work, even if the father is also fully involved in the infant's care. The mother may just have to wait until this difficult infant has slowly but surely adapted to a regular schedule and an additional caregiver. That may take four months or even longer.

The popular media have also to a large extent changed their tune. Claire Etaugh, of Bradley University, compared the child care books and popular magazine articles written for parents in the 1950s and 1960s with those of the 1970s (1980). She found that nearly all the child care books sampled from the 1950s and 1960s (eleven out of fourteen) expressed disapproval of maternal employment in the child's first three years of life. Young children were considered to need the almost continuous presence of the mother, and child care by a substitute caregiver was considered harmful.

Articles in the women's magazines of the same periods were more mixed in their opinions. Seven articles were classified as negative, ten as positive, and four as mixed.

By the 1970s, opinion had begun to shift sharply. Etaugh found that popular magazine writings of the decade generally were more favorable toward maternal employment and substitute caregivers. A number of writers even pointed out that the working mother who spends a few hours of companionship with her child may be a better mother than the housewife, who may not make the effort because she is always there and is also occupied with her household chores. The books by experts, on the other hand, showed less of a shift in opinion. Of the twenty-four books Etaugh surveyed, she considered seven to be positive, eight as mixed, and nine as negative in their opinions on maternal employment. Etaugh speculated that the difference between the books and magazines reflected the shorter publication time-lag of magazine articles; the articles would be more likely to reflect the most recent research findings, as well as shifts in public opinion.

The positive change in expert and popular opinion has continued into the 1980s. A sign of the times is an article by Anita Shrive in the *New York Times Magazine* (9 September 1984) titled "The Working Mother as Role Model," which takes a most positive attitude. It reports,

> Studies suggest that independent and achieving mothers engender similar qualities in their daughters, and that these daughters have higher career aspirations and greater self-esteem than daughters of non-working mothers. Child specialists also believe that as more children grow up in the families of working mothers, both boys and girls will find it easier to balance their masculine and feminine characteristics than their parents did. (p. 39)

The article concludes by quoting Lawrence Balter, of New York University: "Psychiatric theories lag behind social reality. Changing them requires a new generation. People will have to rethink the old. We are on the threshold of that thinking" (p. 54).

This continued shift in the experts' judgments can be attributed to several factors. First, the accumulating serious research studies have with almost no exception found strong evidence that maternal employment as such is not harmful to the children. Some of the studies have emphasized the need for further research to identify specific factors that may influence the attitudes and functioning of individual working mothers, such as job role satisfaction. Such research is desirable, and a good deal is in progress, as in the study by Lerner and Galambos described earlier in this chapter. These new research studies will be valuable in improving our ability to advise individual mothers, but they will not change the established fact that outside employment for mothers is not in itself harmful to their children.

Second, the vast influx of young mothers into the work world has not brought the dire consequences for their children so freely predicted by many experts in the past. The recent studies cited earlier in this chapter falsify those predictions. Finally, and by no means least, the women's movement has effectively challenged the various sexist prejudices that, with one rationalization or another, ended up with the pronouncement that woman's place was in the home. The movement has also played a major role in confronting young fathers with the demand that they share equally with their wives in caregiving responsibilities, giving mothers extra time, energy, and flexibility to devote to their jobs without feeling that their children are being neglected.

But old attitudes die hard. We cannot assume that all young working mothers or their professional advisers view this dual function of nurturing mother and working women as a normal and healthy, though demanding, style of life. Unfortunately, the opposite opinion is still all too prevalent, in spite of the evidence to the contrary.

This observation is confirmed by a recent study by Harold Martin and David Burgess, of Tulane University, together with Linda Crnic, of the University of Colorado (1984). The authors collected questionnaires on attitudes toward working mothers from 448 health professionals, including pediatricians, physicians in family practice, and public health nurses. Eighty percent of the respondents had employed spouses, and 80 percent had children. Eighty-five percent were married. Thirty percent of the sample were women, and 70 percent men.

Analysis of the questionnaire responses showed that the male respondents were significantly more unfavorable toward maternal employment than were the females. Among the male physicians, those who were older, who had children, and whose wives did not work were less favorable toward mothers' working. Overall, they found that gender was more significantly correlated with views about maternal employment than age. The authors suggest that this finding reflects a sexist attitude about the role of women, especially women with children, and wonder quite properly whether "health professionals' attitudes and their advice to mothers are largely based on personal experience and bias rather than knowledge of the research literature" (p. 472).

Brazelton describes vividly the anguish of young mothers who want to or have to go back to work. He recalls the dilemma of one woman who had to go back to work but also had deep feelings about wanting to nurture her baby. These two needs appeared contradictory to her. Brazelton comments that in his practice he frequently hears this kind of distress and ambivalence about returning to the workplace. Young mothers seem to be convinced that they can't combine a successful career with an adequate role as a nurturing mother at home. The woman he cites was a success at both her job and her mothering, despite her fear that she would be a failure at both (1985, p. xvi).

We have also seen this conflict and anguish in competent working mothers. Their own confusions are compounded by the reproaches of friends who are domestic mothers. "What, you're leaving your baby with a babysitter? Don't you realize the harm you're doing to her?" Our reassurances are helpful, but they are often left with a nagging feeling of guilt.

There is also the effect of the bad research that continues to be published. We and others have emphasized that the *good* research consistently finds that a mother's working outside the home does not in itself harm the child. By good research we mean studies that collect accurate information pertinent to the issue being tested, analyze the data according to appropriate methods, and draw conclusions that are warranted from the analyses.

Two recent articles published in leading psychiatric journals will illustrate what we mean by bad research. In one study, a questionnaire survey of a group of first-year medical students of both sexes was used to rate the students on their current or recent feelings of psychological distress. The students were also asked for their recollections of whether during their early childhood their mothers worked outside the home full-time, part-time or not at all (Brodkin et al. 1984). A statistically significant correlation was obtained between the mother's working full-time before the child was six years old and the current level of the student's psychological distress. This correlation was not found for the domestic or part-time working mothers. Can we conclude from such a study that the working mother had an injurious effect on her child that showed up fifteen years or more later? That is what is likely to be quoted, but, no such conclusion is warranted. First, the data on the reasons and details of mother's working was obtained from the student's and mother's memory fifteen years later, and such retrospective memories are known through a number of studies to be notoriously unreliable. Second, there are no data as to *why* the mother worked full-time. Was it because of poverty, divorce, or death of the father? Also, there is no information as to the kind of substitute child care the students of the working mothers received. Finally, in such a relatively small sample (164 students), special life events of even a few of the students might have biased the results, but the authors took no information on such events. One or more of these factors may have been the important influences, and not the mother's working as such. Without these additional data, it is impossible to draw any conclusions about the relationship, if any, between the mother's early work history and the student's psychological state fifteen years later.

In another study (Zappert & Weinstein 1985) questionnaires were obtained by mail from an equal number of women and men who had been graduated from a prestigious business school three years previously. Not surprisingly, the men were earning substantially greater salaries and held higher executive or managerial positions than did the women (the success of women in entering career lines previously closed to them has by no means resulted in equalization of salaries or opportunities for promotion). The authors then report that "even for women without children, work is seen as having a negative impact on decisions about child-bearing, whereas for men, being a parent is reported to have a positive effect on work. In addition, the women we studied reported far more frequently than the men that they worried about home responsibilities at work and work responsibilities at home" (p. 1178). From these findings, the authors conclude that "clear role boundaries may be more difficult for women to maintain" and label this judgment a problem of "role diffusion" for women. These formulations imply that women have some sort of subjective psychological problem that prevents them from keeping "clear role boundaries." Yet one-third of the women reported doing more of the household tasks, whereas only 13 percent of the men reported doing more —a not surprising finding, even in these days when many more men accept a larger share of household chores than in the past. If a woman carries this dual responsibility of job and household more heavily than her husband, is it any wonder that she will be pressed to think and plan about her household duties while at work, and her job responsibilities while at home?

As to the women's conflicts over job versus childbearing, these are women who are struggling to establish their careers. Are they unrealistic, even in these days, in worrying that pregnancy and childbearing may represent a hazard to a woman's career? Will she lose a promotion or a chance for a new job because she will be considered "handicapped" by pregnancy and then by being the mother of a young infant? These are real, objective concerns for career women, and we have known a number who have anguished seriously and realistically over this problem. For a man, of course, fatherhood does not pose this kind of potential threat; it does not jeopardize his competitive job position.

What the authors of this paper have done is to take a set of findings and jump to a psychological explanation without considering an alternative objective explanation that can be readily documented. They have not even bothered to examine their own data to discover whether the women whose husbands shared equally in household and child care tasks had the same "role diffusion" as did those women who bore the major burden of these tasks.

If anything, career women have to be capable of especially clear judgments of role boundaries. Otherwise, they will find it more difficult to manage simultaneously their work and household responsibilities. Unfortunately, we fear that this article will be cited by some opponents of maternal employment to "prove" that women have psychological problems about "role boundaries" that will interfere with their effectiveness in the work world.

Hard Choices

Perhaps in part as a result of the poor research, and certainly in spite of the good research, women continue to agonize over their choices: domestic motherhood versus working outside the home; marriage versus single living; one versus several children; working as a necessity to maintain a decent family standard of living versus not working and accepting a lower family income. And these women receive no help from many mental health professionals who are still bound to the sexist concept, evidence or not, that a mother's place is in the home.

How do women confront the hard choices that face them? How do they decide about work, career, and motherhood? We now have a thoughtful and scholarly study by Kathleen Gerson, a sociologist at New York University (1985). She conducted objective, probing interviews with sixty-three women between the ages of twenty-seven and thirty-seven. Their average age was thirty-one. She is clear that her study has limitations: the sample is small, minority women are underrepresented and no blacks are included, and the interviews relied on the retrospective recall of the subjects' childhood. However, the interview questions were carefully constructed and pretested, the interviews were long and carefully administered, and there was an emphasis on the recent past to minimize any distortions of memory of the childhood period.

Gerson developed three major impressions in her study. First, she found marked variation among the women. "The psychological and social differences among women are large, significant, and consequential. Indeed, they may well be as significant as those between women and men" (p. xiv). Second, she noted a tendency among both feminists and nonfeminists to conclude that one sex excels in specific ways, a view she considers dangerous regardless of which sex is considered better. Third, she discovered important changes in the degree and type of gender inequality. Gerson cites a number of examples: Having children created stress in the marriages of some working mothers; in some cases mothers who wanted to work but found only limited job opportunities wound up staying in the home fulltime even though this had not been their preferred choice; in households where wives took outside jobs out of economic necessity there were various undesired consequences such as postponing children or having fewer children than the couple wanted; and some women who preferred a domestic life experienced conflict over their choice as they saw a growing number of their neighbors, friends, and peers going out to work (pp. 193–95).

Gerson's study turned up some surprises. We have discussed in previous chapters the important function that parents play as role models for their children. But this does not appear to hold for mothers as domestic- or working-mother models for their daughters. Other women are likely to serve as role models in addition to or instead of their mothers.

Gerson found that among those with domestic mothers who remembered having domestic aspirations as children, only 33 percent were oriented toward domesticity as adults. By contrast, of those with either domestic or working mothers who had working aspirations as children, a full 63 percent became domestically oriented as adults. "Remarkably, change was more common than stability. . . . The proportion of changers to non-changers is even higher among the high school–educated group" (p. 67). Whatever her childhood aspirations, a young woman may reinterpret and reevaluate her initial judgments with age and experience. A daughter may feel as a child that her domestic mother is happy with her choice but later see the less happy consequences. As one young woman told Gerson, "I see a woman like my mom. She's a pretty bright lady, and when her kids left, her two babies walked out of the house, she had nothing left in her life. It was all she was geared up for, and it came very close to turning into an almost hate kind of thing toward us for taking away the one thing she had. . . . Look what's happened to her. That's just horrible what's happened to her" (p. 51). Indeed, a vivid description of the "empty nest" phenomenon.

On the other hand, some of the young women who had started with work aspirations found themselves in dead-end traditional jobs—what Gerson calls the "work ghetto" of women. Trapped in occupations that failed to provide significant advancement in their careers, these women experienced declining work aspirations. "Although their jobs often appeared promising at the outset, this initial glow tended toward monotony and frustration as blocks to upward movement were encountered. The resulting demoralization at the workplace dampened their initial enthusiasm for paid work, eased their ambivalence toward motherhood, and turned them toward the home in spite of their earlier aversion to domesticity" (p. 103).

Gerson's study points to some of the inequities that have been a source of special stress to working mothers, as to all working women. In 1939 American working women earned 63 cents for every dollar earned by men. In 1986, after all the gains of the women's movement, this gap remained virtually unchanged—64 cents for the woman, a dollar for the man (Hewlett 1986). Divorce only aggravates the mother's situation. After divorce, the standard of living of men rises 62 percent on the average, while for their former wives and their children there is a fall of over 50 percent. Two-thirds of divorced women receive no child care support from their former husbands (Hewlett 1986).

Sexist bias continues to be blatant, even where women have broken through the barriers to their entry into the professions. A recent New York Task Force on Women in the Courts, set up by the state's chief judge, found pervasive and open prejudice against women lawyers in the courts (Hewlett 1986). The panel reported frequent and shocking episodes of humiliating, offensive, and patronizing behavior toward female attorneys as well as sexual harassment by male judges and lawyers. In divorce settlements, a number of judges minimized a wife's contribution to the economy of a marriage and distributed property unfairly in favor of the husband.

We can assume that such sexist prejudices and behavior are not restricted to lawyers and judges. Sometimes the bias is blatant; sometimes it is subtle and shows up unexpectedly. Several years ago one of us (S.C.) was chatting informally with two male professional colleagues. These two men have been outstanding in their vigorous advocacy for the rights and needs of children and mothers over many years in their professional careers. In the course of our conversation the name of a prominent female professional and mutual acquaintance came up. One of the men commented that she had gone back to work very soon after the birth of each of her children and had managed this burden well. "But," he added, "it was too bad. She missed something by not staying home with her children for at least the first six months." The other man nodded his agreement. It was on the tip of my tongue to ask them, "Didn't *you* also miss something by not staying home with your children for the first six months?" I'm not sure why I kept silent.

As this anecdote illustrates, the care of the infant child is still usually considered the mother's responsibility. The mother feels unjustified in returning to work if the cost of adequate day care for her child, when subtracted from her net income, makes her financial contribution to the family appear insignificant. But why should this day-care cost be charged entirely to the working mother? Why shouldn't the cost be shared equally with the working father?

For the working mother, the father's role in caring for the children makes a crucial difference. In a small percentage of families (16.8 percent), the father assumes the primary responsibility for child care and stays at home while his wife works outside the home (Galinsky 1986, p. 16). Otherwise they share equally, or the mother carries the highly stressful burden of responsibility for two jobs—one at home and one on the outside. The research evidence, as we saw in chapter 17, indicates that fathers can be quite as sensitive and competent as mothers in caring for both young infants and older children. The effects are positive when fathers share equally in child care. For a father with a demanding job, finding the time and energy to act as an active coequal caregiver may be stressful, but no more so than for his working wife.

In Gerson's study, even though many fathers participated actively in caregiving, most resisted equal participation in parenting. When a husband was averse to or unenthusiastic about having children, the wife often felt that the combination of a career and motherhood would be an intolerable double burden and usually decided to remain childless or to have only one child. Other working mothers did come to believe that they could integrate mothering into their lives without significant sacrifice to themselves, their work, or their children. Of special interest is that the decision of these working mothers often resulted from the encouragement and even pressure from their husbands, who wanted to become fathers. The women who were most responsive to such pressure were those who wanted children themselves but needed their husband's urging to avoid feeling guilty or inadequate at being a working mother. Gerson sums up these various patterns by commenting, "These accounts challenge the tenacious view held by social theorists, psychoanalysts, and ordinary people alike that women uniformly become mothers primarily to fulfill strongly felt needs to nurture and men typically seek parenthood grudgingly" (p. 163).

Parental Leave and Substitute Care

More than one hundred countries provide at least partially paid, job-protected time off to new mothers, but the United States is not among them. Some countries, like Sweden, even allow the fathers and mothers to divide the leave-time between them at their own discretion. Efforts by individuals or organized groups to bring the United States into line with this humane policy have thus far been unavailing. The stone wall of opposition is expressed by Frank Benson, a spokesman for the United States Chamber of Commerce: "While we encourage employers to do anything they can, we are not in favor of legislated or mandated benefits that are not connected to job-related injuries or loss of compensation" (Quoted in *New York Times,* 18 September 1985).

The call for paid maternity leave may appear to conflict with the concept that mothers can return to work soon after their baby's birth. But the two ideas are not contradictory. The new mother usually needs weeks and even several months to recuperate physically, if she is to be able to assume the dual responsibility of a job and caregiving. Certain children, such as premature infants, those with extremely difficult temperament, and those born with congenital defects, may require the special attention of both parents for many weeks after birth. In a truly civilized society, a mother should have the option of returning to an outside job quickly or staying home to nurture her baby herself, whether for six months or several years.

When the mother does return to work, especially if her child is still young, adequate substitute care of her child while she is at work is imperative. Actually, the responsibility for arranging substitute care should be just as much the father's responsibility as the mother's. Finding a good child care center outside the home, staying with the child for the first days until she becomes adjusted to this new environment, bringing the child to the center and taking her home, consulting with the teachers when necessary—all of these tasks should be shared equally by the working fathers with their working wives. In some families this does happen, with benefit to the father and the child as well as to the mother. In most families, however, it is still the working mother who shoulders the major and even exclusive responsibility for these tasks.

Substitute child care takes a variety of forms. Fathers can sometimes take up part of the child care load if their work hours do not coincide with their wives' and they are willing to make a real commitment to caregiving. Some mothers and fathers are fortunate enough to have a congenial and affectionate parent or other close relative who has the time, desire, and wisdom to take over the child's care in the mother's absence. Some affluent families may find and be able to afford a full-time caregiver who has a warm and knowledgeable approach to children and who often in effect becomes a member of the family. It goes without saying that in the beginning such a caregiver requires careful monitoring by both parents. A caregiver may come with impressive references and yet be highly unsuitable, or she may appear unimpressive on first contact and turn out to be a gem.

Other families with working mothers have to rely on one or another kind of day-care unit. These vary tremendously in character, from private homes where a single person takes care of a few children to large centers run by public agencies or private nonprofit or profit-making administrators. A few universities, corporations, and other large institutions run day-care centers for the children of their employees. An exciting development is reported from Massachusetts, where a state agency has set aside $750,000 to make loans for setting up child care centers at workplaces. The centers are sponsored by union contributions and private donations. The program was begun by the state governor in 1985, and a year later seven corporations had opened centers and seven more were in the planning stage. As one center director put it, "The center is an absolute necessity for many of these parents. Before it was established they were either unable to work or had to contend with less than adequate day care options. The way that it is set up now is an ideal arrangement for them" (*New York Times,* 4 September 1985). A drop in the bucket, perhaps, but we hope that it is part of a wave of the future.

How successful are these substitute child care centers in providing adequate care for the young children of working mothers? Claire Etaugh has made a thorough review of the extensive reports now available on this subject. Along with others who have studied this issue, she feels that the research literature is still not adequate for a definitive answer, but her "reasonably cautious conclusion . . . is that high quality nonmaternal care does not appear to have harmful effects on the preschool child's maternal attachment, intellectual development, social-emotional behavior, or physical health" (1980, p. 314). Another important review has come from Jay Belsky, of Pennsylvania State University, who represented the American Psychological Association before a congressional committee hearing in September, 1985. "We know that where the staff ratios are reasonable, where the groups of children are not too large and where the caregivers are well trained and attentive to the children, the kids do fine. The outcome is strikingly consistent with what we know about the development of kids raised at home" (Quoted in *New York Times*, 11 September 1985).

An outstanding example of a careful study of the effects of high quality day care on preschool children is the one reported by Jerome Kagan and his co-workers at Harvard (Kagan, Kearsley, & Zelazo 1977). Thirty-three infants attended a child care center created and administered by the research team. The infants were enrolled at three to five months and were studied to age twenty-nine months. A control group of thirty-seven infants, with no day-care experience and matched for age, sex, ethnicity, and social class, was also set up. Extensive data on the psychological characteristics of both groups of children were gathered and carefully analyzed, with the overall conclusion that "Day care, when responsibly and conscientiously implemented, does not seem to have hidden psychological dangers. . . . The assessment of language, memory and perceptual analysis failed to reveal any obvious advantages or disadvantages to the day care experience" (pp. 260–62 passim).

Some may object to drawing conclusions from studies of such special, high quality child care centers as this Harvard unit. If we took the ordinary run-of-the-mill centers, the results might be quite different. But that is just the point. If we want to determine the effects of day care *as such*, we have to use high quality units where the effects on the children will not be contaminated by incompetent or indifferent staff, unsanitary conditions, and a sterile, unstimulating program. Such a research approach is no different from what is done, for example, in testing the effectiveness of a new treatment for a particular disease. We would expect the study to be carried out by competent staff in a high quality hospital or clinic unit. Otherwise, we could not trust the findings.

The children of working mothers deserve high quality child care centers, just as they deserve high quality care at home. This is the demand that should be made on *all* day-care centers. How do we determine what constitutes high quality day care? The report of the American Academy of Pediatrics Committee (1984) gives concise and precise guidelines:

In addition to safety, sanitation, and the provision of proper nutrition, the kind of caregiver to whom a young infant or young child is entrusted is the overriding consideration. This person must be warm, caring, responsible, and able to provide the child the stimulation of new learning experiences. In all cases, parents should talk frequently with the caregiver about the child-rearing practices they desire, especially if the substitute mother is inexperienced or comes from a different sociocultural background. Although the needs of each child in a group setting vary with his or her age and personality, a ratio of one adult to three infants less than two years of age is advised, with the desired ratio increasing to one to four or one to five for older children. (p. 874)

How many child care centers live up to, or even approach, these standards? Shockingly few! Publically funded centers are consistently underfunded, staffed with inexperienced staff, and monitored poorly, if at all, by the funding agencies. Horrendous episodes of physical and sexual abuse of the children have been uncovered in several states, and one can only shudder at the possibility that only the tip of the iceberg has been uncovered. We can expect no better until child care workers are adequately trained and paid a decent salary. But all too many centers pay their workers disgracefully low salaries, sometimes even below the poverty level. It is no wonder that workers in such centers come without child care training and become embittered and frustrated at the heavy work their job demands. Small private day-care units in private homes—"family day-care homes"—are rarely licensed or inspected, and thus their quality varies a great deal.

It is the poor working mothers who need publicly financed child care centers most desperately, and whose children suffer most from their inadequacies. The federal government has refused to take responsibility for this problem. In 1971 Congress passed a bill providing federal funds for day care for the poor, but the bill was vetoed by President Nixon. The federal government does provide the states with block grants that help to subsidize day care in private facilities for children from low-income families. But the Reagan administration is busy cutting funds for social services wherever it can, and the consequences for the ability of states and localities to continue to support the services they have developed are all too easy to predict.

Even many middle-class families find the financial burden of a good child care center difficult or even impossible to meet. Such centers are expensive to run if they are to hire professionally trained child care workers and maintain low ratios of children to workers. Federal tax credits for the working mother who needs substitute child care are helpful but still inadequate in size.

This shameful situation in our country stands in sharp contrast to the attitudes and practices of most European countries. In England, for example, the local communities, even the less affluent ones, are committed to a policy that makes sure that "the least privileged children have loving, considered care" (*New York Times*, 4 September 1985). Nationally, the law in Britain requires local officials to register everyone who takes care of children, whether in a private home or in a day-care center. The law also mandates rigorous inspections of all such facilities and careful checks of people who apply for jobs having anything to do with children.

The United States is sometimes called a "child-centered" society. Nothing could be further from the truth, considering the ways in which we ignore the needs of our young children. Gerson puts it well: "Concern over the welfare of the nation's children is justified, but the blame for children's plight is misplaced. It is not women's equality that threatens children's welfare, but rather the social and economic devaluation of children and those who would care for them" (1985, p. 229). It is time to make the myth of the child-centered society a reality; we need only follow the examples of countries like Great Britain, Sweden, Japan, and yes, even China and Russia.

Hopeful Signs

The overall picture of substitute child care for working mothers is bleak, but there are a few hopeful signs of change. We have already mentioned the program in Massachusetts to develop child care centers at workplaces, to be sponsored by union and private contributions. At the local level, the New Orleans school system has adopted a program in which many of its elementary schools open at 7 A.M. and stay open until 6 P.M. Schools in Boulder, Colorado have worked out an arrangement with the local Y.M.C.A. for a combined program that will care for children from 6:30 A.M. to 5:30 P.M. In New York, one of the Long Island school districts has consolidated its kindergarten and prekindergarten programs under one roof and stays open from 7:30 A.M. to 6 P.M. (Fiske 1986).

More private corporations and other private institutions are beginning to operate child care centers for their working mothers. Even more of them are including in their benefit packages financial plans of various kinds to help their employees meet the costs of substitute care. Many companies have contracted with information and referral services to help their employees locate appropriate child care (Friedman 1986).

We hope that these are straws in the wind, indicating the beginning of a change in attitudes of school systems and private organizations toward recognizing the imperative need for more and better child care centers. But what is also required is a serious commitment to this goal by the federal government. Not only parents but all concerned citizens can be instrumental in achieving this goal by effective lobbying and other campaigns directed at public officials. Only a national commitment can erase the shameful neglect this country now shows toward the needs of its most precious asset—its children.

Recommended Reading

Families in which both parents work face many practical problems as they struggle to cope with responsibilities both at home and at work. Parents need advice in specific management techniques that will help them avoid shortchanging either the baby, their jobs, or the rest of the family. They also frequently need counseling or help in coping with unexpected emergencies.

Some mothers are fortunate in having a wise and experienced adviser, but many feel adrift, especially when they meet with covert or openly expressed criticisms for continuing to work and leaving their babies in substitute care during the day. Three excellent books are now available for working mothers, offering the best kind of support and reassurance— sound practical advice and suggestions that cover the many exigencies that may arise:

The Working Mother's Complete Handbook, Gloria Norris and Jo Ann Miller (New York: New American Library, rev. ed. 1984)
Mother Care/Other Care, Sandra Scarr (New York: Basic Books, 1984)
Working and Caring, T. Berry Brazelton (Reading, Mass.: Addison-Wesley, 1985).

19

Where We Are Now

"There is no absolute knowledge. And those who claim it, whether they are scientists or dogmatists, open the door to tragedy. All information is imperfect. We have to trust it with humility. That is the human condition."
—JACOB BRONOWSKI,
The Ascent of Man

OUR granddaughter Sarah is now a year old, and it is our youngest grandson, Andy, two weeks old, who lies quietly in our arms. As we have seen, a young infant like Andy is a highly competent individual at his own developmental level. He is neither a *homunculus,* an adult in miniature, nor a *tabula rasa,* a blank screen who passively lets the environment write the story of his life. He has come into the world biologically equipped to begin immediately to enter actively into social relationships with his caregivers, a human being in his own right, as dependent as he may be on others for his care. He is already busy learning about himself and the world around him—by conditioning, by imitation of his caregivers, and by his capacity to organize visual, auditory, and touch sensations into definite perceptions in his brain.

Individuality in Development

We also know that each baby will develop his own specific style of behavior, or temperament. His parents are also individuals, and there can be many different ways of being a good parent. The infant's development will be shaped, not by his temperament alone, or his parents alone, but by the goodness or poorness of fit between them. Others also influence his developmental course as well—other family members, age-mates, friends, teachers, outside sociocultural standards, his opportunities or deprivations, his special abilities and talent. Luck and chance can also play a part. With all these factors shaping and reshaping the child's mind and body as he grows through childhood and adolescence into adult life, is it any wonder that we are all so different in our ideals, our values, our ambitions, our goals, and our behavior in our daily lives? Sir Thomas Browne, the British physician and philosopher, said it 300 years ago: "It is the common wonder of all men, how among so many millions of faces, there should be none alike; now contrary I wonder as much how there should be any. He that shall consider how many thousand several words have been carelessly and without study compounded out of 24 letters; withal how many hundred lines to be drawn in the Fabrick of one man, shall find that this variety is necessary" (quoted in Clarke 1975, p. 60).

This has been a guiding theme throughout this book. Any theory of human development must take into account the subtleties, complexities, and richness of individual psychological differences. So many people and situations are influential in the developmental process, so many different outcomes are possible, so many different traits can be significant ones for different individuals, and differently from one person to another, that the search for simple concepts to explain the development of all individuals according to the same formula is doomed to failure.

But this does not mean that the task of identifying the forces that determine individuality in psychological development is an impossible task. Quite the contrary. We have already learned a great deal about these factors—and this book has tried to illuminate some of what we already know. But we have only made a beginning, though an impressive one when we look back to where we were thirty years ago. This is one of the basic challenges to child development research. We can predict that as this research continues, the diversity of individual psychological development will undoubtedly be linked to complexities that transcend our present understanding. Our knowledge of biological factors, temperament, emotion, motivation, perception, thought and language, and the subtleties of environmental influences, as well as of the mutual influence of all these factors, is in its infancy. With increasing understanding of their complexity will come an increased respect for the flexibility of the mind, the variety of ways in which human beings cope with stress and adversity, and the multitude of ways in which they utilize their talents and opportunities.

The complexities of human development will make it untenable to look for simple answers but will also open the way to the formulation of general rules of development that can encompass these diversities and complexities. And so it will be with the parent and child. We already know that there are many ways to be a good parent, and many ways in which goodness of fit between parent and child can and should be achieved. We are confident that with increase in knowledge will come an increased understanding of parent-child relationships. At the same time, we will be able to formulate more specifically the approaches that will ensure goodness of fit between child and environment, the key to healthy child development.

The Virtue of Diversity

We should treasure the fact that different children and adults feel differently, think differently, and behave differently. Because of this diversity, different individuals will see the world differently, and new creative ideas in the arts and sciences can flourish. Even in everyday life it is the differences, as much as if not more than the similarities, that attract us to other people. We recoil with horror from those societies in which uniformity of behavior and thought is rigidly prescribed for all children and any dissidence from established dogma is severely punished in adults. Yet even in our own society, with its traditions of democracy, the positive meaning and significance of human diversity has all too often been negated by hierarchical judgments, in which differences in any category are ranged in a spectrum from the best to better to inferior to worst. Whether it be skin color, sex, national origins, religion, style of life, personal value systems, or material possessions, a constant struggle is necessary to ensure that all these differences are respected as equally normal. This is one important contribution that the science of human development, and perhaps especially that of child development, can make to our society's well-being. Unless clear and definite evidence of antisocial or psychologically pathological behavior becomes evident, diversity in development and in adult outcome are not only desirable but inevitable and should be welcomed. There are many ways to be a healthy child, parent, or grown-up son or daughter.

The Latest Findings of the NYLS

We are completing a new follow-up study of our longitudinal study subjects, now young men and women in their mid- and late twenties. Almost
all of them are settling into fully independent adulthood in their personal,
social, and work lives. We have known these young adults since they were
infants of two or three months of age. What has been most striking to us
is the many different ways these young people have gone through their
earlier lives to reach a productive, mature level of functioning in adult life.

Some have had an easy time all the way—a stable family, easy temperament, high intelligence, absence of any special stresses or tragedies as they
grew up, and definite interests and talents. For this group, the passage
through childhood and adolescence into early adult life has been accomplished smoothly and without turmoil.

Others have had to cope with one special problem or another along the
way—severe conflict between the parents, break-up of the family through
divorce or death of a parent, frequent moves by the family and loss of the
experience of a continued familiar environment, or a serious accident or
illness. Some have had to contend with a parent who was destructively
intrusive in their lives, gave them undesirable social standards to live by,
or set rigid expectations that they could not meet (poorness of fit). Yet most
of these youngsters struggled and coped successfully with these stresses.
Some developed special talents that changed their lives; others found a
supportive adult figure—a teacher, a friend, a co-worker—who gave them
the encouragement and help they had not found in their own families.
Some were able to distance themselves emotionally from an intrusive,
overdemanding, or mentally ill parent as they went through adolescence
and to center their lives productively outside the home.

A relatively small number are still struggling with psychiatric problems
in their young adult lives. Some have had these disturbances since childhood; in other cases the onset was in adolescence or the early twenties. In
some of these cases, the disorder appeared to be entirely psychological,
such as a continuous and escalating poorness of fit between child and
parent. In others, a biological factor appeared to be a prominent feature in
the perpetuation of the problem: brain damage at the time of birth, a
primary depression, or a panic disorder. (In the past such depressions or
panic disorders were considered to be of psychological origin; most psychiatrists, including ourselves, now believe that they have a biological
basis.) Even in these latter cases we have been impressed by how tena-

ciously these people have struggled to lead normal lives in spite of their biological disorders.

Could we have predicted the adult outcome of our 133 subjects from our intimate knowledge of their childhood life? Not at all. All we could say was that if the child's relationship with his parents continued on a positive level, and his level of school interest and achievement was up to his intellectual capacities, and he made good friendships, his outlook for adult life was favorable. But even this formulation contains many ifs, which unusual life experiences or biological changes in the brain could make into a less favorable outcome.

But it must be remembered that our subjects came from middle-class families. These families have the resources and the willingness to support and encourage their children to go on to college and, if necessary, also to professional school. Even if their youngsters have dropped out of college in the late teens and then decide to go back to school to implement a serious goal, the parents are usually delighted and able to help out. It is only in their middle and late twenties that these young adults are expected to become self-sufficient and independent, financially and psychologically, of their parents. This is the prevalent pattern we have found in our current follow-up.

The situation is quite different in working-class families. Here the parents have much more limited resources, and even if they wish to see their son or daughter move upward socioeconomically, the families cannot afford to give their offspring the luxury of dropping out of college and then returning later with a new and more expensive career goal. The ambitious and enterprising young adults in this group are usually limited in their choice of college and must complete their college career uninterrupted, as well as working after school and summers to pay for their education.

In the underprivileged families, especially for minority groups living in inner city ghetto areas, the prospects are much grimmer. The children usually attend mediocre schools at best, and educational advancement does not appear to be a realistic goal. College and often even high school completion appear to be unrealistic goals. When they try to enter the job market, their lack of technical skills and their relative illiteracy leave them only the possibility of low-paying unskilled jobs. It is no wonder that the rates of unemployment, drug addiction, and delinquency are so alarmingly high for these youngsters. But it must be emphasized that this is a social problem, not the result of any inherent inferiority in this group. Enough youngsters make it into the mainstream of life through special talents or indomitable determination to prove that it is possible (Gordon & Braithwaite 1986). We remember one black boy from an underprivileged family who was determined to go to college. He had to battle his family all the way; they kept telling him that college was nonsense for someone with his background and that he should go out and get a job instead. He fought them and did make it into college successfully. Another black boy in Harlem would sneak off to the public library to read voraciously, always afraid that his friends would find out and ridicule him. It is clear, therefore, that decent schools and special support systems could change the present grim and pathological outlook for this group of young adults.

What We Still Don't Know

As much as we have learned in the past thirty years, many questions remain unanswered. Why does a particular stressful event, such as death or divorce in the family, a drastic change in living circumstances, an illness which leaves a physical handicap—to mention only a few possibilities—cause one child to mobilize himself to cope successfully with the problem, while it leaves another shaken, confused, and fearful of the future? Why do two children brought up in similar environments, even in the same stable family unit, so often end up so differently in their personalities, their goals, their life styles, and their feelings for other people? Why do some children, exposed to the high risk factors of poverty, poor education, family instability, even with parents with serious mental problems, not succumb with psychological problems of their own but develop into competent and mature adults? We have seen this positive outcome in some high risk children in our longitudinal study, and so have others who have followed groups of children into adult life. Emmy Werner of the University of California, who, with Ruth Smith of Wilcox Memorial Hospital in Hawaii, did a large-scale study of children in Kauai, Hawaii, calls such youngsters "vulnerable but invincible" (Werner & Smith 1982). Edmund Gordon, of Yale University, has used the apt phrase "defiers of negative prediction" to designate such children (Gordon & Braithwaite 1986).

This is a basic question—the differential response of children to the same unfavorable environment. Sometimes we can identify an answer: goodness or poorness of parent-child fit, special talents or opportunities, the intervention of a new influential person in the child's life. But often we do not know the answer. And answers that are suggested have to be judged according to what Stephen Jay Gould calls "the cardinal principal of all science—that the profession, as an art, dedicates itself above all to fruitful doing, not clever thinking; to claims that can be tested by actual research, not to exciting thoughts that inspire no activity" (1986).

We, and others, have many anecdotes to illustrate our still limited ability to understand the life-history of many people we have known. We will cite two such cases, one a happy story, the other an unhappy one.

Two Stories

Several years ago a car stopped at our country house, and a young couple got out and rang our bell. The young man, in his early 30s, tall, slim, with a neatly trimmed beard, introduced himself with a pleasant smile. "You don't recognize me. I'm Kevin Harris, and this is my wife, Laura." We gasped with delighted surprise and welcomed them in. He explained that he wanted to show his wife the place where he had spent a number of happy summers as an adolescent and also to renew his contact with our family.

We had not seen or heard from Kevin for fifteen years. Circumstances had made for a friendship between him and our youngest son when they were teenagers. But after a few years, their paths had diverged so much that they had lost touch with each other.

In the past we had also known Kevin's parents well, as stimulating and attractive people, to be respected for their ethical standards and professional commitments. But they had truly made a mess of their marriage and their relationship with Kevin. They bickered and argued constantly and openly with each other, couldn't agree on even the simplest issues of daily living, and eventually were divorced. Kevin was the younger son, and his father kept after him persistently and even remorselessly over his many presumed deficiencies. The elder son, Tom, the father's favorite, was constantly held up to the younger boy as a model. "Why can't you be like him?" was the father's standard reproach. As it happens, Tom was a "model" youngster, well-behaved, socially attractive, musically talented, and a good student. Kevin, by contrast, was irresponsible at times, but never seriously, an average student, and often resistant to his parents' requests. The father was convinced that Kevin was a seriously disturbed youngster and had a most pessimistic outlook for his future life. The mother agreed with her husband's judgment but blamed the father for Kevin's problems. She felt that Kevin's gloomy prospects would not change unless her husband changed, and she was sure that would not happen.

Our own judgment of Kevin was quite different. As we saw him, on his frequent visits to our home, he appeared to be an essentially normal teenager with many talents. This was in a relaxed, friendly setting, however, where his company was enjoyed and appreciated. In no way could we convince either parent of our positive view of their son. And knowing the destructive atmosphere in which Kevin lived at home we were indeed unhappy about his prospects.

And now here was Kevin, fifteen years later, having defied all these unhappy predictions. He was poised, self-assured, and immediately friendly. He had earned both M.D. and Ph.D. degrees at an Ivy League university and had already made a significant contribution in a demanding area of basic medical research. He had just accepted a full-time position at a major medical center and was launched on a brilliant and satisfying career. His wife was a medical student, and to all appearances, as we chatted with them, they were affectionate and at ease with each other and had a number of mutual interests.

Kevin was quite clear on how throughout his childhood and adolescence he had been bedeviled by his father, derogated by his mother, and deprived of any support from his older brother, who stayed neutral on the sidelines. We asked him how it was that he had escaped without psychological damage—and this without any psychiatric treatment. He replied without hesitation, "I knew I had to keep my ego intact and keep my distance, otherwise I would go crazy." Somehow or other, he was able to invest his activities and feelings in his few friends and in his own many interests and never let his father's attacks get under his skin. When he went away to college he had a sense of relief and freedom. On returning home after the first year, his father started to harass him again. Kevin told him this had to stop. "I said, 'You have two choices. We can discuss issues when we disagree, come to agreements, and be real friends. Or else, if you can't do that, we will keep our distance from each other.'" What an extraordinary formulation this was for a nineteen-year-old to be able to make to his forceful, articulate, and browbeating father! And this he figured out entirely on his own, without any preliminary advice or counseling from anyone else. His father took the second choice, and since then they have had casually friendly contacts and have gone for long periods without contact.

In the several hours Kevin and his wife spent with us, he was frank and open in discussing his past and present life with us. Clearly he was sharing these with his wife. We could detect no signs of psychological disturbance in his manner, speech, emotional expression, or thinking.

We met Kevin again just recently in a social setting. He was still poised, self-assured, relaxed, and articulate. His career and personal life were proceeding successfully, and again we could not detect any sign of psychological disturbance. On the contrary, he gave every sign of being an impressive young man, beginning to fulfill a promising professional and personal life.

What accounts for Kevin's extraordinary ability to master these most unhealthy and continuous family experiences as he grew up? Why did he come out on top, when so many others would have gone under? Some psychiatrists might offer the explanation that there must have been some subtle but powerful positive bond between him and his father which counterbalanced the criticisms and attacks. But this is circular reasoning. If we ask, "But, what is the evidence for this bond?" the answer would be, "Look at the outcome; that is the evidence." So a cause is invoked to explain a youngster's development, and the evidence to "prove" the cause is the developmental course we are trying to explain. Unfortunately, much psychiatric theorizing tends to be this kind of circular reasoning. Better to say, accurately, that we just don't know the answer.

In striking contrast to Kevin's history is the story of Martin Williams' life. Martin came to consult one of us (A.T.) some years ago when he was in his early forties. A lawyer, he had held many jobs with major companies. The story was always the same. He would start out brilliantly, plunging into the new job with zeal, energy, and a high level of competence. His employer would be highly impressed and hint that a promotion might be in the offing. But then Martin would grind to a halt. After a few months, his interest would wane, and his energy and commitment would dwindle. He soon found he was doing a routine job, feeling bored, and even cutting corners to avoid demanding tasks. He could usually conceal this transformation for some months, but not forever. Either he was finally dropped from the company or allowed to stay on as one more staff member used for simple routine assignments.

Martin at first found all kinds of excuses for his failures: The boss didn't like him, the job really didn't interest him, he was capable of doing much more if he only had the chance, and so on, and so on. But by the time he was forty, these excuses began to wear thin, and he had to face the fact that the problem must lie within himself. With this realization, he came seeking professional help.

In reviewing his life history, it was evident that he had grown up in a modest, stable lower-middle-class family. As he grew into middle childhood and adolescence, qualities of superior intelligence and ease in social situations made him an unusual youngster. He excelled at school, made friends easily, and was the darling of his family for these abilities. He discovered that he could make his way through school with very little effort and even come out with superior grades. I knew his sister at that time; she had a peripheral professional relationship with our research projects. The sister was as different from her brother as could be: quiet, serious, intelligent but not sparkling, and moving ahead slowly but steadily in her own career. She confirmed Martin's story of their family life, his impressive academic abilities, and his talent for making friends easily. He did indeed breeze his way through school and impress his family and friends with his apparent achievements. She remembered vividly taking one high school course with him. She took all the assignments seriously and had a full set of notes by the end of the term. Martin, as usual, coasted through the course, doing a minimum amount of work. The day before the final examination he borrowed her notes, read through them once, and came out with a higher grade than she did!

In an extended series of therapeutic discussions with Martin, his psychological problem became clear. His work habits, or rather lack of work habits, had become ingrained in him by the time he reached the adult world. With a new job, his interest would be stimulated at first, he would perform superbly, but then he would rest on his laurels as he had done throughout his school career. The results were inevitable. Though each job started out with excited interest and intensive activity, he could not sustain his initial level of energy to meet the nitty-gritty, day-by-day details that any job demanded. No other subconscious mechanisms could be detected. He was not afraid of success or of competition, nor did he nurse some derogatory self-image that made him fearful of failure.

But many other youngsters, blessed with Martin's intellectual and social talents, would have utilized them to move full steam ahead consistently in the direction of their specific interests and would have achieved successful and even spectacular careers. Why did Martin choose an opposite course—to use his talents to get by with as little effort as possible? Again, as with Kevin, we have to say we don't know the answer.

To say we don't know why Kevin and Martin developed as they did does not mean we are dodging the issue. In science, to say we don't know is the first stage of knowledge; it is a challenge to find ways to answer the question. As we have quoted from the noted mathematician-philosopher Jacob Bronowski at the beginning of this chapter, "There is no absolute knowledge. . . . All information is imperfect. We have to treat it with humility." We know a great deal about high and low risk factors in the developmental process in *groups* (Garmezy 1983). But we still know relatively very little about why *specific individuals* confound and contradict these group trends in their life course. Our goodness of fit concept is one model through which this issue of individual development can be approached.

But it is only a beginning. We feel that this is a basic problem facing child development research in the coming years. It will be no easy task, but it will be a challenging one. It will explain why Kevin's and Martin's life courses took such opposite directions, and why Ricky and Michael, whom we introduced in chapter 1, were functioning so differently.

A Closing Message

Louise Ames, of the Yale Gesell Institute of Development, a respected authority on child development, has said: "Given the fact that parenthood is probably the most difficult job in the world, I think it's a miracle that mothers do as well as they do. And most do very well indeed" (1983). Ames' purpose is to reassure mothers. Even if parenthood is very difficult, she tells us, most mothers can take comfort from her judgment that they "do very well."

But this last sentence of reassurance cannot cancel out her pronouncement that parenthood is a difficult job and that it is a miracle that mothers do it well. This viewpoint is entirely contrary to the thesis of this book, which we have tried to buttress with authoritative research evidence. Parenthood of a physically or mentally ill or handicapped child may be difficult, but not the parenthood of a normal child. It may be an important job, it may demand commitments of time and energy, but it is not *difficult*. Once the parents know that their child is flexible and adaptable, that they can experiment with different approaches without harming the baby, that they can easily learn to interpret their baby's signals and to communicate with their baby—all tasks which are *not* so difficult—then parenthood can become a relaxed and enjoyable experience.

Let us rather close this book with one of our recent statements, based on our own research findings as well as those from a number of other major longitudinal studies.

As we grow from childhood to maturity, all of us have to shed many childhood illusions. As the field of developmental studies has matured, we now have to give up the illusion that once we know the young child's psychological history, subsequent personality and functioning is *ipso facto* predictable. On the other hand, we now have a much more optimistic vision of human development. The emotionally traumatized child is not doomed, the parents' early mistakes are not irrevocable, and our preventative and therapeutic intervention can make a difference at all age-periods. (Chess 1979)

References

Ainsworth, M.D.S., M.C. Blehar, E. Waters, & S. Wall. 1978. *Patterns of attachment: A psychological study of the strange situation.* Hillsdale, N.J.: Erlbaum.

American Academy of Pediatrics. Committee on Psychological Aspects of Child and Family Health. 1984. The mother working outside the home. *Pediatrics* 73:874–75.

Ames, L.B. 1983. *The American Baby* Nov.: 88.

Anthony, E.J. 1969a. A clinical evaluation of children with psychotic parents. *American Journal of Psychiatry* 126:177–84.

Anthony, E.J. 1969b. The reactions of adults to adolescents and their behavior. In *Adolescence,* ed. G. Caplan and S. Lebovic. New York: Basic Books.

Bank, S.P., & M.D. Kahn. 1982. *The sibling bond.* New York: Basic Books.

Baumrind, D. 1967. Child care practices anteceding three patterns of preschool behavior. *Genetic Psychology Monographs* 75:43–88.

Baumrind, D. 1968. Authoritarian versus authoritative parental control. *Adolescence* 3:255–72.

Baumrind, D. 1979. Current patterns of parental authority. *Developmental Psychology Monographs* 41(1, pt. 2).

Beach, L.R. 1960. Sociability and academic achievement in various types of learning situations. *Journal of Educational Psychology* 51:208–12.

Becker, H.H. 1968. The self and adult socialization. In *The study of personality,* ed. E. Norbeck, D.P. Williams, & W.M. McCord. New York: Rinehart and Winston.

Bell, A.P., M.S. Weinberg, & S.K. Hammersmith. 1981. *Sexual preference: Its development in men and women.* Bloomington: Indiana University Press.

Berlin, I.N. 1982. Prevention of emotional problems among Native-American children: Overview of developmental issues. *Journal of Preventive Psychiatry* 1:319–30.

Berruetta-Clement, J.R., L.J. Sweinhart, W.S. Barnett, A.S. Epstein, & O.P. Weickart. 1984. Changed lives: The effects of the Perry preschool programs on youths through age 19. *Monograph no. 8: High/Scope Educational Foundation.* Ypsilanti: The High/Scope Press.

Bieber, I. et al. 1962. *Homosexuality: A psychoanalytic study.* New York: Basic Books.

Biller, H.B. 1971. *Father, child and sex role.* Lexington, Mass.: Heath.

Birns, B. 1976. The emergence and socialization of sex differences in the earliest years. *Merrill-Palmer Quarterly* 22: 229–54.

Bloom, B.S. 1964. *Stability and change in human characteristics.* New York: Wiley.

Blos, P. 1979. *The adolescent passage.* New York: International Universities Press.

Bowlby, J. 1951. *Maternal care and mental health.* Geneva: World Health Organization.

Bowlby, J. 1969. *Attachment and loss.* Vol. 1, *Attachment.* London: Hogarth.

Bowlby, J. 1982. Attachment and loss. *American Journal of Orthopsychiatry* 52:664–78.

Brazelton, T.B. 1969. *Infants and mothers.* New York: Dell.

Brazelton, T.B. 1973. Neonatal behavioral assessment scale. *Clinics in Developmental Medicine,* no. 50.

Brazelton, T.B. 1985. *Working and caring.* Reading, Mass.: Addison-Wesley.

Bretherton, I. 1978. Making friends with one-year-olds: An experimental study of infant-stranger interaction. *Merrill-Palmer Quarterly,* 24:29–51.

Bretherton, I., & E. Waters, eds. 1985. *Growing points of attachment theory and research.* Monographs of the Society for Research in Child Development 50:1–2, Abstract, p. vi. Chicago: University of Chicago Press.

Brodkin, A.M. et al. 1984. Retrospective reports of mothers' work patterns and psychological distress in first-year medical students. *Journal of the American Academy of Child Psychiatry* 23:-479–85.

Bronfenbrenner, U. 1974. Developmental research, public policy, and the ecology of childhood. *Child Development* 45:1–5.

Brooksbank, D.J. 1985. Suicide and parasuicide in childhood and early adolescence. *British Journal of Psychiatry* 146:459–63.

Bruch, H. 1954. Parent education or the illusion of omnipotence. *American Journal of Orthopsychiatry* 24:723–32.

Bruner, J. 1973. Organization of early skilled actions. *Child Development* 44:1–11.

Bruner, J.S. 1978. Learning the mother tongue. *Human Nature* 1:32–39.

Bruner, J. 1983. *In search of mind.* New York: Harper Colophon Books.

Bruner, J. et al. 1966. *Studies in cognitive growth.* New York: Wiley.

Buss, A.H., & R. Plomin. 1975. *A temperament theory of personality.* New York: Wiley.

Calladine, C., & A. Calladine. 1979. *Raising siblings.* New York: Delacorte Press.

Carey, W.B. 1974. Night wakening and temperament in infancy. *Journal of Pediatrics* 81:823–28.

Carpenter, G. 1975. Mother face and the newborn. In *Child alive,* ed. R. Lewin. London: Temple Smith.

Cattell, R.B. 1950. *Personality: A systematic and factual study.* New York: McGraw-Hill.

Chamberlin, R.W. 1974. Authoritarian and accommodative child-rearing styles: Their relationship with the behavior patterns of two-year-old children with other variables. *Journal of Pediatrics* 84:287–93.

Chase, A. 1977. *The legacy of Malthus.* New York: Knopf.

Chess, S. 1944. Developmental language disability as a factor in personality distortion in childhood. *American Journal of Orthopsychiatry* 14:483–90.

Chess, S. 1978. The plasticity of human development. *Journal American Academy of Child Psychiatry* 17:80–91.

Chess, S. 1979. Developmental theory revisited. *Canadian Journal of Psychiatry* 24:101–12.

Chess, S. 1980. The mildly mentally retarded child in the community: Success versus failure. In *Human functioning in longitudinal perspective,* ed. S.B. Sells, R. Crandall, M. Roff, J.S. Strauss & W. Pollin. Baltimore: Williams & Wilkins.

Chess, S., & M. Hassibi. 1978. *Principles and practice of child psychiatry.* New York: Plenum.

Chess, S., & A. Thomas. 1982. Infant bonding: Mystique and reality. *American Journal of Orthopsychiatry* 52:213–22.

Chess, S., & A. Thomas. 1984. *Origins and evolution of behavior disorders: Infancy to early adult life.* New York: Brunner/Mazel.

Chess, S., & A. Thomas. 1986. *Temperament in clinical practice.* New York: Guilford.

Chess, S., A. Thomas, & H.G. Birch. 1967. Behavior problems revisited: Findings of an anterospective study. *Journal American Academy of Child Psychiatry* 6:321–31.

Chess, S., P. Fernandez, & S. Korn. 1980. The handicapped child and his family: Consonance and dissonance. *Journal American Academy of Child Psychiatry* 19:56–67.

Chess, S., A. Thomas, S. Korn, M. Mittleman, & J. Cohen. 1983. Early parental attitudes, divorce and separation, and early adult outcome. *Journal American Academy of Child Psychiatry* 22:47–51.

Chomsky, N. 1957. *Syntactic Structure.* The Hague: Mouton.

Ciba Foundation. 1982. *Temperamental differences in infants and young children.* Symposium 89. London: Pitman.

Clarke, A.B. 1975. The causes of biological diversity. *Scientific American* 233:50–60.

Colby, A., & W. Damon. 1983. Review of *In a different voice,* by C. Gilligan. *Merrill-Palmer Quarterly* 29:473–81.

Coleman, J.C. 1978. Current contradictions in adolescent theory. *Journal of Youth and Adolescence* 7:1–2.

Coleman, J.S. et al. 1966. *Equality of educational opportunity.* Washington, D.C.: U.S. Government Printing Office.

Condon, W.S., & L.W. Sander. 1974. Neonatal movement is synchronized with adult speech: Interactional participation and language requisition. *Science* 183:99–101.

Condry, J., & S. Condry. 1976. Sex differences: A study of the eye of the beholder. *Child Development* 47:812–19.

Connolly, K. 1972. Learning and the concept of critical periods in infancy. *Developmental Medicine and Child Neurology* 14:705–14.

Conrad, R. 1979. *The deaf school child.* London: Harper & Row.

Costello, A. 1975. Are mothers stimulating? In *Child alive,* ed. R. Lewis. London: Temple Smith.

Curtiss, S. 1977. *Genie: A psycholinguistic study of a modern-day 'wild child.'* New York: Academic Press.

Davis, H.V., R. Sears, H.C. Miller, & A.J. Brodbeck. 1948. Effects of cup, bottle, and breast feeding on oral activity of newborn infants. *Pediatrics* 2:549–58.

Davis, R.E., & R.E. Ruiz. 1965. Infant feeding method and adolescent personality. Paper presented at 165th annual meeting of the American Psychiatric Association, May 1965.

DeJong, A.R. 1985. The medical evaluation of sexual abuse in children. *Hospital and Community Psychiatry* 36:509–11.

Derdeyn, A., & E. Scott. 1984. Joint custody: A critical analysis and appraisal. *American Journal of Orthopsychiatry* 54:199–209.

Deutsch, H. 1944. *The psychology of women,* vol. 1. New York: Grune & Stratton.

Deutsch, M. 1969. Happenings on the way back to the forum: Social science, I.Q., and race differences revisited. *Harvard Educational Review* 39:523–57.

Deutsch, M., C. Deutsch, and associates. 1967. *The disadvantaged child.* New York: Basic Books.

deVries, M. 1984. Temperament and infant mortality among the Masai of East Africa. *American Journal of Psychiatry* 141:1189–94.

Dobzhansky, T. 1966. A geneticist's view of human equality. *The Pharos* 29:12–16.

Drotar, D., & P. Crawford. 1985. Psychological adaptation of siblings of chronically ill children: Research and practical implications. *Developmental and Behavioral Pediatrics* 6:355–62.

Dubos, R. 1965. *Man adapting.* New Haven: Yale University Press.

Dunn, J. 1977. *Distress and comfort.* Cambridge, Mass.: Harvard University Press.

Dunn, J., & C. Kendrick. 1980. Studying temperament and parent-child interaction: Comparison of interview and direct observation. *Developmental Medicine and Child Neurology* 22:484–96.

Dunn, J., & C. Kendrick. 1982. *Siblings.* Cambridge, Mass.: Harvard University Press.

Dunn, J.F., R. Plomin, & M. Nettles. 1985. Consistency of mothers' behavior toward infant siblings. *Developmental Psychology* 21:1188–95.

Eisenberg, L. 1981. Social context of child development. *Pediatrics* 68:705–12.

Eisenberg, L., & F.J. Earls. 1975. Poverty, social depreciation and child development. In *American Handbook of Psychiatry,* vol. 6, ed. D.A. Hamburg. New York: Basic Books.

Eissler, K.B. 1958. Notes on problems of technique in the psychoanalytic treatment of adolescents. *Psychoanalytic Study of the Child* 13:233–54.

Emde, R.N. 1978. Commentary on *Organization and stability of newborn behavior,* ed. A.J. Sameroff. Monographs of the Society for Research in Child Development, vol. 43, nos. 5–6.

Erikson, E. 1950. *Childhood and society.* New York: Norton.

Erikson, E. 1959. Identity and the life cycle. *Psychological Issues* 1:1–171.

Erikson, E. 1968. *Identity: Youth and crisis.* New York: Norton.

Erikson, K. 1976. *Everything in its path.* New York: Simon & Schuster.

Escalona, S. 1952. Emotional development in the first year of life. In *Problems of infancy and childhood,* ed. M.J.E. Senn. New York: Josiah Macy Foundation, 6th conference.

Etaugh, C. 1980. Effects of nonmaternal care on children: Research evidence and popular views. *American Psychologist* 35:309–19.

Fantz, R.L. 1956. A method for studying early visual development. *Perceptual and Motor Skills* 6:13–15.

Fantz, R.L. 1966. Pattern discrimination and selective attention as determinants of perceptual development from birth. In *Perceptual development in children,* ed. A.H. Kidd & J.L. Rivoire. New York: International Universities Press.

Fantz, R.L., & S. Nevis. 1967. Pattern preferences and perceptual-cognitive development in early infancy. *Merrill-Palmer Quarterly* 13:77–108.

Field, T.M., D. Cohen, R. Garcia, & R. Greenberg. 1984. Mother-stranger face discrimination by the newborn. *Infant Behavior and Development* 7:19–25.

Fischer, K.W., & L. Silvern. 1985. Stages and individual differences in cognitive development. *Annual Review of Psychology* 36:613–48.

Fishman, M.E. 1982. *Child and youth activities of the National Institute of Mental Health 1981–1982.* Washington, D.C.: U.S. Government Printing Office.

Fiske, E.B. 1986. Early schooling is now the rage. *New York Times,* April 13, 1986, Sect. 12.

Flavell, J.H. 1976. Metacognitive aspects of problem solving. In *The nature of human intelligence,* ed. L.B. Resnick. Hillsdale, N.J.: Lawrence Erlbaum Associates.

Fraiberg, S. 1977a. *Insights from the blind.* New York: Basic Books.

Fraiberg, S. 1977b. *Every child's birthright: In defense of mothering.* New York: Basic Books.

Freud, A. 1958. Adolescence. *Psychoanalytic Study of the Child* 13:255–78.

Freud, A. 1965. *Normality and pathology in childhood.* New York: International Universities Press.

Freud, S. 1924. *Collected papers,* vol. 4. London: Hogarth Press.

Freud, S. 1933. *New introductory lectures in psychoanalysis.* New York: Norton.

Freud, S. 1940. An outline of psychoanalysis. In *The standard edition of the complete psychological works of Sigmund Freud,* vol. 23, ed. and trans. J. Strachey. London: Hogarth Press.

Freud, S. 1950. Some psychological consequences of the anatomical distinction between the sexes. *Collected papers,* vol. 5. London: Hogarth Press.

Friedman, D. 1986. Corporate support for the child care needs of working parents. In *Group care for young children: Considerations for child care and health professionals, public policy makers, and parents,* ed. N. Gunzenhauser & B. Caldwell. Pediatric Round Table, no. 12. Skillman, N.J.: Johnson & Johnson Baby Products Co.

Galinsky, E. 1986. Contemporary patterns of child care. In *Group care for young children: Considerations for child care and health professionals, public policy makers, and parents,* ed. N. Gunzenhauser & B. Caldwell. Pediatric Round Table, no. 12. Skillman, N.J.: Johnson & Johnson Baby Products Co.

Gardner, H. 1985. *Frames of mind.* New York: Basic Books.

Garmezy, N. 1983. Stressors of childhood. In *Stress, coping and development in children,* ed. N. Garmezy & M. Rutter. New York: McGraw-Hill.

Gerson, K. 1985. *Hard choices.* Berkeley: University of California Press.

Gilligan, C. 1982a. *In a different voice.* Cambridge, Mass.: Harvard University Press.

Gilligan, C. 1982b. New maps of development: New visions of maturity. *American Journal of Orthopsychiatry* 52:109–212.

Goldberg, S. 1983. Parent-infant bonding: Another look. *Child Development* 54:1355–82.

Goldfarb, W. 1943. Infant rearing and problem behavior. *American Journal of Orthopsychiatry* 13:249–65.

Goldfarb, W. 1947. Variations in adolescent adjustment of institutionally reared children. *American Journal of Orthopsychiatry* 17:449–57.

Goodall, J., & D.A. Hamburg. 1975. Chimpanzee behavior as a model for the behavior of early man: New evidence on possible origins of human behavior. In *American handbook of psychiatry,* vol. 6, 2d ed., ed. S. Arieti. New York: Basic Books.

Goodenough, F.L., & D.B. Harris. 1950. Studies in the psychology of children's drawings. *Psychological Bulletin* 47:369–433.

Gordon, E. 1975. New perspectives on old issues in education for the minority poor. *IRCD Bulletin* 10:5–17. New York: Columbia University Teachers College.

Gordon, E., & A. Braithwaite. 1986. *Defiers of negative prediction.* Washington, D.C.: Howard University Press.

Gordon, E.M., & A. Thomas. 1967. Children's behavioral style and the teacher's appraisal of their intelligence. *Journal of School Psychology* 5:292–300.

Gould, S.J. 1981. *The mismeasure of man.* New York: Norton.

Gould, S.J. 1986. A triumph of historical excavation. *The New York Review of Books,* vol. 33, no. 3.

Graham, P., & M. Rutter. 1973. Psychiatric disorders in the young adolescent: A follow-up study. *Proceedings of the Royal Society of Medicine* 66:58–61.

Greenspan, S., & R.S. Lourie. 1981. Developmental structuralist approach to the classification of adaptive and pathologic personality organizations: Infancy and early childhood. *American Journal of Psychiatry* 138:725–35.

Guilford, J.P. 1959. *Personality.* New York: McGraw-Hill.

Guilford, J.P. 1967. *The nature of human intelligence.* New York: McGraw-Hill.

Hall, G.S. 1904. *Adolescence,* vol. 11. New York: D. Appleton.

Harlow, H. 1958. The nature of love. *American Psychologist* 13:673–85.

Hartman, H. 1958. *Ego psychology and the problem of psychology.* New York: International Universities Press.

Hay, D.F. 1985. Learning to form relationships in infancy: Parallel attainments with parents and peers. *Developmental Review* 8:122–61.

Hearnshaw, L.S. 1979. *Cyril Burt, psychologist.* London: Hadden and Stoughton.

Hetherington, M., M. Cox, & R. Cox. 1985. Long-term effects of divorce and remarriage on the adjustment of children. *Journal American Academy of Child Psychiatry* 24:518–30.

Hewlett, S.A. 1986. *A lesser life: The myth of women's liberation in America.* New York: William Morrow.

Hinde, R. 1966. *Animal behavior: A synthesis of ethology and comparative psychology.* New York: McGraw-Hill.

Hindley, C.B., & C.F. Owen. 1978. The extent of individual changes in IQ for ages between 6 months and 17 years in a British longitudinal sample. *Journal of Child Psychology and Psychiatry* 19:329–50.

Hoffman, L.W. 1963. Mother's enjoyment of work and effects on the child. In *The employed mother in America,* ed. F.I. Nye & L.W. Hoffman. Chicago: Rand McNally.

Holinger, P.C. 1979. Violent deaths among the young: Recent trends in suicide, homicide and accidents. *American Journal of Psychiatry* 136:1144–47.

Hunt, J.Mc.V. 1980. Implications of plasticity and hierarchal achievements for the assessment of development and risk of mental retardation. In *Exceptional infant,* vol. 4, ed. D.B. Sawin, R.C. Hawkins, L.O. Walker, & J.H. Penticuff. New York: Brunner/Mazel.

Izard, C.E. 1977. *Human emotions.* New York: Plenum.

Jacklin, C.N., & E.E. Maccoby. 1983. Issues of gender differentiation. In *Developmental-behavioral pediatrics,* ed. M.D. Levine, W.B. Carey, A.C. Crocker, & R.T. Gross. Philadelphia: Saunders.

James, W. 1890. *The principles of psychology.* New York: Holt.

Jencks, C. et al. 1972. *Inequality: A reassessment of the effect of family and schooling in America.* New York: Basic Books.

Jensen, A.R. 1969. How much can we boost IQ and scholastic achievement? *Harvard Educational Review* 33:1–123.

Jersild, A.T. 1968. *Child psychology.* Englewood Cliffs, N.J.: Prentice-Hall.

Kagan, J. 1971. *Change and continuity in childhood.* New York: Wiley.

Kagan, J. 1972. Do infants think? *Scientific American* 226:74–82.

Kagan, J. 1979. Family experience and the child's development. *American Psychologist* 34:886–91.

Kagan, J. 1982. The emergence of self. *Journal of Child Psychology and Psychiatry* 23:363–81.

Kagan, J. 1984. *The nature of the child.* New York: Basic Books.

Kagan, J., R.B. Kearsley, & P.R. Zelazo. 1978. *Infancy: Its place in human development.* Cambridge, Mass.: Harvard University Press.

Kamerman, S.B., & C.D. Hayes, eds. 1982. *Families that work: Children in a changing world.* Washington, D.C.: National Academy Press.

Kamin, L.J. 1974. *The science and politics of IQ.* Potomac, Maryland: Lawrence Erlbaum Associates.

Kardiner, A. 1954. *Sex and morality.* Indianapolis: Bobbs Merrill.

Kaye, K. 1982. *The mental and social life of babies.* Chicago: University of Chicago Press.

Kaye, K., & T.B. Brazelton. 1971. Mother-child interaction in the organization of sucking. Paper presented at the biennial meeting of the Society for Research in Child Development, Minneapolis, 1971.

Keogh, B. 1982. Children's temperament and teacher decisions. In *Temperamental differences in infants and young children,* Ciba Foundation Symposium 89. London: Pitman.

Klatskin, E.H., E.B. Jackson, & L.C. Wilkin. 1956. The influence of degree of flexibility in maternal child care practices on early child behavior. *American Journal of Orthopsychiatry* 26:79–93.

Klaus, M.H., & J.H. Kennell. 1976. *Maternal-infant bonding.* St. Louis: C.V. Mosby.

Klaus, M.H., & J.H. Kennell. 1982. *Parent-infant bonding.* St. Louis: C.V. Mosby.

Kohlberg, L. 1976. Moral stages and moralization: The cognitive-developmental approach. In *Moral development and behavior,* ed. T. Lickona. New York: Holt, Rinehart and Winston.

Kohlberg, L. 1978. The cognitive developmental approach to behavior disorders: A study of the development of moral reasoning in delinquents. In *Cognitive defects in the development of mental illness,* ed. G. Serban. New York: Brunner/Mazel.

Kohut, H. 1977. *The restoration of the self.* New York: International Universities Press.

Kolata, G. 1984. Studying learning in the womb. *Science* 225:302–3.

Kolb, L.C. 1978. Ego assets: An overlooked aspect of personality organization. Menas S. Gregory Lecture, New York University Medical Center, April 20, 1978.

Koluchova, J. 1976. A report on the future development of twins after severe and prolonged deprivation. In *Early experience: Myth and evidence,* ed. A.M. Clarke & A.D.B. Clarke. London: Open Books.

Korner, A.L. 1973. Sex differences in newborns with special references to differences in the organization of oral behavior. *Journal of Child Psychology* 14:19–29.

Kornhaber, A., & K.L. Woodward. 1981. *Grandparents/grandchildren.* Garden City, N.Y.: Anchor Press, Doubleday.

Lamb, M., R.A. Thompson, W.P. Gardner, E.L. Charnov, & D. Estes. 1984. Security of infantile attachment as assessed in the 'Strange Situation': Its study and biological implications. *Behavioral and Brain Sciences* 7:127–47.

Lazar, I., & R. Darlington. 1982. *Lasting effects of early education: A report from the consortium for longitudinal studies.* Monographs of the Society for Research in Child Development, vol. 47, nos. 2–3.

Lerner, J.V. 1983. The role of temperament in psychosocial adaptation in early adolescents: A test of a "goodness of fit" model. *Journal of Genetic Psychology* 143:149–57.

Lerner, J.V., & N. Galambos. 1985. Maternal role satisfaction, mother-child interaction, and child temperament. *Developmental Psychology* 21:1157–64.

Levy, D.M. 1937. *Studies in sibling rivalry.* Research monograph no. 2. New York: American Orthopsychiatric Association.

Lewis, M., & J. Brooks. 1974. Self, other and fear: Infants' reactions to people. In *The origins of fear,* ed. M. Lewis & L.A. Rosenbaum. New York: Wiley.

Lewis, M., & J. Brooks. 1975. Infants' social perception: A constructive view. In *Infant perception from sensation to cognition,* vol. 2, ed. L.B. Cohen & P. Salapatek. New York: Academic Press.

Lewis, M., & L. Michalson. 1983. *Children's emotions and moods.* New York: Plenum.

Lewontin, R.C., S. Rose, & L.J. Kamin. 1984. *Not in our genes.* New York: Pantheon.

Lidz, T. 1968. *The person.* New York: Basic Books.

Lightfoot, S.L. 1983. *The good high school.* New York: Basic Books.

Lorenz, K. 1952. *King Solomon's ring: New light on animal ways.* New York: Crowell.

Lorenz, K. 1966. *On aggression.* New York: Harcourt, Brace and World.

Maccoby, E.E., & C.N. Jacklin. 1974. *The psychology of sex differences.* Stanford, Calif.: Stanford University Press.

Mahler, M.S., F. Pine, & A. Bergman. 1975. *The psychological birth of the human infant.* New York: Basic Books.

Marmor, J. 1974. *Psychiatry in transition.* New York: Brunner/Mazel.

Marmor, J. 1975. Homosexuality and sexual orientation disturbances. In *Comprehensive textbook of psychiatry,* 2nd ed., ed. A. Freedman, H.I. Kaplan & B.J. Sadock. Baltimore: Williams & Wilkins.

Marmor, J. 1982. Review of *Sexual preference: Its development in men and women,* by A.P. Bell, M.S. Weinberg, & S.K. Hammersmith. *American Journal of Psychiatry* 139:959–60.

Marmor, J. 1983. Systems thinking in psychiatry: Some theoretical and clinical applications. *American Journal of Psychiatry* 140:833–38.

Martin, H.P., D. Burgess, & L.S. Crnic. 1984. Mothers who work outside of the home and their children: A survey of health professionals' attitudes. *Journal American Academy of Child Psychiatry* 23:472–78.

Martin, R.R., R. Nagle, & K. Paget. 1983. Relationships between temperament and classroom behavior, teacher attitudes, and academic achievement. *Journal of Psychoeducation Assessment* 1:377–86.

Matas, L., R. Arend, & L. Sroufe. 1978. Continuity of adaptation in the second year: The relationship between quality of attachment and later competence. *Child Development* 49:-547–56.

McCall, R.B. 1977. Challenges to a science of developmental psychology. *Child Development* 48:333–44.

McClelland, D.C. 1973. Testing for competence rather than for "intelligence." *American Psychologist* 28:1–14.

Mead, M. 1962. A cultural anthropologist's approach to maternal deprivation. In *Deprivation of maternal care: A reassessment of its effects.* Public Health Papers no. 14. Geneva: World Health Organization.

Mehrabian, A. 1970. Measures of vocabulary and grammatical skills for children up to age six. *Developmental Psychology* 2:437–46.

Meltzoff, A.N. 1985. The roots of social and cognitive development: Models of man's original nature. In *Social perception in infants,* ed. T.M. Field & N.A. Fox. Norwood, N.J.: Ablex Publishing Corp.

Meltzoff, A.N., & M.K. Moore. 1983. Newborn infants imitate adult facial gestures. *Child Development* 54:702–9.

Miyake, K., S.J. Chen, & J. Campos. 1985. Infant temperament, mother's mode of interaction, and attachment in Japan: An interim report. In *Growing points of attachment theory and research,* ed. I. Bretherton & E. Waters. Monographs of the Society for Research in Child Development 50:1–2. Chicago: University of Chicago Press.

Money, J., & J. Dalery. 1976. Iatrogenic homosexuality. *Journal of Homosexuality* 1:357–71.

Moskowitz, B.A. 1978. The acquisition of language. *Scientific American* 23:92–108.

Murphy, L.B. 1981. Explorations in child psychology. In *Further explorations in personality,* ed. A.I. Rabin, J. Aronoff, A.M. Barclay, & R.A. Zucker. New York: Wiley.

Mussen, P.H., J.P. Conger, & J. Kagan. 1979. *Child development and personality,* 4th ed. New York: Harper & Row.

Myers, B.J. 1984. Mother-infant bonding. *Developmental Review* 4:240–74.

Nisbett, R.E., & A. Gordon. 1967. Self-esteem and susceptibility to social influence. *Journal of Personality and Social Psychology* 5:268–76.

Offer, D., & J. Offer. 1975. *From teenage to young manhood.* New York: Basic Books.

Offer, D., E. Ostrov, & K.I. Howard. 1987. Epidemiology of mental health and mental illness among adolescents. In *Basic handbook of child psychiatry,* vol. 5, ed. J. Call. New York: Basic Books.

Orlansky, H. 1949. Infant care and personality. *Psychological Bulletin* 46:1–48.

Orton, S.T. 1937. *Reading, writing and speech problems in childhood.* New York: Norton.

Parke, R.D. 1979. Perspectives on father-infant interaction. In *Handbook of infant development,* ed. J. Osofsky. New York: Wiley.

Pavenstedt, E. 1961. A study of immature mothers and their children. In *Prevention of mental disorders in children,* ed. G. Kaplan. New York: Basic Books.

Peterfreund, E. 1978. Some critical comments on psychoanalytic conceptualizations of childhood. *International Journal of Psychoanalysis* 59:427–41.

Piaget, J. 1952. *The origins of intelligence in children.* New York: Norton.

Piaget, J. 1954. *The construction of reality in the child.* New York: Basic Books.

Piaget, J. 1963. *The origins of intelligence in children.* New York: Norton.

Pinneau, S.R. 1961. *Changes in intelligence quotient from infancy to maturity.* Boston: Houghton Mifflin.

Previn, L.A. 1968. Performance and satisfaction as a function of individual-environment fit. *Psychological Bulletin* 69:56–68.

Provence, S. 1985. On the efficacy of early intervention programs. *Developmental and Behavioral Pediatrics* 6:363–66.

Pullis, M., & J. Cadwell. 1982. The influence of children's temperament characteristics on teachers' decision strategies. *American Educational Research Journal* 19:65–181.

Redican, H.B. 1976. Adult male–infant interaction in nonhuman primates. In *The role of the father in child development,* ed. M. Lamb. New York: Wiley.

Resnick, L.B. In press. Instruction and the cultivation of thinking. In *Learning and instruction,* ed. E. deCorte. Proceedings of the First European Conference for Research on Learning and Instruction, Leuven, Belgium, 1985.

Rheingold, H., & C. Eckerman. 1973. Fear of the stranger: A critical examination. In *Advances in child development and behavior,* vol. 8, ed. H. Reese. New York: Academic Press.

Ribble, M. 1943. *The rights of infants.* New York: Columbia University Press.

Richardson, S. 1976. The influence of severe malnutrition in infancy on the intelligence of children at school-age: An ecological perspective. In *Environment as therapy for brain dysfunction,* ed. R.N. Walsh & T.W. Greenough. New York: Plenum.

Rigg, M.G. 1940. The relative variability in intelligence of boys and girls. *Journal of Genetic Psychology* 56:211–14.

Robbins, D.R. 1985. Depressive symptoms and suicidal behavior in adolescents. *American Journal of Psychiatry* 142:588–92.

Robbins, L. 1963. The accuracy of parental recall of aspects of child development. *Journal of Abnormal and Social Psychology* 66:261–70.

Rosenthal, R., & L. Jacobson. 1969. *Pygmalion in the classroom.* New York: Holt, Rinehart and Winston.

Russell, G. 1978. The father role and its relationship to masculinity, femininity, and androgyny. *Child Development* 49:1174–81.

Rutter, M. 1966. *Children of sick parents: An environmental and psychiatric study.* Institute of Psychiatry Maudsley Monographs, no. 16. London: Oxford University Press.

Rutter, M. 1979. *Changing youth in a changing society.* London: Nuffield Provincial Hospitals Trust.

Rutter, M. 1980. School influences on children's behavior and development. *Pediatrics* 65:-208–20.

Rutter, M. 1981a. *Maternal deprivation reassessed,* 2d ed. New York: Penguin Books.

Rutter, M. 1981b. Stress, coping and development: Some issues and some questions. *Journal of Child Psychology and Psychiatry* 22:325–56.

Rutter, M., & S. Sandberg. 1985. Epidemiology of child psychiatric disorder: Methodological issues and some substantive findings. *Child Psychiatry and Human Development* 15:209–33.

Rutter, M., B. Maugham, P. Mortimer, & J. Ouston. 1979. *Fifteen thousand hours.* London: Open Books.

Sameroff, A.J. 1979. Learning in infancy: A developmental perspective. In *Handbook of infant development,* ed. J.D. Osofsky. New York: Wiley-Interscience.

Scarr, S. 1984. *Mother care/other care.* New York: Basic Books.

Schaffer, H.R. 1977. *Mothering.* Cambridge, Mass.: Harvard University Press.

Schaffer, H.R., & P.E. Emerson. 1964. *The development of social attachments in infancy.* Monographs Society for Research in Child Development 29:94. Chicago: University of Chicago Press.

Schlesinger, H., & K. Meadow. 1972. *Sound and sign: Childhood deafness and mental health.* Berkeley: University of California Press.

Scott, J.P. 1958. Critical periods in the development of social behavior in puppies. *Psychosomatic Medicine* 20:42–54.

Sears, R., E.E. Maccoby, & H. Levin. 1957. *Patterns of child rearing.* Evanston, Ill.: Row, Peterson.

Shapiro, T., & R. Perry. 1976. Latency revisited, the age of 7 plus or minus. *Psychoanalytic Study of the Child* 31:79–105.

Shaw, C.R. 1966. *The psychiatric disorders of childhood.* New York: Appleton-Century-Crofts.

Siegel, A.E. 1984. Working mothers and their children. *Journal American Academy of Child Psychiatry* 23:486–88.

Siegel, A.E., L.M. Stolz, E.A. Hitchcock, & J. Adamson. 1959. Dependence and independence in the children of working mothers. *Child Development* 30:533–46.

Sokoloff, B.Z. 1983. Adoption and foster care. In *Developmental-Behavioral Pediatrics,* ed. M.D. Levine, W.B. Carey, A.C. Crocker, & R.T. Gross. Philadelphia: Saunders.

Spock, B. 1957. *Baby and child care,* rev. ed. New York: Pocket Books.

Spock, B. 1967. *Baby and child care,* 2d ed. New York: Simon and Schuster.

Spock, B.J. 1976. *Baby and child care,* 3rd ed. New York: Pocket Books.

Sroufe, A. 1977. Wariness of strangers and the study of infant development. *Child Development* 48:731–46.

Steinman, S.B., S.E. Zemmelman, & T.M. Knoblauch. 1985. A study of parents who sought joint custody following divorce: Who reaches agreement and sustains joint custody and who returns to court. *Journal American Academy of Child Psychiatry* 24:554–62.

Stern, D. 1977. *The first relationship.* Cambridge, Mass.: Harvard University Press.

Stern, D.N. 1983. The early development of schemes of self, other, and "self with other." In *Reflections on self psychology,* ed. J.D. Lichtenberg & S. Kaplan. Hillsdale, N.J.: Lawrence Erlbaum Associates.

Stern, D.N. 1985. *The interpersonal world of the infant.* New York: Basic Books.

Sternberg, R. 1985. Human intelligence: The model is the message. *Science* 230:1111–17.

Stolz, L.M. 1960. Effects of maternal employment on children: Evidence from research. *Child Development* 31:749–82.

Svejda, M.J., B.J. Pannabecker, & R.N. Emde. 1982. Parent-to-infant attachment: A critique of the early "bonding" model. In *The development of attachment and affiliative systems,* ed. R.N. Emde & R.J. Harmon. New York: Plenum Press.

Terman, L.M., & M.A. Merrill. 1937. *Measuring intelligence: A guide to the administration of the new revised Stanford Binet tests of intelligence.* Boston: Houghton Mifflin.

Terr, L.C. 1983. Chowchilla revisited: The effects of psychic trauma four years after a school-bus kidnapping. *American Journal of Psychiatry* 140:1543–50.

Thomas, A., & S. Chess. 1957. An approach to the study of sources of individuality in child behavior. *Journal of Clinical Experimental Psychopathology and Quarterly Review of Psychiatry and Neurology* 18:347–56.

Thomas, A., & S. Chess. 1977. *Temperament and development.* New York: Brunner/Mazel.

Thomas, A., & S. Chess. 1980. *The dynamics of psychological development.* New York: Brunner/Mazel.

Thomas, A., S. Chess, & H.G. Birch. 1968. *Temperament and behavior disorders in children.* New York: New York University Press.

Thomas, A., H.G. Birch, S. Chess, & M.E. Hertzig. 1961. The developmental dynamics of primary reaction characteristics in children. *Proceedings Third World Congress of Psychiatry,* vol. 1. Toronto: University of Toronto Press.

Thomas, A., M.E. Hertzig, I. Dryman, & P. Fernandez. 1971. Examiner effect in IQ testing of Puerto Rican working-class children. *American Journal of Orthopsychiatry* 41:809–21.

Thomas, A., S. Chess, J. Sillen, & O. Mendez. 1974. Cross-cultural studies of behavior in children with special vulnerabilities to stress. *Life History in Psychopathology,* vol. 3, ed. D. Ricks, A. Thomas, & M. Roff. Minneapolis: University of Minnesota Press.

Tizard, B., & J. Rees. 1974. A comparison of the effects of adoption, restoration to the natural mother and continued institutionalization on the cognitive development of four-year-old children. *Child Development* 45:92–99.

Tizard, B., & J. Hodges. 1978. The effect of early institutional rearing on the development of eight-year-old children. *Journal of Child Psychology and Psychiatry* 19:99–118.

Torgersen, A.M., & E. Kringlen. 1978. Genetic aspects of temperamental differences in infants. *Journal American Academy of Child Psychiatry* 17:433–44.

U.S. Department of Labor. 1980. *Perspectives on working women: A datebook.* Washington, D.C.: U.S. Government Printing Office.

Vaillant, G.E. 1977. *Adaptation to life.* Boston: Little Brown.

Van Erdewegh, M.M., P.J. Clayton, & P. Van Erdewegh. 1985. The bereaved child. *British Journal of Psychiatry* 147:188–93.

Vygotsky, L.S. 1962. *Thought and language.* Cambridge, Mass.: Massachusetts Institute of Technology Press.

Vygotsky, L.S. 1978. *Mind in society.* Cambridge, Mass.: Harvard University Press.

Wallerstein, J. 1983. Separation, divorce and remarriage. In *Developmental-behavioral pediatrics,* ed. M.D. Levine, W.B. Carey, A.C. Crocker, & R.T. Gross. Philadelphia: Saunders.

Wallerstein, J.S. 1985. Children of divorce: Preliminary report of a ten-year follow-up of older children and adolescents. *Journal American Academy of Child Psychiatry* 24:545–53.

Wenar, C. 1963. The reliability of developmental histories. *Psychosomatic Medicine* 25:505–9.

Werner, E., & R.S. Smith. 1982. *Vulnerable but invincible.* New York: McGraw-Hill.

White, B.L. 1976. *The first three years of life.* Englewood Cliffs, N.J.: Prentice-Hall.

Wikler, N. 1981. Does sex make a difference? New York: N.O.W. Legal Defense and Education Fund.

Wilson, R.S., & A.P. Matheny, Jr. 1983. Assessment of temperament in infant twins. *Developmental Psychology* 19:172–83.

Winick, M., K.K. Meyer, & R.C. Harris. 1975. Malnutrition and environmental enrichment by early adoption. *Science* 1901:1173–75.

Witmer, H.L., & R. Kotinsky, eds. 1952. Personality in the making. In *Fact-finding report of mid-century White House conference on children and youth.* New York: Harper & Brothers.

Wohlwill, J.F. 1973. *The study of behavioral development.* New York: Academic Press.

Wolff, P.H. 1970. Critical periods in human cognitive development. *Hospital Practice* 11:77–87.

Wood, D., J.S. Bruner, & G. Ross. 1976. The role of tutoring in problem solving. *Journal of Child Psychology and Psychiatry* 17:89–100.

Young, K., & E. Zigler. 1986. Infant and toddler day care: Regulations and policy implications. *American Journal of Orthopsychiatry* 56:43–55.

Zappert, L.T., & H.N. Weinstein. 1985. Sex differences in the impact of work on physical and psychological health. *American Journal of Psychiatry* 142:1174–78.

Zigler, E. 1975. Letter to the editor, *New York Times Magazine,* 18 January 1975.

Zigler, E. 1985. Assessing Head Start at 20: An invited commentary. *American Journal of Orthopsychiatry* 55:603–609.

Zigler, E., & E. Butterfield. 1968. Motivational aspects of change in IQ test performance of culturally deprived nursery children. *Child Development* 39:1–14.

Zigler, E., & S. Muenchow. 1979. Mainstreaming: The proof is in the implementation. *American Psychologist* 34:993–96.

Zigler, E., & S. Muenchow. 1984. How to influence social policy affecting children and families. *American Psychologist* 59:415–20.

Index

Abortion, 230, 330

Abuse, see Child abuse; Sexual abuse

Academic achievement: father's role and, 322–23; IQ score and, 208, 274–75; motivation and, 208, 215; parental pressure for, 60, 70, 125; of working mothers' children, 345; see also Schools

Accommodation, 143

Activity level, 13, 33; in the classroom, 207, 209–10, 215–16; defined, 28; hyperactivity vs. normally high, 27–28, 81–82, 215–16; normal range of, 28; parental reaction to, 36; practical management of, 81–82; social factors and, 67

Adaptability: defined, 29; parental handling and, 236; practical management of, 84–85; school functioning and, 205–6, 209

Adolescence, 4–5, 9, 27; divorce and, 332; drug and alcohol use in, 231–32; fads and, 236, 255; generation gap myth and, 228–29; goodness of fit and, 65; guidelines for parents, 235–37; for handicapped children, 254–58; mental retardation and, 257–58; parents and, 228–29, 235–37, 303–4; sex and, 230–31, 300–301; society and, 234–35; suicidal behavior in, 233; transition to, 224–26; turmoil in, 226–28

Adoption, 283, 337–40; meetings between biological parents and adopted children, 338–39

Adversarial parent-child relationship, 78–79, 87, 90

Affects, see Emotions

Aggression: sex differences in, 180, 184; sibling rivalry and, 308

Ainsworth, Mary, 285–86

Ainsworth Strange Situation, 285–86

Alcohol use: by adolescents, 231–32; subcultures and, 69; suicidal behavior and, 233

Allowance, 317

American Academy of Pediatrics, 346, 350, 361

American Psychiatric Association, 192

American Psychological Association, 360

Ames, Louise, 375

Amphetamines, 216, 231

Anal instincts, 165–66, 169, 218

Anomia, 58

Anthropological model of intelligence, 141

Anxiety, 33, 79; fantasies and, 299–300; in mother in prenatal period, 25; in two-year-olds, 164–65

Appeasement of child, 64, 78, 89

Approach or withdrawal: defined, 28; practical management of, 83–84; school functioning and, 209–10

Arousal, 104n

Assertiveness, 180

Assimilation (Piaget), 143

Asthma, 9

Attachment studies, 283–88, 320–21

Attention deficit disorder, 216

Attention span, see Distractibility; Persistence and attention span

Authoritarian parents, 40–42, 91

Authoritative parents, 40–41

Autism, 3–4, 55, 98–99, 158, 251; "blame the mother" ideology and, 8; family stress and, 245, 252–53; sense of self and, 161–62; variability of behavior lost in, 134

Automobile rides, 81

Autonomous ego, 133

Babbling, 108; sense of self and, 159

Babies, see Infants; Newborns

Baby and Child Care (Spock), 349

Baby talk, 297, 308

Balter, Lawrence, 351

Bank, Stephen, 313, 315

Baths, 108–9

Baumrind, Diana, 41

Bedtime, 75, 317; see also Sleep schedules

Behavioral style, see Temperament

Behavior disorders, 5, 19, 66, 218; in adolescents, 192, 225; age of onset of, 221–22; boys more susceptible to, 183; causes of,

Behavior disorders *(continued)*
219; homosexual adolescents and, 192; middle childhood and, 219–20; parental style and, 40; poorness of fit and, 90; school problems and, 215–16; sexual inhibition and, 230; social factors and, 67; therapeutic intervention for, 116
Behaviorism, 55; emotions not studied in, 148; influence and limitations of, 10; origin of, 9–10
Belsky, Jay, 360
Benson, Frank, 359
Berlin, Irving, 222
Binet, Alfred, 259–61, 263, 269
Biological factors: homosexuality and, 190–91; learning and, 197–98; psychiatric problems and, 368; sex differences and, 183–84; temperament and, 24–25
Biological model of intelligence, 141
Biopsychosocial theory, 56
Birch, Herbert, 26–27
Birns, Beverly, 185
"Blame the mother" ideology, 6–9, 287; alternatives to, 11–15; parental insecurity and, 49; psychoanalytic and behaviorist influences on, 10–11, 97
Blind children, 243, 245–47, 251, 253; adolescent, 255; learning in, 134–36
Bloom, Benjamin, 122–23
Bonding, 96, 112–14
Bottle-fed infants, 169; *see also* Weaning
Bowlby, John, 98–99, 157, 280–83, 231, 343, 348–49
Boys, 90–91; *see also* Sex differences
Brain, 95; flexibility and plasticity of, 243, 282; intelligence and, 259–60; language acquisition and, 297–98; learning problems and, 7; object constancy and, 120; *see also* Brain damage
Brain damage: flexibility destroyed by, 136; school problems and, 215–16; sense of self and, 161–62; temperament and, 25; unrecognized, 90
Brazelton, T. Berry, 34, 104, 342, 350, 352–53
Brazelton Neonatal Behavioral Assessment Scale, 104
Breast-feeding, 167; mother-infant interaction during, 106; parental style and, 45–47; sibling rivalry and, 310; *see also* Weaning
Bretherton, Inge, 285
Brigham, C. C., 264–65
Broca, Paul, 259–60
Bronfenbrenner, Urie, 288
Bronowski, Jacob, 365, 374
Brooks, Jeanne, 161
Brothers; *see* Siblings
Bruch, Hilde, 12
Bruner, Jerome, 99–100, 133–34, 143, 243–44, 292; on social context of learning, 127–30
Buck, Carrie, 263–64

Burgess, David, 352
Burt, Cyril, 272–74
Buss, A. H., 25
Butterfield, Earl, 268–69

Carey, William, 34, 85
Carpenter, Genevieve, 102
Catastrophic events, 220–21
Cattell, Raymond, 23
Center for Cognitive Studies, 128
Cerebral palsy, 243, 245, 251, 255
Chamberlain, Richard, 42
Child abuse, 78–79, 349; in child care centers, 362; consequences of, 52; custody issues and, 335; *see also* Sexual abuse
Child care centers, 349, 362; *see also* Substitute child care
Child care support, 357
Childhood schizophrenia, 55, 58
Children's Emotions and Moods (Lewis & Michalson), 149
Child tyrants, 49, 64, 77, 176; abuse of, 79
Chomsky, Noam, 118, 298
Chores, 316, 324
Chowchilla school-bus kidnapping, 220–21
Chukchee people of Siberia, 190
Clarke, Alan, 273
Clarke, Ann, 273
Clinging, 98, 308, 332
Clothing: sensory threshold and, 86; style of, 77, 236, 255, 317
Clowning behavior, 58, 64
Cocaine, 231–32
Cognitive development: emotions and, 137–39, 148; father's role and, 323; goodness of fit and, 61; individual differences in, 143–44; metacognition and, 145–46; and nature of intelligence, 139–41; parental practices and, 152–53; Piaget's model of, 121, 142–43; pressure to speed, 152; school experience and, 205; stimulation of, 120, 210–11; *see also* Learning
Coleman, James, 200–204
Coleman, John, 228
Communal family living, 44
Computational model of intelligence, 140–41
Concrete operations (Piaget), 142, 219
Conditioned reflexes, 10, 55; and adaptive value of stimuli, 126; learning demonstrated by, 101
Condon, William, 103
Condry, John, 185
Condry, Sandra, 185
Congenital heart disease, 245
Congenital rubella, 26, 243, 246, 248, 250, 255–56
Constitutionalist views, 11, 13, 96
Coolidge, Calvin, 265

Courtesy, standards of, 73–75
Crack, 231
Crawford, Peggy, 252
Crawling, 23
Criminal behavior, 184*n*
Critical period hypothesis, 122
Criticisms of child, 176
Crnic, Linda, 352
Crying, 98; as communication, 103, 110–11
Cultural factors: Ainsworth Strange Situation test and, 287; child care practices and, 349; handling of babies and, 110; intelligence and, 141; learning process and, 118, 129; middle childhood and, 221–23; and norms of behavior, speech, and values, 134; temperament and, 25
Cup-fed infants, 167–68
Custody issues, 44, 333–37

Dalery, Jean, 192
Darwin, Charles, 259*n*
Davis, Richard, 168
Day care centers, 350, 359–63; *see also* Substitute child care
Deaf children, 245–46, 248, 251, 253, 255–57; communication skills taught to, 242–43
Death of a family member, 220, 235, 329–30; individual adaptation to, 370
Defense mechanisms, 64–65
DeJong, Allan, 300
Denial, 246–48
Depression, 55; in adolescents, 233; biological factors and, 368
Depressive drugs, 231–32
Derdeyn, Andre, 334
Deutsch, Helene, 179
Deutsch, Martin, 212, 271–72
Developmental aphasia, 297
Developmental dysphasia, 58–59
DeVries, Marten, 67–68
Diabetic children, 251
Diet, 77
Difficult child, 32–33
Disadvantaged children: corrective change possible for, 135–36; IQ tests and, 268–69, 275; language acquisition in, 298; Montessori and, 199–200; schools and, 197, 199, 210, 369–70; *see also* Enrichment programs
Discipline: of adolescents, 236–37; father's role and, 324; parental style and, 40–41; in schools, 203–4
Discrepancy principle, 130–31
Distractibility: defined, 30–31; low persistence combined with, 88; normal range of, 30–31; parental reaction to, 36; practical management of, 33, 87–88; school functioning and, 207–10
Diversity, value of, 367

Divorce, 44; effects of, 331–33; father absence due to, 323; grandparents' role and, 327; individual adaptation to, 370; middle childhood and, 220; sibling bonds and, 313–14; standard of living and, 357
Divorce settlements, 357
Dostoevsky, Feodor, 313
Double bind, 8
Dream interpretation, 9
Dress, *see* Clothing
Drotar, Denis, 252
Drug abuse, 335; by adolescents, 231–32; subcultures and, 69
Dubos, René, 62
Dunn, Judith, 42–43, 150, 159, 164, 288, 307–16
Dyslexia, 183

Early intervention programs, 214–15; *see also* Enrichment programs; Head Start program
Easy child, 32–33
Education, *see* Schools
Educational toys, 119, 125, 210, 268
Ego, 97, 165
Egocentricity, 157–58, 165
Eisenberg, Leon, 343
Elementary schools, 200–204
Emde, Robert, 134
Emerson, P. E., 321
Emotional distancing, 52
Emotions: in adolescence, 226–28; "blame the mother" ideology and, 6–9; cognition and, 137–39, 148; definitions of, 148–50; development of, over life-span, 150–51; ignored by Piaget, 143; individual differences in, 151–52; and the overinterpretive parent, 49–50; parental practices and, 152–53; significance of, 147–48; *see also* Quality of mood
Empathy, 152; defined, 311; development of, 164–65; early onset of, 150; in siblings, 311–14
Empty nest phenomenon, 356
Energy level, 13, 30; *see also* Activity level; Intensity of reactions
Enrichment programs, 123–24, 135, 271; impact of, 212–16
Erikson, Erik, 157–58, 166, 170–71, 219; on adolescence, 227–28; on latency period concept, 223; on weaning and toilet training, 167
Erikson, Kai, 221
Etaugh, Claire, 350–51, 360
Ethologists, 121–22
Eugenics movement, 269–70
Evolution, 259*n*; learning and, 131, 133; neonatal capacities and, 105
Experimental situations, 163

Extended family, 44, 327; *see also* Grandparents

Factor analysis, 139–40
Family, *see* Grandparents; Parents; Siblings
Family therapists, 313
Fantasies, 143, 165; fears expressed in, 299–300; as normal aspect of development, 299; in older children, 170; sexual, 300
Fantz, Robert, 101–2
Father absence, 323, 329
Fathers: "blame the mother" ideology and, 8; infant attachment to, 283; infant interaction with, 107–8; maternal employment and, 358–59; maternal love mystique and, 281; parenting styles of, 43, 47; role of, 110, 320–26, 349; sibling rivalry and, 308–10, 316–18; women's movement and, 352
Fears, 170, 299–300; *see also* Anxiety
Feeding practices, 12
Feeding problems, 308
Fernandez, Paulina, 267
Field, Tiffany, 102
Fifteen Thousand Hours (Rutter), 202
Fighting: between parents, 41, 323, 325–26, 333, 334, 336; between siblings, 317
Finger-nail biting, 42
Fischer, Kurt, 144
Fit and misfit, 61; *see also* Goodness of fit
Flavell, John, 145
Flirtation, 300
Food idiosyncrasies, 77
Formal operations (Piaget), 143
Frames of Mind (Gardner), 140
Free association, 9
Freud, Anna, 157–58
Freud, Sigmund, 97, 133, 158, 167, 180, 184, 283; "blame the mother" ideology and influence of, 9–11; developmental theory of, 166; latency concept of, 224; on mother-child relationship, 280, 342; sexism of, 178–79, 181–82

Galambos, Nancy, 346–47, 351
Games, 119–21, 132; IQ performance and, 268; with sexual overtones, 224, 300
Gardner, Howard, 139–40, 147, 277
Gaze of infant, 110
Gender differences, *see* Sex differences
Gender identity, 189–93
Generation gap myth, 224, 228–29, 303
Genetic factors: and acquisition of culture, 118; *homunculus* concept and, 96; IQ scores and, 270–74; temperament and, 24–25
Genital stage, 166, 218

Geographic model of intelligence, 139–40
Gerson, Kathleen, 355–58, 363
Gesell, Arnold, 100, 260
Gilligan, Carol, 186–88
Girls, *see* Sex differences
Goldberg, Susan, 113
Goldfarb, William, 280, 282, 321, 342–43
Goodenough, Florence, 271
Goodenough-Draw-a-Person Test, 271
Goodness of fit: achieving, 90–91; and changes over time, 65–66; children's protests and, 75–76; concept of, 53, 56–60; formulations of, 60–62; implications of, 62–64; individual development and, 366, 374; other attributes and, 69–70; parental standards and, 68–69, 73–75; quality of life and, 71–73; schools and, 205–8; self-esteem and, 170–71; situational requirements and, 76–77; social context and, 67–68; with various temperaments, 79–89; *see also* Poorness of fit
Gordon, Edmund, 138, 370
Gould, Stephen Jay, 259n, 265, 274, 276, 370
Graham, Philip, 226
Grandparents, 44, 319; maternal employment and, 360; role of, 327–28; sibling rivalry and, 308
Grasp reflex, 97
Greenspan, Stanley, 115
Grown son or daughter, overattached to parent, 304
Guilford, J. Paul, 23
Guilt: cognitive development and, 151; handicapped children and, 244, 250–51, 253; maternal employment and, 342, 353; parental anger and, 289–91; over poorness of fit, 78–79; and suicidal behavior in adolescents, 233

Hairstyles, adolescent, 236, 255
Hall, G. Stanley, 266
Handicapped children, 13, 20, 199–200; adolescent, 254–58; competence and control for, 253–54; denial and overprotection of, 246–48; individual adaptation in, 370; learning in, 134–36; mainstreaming, 249–50; normal development and, 242–45; siblings of, 251–53; and stress on family, 245; support groups for parents of, 250–51
Hand-me-downs, 317
Hands, gazing at and moving, 159
Hardy, Thomas, 117, 121
Harlow, Henry, 320–21
Harvard Grant study, 42
Hay, Dale, 283–84
Head Start program, 199–200, 212–13, 271–72

Health, 62
Hearing, 107–8
Hearnshaw, Leslie, 273–74
Height, 183
Heredity, *see* Genetic factors
Heroin, 231
Herr'nstein, Richard, 184*n*
Heterosexual relationship, modeled by parents, 323
Hetherington, Mavis, 331–33, 335
High schools, 200–204
Hinde, Robert, 122
Holmes, Oliver Wendell, 264
Homosexuality, 189–93
Homunculus, 9, 34–35, 96–97, 99, 105, 365
Horney, Karen, 180
Hospital practices, 112–13
Hunt, J. McVicker, 61
Hyperactivity: boys more susceptible to, 183; normal high activity level vs., 27–28, 81–82, 215–16

Id, 97–98, 165
Imitation, 126; learning and, 129; in newborns, 100–101, 103–4
Immigration Restriction Act of 1924, 264
Imprinting, 122
Impulsive behavior, 83, 330
Incest, 220
Individuality in development, 365–67
Infant bonding, 96, 112–14
Infant psychiatry, 114–16
Infants, 25, 28, 218; attachment in, 283–88; demands of, as expressed needs, 80; early interactions of, 105–7; in institutions, 280, 282–83, 343; intelligence tests devised for, 260–61; learning in, 118–24, 126–31, 291; plasticity of, 109–10; self-awareness in, 156–66; social-cognitive development in, 105–12, 132–33; task mastery in, 132–33; toys for, 118–20; *see also* Newborns
Infants and Mothers (Brazelton), 34, 60
In Search of Mind (Bruner), 243
Insecure parents, 46–49, 53
Instinctual drive, 55, 97, 99, 132, 148, 157, 166–67, 169, 218
Institutional care, 245, 253, 258; infant development under, 280, 282–83, 343
Intelligence, 139–41, 261; criminal behavior and, 184*n*; sex differences not found in, 181; teacher misjudgment of, 205–7; *see also* Cognitive development; IQ scores; IQ tests
Intelligence tests, *see* IQ scores; IQ tests
Intensity of reactions, 13; normal range of, 30; practical management of, 86; school functioning and, 209–10
Interactionism, 55–56

Interpersonal World of the Infant, The, (Stern), 159
Intimidated parents, 49, 53
Intrauterine environment, 25
IQ scores: genetic factors and, 270–74; pressure to increase, 125, 153, 210–11; school achievement and, 208, 274–75; stability of, 122–23, 269–70; of working mothers' children, 345; *see also* IQ tests
IQ tests, 18–19, 144; alternatives to, 275–77; development of, 259–61; social implications of, 263–65, 275; uses and limitations of, 261–63; value of, 274–75; weaknesses of, 128, 266–69; *see also* IQ scores
Israeli kibbutzim, 287, 348

Jacklin, Carol, 180–81, 183–84
Jackson, Edith, 12
James, William, 101
Japanese school system, 222–23
Jealousy: parental, 304; sibling, 305–10, 316–18
Jencks, Christopher, 201–2, 204
Jensen, Arthur, 271–73
Jersild, Arthur, 224
Johnson administration, 212
Joint custody, 44, 333–37

Kagan, Jerome, 126, 143, 152, 156, 285–86, 361; discrepancy principle of, 130–31; on emotional development, 150–51; on parent-infant bond, 343; on role-modeling, 294; on self-awareness in infants, 163–66
Kahn, Michael, 313, 315
Kamin, Leon, 273
Kant, Immanuel, 137
Kardiner, Abram, 342
Kaye, Kenneth, 295–96
Kendrick, Carol, 150, 164, 288, 307–16
Kennell, John, 112
Keogh, Barbara, 209
Kibbutzim, 287, 348
Kindergarten, 199, 217
Kinsey Institute, 190–91
Klaus, Marshall, 112–14
Kohlberg, Lawrence, 186–88
Kohut, Heinz, 157–58, 165
Kolb, Lawrence, 160, 228
Kornhaber, Arthur, 327
Kringlen, E., 25

Lamb, Michael, 287, 322–23
Language acquisition: brain and, 297–98; cognitive development and, 142; in deaf

Language acquisition *(continued)*
  children, 242–43; efforts to speed, 298;
  learning process and, 118, 127, 143; parental role and, 296–98; school problems and,
  215–16; sense of self and, 160; sequential
  development in, 158–59; sex differences
  in, 182–83; *see also* Talking
Language disabilities, 7
Late bloomers, 177
Latency period concept, 223–24
Learning: biological endowment for, 197–98;
  enrichment programs and, 123–24; in infants and children, 118–24, 126–31, 291;
  language acquisition and, 118, 127, 143;
  motivation for, 152–53; in newborns,
  101–3, 117–18, 126, 130, 137; and parents
  as teachers, 291–301; and plasticity in
  human development, 134–36; prenatal,
  137; pressure for success in, 125; process
  of, 126–31; reasons for, 131–33; for social
  competence, 132–33; social context of,
  128–30; for task mastery, 132–33; *see also*
  Cognitive development
Learning disability, 215–16, 279; unrecog-
  nized, 90
Lerner, Jacqueline, 62, 346–47, 351
Levy, David, 305–6
Lewis, Michael, 149–51, 161
Lidz, Theodore, 219
Life events, 13, 97; intelligence and, 143;
  middle childhood and, 220–21; perception
  and, 129; self-esteem and, 177; tempera-
  ment and, 33, 54–55
Life expectancy, 183
Life-span perspective, 56, 141
Life style, 71–72, 236; parental approaches
  and, 42
Locke, John, 96
Longitudinal studies, 16–17
Lorenz, Konrad, 122
Loud horseplay, 73
Lourie, Reginald, 115
Love, 336; adoption and, 339–40; maternal,
  279–81, 283–84; between siblings, 312–14;
  see also Attachment studies; Tender loving
  care (TLC)
LSD, 231–32

McCall, Robert, 122, 288
McClelland, David, 276–77
Maccoby, Eleanor, 180–81, 183–84
Mahler, Margaret, 98–99, 157–59
Mainstreaming, 249–50
Manic-depressive illness, 138
Manners, 73–75
Marijuana, 231–32
Marmor, Judd, 180, 184, 189–92

Martin, Harold, 352
Martin, Roy, 209
Masai infants, 67–68
Masturbation, 224, 230, 300
Match and mismatch, 60; *see also* Goodness of
  fit; Poorness of fit
Maternal Care and Mental Health (Bowlby), 280,
  343
Maternal deprivation, 281–83, 321
Maternal Deprivation Reassessed (Rutter), 281,
  321, 348
Maternal employment: changing attitudes
  toward, 349–55; custody issues and, 334;
  hard choices necessitated by, 355–58; in-
  fant attachment and, 284; and multiple
  caregiver effects, 348–49; parental styles
  and, 44, 46; recommended reading on, 364;
  research findings on, 345–48; sex role
  differentiation as influenced by, 321–22;
  social factors and, 343–44, 356–57; substitute child care and, 345–46, 359–63; traditional view of, 341–43
Maternal-Infant Bonding (Klaus & Kennell), 112
Maternity leave, 359
Mathematical ability, 180, 183–84
Mead, Margaret, 320, 349
Meadow, Kathryn, 242
Measuring Intelligence (Terman & Merrill), 270
Medication, 290; for hyperactivity, 216
Meltzoff, Andrew, 103–4
Memory for locations, 165
Mental age, 260
Mental health professionals, 5, 90, 136;
  "blame the mother" ideology and, 8; concept of temperament and, 35; Deutsch's
  influence on, 179; Freud's influence on, 9–
  10; joint custody and, 335; learning problems and, 215; maternal employment as
  viewed by, 342, 355; maternal love seen as
  panacea by, 279–81; sibling rivalry emphasized by, 309, 313
Mental illness, 55, 58, 368; in adolescents,
  225; adoption and, 338; boys more susceptible to, 183; child abuse and, 349;
  middle childhood and, 220; parental style
  not predictive of, in children, 42; in
  parents, 41, 52–53, 176, 290, 349; school
  problems and, 215–16; sense of self and,
  161–62; unrecognized, 279; variability of
  behavior lost in, 134; *see also individual disorders*
Mental retardation, 26, 199, 246, 251, 253;
  developmental course in, 257–58; low activity level mistaken for, 82; professional
  help in, 116; sense of self and, 161–62
Metacognition, 145–46, 153, 211, 277
Michalson, Linda, 149–51
Mid-Century White House Conference on
  Children and Youth, 14

Middle childhood, 28; cross-cultural variations in, 221–23; goodness of fit and, 65; latency period concept of, 223–24; social context and, 217, 221; special interests and talents in, 235; stability and development in, 219–21; transition to, 218
Miller, George, 128
Mismeasure of Man, The (Gould), 259n
Modeling: adult behavior, 129; thinking processes, 146; *see also* Role models
Money, John, 192
Montessori, Maria, 199–200, 212
Mood, 28–29; *see also* Quality of mood
Moral judgment, 179, 323; sex differences in approach to, 186–88
Mother Care/Other Care (Scarr), 292
Mothers: developmental research emphasis on, 319, 321; father absence and, 323; father's role and, 320–26; infant attachment to, 283–88; infant psychiatry movement and, 115–16; infants' early interaction with, 104–7; rejecting, 42; sibling relationship and, 306, 309, 312, 315–18; and TLC as panacea, 281–83, 290; *see also* "Blame the mother" ideology; Maternal employment; Parents
Motivation, 23–24; IQ score and, 275; learning and, 152–53; school achievement and, 208, 215
Moving, 235
Multiple caregivers, 283, 348–49
Multiple regression analysis, 308
Murphy, Lois, 61
Mussolini, Benito, 199
Myers, Barbara, 113

Nail biting, 42
Name, parents called by, 302–3
Naming objects, 58
Naps, 82; *see also* Sleep schedules
Narcissism, 98, 158, 165
National Academy of Science, 345
National Institute of Mental Health, 115
National Technical Institute for the Deaf, 257
Nature of the Child, The (Kagan), 150
Newborns, 3–4, 25; behavioral integration in, 104; bonding concept and, 112–14; current knowledge of, 100–104; earlier views of, 96–100; as humans, 95–96; imitation in, 100–101, 103–4; learning in, 101–3, 117–18, 126, 130, 137; mothers' and siblings' responses to, 312; sense of self in, 158–62
New experiences, reaction to, *see* Adaptability; Approach or withdrawal
New York Longitudinal Study (NYLS): evaluating temperament for, 26; latest findings

of, 368–70; research methodology for, 18–20; *see also* Temperament
New York Task Force on Women in the Courts, 357
Nixon, Richard, 362
Normal autism, 3–4, 98, 157
Normality, 27–28, 242–45
Nursery schools, 57, 125, 217, 222; characteristics and value of, 198–200
Nursing, *see* Breast-feeding

Object constancy, 120, 157
Oedipus complex, 157–58, 165; adolescence and, 227; middle childhood and, 218
Offer, Daniel, 225–29
Offer, Judith, 227–29
Omnipotence, 158
Oral instincts, 132, 165–66, 168–69, 218
Organic brain disorder, 55, 134, 226
Orlansky, Harold, 11–12
Orton, Samuel, 7
Overachievers, 208
Overinterpretive parents, 49–50, 53
Overprotective parents, 246–48, 302

Pacifier, 17, 100
Parental conflict, 41, 323, 325–26, 333; joint custody and, 334, 336
Parental leave, 359
Parental styles: categories of, 43–53; child outcomes and, 53; insecure, 46–49; intimidated, 49; overinterpretive, 49–50; pathological, 52–53; research into, 41–43; secure, 44–46; temperament and, 39, 43, 53; victimized, 50–52
Parentectomy, 9
Parent guidance, 90–91, 185
Parents: adolescents and, 228–29; 235–37, 303–4; adoptive, 337–40; called by first name, 302–3; and cognitive and emotional patterns of children, 152–53; formal instruction from, 292–94; as friends, 301–4; grown children overattached to, 304; guidelines for, 37–38; of handicapped children, 245–48, 250–51; of homosexual sons or daughters, 189–93; mentally disturbed, 41, 52–53, 176, 290, 349; as role models, 294–95, 323, 356; and self-esteem in children, 175–77; sex differences and, 185–86; and sexual activities of adolescents, 230–31, 301; sexual stereotypes and, 193–95; sibling relationships and, 316–18; single, 44, 329–31, 338; as teachers, 291–301; and the unknowns of human development, 370–75; values of, 68–69; *see also* Divorce;

Parents *(continued)*
   Fathers; Goodness of fit; Mothers; Parental styles; Poorness of fit
Parke, Ross, 320
Path analysis, 190–91, 347
Pavlov, Ivan, 9–10, 14, 97
Peek-a-boo, 119–20
Penis envy, 179–80, 182
Perceptual problems, 262
Permissive parents, 40–41, 222
Persistence and attention span, 33, 172–74; defined, 31; normal range of, 31; parental reaction to, 37; practical management of, 88–89; school functioning and, 207–10
Personality: formation of, 35; psychoanalytic view of, 167; temperament and, 34–36
Pervasive developmental disorder, 252; *see also* Autism
Peterfreund, Emanuel, 99, 158
Phenylketonuria (PKU), 275
Phobias, 10
Physical abuse, *see* Child abuse
Piaget, Jean, 97, 121, 127–28, 135, 141–44, 147, 157, 186, 219, 311
Play, 148; cognitive development and, 129, 132–33; father's role and, 324; learning and, 119–20; mother-child interaction during, 106; in nursery school, 198; between siblings, 312; social competence and task mastery practiced in, 132; symbolic, 165; *see also* Games
Playing doctor, 224, 299–300
Playing house, 299–300
Plomin, Robert, 25, 42–43
Political model of intelligence, 141
Poorness of fit, 219; adolescence and, 229; adversarial parent-child relationship due to, 79–80; defense mechanisms and, 64–65; developmental course and, 366, 368; father's role and, 325; *see also* Goodness of fit
Poverty, 213, 221; child care needs and, 362; IQ tests and, 264; *see also* Disadvantaged children
Praise, 175–77
Pregnancy concerns, 230
Premature infants, 245, 359
Preoperational representation (Piaget), 142
Preschool programs, *see* Enrichment programs; Nursery schools
Previn, Lawrence, 61–62
Problem of the match, 61; *see also* Goodness of fit; Poorness of fit
Protests, children's, 75–76, 78
Provence, Sally, 214
Psychiatric disorders, *see* Mental illness
Psychoanalytic theory: adolescence in, 227; "blame the mother" ideology and, 9–11; and definitions of emotions, 148; development in second year in, 165; development

of self in, 157–58; emotional development of infants emphasized in, 121; infant behavior in, 97–98, 132; middle childhood in, 218; mother's breast emphasized by, 310; newborns in, 97–98; sexism and, 180; temperament concept and, 55; weaning and toilet training in, 166–70
Psychology of Sex Differences, The (Maccoby & Jacklin), 180
Psychotherapy, 5, 66, 69, 91, 279; learning problems and, 215; mistakenly urged on mothers, 6–7
Puberty, 183; *see also* Adolescence
Public Law 94-142, The Education for All Handicapped Children Act, 249–50
Puerto Rican families study, 20, 26, 67, 221–22
Punishment, 76, 89, 237; in schools, 203

Quality of life, 71–73
Quality of mood: defined, 30; normal range of, 30; practical management of, 86; school functioning and, 209–10
Quarrels, *see* Fighting

Racism, 69, 271–72, 295; justified by scientists, 259*n*, 264–65; self-esteem and, 177
Radical egocentrism, 97
Rape, 233
Reading, 7, 197, 294; attempts to accelerate, 292–93, 298; parental pressure and, 125; readiness for, 211
Reagan administration, 362
Reflexes, 97–99
"Refrigerator parents," 8
Regression: divorce and, 332; sibling rivalry and, 306, 309
Remarriage, 327, 331–33, 337
Repression, 167
Research methodology, 15–17
Resnick, Lauren, 145, 152–53
Restlessness, 215–16; *see also* Activity level
Rhythmicity (regularity), 13; defined, 28; normal range of, 28; practical management of, 82–83
Ribble, Margaret, 167
Richardson, Stephen, 123
Ritalin, 216
Role models: aggressive, for boys, 184; for heterosexual relationships, 323; maternal employment and, 356; parents as, 294–95, 323, 356
Rousseau, Jean Jacques, 96
Rubella virus (German measles), 20, 26, 134, 246, 248, 250, 255–56

Rutter, Michael, 201, 203–4, 220, 226, 228–29, 281, 283, 286, 321, 330, 333, 348

Safety, 75–76; for adolescents, 236–37; for distractible infants, 87; for handicapped children, 243, 246, 251; for high-activity babies, 81; middle childhood and, 218; overconcern for, 302; school and, 222
Sander, Louis, 103
Scarr, Sandra, 292–93, 345, 348
Schaffer, Rudolph, 99
Schema, 130
Schematic prototype, 130
Schizophrenia, 8, 55, 290
Schizophrenogenic mother, 8
Schlesinger, Hilde, 242
School phobia, 222–23
School problems, 215–16, 220
Schools: elementary and high schools, 200–204; goodness of fit and, 205–8; handicapped children and, 249–50; IQ scores and, 263, 266; learning process and, 129; metacognition and, 146; middle childhood and, 217; social factors and, 196–98, 200, 215, 369–70; temperament and, 205–10; *see also* Academic achievement; Nursery schools; Teachers
Scott, Elizabeth, 334
Second child, birth of, 305–10
Secure parents, 44–46
Select Committee on Children, Youth and Families, 322
Self-awareness, 286, 289; in middle childhood, 219; origins of, 156–62; in the second year, 163–66
Self-descriptive utterances, 164–65
Self-esteem: development of, 154–55, 166–71; evaluation of, 172–75; in handicapped children, 253–54; importance of, 155–56; language acquisition and, 298; and origins of the self, 156–62; parental influence on, 175–77, 295; school experience and, 205; sex differences not found in, 181
Self-strangulation, 233
Sense of self, *see* Self-awareness
Sensorimotor intelligence, 135, 142
Sensory threshold, 33; defined, 29–30; practical management of, 85–86
Separation of parents, 331–33
Separation anxiety, 120
Separation-individuation, 157
"Sesame Street," 125, 200, 210
Sex differences: in adolescent mental disturbances, 225–26; in adolescent suicidal behavior, 233; biological factors and, 183–84; challenges to traditional views of, 180–82; in moral judgment, 186–88; in sibling

rivalry behaviors, 309; stereotypes about, 189, 193–95; traditional views of, 178–79
Sex education, 300–301
Sexism, 69, 178, 182, 295; justified by scientists, 259*n;* maternal employment and, 352, 355, 357; self-esteem and, 177
Sex role differentiation, 294; stereotyped, 320–21; *see also* Sexism
Sexual abuse, 290, 362; children's reports of, 300; consequences of, 52, 233
Sexual behavior in children: in adolescence, 230–31, 234; homosexual, 189–93; in middle childhood, 223–24; normal range of, 300
Shakespeare, William, 313
Shirley, Mary, 100
Shrive, Anita, 351
Shyness, 33, 50; stress and, 63–64
Sibling Bond, The (Bank & Kahn), 313
Sibling rivalry, 305–10; guidelines for handling, 316–18
Siblings: adult, 313; bond between, 312–14; defined, 305; divorce and, 313–14; of handicapped children, 251–53; implications of research on, 314–15; infant language acquisition and, 296; quarrels between, 317; relationship between, 310–14; rivalry between, 305–10, 316–18; self-esteem in, 176
Siegel, Alberta, 345
Sign language, 242–43, 248, 256
Silvern, Louise, 144
Simon, Theodore, 260
Single parents, 44, 329–31, 338
Sisters, *see* Siblings
Sleep disturbances, 79; in adolescents, 233; sibling rivalry and, 308
Sleep schedules, 75, 84, 317; emotions and, 151–52; goodness of fit and, 72; school and, 222; sensory threshold and, 85; *see also* Rhythmicity (regularity); Sleep disturbances
Slow-to-warm-up child, 32–33; intelligence undervalued in, 205–6
Smiling: sense of self and, 159; as social communication, 103; with task mastery, 164–65
Social competence, 57, 74; attachment to parents and, 284; cognitive development and, 95–116; father's role and, 323; language acquisition and, 297; learning for, 132–33; middle childhood and, 218–19; in school, 205; in working mothers' children, 345
Social factors: adolescence and, 234–35; drug use and, 232; family resources and, 369–70; goodness of fit and, 67–68; homosexuality and, 190; IQ testing and, 263–65, 275; learning and, 127–30; maternal employ-

Social factors *(continued)*
  ment and, 343–44, 356–57; middle childhood and, 217, 221; and norms of behavior, speech, and values, 134; parental values and, 68–69; schools and, 196–98, 200,
  215, 369–70; self-esteem and, 177; temper-
  ament and, 25; *see also* Disadvantaged chil-
  dren; Poverty
Socialization, 98
Sociological model of intelligence, 141
Sokoloff, Burton, 337, 339
Solitary activity, 235
Speaking, *see* Language acquisition; Talking
Special interests and talents, 13, 54, 66, 143,
  331; IQ scores and, 275; middle childhood
  and, 235–36
Special needs, *see* Handicapped children
Spinoza, Baruch, 137
Spock, Benjamin, 17, 342, 349
Spontaneity, 106, 111–12, 116, 289, 294
Sroufe, Alan, 285–86
Standards, appearance of, 163–65
Stanford-Binet Intelligence Test, 260, 264
Steinman, Susan, 334–35
Stepparents, 331–33, 337
Sterilization, 263–64
Stern, Daniel, 105–6, 116, 159–60, 161*n*, 162,
  165
Sternberg, Robert, 138–41, 143
Stimulants, 231–32
Stolz, Lois, 345
Stranger wariness, 50, 130; mother-child at-
  tachment and, 25
Stress: constructive functions of, 63–64, 314–
  15; defense mechanisms and, 64–65; par-
  ental support and, 235; of separation and
  divorce, 331–33; of sibling rivalry, 314–15;
  stuttering and, 299
Stuttering, 298–99
Substitute child care: children as affected by,
  284, 360–63; forms of, 359–60; initial ad-
  justment to, 359; maternal employment
  effects and, 345–46, 359–63; mother-
  infant attachment and, 284; need for, 362–
  63; public policy and, 363; quality of,
  360–63
Sucking, 98, 103, 167
Suicidal behavior, 233
Superego, 97
Support groups, 250–51
Surgery, 245, 253
Symbiosis, 98–99, 157, 159
Symbolic play, 165
Systems theory, 56

Table manners, 75, 77, 316
Tabula rasa, 54, 96–97, 99, 105, 130, 365

Talent, *see* Special interests and talents
Talking, 23, 58, 177; efforts to speed, 298;
  intellectual capacity not correlated with
  age of, 211; sex differences in development
  of, 182; *see also* Language acquisition
Tantrums: case histories involving, 51, 89,
  172–73, 247; parental response and, 63–64;
  temperament and, 32–33
Task mastery, 68–69; learning and, 132–33;
  in middle childhood, 219; in school, 198,
  205; self-esteem and, 170
Teachers, 5, 7, 18, 235; concept of temperament and, 35–36; goodness of fit and, 53,
  62; models provided by, 203; parents as,
  291–301; slow-to-warm-up children misjudged by, 205–6; social environment and,
  197
Teenagers, *see* Adolescence
Temperament: categories of, 27–31; consistency vs. change over time in, 35–36;
  criminal behavior and, 184*n*; developmental theory and, 288; evaluating, 26–27,
  34; hypotheses regarding, 12–13; and
  individual differences in emotion, 151–
  52; in mentally retarded children,
  257–58; and mother's return to work,
  350, 359; nature of, 23–24; origins of,
  24–25; parental practices and, 36–39, 43,
  53; personality and, 34–36; practical management of, 79–89; school functioning
  and, 205–10; sex differences reported in,
  181; sibling rivalry and, 308–9; three patterns of, 31–34; *see also* Goodness of fit;
  Poorness of fit
Tender loving care (TLC): current views of,
  281–83; emphasized in psychoanalytic
  movement, 121; importance of, 288–90; as
  panacea, 278–81, 290
Terman, Lewis, 260, 263, 269–70
Terr, Leonore, 220–21
Thompson, Clara, 180
Thumb-sucking, 17
Tizard, Barbara, 282–83
TLC, *see* Tender loving care (TLC)
Toilet training, 75–76; early, 42; and good-
  ness or poorness of fit, 59–60; parental
  styles and, 43; regression in, 308–9, 332;
  self-esteem and, 166–70; sibling rivalry
  and, 308–9
Tomboys, 191, 195
Torgersen, A. M., 25
Toys, 118–20, 125, 210, 268
Transactionism, 56
Transference (Freud), 9

Underprivileged children, *see* Disadvantaged
  children

Value systems, parental, 68–69, 235–36
Van Erdewegh, Michele, 330
Venereal disease, 230
Verbal ability, 180
Victims, parents who feel like, 50–52, 78–79
Violent behavior, 184
Visual acuity, 107
Visual-spatial behavior, 180, 183
Vygotsky, Lev, 55, 128, 141, 143, 275–76

Walking, 23, 80, 177; intellectual capacity not correlated with age of, 211
Wallerstein, Judith, 313, 327–28, 331–32, 335–37
War, 184
Watson, John, 10
Weaning, 43; self-esteem and, 166–70
Wechsler, David, 260
Wechsler Adult Intelligence Scale (WAIS), 260

Wechsler Intelligence Test for Children, 266
Werner, Emmy, 370
White, Burton, 123–24
Willpower, 36, 38, 88, 208
Wilson, James, 184n
Winick, Myron, 123
Withdrawal, *see* Approach or withdrawal
Women's liberation movement, 182, 352
Word games, 77
Working and Caring (Brazelton), 350
"Working Mother as Role Model, The" (Shrive), 351
Working mothers, *see* Maternal employment
World Health Organization, 280
Writing, 23, 298; parental pressure and, 125

Zigler, Edward, 136, 212–13, 220, 250, 268–69